Psychotherapy and its discontents

Edited by
WINDY DRYDEN
and
COLIN FELTHAM

Open University Press
Buckingham • *Philadelphia*

Open University Press
Celtic Court
22 Ballmoor
Buckingham
MK18 1XW

and
1900 Frost Road, Suite 101
Bristol, PA 19007, USA

First Published 1992

A catalogue record of this book is available from
the British Library

Library of Congress catalog number is available

ISBN 0–335–09677–8 (pbk)
ISBN 0–335–09678–6 (hbk)

Typeset by Graphicraft Typesetters Limited
Printed in Great Britain by Biddles Limited, Guildford and Kings Lynn

From *The Future of an Illusion*, by Sigmund Freud, in the
Pelican Freud Library, no. 12, 1987

What a lot of accusations all at once! Nevertheless I am
ready with rebuttals for them all. (p. 217)

You will not find me inaccessible to your criticism. I
know how difficult it is to avoid illusions; perhaps the
hopes I have confessed to are of an illusory nature, too.
But I hold fast to one distinction. Apart from the fact that
no penalty is imposed for not sharing them, my illusions
are not, like religious ones, incapable of correction. They
have not the character of a delusion. If experience should
show – not to me, but to others after me, who think as I
do – that we have been mistaken, we will give up our
expectations. (p. 237)

Contents

vi *Contents*

List of contributors

MICHAEL BARKHAM is a research clinical psychologist working at the MRC/ESRC Social and Applied Psychology Unit at the University of Sheffield, and is engaged in several large-scale studies investigating the process and outcome in contrasting therapies. He has developed a model of very brief therapy (the Two-plus-one Model) and is involved in a number of collaborative studies evaluating its effectiveness. He has published scientific papers in psychotherapy, clinical and counselling psychology journals and is active in the UK chapter of the Society for Psychotherapy Research.

IAN CRAIB gained his PhD in sociology at Manchester University and lectures in sociology at Essex University. He trained as a group psychotherapist with the London Centre for Psychotherapy, of which he is an associate member, and works with patient and training groups. He is engaged with others in constructing courses with a wider intellectual content than is usual in the psychotherapy world – most notably an MA in sociology and community mental health – and founding the embryonic Essex Institute for Psychotherapy and Analytic Studies.

WINDY DRYDEN is professor of counselling at Goldsmiths' College, University of London. He has written or edited over fifty books and this is his seventeenth book for Open University Press. He is editor of six book series, of which two, *Psychotherapy Handbooks* and *Therapeutically Speaking* are published by Open University Press.

GILL EDWARDS is a chartered clinical psychologist. She worked in the NHS in Britain for ten years, and was a pioneer in community mental health. As a freelance writer she has been widely published since 1978, including more than 200 magazine articles, journal papers and book chapters. After a long spiritual search, her own life was transformed by metaphysics. She has trained in metaphysics and shamanism in Britain, California and Hawaii. Gill runs 'Living Magically' workshops and is a practising metaphysician and shaman.

ALBERT ELLIS is President of the Institute for Rational-Emotive Therapy, New York City. He is the founder of rational-emotive therapy and grandfather of cognitive-behaviour therapy. He is the author of more than 600 articles and over 60 books on psychotherapy, sex, love and marital relationships. These include *The Practice of Rational-Emotive Therapy* (New York: Springer, 1987) with Windy Dryden and *How to Stubbornly Refuse to make Yourself Miserable about Anything – Yes, Anything!* (Syracuse, NJ: Lyle Stuart, 1988).

HANS JURGEN EYSENCK is emeritus professor of psychology at the University of London and was professor of psychology at the Institute of Psychiatry, at the same university, from 1955 to 1983. He has authored over 900 articles which have been published in international medical and scientific journals and has authored or edited numerous books. He is editor of the journal, *Personality and Individual Differences* and has recently published his autobiography, *Rebel with a Cause* (W.H. Allen, 1990).

COLIN FELTHAM is a freelance (eclectic) counsellor, supervisor and trainer. He supervises on the MSc in Counselling at Goldsmiths' College, University of London. He has been a counsellor and supervisor in probation, mental health, alcoholism treatment and private practice settings. From 1988 to 1991 he was conference organizer for the British Association for Counselling. He has been a consumer of primal therapy and psychoanalytically-oriented psychotherapy. He is co-author with Windy Dryden of the *Dictionary of Counselling* (forthcoming).

STEPHEN FROSH is senior lecturer in psychology at Birkbeck College, University of London, and clinical psychologist in the Child and Family Department, Tavistock Clinic, London. He is the author of the following books: *Identity Crisis: Modernity, Psychoanalysis and the Self* (Macmillan, 1991), *Psychoanalysis and Psychology* (Macmillan, 1989), *Child Sexual Abuse* (Macmillan, 1988) with D. Glaser, *The Politics of Psychoanalysis* (Macmillan, 1987) and is co-author of *The Politics of Mental Health* (Macmillan, 1985).

SOL GARFIELD, emeritus professor of psychology at Washington University, received his PhD from Northwestern University in 1942. During World War II, he served as a clinical psychologist in the US Army and then worked as a chief psychologist in three clinical settings of the Veterans Administration. He has also directed three university doctoral programmes in clinical psychology as well as a division of medical psychology. A former editor of the *Journal of Consulting and Clinical Psychology*, he has authored *Clinical*

Psychology: The Study of Personality and Behavior (Chicago: Aldine, 1974), *Psychotherapy: An Eclectic Approach* (New York: Wiley, 1980) and with Allen E. Bergin is the editor of *The Handbook of Psychotherapy and Behavior Change* (New York: Wiley, 1986).

ERNEST GELLNER has been William Wyse professor of social anthropology at the University of Cambridge since 1984. He was professor of philosophy at the London School of Economics from 1962 to 1984. He has held academic appointments in many parts of the world. Since 1974 he has been a Fellow of the British Academy. His many publications include: *Words and Things* (Gollancz, 1959), *Cause and Meaning in the Social Sciences* (Routledge and Kegan Paul, 1973), *Legitimation of Belief* (CUP, 1975) and *The Psychoanalytic Movement* (Paladin, 1985).

JEREMY HOLMES is consultant psychiatrist/psychotherapist at North Devon District Hospital. He was formerly consultant psychiatrist/senior lecturer at University College Hospital, London. He is a member of the Psychotherapy Executive of the Royal College of Psychiatrists, the Guild of Psychotherapists and the Severnside Institute for Psychotherapy. He is the author of *The Values of Psychotherapy* (OUP, 1989) with R. Lindley, *Psychotherapy in Psychiatric Practice* (Churchill-Livingstone, 1991) and *Essays in Psychotherapeutic Psychiatry* (Free Association Books, forthcoming). He is currently working on a study of John Bowlby and his influence on psychotherapy and psychiatry.

PAUL KLINE was appointed professor of psychometrics in the Department of Psychology, University of Essex, in 1986. He has written eleven books and more than 200 chapters and papers in the field of personality and psychometrics. He was awarded the DSc for this work by the University of Manchester. His best known books are *Fact and Fantasy in Freudian Theory* (Methuen, 1971), *Psychometrics and Psychology* (Academic Press, 1979), *Psychology Exposed: The Emperor's New Clothes* (Routledge, 1988). He is currently working on the *Handbook of Psychological Testing* (Routledge, 1992).

KATHARINE MAIR has led a varied career, part of which has included working as a clinical psychologist in many different settings in England and Scotland. She is the co-author of *Voices from the Middle Class* (Hutchinson, 1975) and has contributed to several professional journals. She now runs the Forensic Clinical Psychology Service for Grampian region and has a special interest in the epidemiology of violent and disturbed behaviour.

JEFFREY MASSON is a former psychoanalyst and former projects director of the Sigmund Freud archives. He is the author of *The Assault on Truth* (Penguin, 1985), *Against Therapy* (New York: Atheneum, 1988) and *Final Analysis* (HarperCollins, 1991). He lives in Berkeley, California.

DAVID PILGRIM worked as a clinical psychologist for thirteen years. Towards the end of this period he completed a PhD on NHS psychotherapy and subsequently an MSc in sociology. Currently he works in the Department of Health and Social Welfare at the Open University. His recent publications include a socio-historical critique of his original profession, *Clinical Psychology Observed* (Routledge, 1991) with Andy Treacher, and an account of psychiatric patients' views of services they have encountered, *Consenting Adults?* with Anne Rogers and Ron Lacey.

JEFF ROBERTS studied medicine at Lincoln College, Oxford and King's College Hospital, London and qualified in 1969. He completed his psychiatric training at King's College Hospital in 1977. From 1977 to 1983 he was consultant psychiatrist and psychotherapist at the Ingrebourne Centre, a psychotherapeutic community. In 1983 he became consultant psychotherapist at the Royal London Hospital. Since 1987 he has also been a member of management of the Group-Analytic Practice. He is thus actively involved in the practice and supervision of the psychotherapy of a large number of patients with a diversity of difficulties.

JOHN ROWAN is a founder member and on the board of the Association of Humanistic Psychology Practitioners, and teaches at a number of different institutes. He is on the Council of the UK Standing Conference for Psychotherapy, representing the Humanistic and Integrative Psychotherapy Section. He is a chartered psychologist, a qualified psychotherapist and an accredited counsellor. He is the author of a number of books, including *The Reality Game* (Routledge, 1983), *The Horned God* (Routledge, 1987), *Ordinary Ecstasy* (Routledge, 1988) and *Subpersonalities* (Routledge, 1990). He has co-edited *Human Enquiry* (Wiley, 1981) with Peter Reason, and *Innovative Therapy in Britain* (Open University Press, 1988) with Windy Dryden. He is on the editorial board of *Self & Society*, the *Journal of Humanistic Psychology* and the *Journal of Integrative and Eclectic Psychotherapy*.

DAVID SHAPIRO is a clinical psychologist who has specialized in psychotherapy research for over twenty years. He currently leads a team of research clinical psychologists at the MRC/ESRC Social and Applied Psychology Unit, University of Sheffield; this group's studies of process and outcome of contrasting psychotherapies for depression are prominent in the international scientific literature. He edited the *British Journal of Clinical Psychology* in the early 1980s and is now a co-editor and managing editor of *Psychotherapy Research*.

STUART SUTHERLAND was a visiting professor at MIT from 1961 to 1962 and from 1964 to 1965 and has been professor of experimental psychology at the University of Sussex since 1965. He has written various reviews, articles and journal papers and has authored a number of books including *Animal Discrimination Learning* (1971), *Breakdown* (Weidenfeld and Nicolson, 1977) and the *Macmillan Dictionary of Psychology* (Macmillan, 1989).

Foreword

ANDREW SAMUELS

This profession, which is not one, cannot even be named. Are we discontented with psychotherapy, psychology, depth psychology, psychoanalysis, therapy, counselling, or what? In the plethora of names, schools and institutes we find an uncomfortable echo of the name problem from which our epoch suffers: modernity, late modernity, post-modernism, capitalism, late capitalism, post-Fordism, the information society, etc., etc. Is there a field here at all and, if there is, how can it be defined?

The field of psychotherapy cannot be defined intellectually or ideologically, for there are too many fragmenting tendencies, including rejection of intellectual and ideological definition. Or, if we insist on intellectual definition, we have to take up such a detached and Olympian standpoint that the definition will be academic in all the worst senses of the word. The field of psychotherapy cannot be defined functionally, for its operations display too much variety for that and, in the absence of an intellectual overview, functional definition will certainly be wide of the mark. The field of psychotherapy cannot be defined socially or by means of a cultural analysis – I wish that there were a possibility of a social or cultural vantage point not already hugely coloured by the very existence of the field of psychotherapy. For such has been the cultural success of psychotherapy, rendering untainted discussion of itself impossible.

The field *can* be defined by dispute. Participation in the project of psychotherapy is signified by participation in either the internal disputes of psychotherapy or in attacks and critiques of psychotherapy mounted from the

xi.

outside. Moreover, participation is marked by emotion: if the issues covered by this book energize you, turn you on, then you are already participating in the field of psychotherapy whether you know it (or like the idea) or not. The discontented are part of the field; indeed, by disputing the field as a whole, they help to define it.

Psychotherapy has always been characterized by dispute. As a depth psychologist, I say that psyche's way is to engage in dispute, that the unconscious is structured like an argument, and that the existence of so many competing schools of psychotherapy and equally numerous competing critics is an appropriate analogue or counterpoint to the warring diversity to be found in a person's inner world, wherein competing interest groups engage in negotiation and, sometimes, conflict with each other. Hence I tend to celebrate the competition and dispute-riven flavour of the field of psychotherapy, seeking to temper this only by the working out of an ideology (pluralism) that makes it possible for there to be other outcomes to argument than schism and contempt – though without ruling out schism and contempt as perfectly possible outcomes (Samuels 1989). There is a need to actively combine tolerance and fanaticism, dialogue and commitment – to be fanatical about tolerance, committed to passionate dialogue.

If we look at the contents of this book with an affectionate and optimistic eye, then the cornucopia of opinion and counter-opinion, fact and counter-fact, belief and counter-belief, also radiates a sense of unity, coherence, purpose and, above all, possibility. I realize that the idea of the book as a coherent and united presentation of the field of psychotherapy as a whole will probably shock its editors. But I do not think it is too fanciful to suggest that something has drawn these writers together and that that something can – indeed must – be understood as deeply as possible, in a variety of modes of understanding ranging from the magical to the mechanistic. Something has produced an effect at odds with the original intention. Perhaps it is because of its careful structuring of difference that the book, more than any other single volume I have encountered, has produced a workable federalism and a sense of a field that can wear its differences – if not with ease, then at least with confidence.

If we accept that the overall structure of the book can be reframed so that the discontented are shown to be participants in the field with which they are discontented, then certain obligations emerge. The central one of these – and it is a moral as well as a professional obligation – is to try to integrate some of the criticisms that have been made of psychotherapy so that those criticisms become part of the field but at a conscious, planned-in level. That is, if the critics of psychotherapy are part of psychotherapy, and if participants in psychotherapy are motivated by their tenderness towards psychotherapy (no matter how fiercely this be masked), then what look superficially like stringent and hostile attacks are in fact more accurately regarded as remedies, cures, prescriptions, loving interpretations, communicating high levels of regard for psychotherapy despite the very real problems from which psychotherapy suffers. *The discontented are the therapists of psychotherapy.*

Anyone who has had psychotherapy knows that, for long periods, it is no fun at all. Similarly, allowing these discontented writers to be the therapists of psychotherapy will be no fun at all.

So – if we can work it through to a place where the underlying well-meaning and benevolent strata of discontentment can be reached, it might be possible to indicate the changes, whether pedagogical, technical or intellectual, that will have to be made by the profession of psychotherapy if it is to partake as an active patient/client in its own therapy. I intend to use the licence of writing a Foreword to speculate, in a gentle fantasy, what the outcome of a working, therapeutic alliance with the (discontented) therapists of psychotherapy would lead to.

Jeffrey Masson writes of the widespread personal fallibility and exploitativeness of psychotherapists. If we choose Masson as the therapist of psychotherapy, then even more attention ought to be paid to a person's motives for seeking to be a psychotherapist. Maybe it is no longer enough to rely on 'training analysis' or 'didactic therapy' to deal with the pathological aspects of this particular career choice. Maybe it is time to question the complacency with which psychotherapists entertain the notion that they are all wounded healers, or have neurotic blindspots (shadows, in Jungian parlance) that make them act in unworthy ways. We have to try to work out ethical guidelines for the selection of candidates, not just for the conduct of their work. No matter how naive these will sound, nor how moralistic or even priestly, we have to promulgate these as widely as possible. We need to accept that there is a psychopathology of psychotherapy, involving abuses of all kinds, not just sexual abuse. We might try to focus more acutely on what can go wrong and yet we have to do this in such a way that an over-reaction is avoided. For instance, the absolute necessity of avoiding sexual abuse of the patient/client could easily be taken to mean an avoidance, not only of the inevitable erotic charge between psychotherapist and patient/client as they engage in their intense communication, but also of ordinary human warmth itself. For adherents of some schools of psychotherapy, entering therapy with Masson will mean looking at and making reparation for some of the activities of their founders (see Samuels 1992).

Ernest Gellner writes of the mystically self-protective nature of psychotherapy and its culture. If we choose Gellner as the therapist of psychotherapy, then we are faced with a choice: is psychotherapy a religion or not? That is, we have to discover something about ourselves on an identity level. It may be that a certain kind of acceptance of the religious nature of psychotherapy, no matter how unpalatable to some, could have valuable knock-on effects. These might be in terms of connections to a progressive political and social outlook, bearing in mind that religion has had a progressive as well as a regressive social and political impact. As I see it, psychotherapy is indeed part of a general movement of resacralization that characterizes *fin-de-siècle* Western culture. The role of psychotherapy in resacralization may be critical, first of all for the realism and self-acceptance it brings, and then because psychotherapy does indeed straddle the empiricism–faith divide. Cultural change requires faith in the possibility of change itself. Gellner's critique may also be a clarion call.

Paul Kline and Hans Eysenck write (separately) of the inadequacy of research on the outcomes of psychotherapy and of the possibility that psychotherapy is no more effective than no treatment at all. If we choose either or both of them as the therapist or co-therapists of psychotherapy, then we would have to promise to make something to do with research a mandatory part of psychotherapy training and, indeed, of psychotherapy practice. (For if the research element were to be confined to the training period, it could all too easily be discontinued once independent practice had commenced.) I think that psychotherapists should make an effort to understand why it is that Kline, Eysenck and others express these concerns. No matter how sophisticated a post-Newtonian view of science is embraced, there is still a commonsensical element in the questions that the lovers of research develop. Their scepticism is an antidote to the therapeutic zeal that every psychotherapist knows in theory that he or she must avoid.

Katharine Mair writes of the pretentiousness of therapists' explanations of what they do. If we choose Mair as the therapist of psychotherapy, then the question of identity first raised by Gellner is deepened. What is psychotherapy? Is it art, craft, science, religious ritual, a combination of these, or something *sui generis*? And where within psychotherapy is this question to be discussed? What we need is an effective basis on which to examine the possibility of unwarranted and undesirable influencing of the patient/client. If we are carrying out that kind of examination, then psychotherapy may be able to live more easily with the idea that a degree of suggestion is unavoidable and may not be a wholly negative phenomenon.

Stuart Sutherland writes of the possibility that psychotherapy can be harmful. If we choose Sutherland as the therapist of psychotherapy, then we will be staying close to damage and the fear of doing damage, close to chronicity and incurability, close to the anxiety-provoking realization that 'we' are as mad as 'they' are. In practical terms, there should be regular training sessions on the corruption and inefficiency of all the mental health institutions in the hope of improving them, statutory legislation governing the profession of psychotherapy, and some kind of Ombudsman-type system to handle complaints on which lay persons would sit.

Gill Edwards writes of the detachment of much psychotherapy from new age thinking, psycho-spirituality, and transpersonal psychology. If we choose Edwards as the therapist of psychotherapy, then we have to rid ourselves not only of specific ways of thinking, but also of the world view that promotes mechanistic, anthropocentric, hyper-rational ways of thinking. Merely embracing new ways will not be enough; the underlying dynamo of old-style thought has to be stilled. From the standpoint of a therapist of psychotherapy, the point is that the old paradigms are actually harmful to the health of psychotherapy. The new and newer paradigms, on the other hand, will enable the full potential of this patient/client to be realized. I imagine that Edwards would see the transpersonal, spiritual and ecological potentials of psychotherapy as *already there*, within the patient called psychotherapy, requiring therapy to be released. It is surely not a question of putting these potentials *into* psychotherapy, a hypodermic approach to the new age. We need to see that mechanistic ways of thinking and the practices based on them are neurotic, in the sense of one-sided and over-developed. It is the old ways that restrict the flowering of psychotherapy. Edwards's therapeutic concern is a teleological one, concerned with outcome and futurity. It follows that psychotherapists should study, engage with, explore general areas such as mysticism, visionary experience, the numinous, and spirituality. The search for meaning is not to be confined to 'the patients' alone.

David Pilgrim writes of the lack of political credibility of psychotherapy. If we choose Pilgrim as the therapist of psychotherapy, then we are confronted with psychotherapy's neglect (denial, repression) of the political factor in human experience and the manner in which the political dimension inflects all of human experience. The realization that the social realm is a source of what looks like the psychology of the individual leads to an understanding of the limits of psychotherapy on an individual level as a means of bringing about political change and an increase in social justice. Moreover, psychotherapists as a group need to become more conscious of their entrenchment in a social system that is proving itself to be advantageous to them. Pilgrim is underlining the fact that there is an inflation within psychotherapy, an offensive pan-psychism and psychological reductionism that, far from being just a habit of mind, evacuates the political strain from any problematic. Psychotherapists thereby create an illusion or even a delusion that there is a politics-free zone within which we can operate. But the idea that there is a politics-free zone is not a politically neutral idea. Pilgrim identifies a primitive omniscience with which we are afflicted when psychotherapy puts forward its claims for mastery in universalist terms. Psychotherapists engage in an act of enormous violence and destructive aggression when they overlook the psychological specificity of people's social experience as members of a particular race, class, gender and so on. Pilgrim's therapeutic offering is the suggestion that, symptomatically speaking, the possession of wealth and psychological-mindedness are linked. If psychotherapy can face being a patient/client of Pilgrim's, it will have to question its entire *raison d'être* and turn maximum attention to an exploration of its location on the socio-political landscape. Psychotherapy will, in a sense, have to try to develop a relatedness towards other institutions and movements similar to the relatedness it works upon so effectively with its patients and clients.

I am sure that these reactions to each chapter of the book will not meet the discontentment of the particular writer in question. And I am aware that the editors have been exceedingly careful to state that this is not a homogeneous collection. However, I did declare at the outset that this Foreword incorporated a gentle fantasy of a unified field in which the discontented critics of psychotherapy were gathered into the field of psychotherapy as its therapists.

References

Samuels, A. (1989) *The Plural Psyche: Personality, Morality and the Father*. London and New York: Routledge.

Samuels, A. (1992) National psychology, national socialism, and analytical psychology: reflections on C.G. Jung and anti-Semitism. *Journal of Analytical Psychology* **37** (1 and 2).

ONE

Psychotherapy and its discontents: an introduction

WINDY DRYDEN AND COLIN FELTHAM

Why compile a book on the shortcomings of psychotherapy? Aren't there enough around? Why do people want to indulge in such distasteful, disloyal and gratuitous attacks? And who is this book for, anyway? These are some of the questions we hear and anticipate hearing in connection with this book. It is certainly true that there have been a number of critiques of psychotherapy over the years, but we became aware that no one single volume attempted to bring these together. Few people would deny that psychotherapy does have its shortcomings. Many people within the profession of psychotherapy, however, react strongly against the idea that these should be paraded and systematically analysed. We believe this is an unhealthy position and an unnecessary one. Neither can the door be closed on dissent by simply attributing its motives to unresolved Oedipal conflicts, envy, or other unconscious phenomena.

Psychotherapists are engaged with their clients in a search for truth, clarity and rationality; they stand with the truth-seeking, fear-confronting, cobweb-clearing parts of their clients 'against' the fearful, superstitious, addictive and avoiding parts of their clients. Therefore it would be illogical of us to resist or fear examination of some of the more addictive, superstitious or cobweb-like parts of our profession. As well as illogical, it would be a disservice to our clients if we refused to examine and improve areas of psychotherapy that need examination and improvement. We hope, therefore, that this book will contribute towards the betterment of psychotherapy, and that it will stimulate therapists, trainees, clients (and even some readers who do not constitute any part of the mysterious dyad of psychotherapy!) to question assumptions about psychotherapy. As well as suggesting a need for reform, however, we are asking that radical questioning of the foundations of psychotherapy be taken seriously. 'Immunity from scrutiny' does not, as Broad and Wade (1985) showed, ultimately benefit anyone.

Structure of the book

We have invited eight distinguished critics of psychotherapy to outline their views succinctly. We have sought to bring together the well-established critique of Eysenck, the recent radical critique of Masson, with others representing discontentment from different perspectives. Thus you will find views from the perspectives of psychometrics, politics, philosophy and psychology. You will also read the views of both practitioner and consumer. We do not claim that this is a comprehensive collection of critiques but see it rather as sufficiently representative of arguments against psychotherapy. It will also be apparent that the eight critics form a heterogeneous group: there is no suggestion that they agree with each other's views. We have not sought to produce a particularly anti-Freudian bias and where the weight of our critics' arguments is thrown against psychoanalysis more than against other forms of psychotherapy, this is probably due to its being the most mature and well-known model.

In order to inject some balance into the book we have also invited eight psychotherapists to offer brief commentaries on the critiques. In doing so, we hope to achieve a sense of dialogue; to make clear some of the inevitable areas of misunderstanding; and to offer a way forward from any entrenched pro-psychotherapy versus anti-psychotherapy stalemate into a more ecumenical debate. We are aware of certain gaps in our presentation of the debates surrounding psychotherapy and have attempted to address some of these in our summary.

Psychotherapy's discontents in context

Ellenberger's (1970) extensive history of 'dynamic psychiatry' shows the evolution of psychoanalysis up to and beyond Mesmer, Charcot and Janet to Freud; and thereafter of the evolution of individual psychology and analytical psychology with Adler and Jung respectively. No doubt early psychoanalysis *evolved* as all movements do, but it is also marked by obvious personal and ideological conflicts between many of its leading figures. The conflicts surrounding both Melanie Klein and Karen Horney, for example, are well documented. It is interesting to consider the events of Horney's split from the New York Psychoanalytic Institute. Following publication of her *New Ways in Psychoanalysis* in 1939, Horney came under mounting pressure from the Institute. According to Quinn (1987), Horney's book drew 'nearly unrelieved hostility' from members of the Institute. When she was actually demoted from her position of Instructor, she and four others resigned. In their letter of resignation, they complained that 'reverence for dogma has replaced free inquiry; academic freedom has been abrogated; students have been intimidated; scientific sessions have deteriorated into political machinations' (Quinn 1987: 349). This was and, we believe, still is the kind of ethos that prevails in many training institutes.

While we do not intend to dwell on the inter-school conflicts and their origins, it is worth noting that founders of schools as diverse as Perls, Reich, Assagioli, Berne, Ellis, Beck and Janov began their careers within the psycho-analytic tradition. Each for his own reasons radically rejected psychoanalysis. Each went on to found a distinctive model of psychotherapy. Each of these models was claimed to be more effective, comprehensive or accessible than psychoanalysis. Some of these models, within a few decades, have survived well enough to foster schisms within their own back-yards. Does this demonstrate a healthy plurality of rich veins of free inquiry? Or does it suggest that psychotherapy is often based on the enthusiastic assertions of founders and proselytes, and that these assertions do not remain acceptable for very long? The psychotherapeutic enterprise is relatively young, and many new therapies have been in existence for only two or three decades, yet bold claims to new knowledge and healing methods are made with apparent ignorance of the centuries of philosophical struggle that has been devoted to examining problems regarding human nature, self-knowledge, suffering and hope. In other words, many therapists tend to act and write as if they had discovered the wheel!

Freud initially faced considerable hostility for his ideas but within decades many of them have become popular currency. Along with enthusiasm for psychoanalysis, and uninformed or defensive rejection of it, has gone its assimilation into the post-theistic culture of the West. Psychotherapy has slowly become accepted fairly widely as a respected professional activity. Perhaps a major implicit criticism has been that expressed through the medium of jokes and caricatures: psychiatrists and psychotherapists have frequently been depicted as crazy and eccentric on the one hand, and as mind-reading savants on the other. The dismissing of therapy as 'psycho-babble' (following Rosen 1978) is part of this popular scepticism. In the scientific community, research into how therapy works and whether it works was slow in developing but is now well under way (if still inconclusive). Eysenck is largely responsible, from the 1950s, for the focus on whether psychotherapy actually works.

In a colourful and challenging review of 'madness in our time', Friedrich (1977) searched historical and contemporary literature and interviewed many people who were suffering, or had suffered, from some kind of mental ill-ness or breakdown. In his concluding remarks Friedrich summarized much of the discontentment felt towards psychotherapy and it is worth repeating some of his remarks:

> I must confess I am prejudiced against psychiatry, both the traditional sort and the new variations of people like Laing . . . After more than

half a century of psychiatry triumphant, its power to cure insanity, or even the lesser torments, still seems extremely uncertain. One reason, which is not much publicised, is that the profession, by its very nature, has attracted a lot of neurotic or simply incompetent practitioners. . . . [There are] so many dissident factions that it is now largely a matter of pure chance whether somebody on the way to a breakdown ends up in the custody of a transactional analyst, a primal therapist, a Gestaltist, or a marathon-encounter group, or even, for that matter, the gurus of transcendental meditation. . . . In my talks with people who have gone crazy, I have found that about one third were cured mainly by psychiatry, about one third mainly by drugs and vitamins, and about one third (perhaps slightly more than one third) by being left alone to work out their own problems.

(Friedrich 1977: 353–7)

Occasional salvoes against therapy have included Sargant's (1957), who ranked psychotherapy alongside religious and political brainwashing and conversion phenomena. Rycroft (1968) attempted to put psychoanalysis under the micro- scope but decided against using the title *Objections to Psychoanalysis*, in favour of the neutral *Psychoanalysis Observed*. The Jungian, Guggenbühl- Craig (1971) incisively warned therapists against ignoring their own 'char- latan shadow' but also, arguably, reinforced a myth of the therapist as heroic challenger of her hydra-headed shadow. Strupp *et al.* (1977) looked at 'the problem of negative effects' in psychotherapy, collecting testimonies from leading therapists as to what can and does go wrong in therapy, and why. Strupp *et al.*'s study no doubt shook the profession momentarily and cer- tainly suggested important lines of research, but there is little evidence, still, of any substantial impact of such criticism. Farrell (1981) contrasted the insights gained from psychoanalysis with those from common sense, and attempted an interesting hypothetical comparison of a 'Kleino-Freudian' with a Horneyian approach to the same client, thus demonstrating vividly the problem of clinical epistemology. In the 1960s we saw a wave of anti- psychiatric literature, which if anything boosted the reputation of psycho- therapy. One might have expected supporters of Illich (1977) to extend his critique of the professions and their disabling nature to the field of psycho- therapy, but there is little evidence of that having happened. Illich himself noted that the positions of Goffman, Szasz and Laing were paradoxically at odds with his own because, in playing down the reality of mental illness, they tended ironically to bolster the domain of physical medicine. Szasz has kept up a thoroughgoing demythologizing programme since the early 1960s, but not one that satisfies either Illich (1977) or Masson (Chapter 2 in this book).

The multiplicity of psychotherapies in the market-place is now giving some cause for concern. Consumers are naturally confused. The more estab- lished therapists are often suspicious of the new therapists and their un- conventional methods. Government bodies responsible for regulating the activities of therapists rightly put direct or indirect pressure on them to explain and organize themselves. Unfortunately this does not necessarily lead to better therapy – it may just lead to better 'public relations'. However, there are signs that public awareness of how psychotherapy can be abused (see Masson 1988; Striano 1988; Austin *et al.* 1990) may force the profession as a whole to put its house in order. The present book, in a spirit of 'opposition is true friendship', aims to be a part of this process.

What is psychotherapy?

Definitions of psychotherapy abound and none is completely satisfactory. In this book we have assumed a broad definition, broad enough to encompass the work done by psychoanalysts, psychotherapists, clinical psychologists, counsellors and (at least in part) by psychiatrists and social workers. While there is little direct comment on group or family therapy, it may be assumed that much of the criticism aimed at individual therapy can be equally applied to other arenas. We have touched on, but not highlighted, the contested differences between psychotherapy and counselling. It will be evident from Chapter 7 by Sutherland that we have included both psychoanalysis proper and the more general psychotherapeutic ethos of psychiatric in-patient care. (This chapter may help to question the myth that the one is more effective or humane than the other.) For present purposes, therefore, we regard all formal talking-centred treatments or attempted treatments of psychological difficulties as forms of psychotherapy.

References

Austin, K.M., Moline, M.E. and Williams, G.T. (1990) *Confronting Malpractice: Legal and Ethical Dilemmas in Psychotherapy.* Newbury Park, Calif: Sage.

Broad, W. and Wade, N. (1985) *Betrayers of the Truth: Fraud and Deceit in Science.* Oxford: Oxford University Press.

Ellenberger, H.F. (1970) *The Discovery of the Unconscious.* New York: Basic Books.

Farrell, B.A. (1981) *The Standing of Psychoanalysis.* Oxford: Oxford University Press.

Friedrich, O. (1977) *Going Crazy: An Inquiry into Madness in Our Time.* New York: Avon Books.

Guggenbühl-Craig, A. (1971) *Power in the Helping Professions.* Dallas, Tex: Spring Publications.

Horney, K. (1939) *New Ways in Psychoanalysis.* New York: W.W. Norton.

Illich, I. (1977) *Limits to Medicine.* Harmondsworth: Pelican.

Masson, J.M. (1988) *Against Therapy.* New York: Atheneum.

Quinn, S. (1987) *A Mind of Her Own: The Life of Karen Horney.* London: Macmillan.

Rosen, R.D. (1978) *Psychobabble: Fast Talk and Quick Cure in the Era of Feeling.* New York: Atheneum.

Rycroft, C. (1968) *Psychoanalysis Observed.* Harmondsworth: Pelican.

Sargant, W. (1957) *Battle for the Mind.* London: Heinemann.

Striano, J. (1988) *Can Psychotherapists Hurt You?* Santa Barbara, Calif: Professional Press.

Strupp, H.H., Hadley, S.W. and Gomes-Schwartz, B. (1977) *Psychotherapy for Better or Worse.* New York: Aronson.

TWO

The tyranny of
psychotherapy

JEFFREY MASSON

After the publication of *Against Therapy: Emotional Tyranny and the Myth of Psychological Healing* (Masson 1988) the most common criticism I heard as I lectured around the United States was that my book was merely a list of all the worst therapists who have ever lived, and that it was as if I had set out to uncover the worst abuses these worst therapists had ever perpetrated.[1] This was generally followed by a comment such as the following:

Speaker: I have been seeing a little-known therapist, in fact, he is completely obscure. You will certainly never have heard of him. He has published no books. He writes no articles. He appears at no conferences. He is simply a good therapist, with none of the pretension and arrogance you describe with such abandon. What do you say to that?

Me: Well, it is of course always possible that you have, against all the odds, run into such an individual, though this is not very likely. I have to tell you also that it is not verifiable. This is a problem that concerns me very much. How do I know that you are right? I mean, how do I know that the person you describe is really the way you describe him to be? The reason that I can judge the 'famous' names I denounce in my book is that I need not know them personally, I don't have to depend on gossip (good or bad) to make certain judgements about them, since I have their record before me.

And in fact it is really not very difficult to unmask therapists, especially if they have achieved any fame. All you have to do is read what they write, and sooner or later you will come across what you need. That is what was so astonishing about reading, for example, Fritz Perls: he himself told, in embarrassing detail, and obviously with considerable pride, how he enjoyed belittling, sexually assaulting and in general abusing his patients. When I was at Esalen, where Perls reigned, I heard many eye-witness accounts of people he ridiculed who committed suicide as a result. But I also heard, not infrequently, comments like the following: 'Well, yes, Perls did all the things you accuse him of, and many more and worse; still, that does not mean he was not a good therapist. After all, a therapist does not pretend, or should not pretend, to be a perfect human being.' Perfect? Surely it is asking less than perfection to expect a therapist to remain civilized and courteous in exchanges with patients, not to hit them, or ask them for sexual or financial favours, or drive them to suicide.[2] Moreover, to claim, as many of my critics did, that I was engaging in *ad hominem* attacks is to forget that the instrument of a therapist is his or her person, and if that person is corrupt, then the psychotherapy is bound to reflect that corruption.[3]

What undoubtedly lies behind Perls's belief that he could act with impunity was the idea, widely accepted in our society, that therapists, by the very fact of their bearing this label, have access to some greater wisdom about the human mind and are therefore entitled to make pronouncements that the rest of society would otherwise regard as pompous, arrogant and unwarranted. A typical example comes from the popular book by Anne Wilson Schaef, *When Society Becomes an Addict*; she tells the following anecdote:

> I once had a recovering alcoholic client whose husband had had an affair. Whenever she slipped into her disease [*sic*] or fell into her dry drunk mode, her thinking became very circular and went something like this: 'I know that he is no longer in this affair ... yet I am afraid that he is lying to me ... What if he wants to get back into it? ... What if he is *already* back into it? ... I drove around for an hour today, trying to find them together ... I know this is crazy, but I can't stop ...'. She would then ask me, 'What do *you* think?' I would say, 'Well I have been seeing him [as a client], too, and I know that the affair is over.' To which she would reply, 'Yes, I know that's right ... but what if it isn't?'
>
> (Schaef 1988: 60)

Schaef has no business seeing both people simultaneously, and even less business telling about what happens in one person's therapy to another (professional misconduct). Schaef has no way of knowing, for certain, whether the man is not lying to her, as he might well be lying to his wife. Why should Schaef pass herself off as the arbiter of human truth? What gives her the right to believe that she knows what is true whereas other people only have what she calls 'obsessive thinking'? It is a blatant example of overweening psychological arrogance.[4]

It bears repeating that the great names of psychotherapy do not fare very well in the cold light of objective history. Freud (think of how he sided with

Dora's tormentors, though he knew that her version of reality was correct; think of Emma Eckstein who nearly died from a botched operation that Freud approved and then helped cover up; and as I elaborate later, the Wolf Man, Schreber, and others),[5] Carl Jung (his collaboration with the Nazis), Ludwig Binswanger (the many well-known individuals whose lives were destroyed because they were 'treated' at his famous clinic, the Bellevue in Kreuzlingen), Fritz Perls (the sexual abuse, the physical abuse), John Rosen (patients dying under odd circumstances), Milton Erickson (whose insults to women were taken as therapy). (I detail these charges in *Against Therapy*.)[6] Since these are the very people whose doctrines and books are taught in psychotherapy training institutes, surely it matters more than simply unmasking the case of the corner therapist (who rarely impinges enough on the world to warrant the kind of scrutiny necessary to discover what he is doing wrong). The more we learn about most of these great names in therapy, the more tarnished do their images become. Moreover, new information is constantly becoming available to support this view.

My chapter on Jung has caused much consternation, especially among Jewish Jungian analysts. For this reason, I returned to the library and again took out the volumes of the *Zentralblatt für Psychotherapie* that Jung edited, to make absolutely certain that I was being fair to Jung. My impression is simply strengthened: Jung was involved in an activity that could not but give pleasure to his Nazi hosts and grief to all Jews. For Jung to state that Göring published his remarks without permission is nothing short of hypocrisy. The volume for 1936 prominently displays on the cover both Jung's name and that of Professor Dr M.H. Göring as *joint* editors. Jung is hardly distancing himself from this man. Nor can there be any doubt of Göring's loyalty to Hitler. In that same volume, in an article by Göring titled 'Weltanschauung und Psychotherapie', he writes about the differences between Jewish and Aryan patients:

> The question why Aryan patients do not dream and associate in a racial manner can also be answered in another way. Rosenberg, at the 1936 Reichs Party Day, pointed out that in many of the large cities of the world live hundreds of thousands of deracinated intellectuals for whom 'Blood', and 'Boden' have no meaning. It is precisely these people who do not dream and associate in a racial manner, and precisely these deracinated people are often our patients. We must guard against using them as examples of the Aryan soul.
>
> (Göring, in Jung 1936, vol. 9: 293)

Later in the same essay he writes:

> Thus it will be our task in lectures, class and seminars to attempt to work out a clear distinction between the Jewish and the Aryan-Germanic world view.

At the seventh Congress for Psychotherapy, Jung was almost the only non-German to attend. In the report of Göring's concluding remarks we read:

Reference to Hitler's *Mein Kampf*: the value of a book does not depend on its scientific statements, but on its internal content. The most important part is the intuitive. I beseech the foreigners in the audience to disseminate the following impression in their own country: the complete agreement on the part of national socialist physicians with the ideas of Hitler, out of love for the Volk.

(Göring, in Jung 1934, vol. 7: 133)

Göring also began the conference on this note, as we see from his address (summarized in Jung 1934, vol. 7: 130), where he actually quotes from Hitler.

Jung seemed to have no problem printing K. Gauger's speech on 'Psychotherapy and the political world view', which begins with these words:

It is perfectly clear to you that the meaning of my address is a political one, since I stand before you in the uniform of a political soldier, that of an SA man.

(Gauger, in Jung 1934, vol. 7: 158)

I should say a word here about the excuses offered by Jewish Jungian analysts. *The Journal of Psychology and Judaism* devoted a special issue in 1982 to Jung and the Nazis: one article was by James Kirsch, who knew Jung. I am not impressed. Basically Kirsch gives us personal anecdotes as 'proof' of Jung's change of heart:

The first time I saw Jung after the war in July of 1947, the first thing that Jung did was to remember this conversation and to apologize to me [for his statement that there would be a positive outcome of the Nazi movement] and to apologize for some things he had written at that time. I regret very much that this apology was made only to me personally but was never put in public writings.

(Kirsch 1982)

I regret it too, but I cannot regard it as sufficient. Kirsch makes it sound as if Jung's published statements were a personal insult to him, and a rather minor matter after all. But Jung did not owe Kirsch an apology: he owed it to the world. And he did not offer it.

The internationally known co-founder of Neuro-Linguistic Programming (NLP, a controversial approach to psychology and communication), Richard Bandler, was arrested and charged with the murder of Corine Christensen, a Santa Cruz prostitute on 3 November 1986. She had been killed by a single bullet shot through her nose and into her brain fired from the barrel of a .357 Magnum revolver. The two men with her at the time were her former boyfriend, James Morino, an admitted cocaine dealer and convicted burglar, and Richard Bandler. Bandler's trial, which lasted nearly three months, brought out many of his followers and patients, all testifying to his greatness as a therapist. On 28 January 1988 he was acquitted of murder. He admitted that he had indeed threatened the woman with murder, and that, at the very least, he left her alone to die, then drowned his sorrows in gin and cocaine. He may already have forgotten. Just as Bandler has often reimagined his past, he might have found it useful to re-create the events of November 3, 1986 – for the truth has disturbing implications, whether he is innocent or guilty. Here too NLP offers solace: it is 'the *right* and *duty*' of your unconscious mind, he and John Grinder once wrote, 'to keep from your conscious mind anything that is unpleasant'. When Bandler awoke the morning after the acquittal, he found a sea of roses outside his house. Eleven dozen flowers covered the doorway, the lawn, and the two cars in the driveway. They were, said a colleague who had scattered them, the sign of a new beginning. Bandler moved to San Diego and continued his NLP work.[7]

A more important case in point is the new information that has recently come to light about Bruno Bettelheim. When Bettelheim committed suicide in a Maryland nursing home in March 1990 at the age of 86, obituaries in the *New York Times* and elsewhere could not praise him highly enough. Without exception, he was called one of the United States' great psychoanalysts, and the man who had pioneered child psychotherapy, a brilliant theoretician, a man of enormous compassion and love, etc., etc.[8] Of course psychoanalysts knew that he was never a psychoanalyst, merely somebody interested in psychoanalysis.[9] (It would be like my calling myself a medical doctor on the grounds that I was interested in and had contributed to medicine, even though my degree is in Sanskrit.) As for his compassion to children, we heard this mainly from Bettelheim himself, in his many books, e.g. *Love is Not Enough: The Treatment of Emotionally Disturbed Children* and *The Uses of Enchantment*. We had not yet heard from the children. Well, many of the children who were in the Sonia Shankman Orthogenic (a prejudiced word, that refers to so-called 'mental defects' that need correction) School at the University of Chicago, originally diagnosed as 'autistic' or 'chronic schizophrenic' (now miraculously cured; would Bettelheim claim that their current anger is proof that he 'cured' them?) have now started to come forth and speak: the story they tell is a chilling one, in complete contrast to the ones that Bettelheim told about himself. Articles in the *Chicago Reader*, *Commentary* and the *Washington Post* reveal a different Bruno Bettelheim.[10] Alida Jatich, for example, who was in the school from 1966 to 1972, and is now a computer programmer in Chicago, wrote in the Chicago Reader:

> In person, he was an evil man who set up his school as a private empire and himself as a demigod or cult leader. He bullied, awed, and terrorized the children at his school, their parents, school staff members, his graduate students and anyone else who came into contact with him.
>
> (Jatich 1990a)

He made no secret of the fact that, a clumsy man himself, he abhorred clumsiness in others. You see, Bettelheim theorized that awkwardness was a sign of hidden aggression, and all aggression, even unconscious aggression, must be punished. Here is her story in her own words:

I was at his school from 1966 to 1972 and I lived in terror of him. He beat me for bumping into people, on the theory that there is no such thing as an accident. Another time he dragged me out of the shower without any clothes on and beat me in front of a roomful of people. No, I don't understand what prompted him to do that, and I don't suppose I ever will. I didn't dare try to defend myself. Children who didn't 'behave' would be threatened with being sent to a state asylum where they would be given shock treatments and drugs.

(Jatich 1990b)

Ronald Angres (1990) writes that Bettelheim was 'widely mourned as a paragon both of insight and of compassion; but to me, in the twelve years I spent as his student/patient, he was a bully, a tormentor, and a liar'. Angres, a fine writer and a man of enormous astuteness, wrote that

though Bettelheim routinely proclaimed in print and speech that no one should *ever* use corporal punishment on children, he himself just as routinely administered it. And so I lived for years in terror of his beatings, in terror of his footsteps in the dorms – in abject, animal terror. I never knew when he would hit me, or for what, or how savagely. For Bettelheim prized his unpredictability, no less than his unconventionality: as someone who saw into the secret depths of men's souls, he gloried in defying ordinary notions of which offenses were important, or even what constituted an offense. 'What a hostile character!' he would say of me, and countless other boys, as he beat us publicly. These beatings, which made the greatest impression on me of anything that I have known in life, stick in my memory as grand performances of exultant rage.

(Angres 1990)

This outstanding article in *Commentary* called down the wrath of Ernst Federn (the psychoanalyst Paul Federn's son), who wrote an almost incoherently angry letter to the editor in which he says:

Bettelheim was a pioneer in what in the field is called 'milieu therapy', the only effective form of therapy for severely disturbed patients. Anyone who has some knowledge or experience with this type of treatment knows that it cannot exclude violent acting out, not only from the side of the patients but from the therapists and the caretakers as well. This violence is not corporal punishment in the sense of chastisement but the consequences of the disturbed behavior and is integrated into the therapy itself.

An astonishing letter.[11] Bettelheim first attracted the attention of American academics when he wrote a bizarre paper entitled 'Individual and mass behavior in extreme situations' (Bettelheim 1943) about his experiences in Dachau and Buchenwald (he was there in the late 1930s for several months), one of the first, perhaps the very first, article to blame the victims, by stating that to some degree the Jews provoked some of the actions of the

Nazis. (This was a theme later taken up with a vengeance by Raul Hillberg in his book *The Destruction of the European Jews* and by Hannah Arendt in her equally outrageous *Eichmann in Jerusalem*, a book that Bettelheim defended in print when other more careful scholars distanced themselves from her views.)

In Bettelheim's obituary in the *New York Times* (13 March 1990) a close friend of Bettelheim, the psychoanalyst Rudolph Eckstein, is quoted as saying that

> He told me that once you were in a camp, you could never escape the cruelty. He turned it upside down when he started his school for disturbed children. It was a protected, caring environment, the mirror opposite of the camps. The door was locked to the outside, but always open from the inside.

In fact, Bettelheim seems to have turned the school into yet another version of a concentration camp, as Angres (1990) and other survivors of his school point out. (Of course Bettelheim has been defended by the staff and the present director of the school, Jacquelyn Sanders.)[12] This was recognized in an excellent letter to the *New York Times* by Roberta Redford, who was an inmate in the school from 1967 to 1974:

> Perhaps it was the power he held over so many lives for so many years that corrupted him. I would like to believe that at the beginning his motives were pure. By the time I knew him, he was a megalomaniac, twisted and out of control. We were terrified of him, and lived for those days when he was out of town. . . . We had nobody on our side. We were falsely imprisoned, falsely labeled as insane and then publicly beaten and humiliated. This was a loving milieu that was supposed to turn the Nazi methods upside down? No. This was a replica of the Nazi milieu Bettelheim supposedly loathed.
>
> (Redford 1990)

Is the fact that Bettelheim beat the children news? Not really. As Ron Angres points out:

> Everyone who worked at the Orthogenic School knew. His beatings, after all, were usually performed in front of staff members and, almost as often, in front of classmates or dorm mates. Yet those who observed these scenes for the most part kept silent.
>
> (Angres 1990)

Newsweek (10 September 1990) in an article entitled 'Beno Brutalheim?' pointed out that 'there are indications that at least the local psychiatric community knew exactly what was going on, and did nothing. Chicago analysts scathingly referred to the doctor as "Beno Brutalheim".' But not, note, in print!

Of course my critics can always claim, indeed they do, vociferously, that no matter how many individual examples of corruption among psychotherapists

I can provide, this does not necessarily reflect on the discipline of psychotherapy as a whole.[13] I am not sure this is true. After all, there are a finite
number of psychotherapists, and after a while, when you continue to find
evidence of abuse, you begin to ask yourself whether there is not something
inherently corrupting about the very process of becoming a psychotherapist.
It seems that the less we know about an individual therapist, the more
likely we are to worship him or her. Knowledge inevitably leads to disillusion.
And it usually takes some years for this information to become available.
Especially during the lifetime of powerful psychotherapists, people are reluctant to come forward to bear witness to their own negative experience.
For example, Esther Menaker (1989), in her book *Appointment in Vienna:
An American Psychoanalyst Recalls her Student Days in Pre-War Austria*,
is the first intrepid analysand of Anna Freud to point to serious flaws in that
great daughter of Sigmund's method of analysis:

> Anna Freud must have sensed my attachment to Elizabeth and ex-
> perienced it as competitive with her relationship to me, for she reacted
> strongly, even unprofessionally, to a trivial incident. Elizabeth had
> given me a rather chic silk dress that had become too small for her.
> I remember it well: a black silk print with a small yellow flower, close-
> fitting and rather elegant on a slim young figure. One day, for reasons
> I no longer remember, I wore it to my analytic session. Feeling that it
> was not particularly appropriate for the occasion, I made some com-
> ment about this, referring to the fact that it was a gift from Elizabeth.
> With considerable emotion and a palpable sense of relief, Anna Freud
> said, 'I thought the dress was not yours. It's not your style or taste'.
> The remark left me somewhat conflicted, although I said nothing. (I
> must have been learning that I could not be outspoken with impunity.)
> Actually, I liked the dress, although it did differ from my usual style.
> But it was precisely this change that I enjoyed. Anna Freud's lack of
> joyousness, of abandon, of even a bit of flamboyance, put a damper on
> some of my natural inclinations in these directions.
>
> (Menaker 1989)

The problem of Anna Freud's understanding of her own sexuality has come
to play some role in probing the limits of her understanding of other people's
sexuality. David Viscott, a prominent psychiatrist in Los Angeles with his
own radio and television show, recently suggested the possibility that Anna
Freud was sexually assaulted by her father, Sigmund Freud. He does not
have any direct evidence, only circumstantial. This is not the place for me
to address this intriguing question, but I merely wish to note that in 1981,
the year before she died, Anna Freud contributed two pages to the book
Sexually Abused Children and Their Families edited by Patricia Beezley
Mrazek, Instructor of Pediatrics at the University of Colorado Health
Sciences Center, and the late C. Henry Kempe, Professor of Pediatrics at the
Medical School of the University of Colorado. The last paragraph of her
contribution is worth quoting in full:

Far from existing only as a phantasy, incest is thus also a fact, more widespread among the population in certain periods than in others. Where the chances of harming a child's normal developmental growth are concerned, it ranks higher than abandonment, neglect, physical maltreatment or any other form of abuse. It would be a fatal mistake to underrate either the importance or the frequency of its actual occurrence.

(Anna Freud, in Mrazek and Kempe 1981: 34)

The last sentence is particularly important: if it is really a 'fatal mistake' to underrate the importance or the frequency of its actual occurrence, what explanation would Anna Freud provide for the fact that over her entire illustrious career, she did precisely this? In her voluminous writings about children (more than eight volumes) during a long and successful career, apart from this one outstanding statement, Anna Freud consistently failed to address the question of the sexual abuse of children.[14] Are these words intended to be self-incriminatory? Or is she looking beyond herself, possibly to her father? Could this, in fact, be a kind of veiled accusation? After an initial courageous stance, her father wound up underrating both the importance and the frequency of the actual occurrence of the sexual abuse of children. In fact, so successful was Sigmund Freud's 'reasoning' on this point that he convinced generations of psychiatrists that the sexual abuse of children was neither important nor frequent. I need not remind my readers that the standard *Comprehensive Textbook of Psychiatry* as late as 1975 was still speaking about the actual incidence of incest as one per million in the general population (Henderson 1975: 1,532; see also Herman 1981). The latest edition of the *New Harvard Guide to Psychiatry* (Nicholi 1988) lists in its index, under incest, only one entry: 'Delusional disorder'. By contrast, Diana Russell's (1983) sophisticated research shows that the actual prevalence of sexual abuse before the age of 18 is something like 38 per cent of the female population.[15]

Again, people have come to me with the objection that even if Freud were wrong about sexual abuse, this need not compromise his other contributions. It is worth considering for a moment whether this is so. It cannot be denied, I think, that Freud's views on women were compromised from the beginning by his characterizing women's genuine memories of sexual abuse as mere fantasies. His theories on female sexual development were tainted by his belief that these 'imaginings' must be grounded in psychological need (the 'Oedipus Complex'), which also vitiated his view of childhood sexuality. Since he could not acknowledge that men were violating women and children in fact and not just in fantasy, he was unable to give a convincing portrait of male sexual development either. None the less, these very real and important systemic defects did not prevent Freud from certain recognitions that have proved real and enduring: the reality of the unconscious; the reality of certain psychological devices to protect us against unbearable emotional pain, the importance of trauma as a factor in human misery, the importance of early childhood experiences in general, the fact that dreams are significant, and can reveal important biographical information, and so on. These are theoretical advances. They do not, however, translate directly into therapeutic devices. Thus while recognizing the reality of the unconscious, it does not follow that the ability to interpret another person's unconscious is easily achieved, learned, or passed on. This general statement is also true of interpretative efforts in general. Too often interpretations are used as disguised insults, or ways of forcing another person to accept the analyst's opinions. 'Insight' comes no easier to the so-called analyst than it does to the so-called patient. Freud's own 'insights' were often shockingly manipulative. One has to think only of the great case histories to realize how often Freud was wrong: he handed over his first analytic patient (Emma Eckstein) to a quack (Wilhelm Fliess) who performed a disastrous operation that disfigured her, yet Freud could never acknowledge what happened and insisted the injuries were psychosomatic in origin; he dismissed Dora's real problems as hysterical in nature and only grudgingly recognized her insights into the politics of her own family; he assured the Wolf Man that he would recover memories to vindicate Freud's interpretations (such memories never came); he analysed Schreber's so-called delusions on the basis of unconscious homosexual longings for his father, instead of on that father's sadistic physical manipulations of the young boy, and so on. It would be a good idea if all therapists could acknowledge that if the founder of their 'science' was so prone to errors in psychological judgement, apparent to most of us fifty years later, their own efforts might be viewed in a similar light some years hence. Humility and scepticism should be the order of the day in all psychology.

I have also had to come to terms with the fact that people with whom I am in almost complete agreement, for example Thomas Szasz, part company with me when it comes to the value of therapy. When I decided to publish my unpopular views about child sexual abuse, it was Alice Miller who first came to my aid, encouraging me to stand up against the combined might of the psychoanalytic establishment. In many conversations, however, it became obvious to me that while Alice Miller could break decisively with orthodox psychoanalytic theory, it was not possible for her to include psychotherapy in general in her criticisms. This has become increasingly clear in her last three books, the most important of which, *Banished Knowledge: Facing Childhood Injuries* (Miller 1990), recently came out in the United States. In that book she tells how she was finally able to be 'healed' and face her own childhood abuse (though what, precisely, it consisted in we are never told) by seeking out a Swiss psychotherapist who practises a form of primal therapy which he calls Primäre Therapie. This man, J. Konrad Stettbacher, is known in the United States only through Alice Miller's references to him. Indeed, he was more or less unknown in Switzerland as well until Alice Miller wrote about him in her last books. (I understand that he is booked for life now.) He has just published a book, still available only in German, entitled *Wenn Leiden einen Sinn haben soll: Die heilende*

Begegnung mit der eigenen Geschichte (If Suffering is to have Meaning: The Healing Encounter with one's own History) with a foreword by Alice Miller (Stettbacher 1990). In her four-page Introduction, Alice Miller cannot praise the book enough. She says, for example, that it is 'a breakthrough to an entirely new concept of help and self-help, without any trace of pedagogy, and at the same time a breakthrough to a new view of man, to an anthropology with as yet unimagined perspectives'. Such extravagant praise is completely out of place. The small book is filled with prescriptions about what to do and not to do when undergoing his form of psychotherapy (which he warns is very expensive). The therapist, of course, is to be obeyed, as long as the therapist is 'well trained' and, lo and behold, how does one know if a therapist has been 'well trained'? If he has been trained in the Stettbacher method! It is a modified version of primal therapy crossed with Miller's own views about childhood (which, in and of themselves, that is divested of their therapeutic cloak, I find unobjectionable). The dust-jacket of the book (in German) tells us little about him: 'J. Konrad Stettbacher was born in 1930 in Bern, Switzerland, and since 1972 has had a private practice in "primary" psychotherapy, something he himself developed'.

One has to ask the broader questions. How can clients or patients really know to whom they are talking? What can be asked? 'Are you faithful to your wife? Are you a good father? Do you frequently lie, cheat, steal? What are your politics? How do you feel about animals, race, the war?' And can honest answers be expected in the unlikely event that the therapist would answer such questions? What is involved in full disclosure? Can we expect honesty and introspection about all those signs which point to bias, prejudice and a lack of objectivity? Can these qualities be reasonably expected in therapy? Can therapy proceed without them? And what guarantee can there be beyond blind faith that such qualities will be available, merely because the practitioner was 'well trained'? (As if anybody will admit to poor training.) What is training, anyway? Can there be an institute for the instillation of human kindness? Can such matters ever be taught? Yet without them, is therapy not dangerous? At most colleges and universities today, the students put out a guidebook, grading their teachers openly and frankly, in a way that cannot be found in the more formal publications put out by the universities themselves. There is no equivalent consumers' guide to therapists, warning them away from the dullards, the frauds and the narcissists. A guild protects its members from such possible narcissistic wounds. And a guild needs to feed on itself to survive, hence the cult-like atmosphere evidenced in all training institutes. There is reverence for a founder around whom legends accrue. These legends are then passed on. They are not just about Freud. Many of the lesser names, as time passes, take on some of the reflected glory of the first master, and so we think, with some reverence, of Adler, Rank, Stekel, and so on, though if we read their actual words (as spoken during the famous Wednesday night meetings, in the published Protocols, for example) we are reminded of how human, humanly flawed that is, they were. Most of their comments were banal, some were downright silly, others were dogmatic, irrelevant or plain wrong. But this council of elders, the further it is removed from us in time, takes on an aura of sanctity and wisdom. Freud began passing on rings to his favourite disciples. These ring-bearers then bequeathed their rings to favourite disciples, and otherwise reasonable people see them as possessing some fetishistic essence. Old values are then conserved and the penalty for questioning them or revolting is disbarment. We are no longer in the realm of science. It is the mythical world of fairy-tales we have entered. In this sense psychoanalytic institutions are not at all like a university. In a university, tolerance and diversity are greater. There is an avenue to seek redress and air grievances. There is no such thing as an ombudsman in psychoanalytic institutes. How, then, can individuals be protected from the power imbalance that exists in their own analysis? The temptation to abuse, misuse, profit from and bully is constant. All access to power offers the opportunity for corruption. Within the thera-peutic setting, emotional power, at the very least, is almost absolute.

This 'impossible' profession makes demands that simply cannot be met. No therapist can consistently and permanently avoid the temptation to abuse the inevitable and inherent power imbalance. Even the kindest therapist may well experience envy of somebody else's capacity for love, or anger that they are leading a more interesting life, or that they are richer, smarter, better looking, deeper, happier, more amusing, or whatever quality they have and the therapist lacks. We may be tested and tempted by our friends in this same regard in real life, but we have no strangle-hold on them, nothing that is built into the relationships we do or do not form. But in therapy that strangle-hold is pre-ordained.

Freud is supposed to have told Richard Sterba that

> During my whole life I have endeavored to uncover truths. I had no other intention and everything else was completely a matter of indif-ference to me. My single motive was the love of truth.
>
> (Freud, in Sterba 1982: 115)

A noble sentiment, no doubt, but is it true? One can't help but wonder how somebody could be so clear as to his motivation, and yet so rigid when it came to contemplating another point of view. Freud had few minor foibles. But he had large ones. He had a superb intellect, but a small heart. And this means there were things he simply could not understand. Such as another person's suffering.

The message I wish to reinforce is that the consent we presumably give to psychotherapy must be genuinely informed. In order to be informed, we must hear more from the critics of psychiatry and psychotherapy than we have been accustomed to.[16] It is alarming to see how far from this ideal practising psychiatrists can be. The most flagrant example I have seen is from a Chicago psychiatrist, J. Dennis Freund, who is quoted by the *Chicago Tribune* as saying in a new book, *A Psychiatrist Speaks Out*, that 'I am strongly for civil rights, but a patient who is deprived of reality, whose mind is suffused with delusions, has lost her civil rights. Only a hospital, and a physician, can give her her civil rights back.' I am alarmed at psychiatry's fear of taking an unsentimental and unflinching look at its own past. The role of psychiatry in Nazi Germany, where over 300,000 mental patients were killed by psychiatrists, a prelude to the killing of Jews and Gypsies, has been glossed over or ignored by world psychiatry until very recently, and even now, the best research is coming, not from the psychiatrists, but from people outside the field.[17] Anna Freud, in an article entitled 'Child observation and prediction', wrote:

> I was impressed by the story of a boy who, at $4\frac{1}{2}$ years, had escaped with his family from enemy-occupied territory. A subsequent analysis showed which elements of the experience had been singled out for traumatic value: he had suffered a severe shock from the fact that the invaders had deprived his father of his car. This, to him, meant that the father had been robbed of his potency. Besides this all-important oedipal experience, everything else (loss of home, security, friends) paled into insignificance.
>
> (Anna Freud 1958)

This is a good demonstration of the incapacity of analysts to see beyond their theoretical constructs. It is typical that psychoanalytic interpretations avoid external reality and focus on predetermined events that *must* loom large in the child's psyche. Psychoanalysts were well prepared, because for so many years they too had ignored the real world that National Socialism created around them.

Klaus Hoppe, a psychoanalyst in Los Angeles who specializes in treating Jewish concentration camp survivors (in spite of the fact that he admits to having been a member of the Hitler Youth: Luel and Marcus 1984: 94) writes:

> Sometimes the expert may use a combination of projection upon and identification with the survivor, i.e. 'altruistic surrender'. He thus gratifies his own libidinal needs and simultaneously liberates inhibited aggressive drives. In addition, he puts himself into the role of an alter ego of the survivor: he attacks the German officials, giving in to the manipulative wishes of the survivor, who is still afraid of the authorities.
>
> (Hoppe, in Luel and Marcus 1984: 105)

In other words, if a concentration-camp survivor wishes to receive compensation from the German government (*Wiedergutmachung*) for his suffering, Hoppe would 'interpret' this as a 'manipulative wish' and warns the psychiatrist against a desire to help out of an aggressive drive against the Nazis! Here psychoanalytic theory is enlisted as an aid to salve the conscience of a German psychoanalyst at the expense of the real needs of those who suffered the most, namely his Jewish patients.

Psychiatry has not distinguished itself by fighting in the front lines for social justice and against human oppression. It is time this fact was recognized and the implications drawn. A final historical example: there is a letter that Freud wrote to his daughter Anna (on 3 September 1932) that is now in the Library of Congress in Washington DC. It is, curiously enough, the one passage in the entire correspondence between father and daughter where Freud clearly speaks with some passion about an event in psychoanalysis that seems to have exercised him more than any other. It is found very late in the letters. It concerns Sandor Ferenczi, Freud's favourite disciple and the most beloved of all the analysts, and his turning from orthodox Freudian doctrine. I have given all the details of this strange case in my book *The Assault on Truth* (Masson 1985). But at the time, of course, I had not seen this letter to Anna Freud. It does not change the story, but it does add some interesting details, and it is fascinating in the context of the letters. This is because Freud is writing on a rather delicate subject, the sexual abuse of children, to his own daughter, Anna, and the person about whom he is writing is somebody he once called 'my beloved son' and somebody who he had once hoped would marry Anna! Moreover, Anna Freud made no secret of the special affection she held for Ferenczi. She told me about it quite openly, and was visibly shaken when I told her that the letters I found in her father's desk revealed clearly that Freud had not been fair to Ferenczi. The letter is worth quoting in full:

The two of them came in before 4. She was as charming as always, but from him there emanated an icy coldness. Without further question or any greeting, he began: I want to read you my paper. He did so, and I listened in shock. He has suffered a total regression to the etiological views that I believed in 35 years ago and renounced, [namely] that the general cause of the neuroses are severe sexual traumas in childhood, and he said it almost with precisely the same words I used at the time. No word about the technique by means of which he retrieves this material. It also contains remarks about the hostility of patients and the necessity of accepting their criticism and admitting one's errors in front of them. The results are confused, unclear, artificial. The whole thing is really stupid, or seems so because it is so dishonest and incomplete. Well, by now you have already heard the paper and can judge for yourself. In the middle of his reading Brill came in (he later caught up on what he had missed). The paper seemed to me harmless, it can hurt only him, and will certainly spoil the mood of the first day [of the Congress]. I asked only two questions. The first, I said, would be asked as well by his audience. How did he come by these trance phenomena which the rest of us never see? His answers were evasive and reticent; when he was asked about his contradictions [*sic* – i.e. objections?] against the Oedipus Complex etc., he explained that Brill's comments were incomprehensible, and admitted certain deviations from his views that I however could not understand. Brill whispered to me: 'He is not sincere'. [In English in the original.] It is the same as with Rank, only much sadder. My second question was what he had in mind in reading me the paper? Here also he revealed his coldness. It came out that he does want to be president [of the International Psycho-Analytical Association] after all. I told him that I would not attempt to influence the vote. My only motive against him is that in this case you could unburden yourself of your position; I think, though, that his paper will create hostility toward him.

It is impossible for a modern reader to read these words without thinking how profoundly right Ferenczi was and how completely mistaken Freud was. Ferenczi's paper is a gem, one of the great documents in the history of psychology. Never before (or since) had any man penetrated so deeply into the mysteries of the sexual abuse of children. The very trance phenomena that Freud claimed never to see is commonly referred to by victims of sexual assault: they go into an altered state as a means of warding off the full reality and thus the full impact of the attack. When this state is deliberately or accidentally achieved in analysis, buried memories of the event become available.

What was it about this paper that Freud feared would spoil the mood of the Congress in Wiesbaden in 1932? Simple: Ferenczi was asking deep and important questions about psychoanalysis that no analyst, including Freud, wanted to hear. He was really calling into question his own practice and the very fabric of psychoanalysis. If psychoanalysts from Freud onwards could miss something so common and so essential to childhood, then how could it possibly be what it claimed to be, a method of discovering truth? The greatest truth it had seen (and Freud had seen it clearly in 1896) it had repudiated. Ferenczi in his paper talks openly about the hypocrisy of the analysts, and how important it was to recognize that patients knew more about the truth than did the analyst. Freud was incensed. It clearly offended his sense of dignity to be asked to recognize errors in front of a patient. Freud, certainly by then, was no seeker of truth; Ferenczi, to his everlasting credit, was.

What happened to psychoanalysis? Why did it become so dry and so inhuman? It did not begin that way. The early letters of Freud, those to his fiancée, and those to his best friend, Fliess, are filled with life, passion and emotions. Not so, though, the later letters. Once Freud had 'made it', once psychoanalysis was a recognized science, something happened both to him and to his discovery. They both aged. They lost something essential. Freud and psychoanalysis slowly became respectable and that may have squeezed the life out of both. Reading the early Freud, from the *Studies on Hysteria*, the great essay 'The aetiology of hysteria', 'Screen memories' to *The Interpretation of Dreams*, is to enter an exciting, passionate world. The later Freud is always elegant and eloquent, but something has gone out of it, something is missing, some essential passion has disappeared.

Finally, I must address the concern, widely expressed, that I have not offered any alternative to psychotherapy. I have repeatedly expressed my resistance to being placed in the position of pretending to have a solution.

I did not and still do not feel that in order to criticize the current state of affairs in psychotherapy I must offer a better alternative. Still, I have been forced, by the large number of people who have challenged me in this matter, to think about it more than I had when I wrote *Against Therapy*. Exposing oppression, injustice and all the many evils our times are subject to is itself a healthy activity. In fact, I cannot think of a better therapy than exposing the inadequacies of psychotherapy itself. Politicizing oneself by joining with other survivors in political actions is an excellent antidote to the powerlessness that psychiatry induces in its subjects. Becoming active in the struggle against psychiatry (and other forms of injustice) even in one's own mind, is a good alternative to the helplessness that psychiatry encourages in patients. Writing up one's own story, even if only for the instruction of other friends, especially if nothing is omitted, is to offer people the other side of the official story. (More of these personal stories are being published every year.) Finally, becoming informed, the hard way, by active investigation is still the best way of exposing the truth.

Notes

1 So far none of my critics has suggested that I was wrong about the abuse that I detail in the book: they seem merely to disapprove of my writing about it, or drawing any conclusions from it. Often the writers simply repeat my allegations, as if recounting them was enough to demonstrate their patent absurdity. A typical example is by Peter L. Giovacchini, MD, Clinical Professor in the Department of Psychiatry, University of Illinois College of Medicine, and a practising psychoanalyst. His books include *A Narrative Textbook of Psychoanalysis* and *Developmental Disorders: The Transitional Space in Mental Breakdown and Creative Integration*. In his review, entitled 'The good, the bad, and the truth' (Giovacchini 1989), he says: 'Masson attacks Jung for his "affair" with a patient and his opportunistic acquiescence to the Nazis, denounces Freud's defense of Fliess and depreciation of patients, and cites scandals such as John N. Rosen's and others' brutal attacks on and exploitation of patients', as though every sober person will understand how outrageous such claims are. But to repeat an argument is not to refute it. I have been accused of worse crimes. Jacqueline Rose (1989) seems to suggest (though the wording is so obscure it is hard to know what she means) that I am responsible for sexual violence: 'What the two have in common [Masson and Reich] is the utterly unquestioned image of sexual difference whose rigidity is, I would argue, the real violence and, in Masson's case – with a logic to which he is of course totally blind – leads directly to it.'

2 A woman named Judith Gold drowned herself in the baths, early in 1969. One of the residents, Jacqueline Doyle, was in the baths the morning it happened and said: 'She came into Fritz's group and was told to take the hot chair . . . she was degraded aloud and mocked by Fritz. Which was not an unusual thing for him to do. He could be quite verbally malicious. She left the group that night very distraught. Later, I believe, she called her husband, talked to him, expressed to her roommates her betrayed feeling – and went down the next morning and drowned herself in the baths . . . Everyone there was totally frightened and spooked

by this, and there was a lot of confusion of feelings toward Fritz. Fritz was being very offhand and callous, no grief being expressed. Just: "Ach, people who play games –" You know, his way.' Cited by Anderson (1983: 201). Another suicide was Marcia Price, who had been both a patient and a mistress of Fritz's: 'Fritz had rejected her as patient and mistress' (Anderson 1983: 200).

3 It is true that I have not enjoyed the personal criticisms directed against my person that have greeted my books. I have argued that whether they are true or false is irrelevant to the criticisms I bring to bear against psychiatry. 'So you see,' say these same critics, 'you do not believe that your arguments are vitiated by anecdotes about your person.' This is true. The difference is that my points are generally historical, that is, the criticisms I bring to bear against psychiatry have to do with historical documents. The kind of person I am is irrelevant to the truth of these documents. I often have to remind my psychoanalytic critics that I did not write Freud's letters about Emma Eckstein: I simply found them and published them. I can, of course, be wrong in my understanding of their importance or relevance, but evidence for my mistakes must be found outside of my person. The situation is different, however, if I make claims about my character, that is, if I am a therapist pretending to have overcome the normal human frailties of dishonesty, bias, prejudice, etc. Then any evidence that I have failed in this stated task is important in evaluating my right to propose myself as a model, which is, to some extent, what all therapists do, much to their own peril. Therapists do not, after all, only write books. They tell people, overtly or covertly, how to live and this opens them up to the kind of scrutiny I employ in *Against Therapy*. The only relevant criticism, then, is whether the documents I use are reliable and whether the conclusions I draw from them are valid.

4 Many feminists have complained to me that while they back the ideas in my books that are against *men* they draw the line when I criticize women. Now it is certainly true that psychotherapy has been dominated by men. (The very title of a well-known book in the field, *The Mind of Man: A History of Psychotherapy and Psychoanalysis* by Walter Bromberg, bears this out.) So it is probably true that most of the damaging ideas already in psychotherapy are the product of men. But it should be pointed out that the hatred is not necessarily directed to women. A title such as Victor R. Small's *I Knew 3000 Lunatics* shows an admirable impartiality. It certainly does not follow that women will automatically rectify these wrongs, as the passage quoted above demonstrates. Moreover, the mere fact that a woman calls herself a feminist does not mean that she upholds feminist values. (The mere fact that Margaret Thatcher was a woman did not necessarily translate into better legislation for British women.) Therapy, it seems to me, is antithetical to what I regard as feminist principles, and so I stand by my criticism of feminist therapy in the book. Psychologists in the United States are not allowed to dispense anti-psychotic drugs, and so, on the whole, they have not been as eager as medical psychiatrists to approve their use wholesale. Now, however, the American Psychological Association is demanding that PhD psychologists be allowed to prescribe medication. One can be certain, therefore, that in the future this criticism of psychiatric drugs will be muted because of economic self-interest.

5 The latest 'scandal' has not even broken yet. In the recently published *The Letters of Sigmund Freud to Eduard Silberstein, 1871–1881* (Boehlich 1990), Silberstein's granddaughter, Rosita Braunstein Vieyra ('Biographical Notes on Dr Eduard Silberstein'), points out something that was not previously known, namely that Silberstein 'fell deeply in love with Paula Theiler, a young girl from Jassy

[Romania]. Sadly, their marriage was a short one. She soon became mentally ill, was treated unsuccessfully by his friend Sigmund Freud, and threw herself from a window in Freud's apartment building. This tragedy was corroborated by Anna Freud, who invited me to visit her in 1982, a few months before her death' (Boehlich 1990: 192). Of course there is no known reason to blame Freud, but this is yet another instance of the history hidden behind the official history of psychoanalysis. Cases of Freud that ended in suicide or total failure are rarely publicized. They represent the hidden underbelly of psychoanalytic history.

6 These figures seem to be joining the ranks of other culture-heroes whose images have been tarnished recently by disclosures of their extreme right-wing (often anti-Semitic) leanings, e.g. Joseph Campbell (see the article about him in Brendon Gill's new book *A New York Life: Of Friends and Others* (1990), the 'distinguished' historian of religion at the University of Chicago, Mircea Eliade (who was a high-ranking member of the Iron Guard in Romania during the Second World War, and wrote a series of vicious diatribes against Jews). Adriana Berger, who had been Eliade's research assistant at the University of Chicago, found these articles and has written a biography of Eliade based on the new material: see her piece entitled 'Fascism and religion in Romania' (Berger 1989). I was able to confirm that the Office of Special Investigation in the United States Department of Justice has a file on Eliade, though they would not reveal to me what it contained. The British Secret Service evidently also contains such a file. (See also Strenski 1982.) Even more significant is the new information recently available about Martin Heidegger (Farias 1989) which proves beyond doubt that Heidegger remained a member of the Nazi party throughout the war, and even attempted to induct his own students into the movement. Paul de Man, the founder of 'deconstruction' in the United States, has been revealed in a series of widely publicized articles to have an equally unsavoury past in Belgium, where he wrote anti-Semitic articles.

7 See the outstanding piece of investigative journalism by the Los Angeles writers Frank Clancy and Heidi Yorkshire (1989).

8 One example among many: 'For Bettelheim, the privilege of being a psychoanalyst and of practicing, teaching, transmitting, and modifying psychoanalytic theory and practice, consisted in a deeply ingrained respect for the human being, for his or her own privacy, individual uniqueness, struggles, quest for truth, aspirations towards personal forms of liberation, creativity, and playfulness' (Fisher 1990: 628).

9 I have often heard people say that Bettelheim did not refer to himself as a psychoanalyst, only others did so. But this is not entirely true. For example, in *The Informed Heart*, on p. 10 he writes 'It took several years of intensive analysis, and many more years of its practice, to teach me how far psychological experiences can change the personality of a man', which certainly implies that he practised psychoanalysis. Moreover, in the last interview he gave before his death, 'Love and Death' to Celeste Fremon (*Los Angeles Times Magazine* 27 January 1991: 21), Bettelheim said: 'Now, I will not say that psychoanalysis doesn't help in many ways. After all, if I didn't believe that, I wouldn't be a psychoanalyst.' In fact, he was not a psychoanalyst.

10 The letter that started the discussion was printed anonymously in the *Chicago Reader*, under the title 'Brutal Bettelheim' on 6 April 1990 and stated, among other things, that 'it's agonizingly difficult to write about this. I've been trying to put these memories behind me for a long time. These memories have robbed the

joy from my life. But when I saw those obituaries that painted Bettelheim as a hero, I could keep silent no longer . . . Bruno Bettelheim did not help children at his school; instead, he damaged everyone he came in contact with. Bettelheim and his life's work is a fraud.' The writer was Alida M. Jatich (personal communication). Charles Pekow, another inmate, wrote the next article, in the *Washington Post*, entitled 'The other Dr Bettelheim: the revered psychologist had a dark, violent side' (26 August 1990). Pekow's fine article reveals the same world: 'In the four books he wrote about the school, Bettelheim never mentioned hitting. But he created a climate of fear – we could never tell when he would attack us for any arbitrary reason. Once, after a boy returned from a visit home, Bettelheim spent five minutes slapping him in the face, hitting him in the sides with fists and pulling his hair. Midway through, he revealed why: the lad had told his brother to "do well in school". He had no right to "push" his brother around. To be sure, the blows he struck, though often painful and humiliating, did not physically damage people. But I often saw Bettelheim drag children across the floor by their hair and kick them. He even hit autistic children who couldn't speak clearly. . . . I heard him proclaim that even sporting collisions were always the result of deliberate aggression (even from children with motor problems lacking normal nerve controls). And I saw him hit children who had such accidents.' Pekow also pointed out that Bettelheim's methods were similar to those used in concentration camps. All of these articles are excellent; the one by Ronald Angres (1990) is especially beautifully written and tightly argued. Much to be recommended, too, is a fine article by Ron Grossman (1990) who points to the puzzles in Bettelheim's degree (it is not at all certain he had any degree at all in psychology) and reveals that 'the senior counselors also regularly laid down on Bettelheim's couch to be analyzed, with Bettelheim sharing the results with the rest of the staff'. See too a good article by Richard Bernstein (1990).

11 The letter, sent to the editors of *Commentary*, was not published. I have seen it through the courtesy of Ron Angres. The editors did publish (February 1991) a large number of letters on this article, along with a fine response by Angres. Most of the letters, many from former patients, were supportive, but there were a few like that by Federn.

12 Sanders wrote a memorial tribute, which ends with these words: 'Not only did Dr. B. know what I had to say about him, he also knew of the plan to establish a Bettelheim Center for Research and Training at the Orthogenic School, so that there can long continue to be, in his name and in his memory, a very personal place that, as part of a great University, can bring heart and mind together so that the light necessary for us and others on similar quests to explore the dark shadows of children's suffering can continue to grow' (Sanders 1990: 2). She is not, needless to say, referring to the suffering caused by Dr Bettelheim.

13 Glenn Collins (1988), for example, in his review of *Against Therapy*, accuses me of taking the reader on 'the grand tour' of horror stories in therapy, as if this were some fundamental failing in my character, or evidence of sadism directed at the reader. He seems to feel it was wrong of me to 'revive assertions that Carl Jung collaborated with the Nazis during World War II' as if this were somehow a lapse in good taste, or to point out that the 'founding deities of therapy were paternalistic, sexist, authoritarian and all too fallible'. But he never says I am mistaken, or why, precisely, it is wrong to raise these questions. Most importantly, Mr Collins writes that I 'suggest that psychotherapy has not come to terms with sexual assault, child abuse, rape, battering, torture, concentration camp victimization

and other atrocities'. I do more than suggest it: I state it flat out, many times. I believe it, and I believe it on the basis of much historical evidence. I can go even further, and suggest that any new-found concern for oppression on the part of the profession of psychiatry should be viewed with a generous degree of scepticism, especially when the primary oppressors have been the psychiatrists themselves: lobotomy, electroshock, medications that cause tardive dyskinesia (a grotesque and irreversible Parkinsonian neurological impairment), forced incarceration in psychiatric institutions, sexual abuse of patients: the list goes on and on. True, recently, psychotherapists are eager to exploit the new public interest in sexual abuse. They say, for example, that they are 'experts' in its treatment, and that women need to seek a psychiatrist to be 'healed'. But permit me to be sceptical of a profession which claims expertise in child abuse when a few years back they claimed it hardly existed!

14 It is widely recognized that Anna Freud had little interest in the actual circumstances of her patients. 'She also places all of adolescent pathology in the young people's inner space, with very little interest in their social environment. During a Hampstead Clinic discussion of a clinical presentation, she was troubled when some clinicians suggested that the source of pathology might be located in the adolescent's family, and she pointed out that the parents were clearly well-meaning, middle-class, and benevolent, overlooking that none of these qualities negated a possible pathological family system' (Sophie Freud 1988: 304). However, Sophie Freud, the daughter of Esti Freud, Freud's daughter-in-law, does not agree with my criticisms: 'Yet the recent criticism that Sigmund Freud or Anna Freud relegated all accusations against parents to the realm of fantasy is unjustified' (p. 314), evidently a reference to me, and she cites a passage from Anna Freud to prove it: 'In actual life it is as a rule far more important to protect the child from the father's violence than the father from the child's hostility'.

15 Russell (1983) is generally considered the most serious and reliable of the studies in this area, and it has now been replicated several times. Her conclusion reads: 'Over one quarter of the population of female children have experienced sexual abuse before the age of 14, and well over one-third have had such an experience by the age of 18 years' (Russell 1983: 145). Her definition of extrafamilial child sexual abuse is 'one or more unwanted sexual experiences with persons unrelated by blood or marriage, ranging from petting (touching of breasts or genitals or attempts at such touching) to rape, before the victim turned 14 years, and completed or attempted forcible rape experiences from the ages or 14 to 17 years (inclusive)'. Her definition of intrafamilial child sexual abuse was defined as 'any kind of exploitive sexual contact that occurred between relatives, no matter how distant the relationship, before the victim turned 18 years old'.

16 On the plus side are the few new books that raise fundamental questions concerning psychiatry. I would in particular recommend Kate Millett's new book *The Loony Bin Trip* (1990), a powerful indictment of forced commitment. Peter Breggin's new book *Toxic Psychiatry* is one of the most scathing critiques of psychiatry ever to appear. Also being reprinted is what I consider the single best book against psychiatry ever written, Janet and Paul Gotkin's *Too Much Anger, Too Many Tears*. I too have recently published *Final Analysis: The Making and Unmaking of a Psychoanalyst*, which tells the story of my analytic training and the reasons why I left the field.

17 See the outstanding book by the geneticist Benno Mueller-Hill (1988) *Murderous Science: Elimination by Scientific Selection of Jews, Gypsies, and Others, Ger-*

many 1933–1945. I consider Robert J. Lifton's (1988) *The Nazi Doctors* to be something of a whitewash of psychiatry. Lifton, an American psychiatrist, does not make it clear who, precisely, the perpetrators were, and certainly never indicts anybody outside of Germany, though the silence of the international psychiatric community deserves condemnation. (I know of no study yet of the reaction, though preliminary research I have done shows that there were almost no voices of protest raised outside of Germany either.) In fact, psychiatric professionals (including holders of prestigious chairs of psychiatry in German universities) enthusiastically pursued the elimination of about 80 per cent of the population of psychiatric institutions. In 1942 Foster Kennedy, Chief of Neurology at Bellevue Hospital and President of the American Neurological Association wrote about 'unfit and feeble-minded children of at least five years' whom he described as 'useless and foolish and entirely undesirable' and thought they should be euthanized. The *Journal of the American Psychiatric Association* in July 1942 endorsed this view! Recently, some new information has come to light about the French killing of mental patients too: see Lafont (1987).

References

Anderson, W.T. (1983) *The Upstart Spring: Esalen and the American Awakening.* Reading, Mass: Addison-Wesley.
Angres, R. (1990) Who, really, was Bruno Bettelheim? *Commentary* October, **90**(4): 26–30.
Arendt, H. (1977) *Eichmann in Jerusalem.* Harmondsworth: Penguin.
Berger, A. (1989) Fascism and religion in Romania. *Annals of Scholarship* (issue on Religion and the Humanities) **6**(4): 455–66.
Bernstein, R. (1990) Accusations of abuse haunt the legacy of Dr Bruno Bettelheim. *New York Times* 4 November: E 6.
Bettelheim, B. (1943) Individual and mass behavior in extreme situations. *Journal of Abnormal and Social Psychology* 38. Reprinted in Bettelheim (1960) *The Informed Heart: Autonomy in a Mass Age.* Illinois: The Free Press.
Bettelheim, B. (1950) *Love is Not Enough: The Treatment of Emotionally Disturbed Children.* New York: Free Press.
Bettelheim, B. (1960) *The Informed Heart: Autonomy in a Mass Age.* Illinois: The Free Press.
Bettelheim, B. (1976) *The Uses of Enchantment.* New York: Alfred A. Knopf.
Boehlich, W. (ed.) (1990) *The Letters of Sigmund Freud to Eduard Silberstein, 1871–1881*, trans. A.J. Pomerans. Cambridge, Mass: Harvard University Press.
Breggin, P. (1991) *Toxic Psychiatry.* New York: St Martin's Press.
Bromberg, W. (1954) *The Mind of Man: A History of Psychotherapy and Psychoanalysis.* Philadelphia: Lippincott.
Clancy, F. and Yorkshire, H. (1989) The Bandler Method. *Mother Jones* February/March: 23–64.
Collins, G. (1988) Review of Masson, *Against Therapy. New York Times* 13 November.
Farias, V. (1989) *Heidegger and Nazism.* Philadelphia, Pa: Temple University Press.
Fisher, D.J. (1990) Homage to Bettelheim. *Partisan Review* **57**(4): 628.
Freud, Anna (1958) Child observation and prediction. *Psychoanalytic Study of the Child* **13**: 112–16.

28   *Jeffrey Masson*

Freud, Sophie (1988) *My Three Mothers and Other Passions*. New York: New York University Press.
Gill, B. (1990) *A New York Life: Of Friends and Others*. New York: Poseidon.
Giovacchini, P.L. (1989) The good, the bad, and the truth. *Readings: A Journal of Reviews and Commentary in Mental Health* 4(1): 9–12.
Gotkin, J. and Gotkin, P. (1975) *Too Much Anger, Too Many Tears*. New York: Quadrangle.
Grossman, R. (1990) Quoted in the *Chicago Tribune* 11 November.
Henderson, D.J. (1975) Incest, in A.M. Freedman, H.I. Kaplan and B.J. Sadock (eds) *Comprehensive Textbook of Psychiatry*, 2nd edn. Baltimore, Md: Williams and Wilkins.
Herman, J.L. (1981) *Father–Daughter Incest*. Cambridge, Mass: Harvard University Press.
Hillberg, R. (1985) *The Destruction of the European Jews*. New York: Holmes & Meier.
Jatich, A.M. (1990a) Brutal Bettelheim. *Chicago Reader* 6 April.
Jatich, A.M. (1990b) Letter. *University of Chicago Magazine* October.
Jung, C.G. (ed.) (1934, 1936) *Zentralblatt für Psychotherapie und ihre Grenzgebiete*, vols 7 and 9.
Kirsch, J. (1982) Carl Gustav Jung and the Jews: the real story. *Journal of Psychology and Judaism* 6(2): 113–43.
Lafont, M. (1987) *L'Extermination douce: la mort de 40,000 malades mentaux dans les hôpitaux psychiatriques en France, sous le Régime de Vichy*. Paris: Editions de l'Arefppi.
Lifton, R.J. (1988) *The Nazi Doctors*. New York: Basic Books.
Luel, S.A. and Marcus, P. (1984) *Psychoanalytic Reflections on the Holocaust: Selected Essays*. New York: Ktav.
Masson, J. (1985) *The Assault on Truth*. Harmondsworth: Penguin.
Masson, J. (1988) *Against Therapy: Emotional Tyranny and the Myth of Psychological Healing*. New York: Atheneum.
Masson, J. (1991) *Final Analysis: The Making and Unmaking of a Psychoanalyst*. London: HarperCollins.
Menaker, E. (1989) *Appointment in Vienna: An American Psychoanalyst Recalls her Student Days in Pre-War Austria*. New York: St Martin's Press.
Miller, A. (1990) *Banished Knowledge: Facing Childhood Injuries*. New York: Doubleday.
Millett, K. (1990) *The Loony Bin Trip*. New York: Simon & Schuster.
Mrazek, P.B. and Kempe, C.H. (eds) (1981) *Sexually Abused Children and Their Families*. Oxford: Pergamon.
Mueller-Hill, B. (1988) *Murderous Science: Elimination by Scientific Selection of Jews, Gypsies, and Others, Germany 1933–1945*, trans. G.R. Fraser. Oxford: Oxford University Press.
Newsweek (1990) Beno Brutalheim. *Newsweek* 10 September.
Nicholi, A.M. (1988) *The New Harvard Guide to Psychiatry*. Cambridge, Mass: Harvard University Press.
Pekow, C.P. (1990) The other Dr Bettelheim: the revered psychologist had a dark, violent side. *Washington Post* 26 August.
Redford, R. (1990) Bettelheim became the very evil he loathed. *New York Times* 20 November.
Rose, J. (1989) Where does the misery come from?, in R. Feldstein and J. Roof (eds) *Feminism and Psychoanalysis*. Ithaca, NY: Cornell University Press.

Russell, D.E.H. (1983) The incidence and prevalence of intrafamilial and extrafamilial sexual abuse of female children. *Child Abuse* **7**: 133–46.
Sanders, J. (1990) Tribute to Bettelheim. *University of Chicago Chronicle* 25 October: 2.
Schaef, A.W. (1988) *When Society Becomes an Addict*. New York: Harper & Row.
Small, V.R. (1935) *I Knew 3000 Lunatics*. New York: Farrar & Rinehart.
Sterba, R.E. (1982) *Reminiscences of a Viennese Psychoanalyst*. Detroit, Mich: Wayne State University Press.
Stettbacher, J.K. (1990) *Wenn Leiden einen Sinn haben soll: Die heilende Begegnung mit der eigenen Geschichte*. Hamburg: Hoffmann & Campe.
Strenski, I. (1982) Love and anarchy in Romania. *Religion* **12**: 391–403.

RESPONSE – Jeremy Holmes

It is difficult to show gratitude when someone is spitting in your face. Yet the psychiatric and psychotherapeutic world is indebted to Jeffrey Masson. His highlighting of the reality – as opposed to the phantasy – of sexual abuse, the commonness of its occurrence and psychoanalytic prevarication about this, whether through ignorance or, as Masson suggests, cowardice, has contributed to a reversal of public and professional opinion. What was previously denied or forgotten is now openly discussed and the traumatic impact of abuse is a major focus of psychiatric and psychotherapeutic concern.

Any acknowledgement of this indebtedness seems to have gone unnoticed by Masson. His assault on the psycho-professions has continued in *Against Therapy* and the present chapter, which summarizes and extends its attack. Embedded in his invective are some valid and useful points, but he has delivered them with such violence that the psychotherapeutically minded reader has to make considerable efforts if he is not to respond in kind, and so dismiss Masson's whole project as the outpourings of a disappointed and unbalanced man.

Masson's critique can be divided into four main areas: the question of real trauma versus phantasy; the problem of informed consent in psychotherapy; the selection and training of psychotherapists; and the abuse of patients by therapists. Let us consider each in turn.

Real trauma versus phantasy

Masson is undoubtedly right in his thesis that the earlier analysts, perhaps including Freud post-1900, tended to underplay the impact of real trauma in childhood, and to emphasize instead childhood *phantasies* of seduction and cruelty, thus reinforcing the parental turning of a blind eye which may have allowed the trauma to occur in the first place. This charge, however, could hardly be levelled at the post-war generation of British psychoanalysts, including Bowlby, Fairbairn, Winnicott and Laing, all of whom strongly emphasize the importance of real loss and parental failure in the origins of adult mental illness and emotional distress.

Within contemporary psychotherapy there is an enormous emphasis upon childhood sexual abuse, and the problem is no longer the denial of its existence, but the evaluation of its impact and meaning, and the implications for therapy. Identification with the victim, with her pain, rage and despair, is essential; in many cases it may be sufficient for her to feel that her trauma has been recognized and, where possible, the perpetrator punished. But, as anyone who has worked clinically with such patients knows, this is often not enough. For the patient's guilt and shame to be reached and overcome there has to be an understanding of how the outer trauma has had its impact on the inner world, of how reality reinforced the phantasy, of how the little girl's longing for closeness (perhaps a consequence of an absent or depressed mother) was so painfully and ambivalently exploited by her abusing father. Analytic understanding remains indispensable if this level is to be reached and patients are to be moved on from the paranoid position of the permanent victim.

The problem of informed consent in psychotherapy

Difficulties surround the question of informed consent throughout the helping professions. British and US law differs, for example, in the extent to which physicians are expected to explain in advance every detail of possible adverse consequences of a procedure or treatment. Informed consent in psychotherapy is particularly problematic (Holmes and Lindley 1989). First, the patient in search of psychotherapy may well be in a vulnerable and emotionally aroused state, and so unlikely to be able to make balanced judgements about the suitability of the particular form of therapy being offered, and his or her compatibility with the therapist who is offering it. Second, unlike medical procedures, the varieties of psychotherapy tend to be poorly understood by the general public and the media who still, at least in Britain, tend to associate psychotherapy with couches, Viennese accents and interminability. Third, the lack of any generally agreed standards of training and practice or regulatory procedures in psychotherapy means that there are no external criteria against which a particular therapy can be assessed. Fourth, there are special problems of consent associated with particular therapies. Systemic therapies using paradox may lose their effectiveness if fully explained in advance. In psychoanalysis some degree of 'opacity' is necessary if transference is to be worked with, and in assessing patients for treatment psychoanalysts have to strike a balance between proffering legitimate information on the one hand and upholding their technique, not to mention their privacy, on the other. Questions about the length and timing of sessions, the likely duration of therapy, and perhaps about therapists' professional background and training will need to be answered, indeed offered. A very different response is required to the Massonic interrogation: 'Do you frequently lie, cheat, steal? What are your politics? How do you feel about animals, race, the war?' These questions should be taken seriously and not evaded, but to demand a direct answer is totally to misunderstand the nature of the analytic process, in which the *meaning* of the question for the patient is the important issue, not its factual answer, and, in Masson's case, the need would be to help him to try to understand the origins of the fury and bitterness which his questions reveal.

Despite these difficulties, the problems of consent in psychotherapy are far from insuperable. Recognized standards of training and practice would help, which is why most psychotherapy organizations in Britain favour the establishment of a state-recognized profession of psychotherapy, and are actively engaged through the United Kingdom Standing Conference on Psychotherapy in trying to bring this about. No doubt Masson's 'guild protectionism' plays its part, but unless one believes that all professions are inherently self-serving and a danger to the public, then this must be seen as an important step forward. Masson's suggestion of a 'psychotherapeutic ombudsman' is a good one, and should perhaps be taken up by the psychotherapy profession. But even without state recognition and regulation the situation is not perhaps as bad as Masson depicts. Most patients probably gravitate to therapists and therapies with which they feel comfortable, and, as in the building trade (another unregulated service industry), personal recommendation and word of mouth remain important. Also, psychotherapy clients are not often so totally in thrall to their therapists that they cannot get up off the couch (unlike a surgical operating table) if they are dissatisfied with their treatment, and payment for psychotherapy, unlike for used cars, is in instalments so that all is not lost if the client wishes to abandon therapy.

Selection and training of psychotherapists

Masson appears to take seriously the view once jokingly expressed by James Glover that 'no one ought to practice psychotherapy unless he has the wisdom of Socrates and the morality of Jesus Christ'. He talks about the 'inherent corruption about the process of becoming a psychotherapist'; he questions whether 'the ability to interpret another person's unconscious is easily achieved, learned, or passed on?'; and asks, 'Can there be an institute for the instillation of human kindness?' Here, while raising some important questions, Masson reveals his lack of understanding of the nature of psychotherapy. While 'human kindness' may well be a prerequisite for an effective therapist, a certain toughness is needed too. Psychotherapy is not just about being 'kind' to patients; indeed it is usually the lack of success produced by ordinary kindness offered by non-psychotherapeutic helpers, friends and family that leads people into therapy in the first place. While human kindness may not easily be 'instilled', it can certainly be cultivated:

there are numerous scientific studies showing how therapeutic effectiveness, including the Rogerian categories (not unrelated to 'human kindness') of empathy, genuineness and non-possessive warmth, can be enhanced by training (Margison 1991). Nevertheless Masson does raise the important issue of the ethical – as opposed to the technical – attitudes of therapists both in their work and their private lives (Holmes and Lindley 1989).

The selection of therapists is another important and contentious issue. (Masson's former analytic colleagues might ruefully be wondering about their selection methods!) Should training be confined to psychiatrists and psychologists? Should non-graduates be excluded? Should there be a minimum and a maximum age? How can maturity and balance be ensured? These are issues of active debate among psychotherapists, and in the UK there is a move towards nationally agreed standards of entry and training among the different psychotherapies. Simply to discredit the whole enterprise, as Masson does, is to conflate the difficult with the impossible, and sounds less like constructive criticism than a Mercutio-like plague-on-all-your-houses of a glittering but unfulfilled man whose star has fizzled out too soon.

Similarly, Masson is no doubt right when he criticizes some psychoanalytic training institutions for being less than open in their intellectual atmosphere. Few would disagree with the view that 'humility and scepticism should be the order of the day in psychology'. But despite the persistence of some arcane and outdated intellectual baggage, there undoubtedly is a firmly established corpus of knowledge in psychotherapeutic theory that can confidently be imparted to students. When it comes to the need for humility (not one of his most obvious virtues) once again Masson appears to be out of touch with contemporary psychotherapy and to be tilting at windmills. Many British analysts, including Winnicott, Rycroft, Bion and Casement, have emphasized the importance of 'not-knowing', of entering a session with a patient in a state 'beyond memory and desire', and cite Keats's notion of 'negative capability' as a suitable condition for analysts to be in when approaching their patients.

The abuse of patients by therapists

Exploitation and abuse of patients by therapists undoubtedly occurs, and can take many forms – sexual, financial, or simply the encouragement of an unnecessary dependency upon an ineffective or inappropriate method of therapy. Masson cites the well-known cases of Rosen and Perls and rushes to a rather hasty condemnation of Bettelheim based on a few letters from former pupils (the one supportive letter is relegated to an end-note). It is quite clear that in Masson's mind *all* therapists are tarnished with evil, especially those who purport to be innovators and leaders.

Several points need to be made here. First, exploitation and abuse are by no means confined to the psychotherapy profession (Rutter 1990). Lawyers exploit their clients financially and commit crimes themselves; university teachers demand sexual favours in return for good grades; priests seduce parishioners; doctors neglect, misdiagnose and sometimes sleep with their patients, as well as abusing alcohol and drugs. All this is recognized by the professions and all, including reputable psychotherapy organizations, have ethical standards and codes of practice (far more stringent than the law of the land), with disciplinary bodies which impose severe punishments, usually expulsion from the profession, for those who transgress. No one would suggest that these professions are entirely discredited by the small minority of practitioners who abuse their position of power. It might be argued that psychotherapists should be especially sensitive to the issue of exploitation, first, because of the emotional vulnerability of their clients, and second, because in the notion of counter-transference, they have a theory which can account for, and to some extent safeguard against, their own exploitative behaviour. Part of the purpose of personal therapy and supervision is to help therapists to become aware of their own exploitative potential, and to understand how the intensity of the therapeutic relationship renders both themselves and the patient vulnerable to unconscious forces which, if acted upon, could lead to abuse. Rosen, Perls, and to some extent Bettelheim could all be seen as examples of 'wild' analysts who put themselves outside the constraints of professional affiliation or supervision. The sensible core to Masson's desperate attempt to prove that all the gods of therapy have feet of clay is the view that no therapist, however experienced or distinguished, is above the laws of the unconscious, and all should have access to supervision and work within a framework of proper professional practice.

Again, in contrast to Masson's caricature of the dogmatic and overbearing analyst, contemporary psychoanalytic thought increasingly recognizes the reciprocity of the psychotherapeutic relationship and sees a 'bipersonal field' (Langs 1978; Casement 1985) in which the analyst, while playing a different role from the patient, is not exempt from envy, hatred (Winnicott 1965) or sexual arousal, alongside pity, compassion and love. The task of the therapist is to use these feelings in the service of understanding and containment, not to reveal, act on or ignore them. Acknowledgement of the 'real' aspect of the therapeutic relationship and the importance of counter-transference as a safeguard against exploitation and as a guide to the patient's inner feelings, are key themes in modern psychoanalytic psychotherapy and can be traced back through the work of Balint and Winnicott in Britain, and Searles and Sullivan in the United States to Masson's hero Sandor Ferenczi.

Masson refers to Ferenczi's paper 'Confusion of tongues between adults and children' (Ferenczi 1932) as a 'gem, one of the great documents in the history of psychology'. It is a discursive paper, ranging over several important topics. These include Ferenczi's insistence on the reality of sexual abuse by adults of children; the 'professional hypocrisy' of analysts who offer their patients a cold and correct politeness rather than being honest about their own resentments; the importance of analysts being able to admit to their mistakes and how this can 'loosen the tongue' of the patient in a helpful way. The paper describes how the abused child, through identification with the aggressor *introjects* the abusing parent or adult and thus takes in all the guilt and shame associated with the abuse, thereby losing the innocence of his childlike 'tongue' which becomes contaminated (perhaps literally as well as metaphorically) with adult sexuality and hatred. The central point of the paper is to point out how a similar process may occur in analysis whereby the patient introjects the analyst's hatred and resentment, and becomes submissive and compliant, entranced by the analysis, and so loses rather than finds her own voice. Analysis then becomes Kraus's 'disease of which it purports to be the cure'. Masson makes much of Freud's opposition to the paper, but acceptance of it poses little problem to the present-day therapist. Winnicott's (1965) classic paper 'Hate in the counter-transference' was probably influenced by it, and it is a commonplace of psychotherapeutic technique that a sexually abused patient may well be compliant, out of touch with her aggression, and vulnerable to exploitation in therapy – indeed may actively, though unconsciously, seek out therapeutic situations that lead to abuse.

Ferenczi's picture of the abused child is of one who can react only with compliance or defiance: 'a form of personality consisting only of id and superego'. The introjected object can only be identified with or expelled. None of the ego-based functions of assimilation, digestion, sifting of good from bad, evaluation, balance and adaptation is possible. The object must be either swallowed whole, or spat or shat out. Ferenczi was certainly ahead of his contemporaries, including Freud, in his appreciation that the analyst must act as a temporary auxiliary ego for these very damaged individuals until such time as they can introject the ego-function and move on to more classical Oedipal themes in their analysis (Kohut 1984).

If we look now at the *tone* and manner of Masson's attacks they seem eloquently to exemplify this Ferenczian picture of the helpless and traumatized child. Masson's project appears to be to expel the entire psychotherapeutic movement in one undifferentiated bolus from his system. But once he has done so he is confronted by an inner emptiness, for he has nothing to put in its place. He offers no real alternative to psychotherapy; for all its uncertainties there is often no better way of confronting and trying to resolve unhappiness and conflict. Trapped in a sisyphean cycle of swallowing and spitting, he is condemned to alternate between disillusionment and desolation.

Masson's logic is that of the primary processes: condensation, and the taking of a part for the whole. He conflates psychiatry, psychoanalysis and psychotherapy. If psychiatrists have given their patients ECT without consent, if Nazi doctors tortured their patients, then this makes psychoanalysts into terrorizers and torturers. If one psychotherapist is corrupt or abusive then they all are. There is no balancing of primary process with secondary process, tempering of id by ego. Masson's child's tongue pours out the invective and we watch, painfully but with some fascination as his claims become more and more wild and outrageous, rather as one might witness a child in a rage laying waste to his immediate surroundings, hitting out at anything in sight, especially at the parents whom he holds most dear, and by whom he feels most let down. No one is spared: Jung was a fascist, Bettelheim a Nazi, Freud had an incestuous relationship with Anna. Any attempt to evaluate or sift through these claims, some of which contain important grains of truth, is impossible. We are in a perverse and faecal world (Chasseguet-Smirgel 1985) in which everything is smeared and besmirched, in the discourse of graffiti where if you are not part of the solution you are part of the problem.

It is the lack of a calm and neutral stance that makes Masson's work so alien and unconvincing to the psychotherapeutic reader. One longs for evidence of that observing and self-reflective ego which would enable him to understand and take into account the unconscious motives and confusions which underlie, distort and ultimately discredit even the valid parts of his project. One feels for his sadness and despair: 'knowledge inevitably leads to disillusion' is his leitmotiv. One feels that he has been deeply traumatized by his analytic experiences, as are a small but significant proportion of analytic patients. This is usually a result of a pathological resonance between the patient's unconscious and that of the therapist, described by Racker (1968) as 'complementary counter-transference'. Therapist and patient become locked into a pathological dyad: in Masson's case, that of 'persecutor' and 'victim'. The omnipotent wishes of the patient – for absolute power and total admiration for example – cannot be tempered by reality into a 'good-enoughness', but evoke a comparable omnipotence in therapists who delude themselves into believing that psychotherapy can solve any problem and cure every ill.

Ferenczi describes how the traumatized child, burdened with knowledge beyond his years, can become a 'wise baby', and links this with legends in which

> an infant in its cradle suddenly begins to talk and indeed teaches wisdom to all the family. Fear of the uninhibited and therefore good as crazy adult turns the child into a psychiatrist, as it were.
>
> (Ferenczi 1932)

Perhaps those who are attracted to the psycho-professions have something of the wise child in them, a combination of helplessness and sideline power. Masson is undoubtedly such a wise baby, the boy who has dared to say that the emperor has no clothes. But what happens to that little boy when he grows up? Does he become petrified at the moment of his precosity? Is he left to shout to the empty streets about the emperor's nakedness long after the procession has passed on and the tricksters have left town? And what will become of him when the psychotherapeutic crowd start to drift away, returning to their daily task of applying limited but real skills and knowledge to the urgent needs of their patients?

References

Casement, P. (1985) *On Learning from the Patient*. London: Tavistock.
Chasseguet-Smirgel, J. (1985) *Creativity and Perversion*. London: Free Association Books.
Ferenczi, S. (1932) Confusion of tongues between adults and children, reprinted in J. Masson (1985) *The Assault on Truth*. Harmondsworth: Penguin.
Holmes, J. and Lindley, R. (1989) *The Values of Psychotherapy*. Oxford: Oxford University Press.
Kohut, H. (1984) *How Does Analysis Cure?* London: University of Chicago Press.
Langs, R. (1978) *The Listening Process*. New York: Aronson.
Margison, F. (1991) Learning to listen, in J. Holmes (ed.) *Textbook of Psychotherapy in Psychiatric Practice*. Edinburgh: Churchill Livingstone.
Racker, H. (1968) *Transference and Counter-transference*. London: Hogarth Press.
Rutter, P. (1990) *Sex in the Forbidden Zone*. London: Unwin-Hyman.
Winnicott, D. (1965) *The Maturational Process and the Facilitating Environment*. London: Hogarth Press.

REBUTTAL – *Jeffrey Masson*

Jeremy Holmes agrees with me that 'earlier analysts tended to underplay the impact of real trauma in childhood' but says that 'this charge however could hardly be levelled at the post-war generation of British psychoanalysts including Bowlby, Fairbairn, Winnicott and Laing'. Now while it is perfectly true that all of these analysts recognize the importance of real trauma in childhood, not one of them ever wrote about childhood sexual abuse. It is strange, after all, that they could acknowledge Freud's failure in some areas, but not in this crucial one. It is not only that they failed to see Freud's loss of moral courage, but also that they themselves then seemed unable to turn their gaze upon this crucial problem. It is puzzling: all analysts hear and have always heard cases of real sexual assaults, on a more or less daily basis. How did they listen to them? What thoughts went through their minds? It would be, from both a sociological and a philosophical view, of value to know how they managed to still their own conscience as they dismissed these accounts as fantasies. Of course many of them claim that they agonized over the problem, or even secretly rebelled against Freud and the Freudian doctrine of fantasy. But they never did so publicly. Their private thoughts cannot be verified and thus possess no historical significance.

Holmes makes much of the point that he accepts the reality of childhood sexual abuse, breaking with earlier orthodox psychoanalytic doctrine. But the way he writes and what he says indicates that his break is imperfect at best. Perhaps unwittingly he falls into analytic jargon. For example while acknowledging an 'outer trauma' he also says that the reality often only reinforced the fantasy. Once again we are back in the analytic world where there can be no such thing as a purely external event. The victim must always be partly to blame. So if there is a sexual assault, it must be accompanied by a fantasy. This is what men were saying about rape some years ago, but no longer dare to say aloud. Not every victim of a murderer secretly longed to be murdered. There can be sexual assault without an accompanying fantasy. Maybe what the 'patient' needs is not help with her guilt and shame, but somebody to recognize that what happened to her was something that had nothing to do with her, that it was undeserved, unasked and completely traumatic. For help of this kind, analysts are less well equipped by tradition, training and inclination than just about anybody else.

Holmes speaks of the indispensable 'analytic understanding if patients are to move on from the paranoid position of the permanent victim'. The language is alarming. What is a 'permanent victim'? Somebody who feels, for a long time, victimized? Such as, what, a survivor of a concentration camp? An incest victim? Do Holmes and other analysts possess a secret chart that tells them how long a person can feel victimized without being seen as paranoid? One month? A year? Ten? Who are these people to tell other people how long they can feel the pain of their own suffering? How are any of us to tell another person: 'Enough already'? It is not our prerogative, nor that of any therapist. Moreover, is it really paranoid to recognize what has been done to you, and to speak about it? What a limited perspective to believe that some 'professional' can tell you when you must stop believing in the reality or importance of your own past, and 'get on with it'. Would the therapist fault Primo Levi, Jean Améry and Tadeus Borowski for committing suicide after coming out of the concentration camps? Would Holmes have set them straight by telling them: 'Stop whining'?

Holmes seems to agree with me that secrecy is a bad thing in psychotherapy. But does he really? He writes that 'systemic therapies [whatever those are] may lose their effectiveness if fully explained in advance'. One could say as much for any form of tyranny. After all, any therapist could argue that what he was doing, no matter how unethical (he would say 'paradoxical'), was part of the treatment programme, and could not be judged from the outside. 'Paradox' can cover for a multitude of deficiencies in the therapist. It reminds me a little of 'confrontation therapy', in vogue a few years ago in the United States, which in effect gave the therapist free rein to say any offensive thing he liked to a patient and rationalize it as being part of the therapy.

Holmes does little to allay my fears that he is playing shrink (this is a common put-down in the United States – 'Don't play shrink with me', an example of common wisdom where the general public recognizes that there is something unpleasant about analysing another person who did not ask for the analysis) when he resorts to a particularly virulent form of the *ad hominem* argument. I am referring to the many times Holmes feels compelled to analyse me. At one point he calls me 'a glittering but unfulfilled man whose star has fizzled out too soon'. It is hazardous to analyse anybody, under the best of circumstances. But to analyse somebody you have never met, on the basis of a paper he has written critical of your profession, is particularly liable to error. Because I suggested that any prospective patient of psychotherapy question the therapist very closely on whatever issue happened to be important ('How do you feel about animals, race, the war?' etc.) Holmes writes that 'the *meaning* of the question is the important issue, not its factual answer, and, in Masson's case, the need would be to help him to try to understand the origins of the fury and bitterness which his questions reveal'. Really? The arrogance behind this assumption is revealing, because it is the arrogance which I accuse the profession of harbouring, indeed, encouraging. How does Holmes know that I am bitter about these issues, as opposed to simply passionate about them? If you or I feel strongly about racism, does this necessarily imply bitterness, or even personal exposure? Is it impossible, in Holmes's world, to feel the sting of social injustice without having experienced it directly? And what is this preoccupation with 'origins'? Would it not be enough to know that something bad happened? Suppose you learned something about the terrible conditions under which battery hens or veal calves are raised in Britain and you were, understandably, furious. What would it mean to question the origins of this fury? Would you have to have been a battery hen yourself? Could you not simply feel very strongly, because you think it is wrong to cause unnecessary suffering to battery hens or veal calves?

There must be some reason why psychoanalysts, by and large, are not active participants in movements calling for social justice in the world. And I do not think it is because they are uncommonly reflective about motivation, their own and others. No, I think it is because it is in the very nature of psychoanalysis to ascribe greater force to internal factors than external ones, to slight the outer world in favour of the inner one.

This disagreement about the origins of human suffering informs many of Holmes's points. Holmes writes: 'Psychotherapy is not just about being "kind" to patients; indeed it is usually the lack of success produced by ordinary kindness offered by non-psychotherapeutic helpers, friends and family that leads people into therapy in the first place.' This view presumes that people can 'fall ill' in spite of a perfectly kind environment and up-bringing. I don't believe this. I think people become unhappy because of things that happen to them, and ideally, the therapist should help them uncover those past hurts that still cast a shadow in the present. I naively believed, at first, that this was Freud's position, and that of the analytic world in general. I realize now I was wrong, and the analyst is more often an adversary (though a secret one) representing the interests of the family and of society, in an effort to convince, the patient, at some deep level, that the fault lies within. Going to the heart of our disagreement is the question of what kind of person should be a therapist. Holmes thinks all I ask is that a person be kind to a patient. No. Kindness is not something you do 'to' somebody. Kindness, as a deep human characteristic, is, in my view, essential to therapy. But how do you ever guarantee that somebody possesses such a mysterious quality as kindness? It is not, after all, something we learn in school. You cannot pass an exam in it. You have it, or you don't, and I know of no test for it. But without it, surely any therapy has a poor prospect of succeeding.

Humility is a virtue I align with kindness because its opposite, arrogance, is so often accompanied by violence, intellectual or otherwise. When I say, for theoretical reasons, that humility is a virtue lacking in therapists, Holmes says that I am out of touch with contemporary psychotherapy: 'Many British analysts including Winnicott, Rycroft, Bion and Casement emphasized the importance of "not-knowing", of entering a session with a patient in a state "beyond memory and desire".' I am familiar with these views, and I consider them nonsense. Bion actually goes so far as to state that if you recognize a patient when he or she comes into your room, you have already fallen from therapeutic grace. In fact, all of us bring our memories and our desires to all encounters, therapeutic or otherwise. People who *claim* to be beyond such ordinary human foibles are rarely doing more than simply proclaiming it.

Holmes's method of dealing with my criticism of individual therapists is to point out that there is another side to therapy. For every therapist who abuses a patient, there is surely one who does not. He says that I condemn Bettelheim on the basis of a few letters from former pupils. But what is important is not how many letters there are, but what they tell us. Dozens of Bettelheim's former patients/students have come forward to talk about having been slapped, pushed, pulled and beaten by him, on a regular basis. The fact that there are some who were not is surely a rather weak defence of Bettelheim. Moreover, none of his former colleagues, many of whom knew of these beatings, ever said anything about it in print. Bettelheim himself wrote, over and over (as recently as November 1985 on the cover story of the *Atlantic Monthly*), that a child must never be beaten, yet he routinely did so. Why did no therapist ever challenge Bettelheim? Why did we have to wait for his own patients to do so (having tried while he was alive, but finding no magazine or newspaper that would print their stories)? Does this not tell us something beyond Bettelheim, about the profession itself? Moreover, Holmes does not answer my criticisms directly. All he does is repeat them. He writes: 'No one is spared: Jung was a fascist, Bettelheim a Nazi, Freud had an incestuous relationship with Anna.' Actually, only the first criticism is correct. I did not say that Bettelheim was a Nazi, and I did not say that Freud had an incestuous relationship with Anna. But surely the point is to answer my charges, not simply repeat them. If I am wrong about Jung, then I must be corrected. So far, nobody has come forward with counter-documents. When I write about Nazi doctors, I do not claim that their existence makes 'psychoanalysts into terrorizers and torturers'. But surely the Nazi doctors were. And the fact that their colleagues were more interested in covering up their crimes than in denouncing them is worthy of some serious attention. Why does Holmes think it is impossible to evaluate these claims? All he need do is read the relevant literature and come to some conclusions of his own. Instead, he prefers to give an interpretation: my criticism is part of 'a faecal world in which everything is smeared and besmirched'.

Holmes constantly substitutes interpretations (straight out of a primer on psychoanalysis) for argument. It is, not surprisingly, just what therapists do when confronted with criticism of their own behaviour in a psychotherapeutic session. It is a debasement of language (all criticism becomes 'resistance') and of the intellect, and demonstrates with convincing clarity the moral bankruptcy of psychotherapy.

THREE

Psychoanalysis, social role and testability

ERNEST GELLNER

Psychoanalysis is, in a very strict sense of the term, a mystical experience. Mystical experience can best be defined as follows: an intense emotional experience, which at the same time purports to be and is felt as being the acquisition of knowledge which is important, privileged and out of the ordinary. The knowledge so acquired is not, so to speak, common or garden information: rather, it is supremely important illumination, revealing, to its possessors, both the basic nature of the world they inhabit, and their place within it, and the path to whatever salvation is available to them. The intensity of the experience is both the herald, and the vindication of the authority and reliability, of the knowledge so acquired.

The knowledge does not consist simply of a representation of the reality to which it refers: on the contrary, it consists of direct contact with, permeation by, fusion with, and penetration of, that reality. It is this intimacy of contact between known and unknown which gives the knowledge its special character. The acquisition of such knowledge transforms the knower, endows him or her with new power and a new identity, and the possession of the knowledge is such that – in cases of a genuine mystical experience – doubt is, by the very nature of the experience, excluded.

The experience has a content which is vindicated by the luminous inner authority of the experience itself, even though this content goes beyond that experience. The content in turn validates and confirms the experience. Mystical experience *can* come unannounced and unheralded, spontaneously, from within, endogenously, as it does with the Founder of the Movement; or it can be induced by the suitable technique, which is the form appropriate for ordinary mortals and followers. In the latter case, Qualified Masters of the technique are naturally endowed with a special status as Givers, as people capable of bestowing an extremely valuable boon on their fellows. Their own selection for this status may have been spontaneous and self-validating, like mystical experience itself, or it may be formally, more or less bureaucratically, conferred on them by a licensing authority, a guild of practitioners, after they had successfully undergone the appropriate initiation.

It is widely recognized – and, indeed, inherent in the logic of the situation – that, though the mystical experience is self-authenticating when genuine, there are also spurious, counterfeit versions of it, much to be feared, and to be guarded against. So there are spurious or inadequate initiators or putative masters of initiation, and there are even entire guilds or corporations of such frauds. The inexperienced searcher after Illumination must carefully beware of these fraudulent imitations. But there appear to be no public, external criteria of validity and fraudulence: the marks of legitimacy are internal to each competing system. Neutral and external tests are not available: if they were, the revelation-experience would no longer be self-validating and sovereign, but subject to general criteria, and thus lose its standing.

All this is inherent in the very idea of uniquely powerful knowledge, acquired in exceptional circumstances and accompanied by exceptional emotional states, discontinuous from (more powerful and more dangerous than) ordinary cognition, governed by its own and very distinctive rules, and capable of being induced by a complex technique, which constitutes the professional arcana of a body combining the features both of a profession and of a sacramentally distinct priesthood.

The attribution of the characteristics here listed is not, it seems to me, in any way contentious. If challenged, it will be more, I suspect, because of the neutral, so to speak external terminology employed, which inherently places psychoanalysis alongside other historically similar phenomena. By this very fact, it suspends judgement concerning the validity of the claims implied by the terminology internal to the system, as deployed by its adepts, adherents, practitioners and enthusiasts. A terminology which suspends judgement does not endorse the claims contained by the system, thus implying that they *might* be false, even though it does not imply that they *are* false, is unacceptable to the adept. It seems to leave out something essential, 'not to understand'. The external terminology does not necessarily prejudge the question of validity, or strictly imply that the claims are invalid; but its very neutrality or suspension of judgement, and the suggestion that the claims made are formally similar to many others, including some no longer fashionable and appealing – all this is liable to give those 'inside' the feeling that their characterization is ironic, hostile, and is meant to be a kind of 'put-down'. By contrast, 'internal' language links the characterization of the experience to a background picture, which in turn validates the authority of the experience and the validity of the claims contained in it.

If, however, it be granted that psychoanalysis does share these features with other species of mystical existence, it must be stressed that psycho-analysis (jointly with all its cousins in what might be called the depth psychology family) is also distinguished from those other kinds in at least one important way: its theory and background assumptions can be and are articulated in impeccably naturalistic terms. Other forms of mysticism, if given to explicit theorizing at all, explain both the intensity of the experience, and the special and authoritative nature of the knowledge acquired in the course of it, in terms of penetration on the part of the mystic, of *another* realm of reality altogether, one superior to the humdrum world of daily life, though also liable to dominate it in mysterious ways. The mystical prac-titioner penetrates or is penetrated by (or both) another realm. Psychoanalysis, on the other hand, was founded by a man who shared what might be called the positivistic or scientistic or materialistic coventional wisdom of the nineteenth century, and felt no inclination at all to contest it. He formu-lated his ideas in terms of that vision. Psychoanalysis does indeed consist of the penetration of a Special Realm, discontinuous from the ordinary world though dominating it, and accessible only to forms of exploration distinct from those prevalent in the ordinary world: success is heralded by intense emotion, and a deep transformation of the knower himself. All this it shares with older forms of mysticism. But: this Other Realm *is part of Nature.* This is mysticism with a naturalistic face. That is one of the proudest boasts of the system. Freud is acclaimed as the last term in a progression, whose earlier links are Copernicus and Darwin. He is the Seal of the Prophets of naturalism, heralding the definitive unification of all nature and the final inclusion of humankind, in all their aspects, within it. The claim to any even partially extra-territorial status for us is repudiated, with great emphasis.

The duality (or multiplicity) of realms, in the pre-materialist or pre-positivist period of human thought, had been endowed with intimate links to the provision of therapeutic and pastoral care. People seeking counsel in crucial decisions, consolation in tragic bereavements, cure in painful ailments, or preventive action in the face of grave external dangers, in the past sought the aid of priests or shamans who claimed knowledge of, and at least partial power to control or propitiate denizens of the Other Realm. But if the Other Realm is with us no longer, this doesn't mean that we are free of tragic and perilous predicaments. Not at all. Their nature may have changed, but life is as frightening as ever it was, even if the menaces are often new ones. Freud's real discovery concerns, really, the new nature of the Other Realm, and of new techniques for its exploration, propitiation and manipulation.

This is the real basis for the claim that he completes the important Copernicus–Darwin–Freud progression. Many naturalists, positivists or materialists have proclaimed the Unity of Nature, and Freud has not really contributed any important new arguments or formulations to that position. What he did do was to make possible, within that Single Nature, of what might be called Therapeutic and Cognitive Mysticism: intensely personal and individual problems were to be handled by a technique discontinuous from ordinary knowledge. It would claim to attain knowledge by a unique and unusual path. It was accompanied by intense emotion and a ritual suspension of the humdrum world, a suspension such as had ever been associated with mysticism. He had found a Realm ('the Unconscious') which possesses precisely those properties which had previously made transcendent realms into the appropriate working partners, the area of operation, the tools of trade, of pastoral mystics. It was a Realm open to *selective* penetration, by some men only – and the reward of such aided penetration was illumination and an at least partial escape from mundane ills, a 'cure'. He did not discover or establish the Unity of Nature; he made shamanism possible within it, endowing it with a new rationale, technique and terminology.

He was by no means the actual discoverer of this New-Found Land: there is a long pre-history of speculation about the Unconscious, including such names in the history of thought as Schopenhauer, Nietzsche and von Hartmann. But these men had merely affirmed its existence, in one terminology or another, but had not proposed any technique for handling it, for exploiting their discovery, so to speak. They were discoverers devoid of any ideas for the practical exploitation of what they had found. With Freud it was the other way around: he had not made the discovery in the abstract. He had made it only in the course of therapeutic practice in the pursuit of concrete and immediate aims, and in a manner inseparable from his practice. In Freud's thought, the nature of that realm, its discovery, its penetration, its role in human suffering and tragedy, the nature of its exploration *and taming* – all these form one indissoluble whole.

Theoretically it would, I suppose, be possible that one thinker should have discovered the Unconscious and persuaded humankind of its existence, and that some Academy would then have offered a prize to the first person to map its laws and devise techniques for manipulating it. But that was not at all how it happened. Humankind became persuaded of the existence and importance of this new continent, not by the men who had originally stumbled upon it, but by the man who claimed, at first rather persuasively, that he knew just how to handle it. Karl Marx had observed, in quite a different context, that humankind sets itself only such problems as it can solve. I rather doubt whether this is true in general, but it does seem to apply in this case. Humankind became widely persuaded of the existence and importance of the Unconscious only when it was reported by an explorer who said he also knew how to control it. People listened with attention or rapture, not to the discoverer, but to the beast-tamer.

The conventional account of Freud's discovery rather misinterprets it, and in effect inverts its real significance. It is normally said that Freud discovered that the mind 'had an unconscious'. But this had never been in doubt. Everyone knows that there is an enormous amount that goes on within us which is not accessible to consciousness. What Freud really reported was that *the unconscious had a mind*: that the processes which are by common consent not accessible to consciousness, or at any rate an important group of them, comport themselves *as if they had a mind*, that is with great cunning. They have aims, are sensitive to information, and form their aims with reference to persisting situations, notably interpersonal relations. The kinds of aims they have, the manner in which they are sensitive to information, differ a little from the principles observed by, or aspired to, by the conscious mind: they lack the discipline, tidiness, respect for logic which our mind, at least in its more sober and well-behaved moments, tries to observe. But that is another matter. This is a form of animism – applied to human beings themselves.

Freud did not establish the unity of nature, or even the incorporation of humankind in its entirety, within that realm. He made it incomparably more habitable. What he did was to find a method of living with and within that unity. He found a sub-zone within nature, which could be credited with governing our fates, much in the way in which the transcendent Other world had previously been credited with ruling us. So Freud did not complete the naturalization of humankind: he merely made it tolerable, habitable or domesticated, so to speak. The naturalization of the world had previously led to the famous icy disenchantment, the recognition of a world governed by cold indifferent laws, and offering neither succour nor consolation nor support. Now, within an impeccably natural world, a measure of moral order was restored. There was a technique and an accredited clerisy to whom one could turn in distress. The severely natural world turned out to be tolerable after all: it contained a technique and practitioners of it, to whom one could turn in anguish. A world without shrines was endowed with the charismatic couch.

The discovery of the dread sub-Realm and the accreditation of the guild of intermediaries giving access to it and making propitiation, even manipulation, possible, was all of a piece, and linked to each other with a logically tight elegance. The Unconscious is not just a hypothesis: it is a suspension of all other hypotheses. It affirms that we know not what we do, and, above all, know not what we really think, and why we think it, and whether we have any right to think it. If the hypothesis is valid, it really amounts to the cognitive disenfranchisement of us all. We suffer from an intellectual Original Sin, which we cannot – or at any rate, most of us cannot – purge unaided. We cannot recover cognitive licence unaided, especially when it comes to making assertions about our own psychic states.

Like many key premises, all this is really a little bit stronger than is comfortable: it must be used in moderate doses if it is not to be fatal. Used with uncompromising consistency, it could lead to total scepticism. If our conscious life is governed by forces inhabiting a far away country of which we know little, how can we trust anything we think? We cannot.

Freud's particular path to the discovery of this realm was intimately and indissolubly combined with the discovery of a technique for unmasking and controlling the forces which otherwise held sway over us. He promptly patented this discovery, making it the exclusive property of the guild he founded and which he was to govern, with the help of a secret inner council. If this monopolistic patent had been respected, and its claims upheld, logically there could have been no way forward for mankind other than appointing Freud the Enlightened Despot of humanity. In fact, people who take psychoanalysis seriously do sometimes wonder – and given their premises, they are right – about the oddity of the existing political systems, which allows ordinary un-analysed people, as neurotic as they come (true enough) to decide our destinies.

The concept of the Unconscious implicitly allocates status: those who have mastered it, or at least are privy to its secrets, should rule, those who are its dupes should obey. This is inherent in the logic of the situation: the one-eyed should indeed lead the blind, and the doctrine of the Unconscious, like some naturalistic and cognitive version of the doctrine of Original Sin, consigns all of us to blindness, in its full rigour in all contexts: it is applied fully only in the therapeutic/pastoral situation. There, on the other hand, it is applied with special force.

One of the marked features of psychoanalysis is what might suitably be called 'de-proceduralization'. The point is this: in other activities, notably in inquiries and investigations, due process has to be observed, and the proper procedure is not itself *sub judice*. It provides the fixed framework within which the inquiry takes place and which sets its rules. Not so for individuals fully involved in the analytic experience. Anything, including – above all, including – their doubts and feelings about the process itself and the practitioner, must be investigated and related to their deeper motives (and not to their possible validity), *within* the investigation and by its rather peculiar rules.

What goes on *inside* the technique trumps and devours any external, formal, procedural rules or evaluations which might take place outside it, and possibly check it. No appeal is possible to anything outside. Doubts about the technique itself and the theory underlying it are treated as symptoms *within* the process, and their face value is held to be irrelevant. All this is an oblique way of placing the technique itself beyond the reach of doubt – but it is a perfectly logical corollary of the basic picture itself. The Unconscious is all-pervasive and well informed, and only too able and willing to use seemingly rational, theoretical doubts, as devices to obstruct therapy. In this way, the key ideas of the technique create a world within which scepticism concerning the technique itself is out of bounds. Psychoanalysis does not allow any Reserved Area, exempt from depth probing: this proscription of any redoubt assures it of undisputed sovereignty, for within its own zone, it alone can decode the deceptions imposed by the wily Unconscious, and identify the residual truth. So what is presented as a temporary therapeutic device – the depth interpretation of simply anything – is an indirect way of absolutizing the claims of the technique and the associated theory. The absolutization of the theory need not be overtly affirmed (though on occasion it is): it follows from the basic picture in terms of which the technique operates. In other activities, the basic procedural principles, the evaluation of the cost-effectiveness of the operation itself, cannot be challenged from within the game: in psychoanalysis, all this is suspended. Truth is only to be found inside, and trumps decisions, evaluation, made in unenlightened, Unconscious-dominated Outside. In this respect, psychoanalysis resembles Marxism, which also – using a different terminology – believed that substantive justice, the considerations of the class struggle, rightly trumped mere formal, procedural considerations. The imperatives of the class struggle, revealed *inside* the theory, trump consideration of more formal justice. Similarly, bourgeois legal function is only a device for obstructing true, substantive, proletarian revolutionary justice: attempts to judge the corporation possessed of the psychoanalytic revelation and the revelation itself are mere cunning and intolerable attempts to hamper substantive justice. The substantive revelation is triumphant in each case.

Psychoanalysis not only puts people in their place – by first depriving them of cognitive status in virtue of being dupes of the Unconscious, and then readmitting them to rationality only on condition of submitting to a process which recognizes only its own authority, but suspends all neutral procedural rules – but also *puts down* data, so to speak. One of the elementary principles of scientific activity is the 'operationalization' of data. This simply means that there must be rules concerning what a given term means and does not mean, rules applied impersonally and not subject to the whim of the investigator. Notoriously there are problems about operationalization: not all concepts actually in use in science can be directly related in the approved manner to observationally or experimentally defined facts, and those not so linked to the world must then be justified – in accordance with philosophic preference – either as relating to unobservable but inferred entities, or in terms of their service role within the explanatory system, 'instrumentally'. There is also the problem arising from the fact that 'operationalization' is liable to be circular: the terms used to relate a given notion to data may themselves in turn be defined in terms of the explicated notion. Notwithstanding these and perhaps other problems, operationalization is a well-established requirement of scientific inquiry. Without it, there is no guarantee that terms are employed in a consistent and stable manner, and that affirmations retain their meaning from one case to another.

It is not widely recognized that psychoanalysis and its key idea of the 'Unconscious' inverts all this: covertly, it consists of an omnibus *de*-operationalization of all concepts. The background situation in which it sees itself functioning, and which justifies such *de*-operationalization is this: it is engaged in a struggle with an extremely cunning, devious, deception-addicted agency known as the Unconscious, which is, above all, an expert in camouflage and disinformation. It is constantly shuffling the 'meaning' of observable data. The data it presents to a repressive consciousness are disguised in order to pass a severe internal censorship, and its cyphers are certainly resistant to any mechanical decoding. The Unconscious is quick to find new codes, as soon as the conscious mind finds itself on the scent of the earlier mystifications practised by the malignant inner demon. Hence, in the very nature of the situation, there can be no general operationalization of psychological concepts, no general linkage of abstract classificatory terms to psychic content. The 'meaning' of the data is variable, not fixed. The linkage has to be idiographic, effected in the individual case, and it can never be generalized. The linkage of data to concepts is being ever revised by the practitioner: impersonal operationalization is impossible.

So psychoanalysis lives a double life. It is, from one viewpoint, a hypothetico-deductive system like any other, a structure of general theories and middle-range generalizations, purporting to cover the data of our comportment and our psychic life. But at the very same time, it is a mystical technique directly relating the investigator to an individual's concrete and living reality, and moreover one which precludes, for the reason stated, deference either to the authority of extraneous procedural rules, or to the stable operationalization of concepts. It has its own inner self-sustaining authority. One never knows which of these two aspects one is dealing with; no rules exist for deciding which it is to be at any given time. Invocation of 'resistance' appears to be in order in a scientific discussion to devalue an opponent's view. It is this general situation which leads to the well-known and frequently noted tendency of psychoanalysis to evade all testing. This tendency may be present in all theorizing, but in other spheres an excessive use of it suggests that the investigator or theorist in question is, by temperament, a committed dogmatist, unable to face the falsification of his or her own ideas. In psychoanalysis, this tendency does not really reflect on the personal idiosyncrasy of any one practitioner: it is very deeply inherent in the very logic of the central ideas themselves.

This point can also be made in another way. Many theoretical systems in science (perhaps all of them) contain both horizontal and vertical connections. By horizontal connections I mean links between things and things, or events and events. By vertical ones I mean links between things and the observer. Physiological theories, for instance, not only contain affirmations about the connections between diverse objects, but also contain ('vertical') connections between objects and the human senses, or our perception of those objects; those latter then of course also govern the manner in which observers interpret what they 'see'. In theory, this introduces the danger of circularity: the theory which determines how we interpret 'what we see' *might* be so constructed as to ensure that what we see always confirms the theory itself.

In practice, this danger is generally avoided. It is avoided because 'vertical' connections make up only a relatively small part of the system, are required to be consistent with the horizontal elements of the system, and above all, they do not single out some observers over others, and thereby engender a, so to speak, cognitive ranking between them. No physiological theory affirms that what is seen by a Professor of Physiology is more authoritative than what is seen by a person of lower university rank.

In psychoanalysis, all this is radically different. Vertical affirmations about the differently distorted perceptions of psychic content make up a very large proportion of the theoretical structure: in fact, they make up its central part, the very heart of the theory. Psychoanalysis is, above all, a doctrine about the manner in which, thanks to the Unconscious, the true state of psychic affairs is quite different from what it appears to be to the naked, unenlightened eye (or I). In a sense, it is above all a theory about the distortion of our perceptions. Second, the vertical generalizations do most emphatically distinguish the veridicity of perceptions in accordance with the rank of enlightenment, attributed to the observer in the guild of enlightenment. Under these circumstances, the potential for circularity, logically carried by any presence of vertical elements in a system of explanation (but avoided thanks to, in the long run, the equality of all investigators, and the predominance of other elements), is liable to be exploited to the full.

The ethical theory or precepts contained within psychoanalysis is of the Stoic variety. The key idea is that at least relative contentment or inner peace can be attained by recognizing reality, rather than struggling unavailingly against it: congruence between desire and fact can best be won by modifying our desires in the light of reality, rather than trying to bend reality. Psychoanalysis differs from other versions of this doctrine – such as that taught, for instance, by the seventeenth-century philosopher Spinoza – in one important respect: the recognition of the inner realities which are to be accepted is no easy matter, and cannot normally be achieved by the individual unaided by the specific technique invented for the purpose of penetrating the said inner reality. Unaided conscious thought is simply not capable of performing this feat. The great psychoanalytic promise is that it can help the neurotic sufferer both to identify the inner reality and to accept it. Such is the nature of the cure. The Stoic view was that the good man (by Stoic criteria, one who accepts reality and adjusts his desires to it) could be happy even on the rack. As an undergraduate allegedly said to Dr Jowett, this would require a very good man on a very bad rack. Psychoanalysis does not promise either to remove the rack or to diminish the physical pain it induces: but it does promise to free the sufferer from anxiety by laying bare the unconscious meanings which the rack may have for him.

The trouble with this promise is that it too evades testing. The deoperationalized nature of that very knowledge, which is to secure acceptance of reality, already ensures that there can never be a confident and above all neutral, independent way of establishing whether the knowledge has really been attained, so that we can see whether this secures the promised effects: so failure of the appearance of the promised reward of the attainment of this knowledge, *for which there is never any deadline*, can always be blamed on the non-attainment, as yet, of the genuine illumination. But psychoanalysis also insists on the importance of the distinction between mere intellectual knowledge and a genuine inner adjustment to it – another ever-available let-out. If it fails to work, the conditions have – ex hypothesi – not been met.

Freud insisted on the difference between neurotic and merely ordinary unhappiness, and refrained from promising, plausibly enough, to alleviate the latter. But what is the operationalizable, independent criterion for distinguishing the two? Dissatisfied clients of the technique show by their very dissatisfaction, that they have not learned to accept the ordinary unhappiness which is the human lot. So, in practice, the real and adequate application of technique is judged, not by any independent criteria of therapeutic effectiveness, but by whether patients accept the adequacy of the technique and the effectiveness of its practitioner, by consenting henceforth not to ask for any more, and to treat their discontents as appropriate, 'ordinary' unhappiness. Only satisfied customers have met the conditions of the guarantee. The de-proceduralization of the practice, the insistence that everything of importance must be 'looked through' *within* the therapeutic relationship, precludes any appeal to outside validation or quality control. The tacit operationalization of the concepts of 'cure' and 'neurosis' are such that the application of the requirements of the technique has been properly performed only if the recipient endorses the technique and is satisfied with its result. The success of the technique, within the system of its own concepts and their implied definitions, is a tautology.

The question may legitimately be asked – if psychoanalysis has these (and other) defects, how it has come to have the impact both on the general intellectual climate and on therapeutic practice which, indisputably, it has? The answer to this question has a number of quite distinct elements, which deserve separate formulation.

Acute need

Marx, as already mentioned, once observed that humankind sets itself only such problems as it can solve. In general, this strikes me as totally untrue. On the contrary, humankind normally finds itself face to face with problems which it simply has no means of solving. The problems do, of course, change in character from period to period. But when confronted by the anguish of an insoluble and tragic problem, few of us have the strength to face such bleak reality unaided. The problems faced by people living in a modern, secularized, naturalistic and largely atomized society are rather different from those which overwhelmed their ancestors, and they are acute.

As stated, Freud is not really responsible for the definitive incorporation of humankind in a cold nature, obedient to its own laws, and replacing the much warmer previous cosmos, purposefully designed by a supposedly benevolent, though somewhat mysterious and wayward creator. This reallocation of humankind had been done by others. But our new habitation carries its own and most disturbing problems. For one thing, it contains no guide posts and no signs, no indications of the proprieties of conduct, inherent in the overall structure, and at least liable, if properly observed, to reward the respectful citizen of the cosmic order with some prospect of contentment. Moreover, the laws governing this new and cold nature are largely unknown, at any rate in their application to the psychic and social spheres, and so do not permit effective manipulation of circumstance with a view to avoiding disaster. Altogether, this is a rather uncomfortable situation.

And there is worse to come. Pre-industrial societies were, all in all, endowed with well-defined structures, assigning roles and positions to their members, who could then really observe an ethic of their 'station and its duties'. But that is now largely gone. An occupationally mobile society, endowed only with loose sub-units, leaves its members to find their human contacts and warmth as best they can, and many of them fail. In developed affluent societies, the threats of hunger and pestilence have lost much of their sting. They have, however, been replaced by the fear of personal, psychological inadequacy. A need for support and solace which is so widespread will inevitably provoke attempts to meet it. Who better suited to meet this need, and supply the new secular pastoral care, than the experts at communication with that dread realm within which our capacity to 'get on' with spouses, lovers, kin, colleagues, is notoriously decided?

One of the major events of recent decades is the emergence of a major new (and I suspect, largely uncharted) profession of 'counsellors'. The conceptual equipment these new pastors bring to their task is, I suspect, in the main Freud-and-water, a diluted and context-adjusted employment of the central intuitions of Sigmund Freud. These ideas carry both a hope of effective manipulation of recalcitrant psychic processes, and the promise of moral direction – no longer based on transcendent command, but on the authority of the sovereign psychic deep.

Suggestiveness of the idiom

The general language in which psychoanalytical ideas are articulated unquestionably does more justice to the reality of our inner lives and our absorbing personal relations, than did the stilted language of academic psychology, the anaemic schemata of associationism, or the language of common sense. Psychoanalysis does great justice to two salient features of our lives: the strength of instinctual drives such as sex, domination and resentment, *and* the extraordinary complexity, volatility and deviousness of the semantic structures in terms of which we see ourselves. It does justice to *both* of these: rival psychologies tend to ignore one or the other of them, and sometimes both of them at once. Moreover, psychoanalysis plausibly relates the two to each other: the Unconscious is the place where instinctual drives and convoluted, devious meanings meet each other. As predictive and genuinely explanatory structures, the theories of psychoanalysis are not very impressive; as a phenomenology, as a system of descriptive and suggestive terms, they seem to be the best we have, and their conquest of our language is not only unchallengeable, but also probably well deserved.

The discovery of mystical technique

While the therapeutic effectiveness of psychoanalysis and related techniques is evidently questionable, there can be little doubt concerning the fact that

52 *Ernest Gellner*

'transference' does very frequently occur and is exceedingly powerful. *Why* this is so is unknown: Freud's own explanation shows only the very low level of his own sophistication concerning what can count as an explanation, and his inability to distinguish between a real explanation and a mere simple-minded physical metaphor for a psychic process.

It is amusing to reflect how closely the psychoanalytical technique illustrates certain anthropological theories concerning the method of engendering heightened emotion: the use of a dramatic inversion of the most sacred proprieties. Modern humans, unlike their peasant ancestors, are drilled and obliged to respect an astonishingly high standard of logical order. Human work requires it, human education prepares them for it. But when, in distress, they seek their shepherd, they are instructed to abandon all semantic restraint, and display not only their intimate and shameful secrets, but also the total and deplorable chaos of their mental content, which otherwise they must strive to hide. They must 'free-associate'; then, it would seem, they develop feelings towards the person in whose presence they have so utterly revealed and abased themselves. The intensity of the feeling so generated in turn appears to confirm the validity both of the theoretical and the specific insights attained in the course of the therapeutic sessions, thus producing that characteristic blend of strong feeling and sense of cognitive and liberating illumination, which defines mystical experience.

Note

A fuller exposition of these points, accompanied by a bibliography, is to be found in Gellner (1985) *The Psychoanalytic Movement*, London: Paladin.

RESPONSE – Stephen Frosh

Persuasion is a masterly art. How do we decide what is true? Sometimes it is through the irrefutability of a material demonstration of the reality of a phenomenon, an absolute concreteness before which all scales fall from all eyes, at least until the next, more concrete but different demonstration. Sometimes, what persuades us is a 'mystical experience' of the kind which Professor Gellner so elegantly evokes at the beginning and end of his chapter. This kind of persuasion is based on a lived experience of transformation, something internal which is experienced as so irrevocable and so compelling that it cannot be false – even if all the external signs are that, in reality, it is. Sometimes, we accept the validity of an argument, hypothesis or theory, because of a mixture of the external signs and the internal logic of the argument, accompanied by a partially transformative experience. This experience is best thought of as a personal resonance or movement produced by the theory, not strong enough to outweigh compelling intimations of reality, but powerful enough to make us entertain the possibility that what we see, hear or feel might be true. Much of the best kind of knowledge falls into this last category; indeed, one could argue that the best kind of *psychological* knowledge must be like this – transformative, making a difference to us, making us reflect on our own experience, resonating subjectively, operating as more than just an addition to an intellectual jigsaw. Psychological knowledge, as we acquire it through our scientific investigations and through our personal explorations, is at its best a reflexive kind of knowledge; it changes us because it is about us.

Professor Gellner places psychoanalysis as 'a mystical experience', arguing that it is based on an intense emotional experience leading to special knowledge which is impermeable to evaluation by external criteria. Indeed, he suggests, it is the very intensity of the experience, for example as encountered through transference during analysis, which is taken as evidence of the validity of the theory, so confusing emotion with truth. The danger of this confusion is that something which answers emotional needs, offering various kinds of consolation in an admittedly persecutory world, will be taken up and believed in even if it has nothing to do with reality. Professor Gellner does not deny that psychoanalysis might have something to do with the real world, that its theories might be 'true'; but he does suggest that people believe in it because of its emotional power, not because of its potential validity – and that the premises and postulates of psychoanalysis, particularly its notion of the unconscious, make it impossible ever to find out if this belief is justified. This is what makes it 'mystical'.

He may, of course, be right; we cannot know for sure. His prose is elegant, ironic, amusing, balanced and persuasive. It stirs up feelings and articulates doubts which I and, I am sure, others share; it reminds us of the ambiguities of the psychoanalytic procedure, its reliance on rhetoric and binds, emotional upheaval and interpersonal power. There are no purely external criteria for evaluating Professor Gellner's contribution. On the other hand, it is not a completely mystical phenomenon: there are some points on which we might take hold, as with psychoanalysis, I would say. I want to take hold of some of these points, focusing as is expected of me on the disagreements although also conceding some of Professor Gellner's arguments. First, however, a simple statement which is not, it seems to me, in any way contentious. The emotional power of a theory does not guarantee its validity, but if that theory is a psychological one, its emotional impact is one important source of information on how valid it might turn out to be.

On consolation

Professor Gellner at various points attributes the hold of psychoanalysis over its adherents to its consoling power. For example, he suggests that the naturalized version of the unconscious put forward and managed by Freud is a major reason for the persuasiveness of his approach as compared with that of his precursors – Schopenhauer, Nietzsche, von Hartmann and the like. 'Men listened,' he writes, 'not to the discoverer, but to the beast tamer.' Later, having diagnosed the mysticism in psychoanalysis more fully, Professor Gellner returns to this theme: 'The great psychoanalytic promise is that it can help the neurotic sufferer both to identify the inner reality and to accept it'. Finally, Professor Gellner remarks on what he compellingly pigeon-holes as 'Freud-and-water' counselling, carrying 'both a hope of effective manipulation of recalcitrant psychic processes, and the promise of moral direction'.

What one says is not necessarily what one does, but for what it is worth here is Freud's view of the appeasements immanent in psychoanalysis.

> I have not the courage to rise up before my fellow-men as a prophet, and I bow to their reproach that I can offer them no consolation: for at bottom that is what they are all demanding – the wildest revolutionaries no less passionately than the most virtuous believers.
>
> (Freud 1930: 82)

Freud was a great ironist, but he did often mean what he said. It has been a well-charted fate of psychoanalysis to have had its radical dimension disowned or adulterated – to have become a method of reconciliation with reality rather than a critical engagement with the impact of the social order on personal possibilities (e.g. Marcuse 1955; Jacoby 1975; 1983; Frosh 1987). Freud himself was not an advocate of particularly radical practices – he tended to side with what he saw as reality over pleasure, tended to think that the optimal basis for healthy living was to exert conscious, egoic control over unconscious impulses, or in the social domain to behave towards others with sufficient decorum to enable society to survive. Nevertheless, his 'discovery' partly involved the identification of a domain of personal life that is always at odds with the world, always has a critical stance towards it, is always striving for something other than what it has or is offered. In this light, as many commentators have pointed out (e.g. Rieff 1959; 1966; Richards 1989), Freud's vision is a tragic one, not a consolatory one – individuals have to live without gods who can save them, maintaining an 'analytic attitude' that involves adoption of an ironic and mistrustful stance towards all communities of commitment, including psychoanalysis itself. Freud-without-water forces our attention on this: to what extent can the real needs of the human subject be met within the current social order; the consolations of the post-Freudian revisionists and humanists are Freud-watered-down precisely because they and their adherents cannot bear so much reality.

Psychoanalysis makes some kind of sense of our contemporary confusions, gives us a set of narratives to live by, but it is because these narratives are uncomfortable that psychoanalysis sometimes loses its way. Professor Gellner is undoubtedly correct to point out how strongly people desire consolation, but psychoanalysis is more like those fairy-tales that conjure up demons than like those that wish them away.

A brief note on social status

'Poor ourselves, and socially powerless' is Freud's (1917/1974: 483) verdict on the social status of psychoanalysis; indeed, like the bringing up of children and the governing of nations, psychoanalysis is an 'impossible profession'. Professor Gellner has a point when he implicitly questions these protestations and suggests that premises of psychoanalysis make it appear that 'those who have mastered [the Unconscious], or at least are privy to its secrets, should rule, those who are its dupes should obey' – at least, that is the way psychoanalysts sometimes behave. But, first, many psychoanalysts recognize that the quality of functioning of psychoanalytic institutions does not instil confidence and that it would be a good thing if they tried their hands at larger social tasks. Second, and more to the point, psychoanalysis has a domain to which it is relevant – the large domain of psychological investigation and its sub-domain of therapeutic practice – but it is not necessary for everything. Because psychoanalysis eschews the notion of 'cure' (Professor Gellner himself quotes the famous passage suggesting that 'common human unhappiness' is all that can be hoped for), people can be ranged only along a continuum of more or less successful functioning. Depending on the psychoanalytic school involved, this means more or less high-quality engagement with work and love, more or less consciousness of one's inner motives, more or less fulfilling personal relationships, and so on. 'Mastering the Unconscious' might be relevant to this, but some people seem to manage all right without it, and not everyone needs help. The question of mastery *within* the psychoanalytic movement is another matter: as Professor Gellner suggests, there it does seem to be the case that the more senior an analyst is, the closer to the truth she or he is thought to be – although whether this is actually that different from what goes on in the institutions of the 'objective' sciences is a moot point. This is a larger argument, however, pertaining to the central issue in Professor Gellner's chapter, the issue of whether psychoanalysis allows any external criteria of validation to operate upon it.

Procedures and operations

De-proceduralization and a failure to operationalize concepts: these are crucial criticisms of psychoanalytic theory and practice. Attack the views of a psychoanalyst and you are accused of being defensive, or unconsciously envious, or insufficiently analysed – even if you are an analyst yourself. Suggest criteria for evaluation and the complaint comes back: 'the Unconscious is not the kind of thing which can be inspected; nor are the consequences of psychoanalytic treatment the kind of consequences which can be measured and displayed'. Professor Gellner certainly has a point.

However, I think he overdoes it, not – I hasten very diligently to add – because he is defensive, or cathects an alternative theoretical/therapeutic empire, but because he fails to recognize the heterogeneity of positions and levels within psychoanalysis itself, the vibrant nature of its internal disputes, critiques, reconciliations and efforts towards understanding, and the possibility of there being some important differences between therapeutic practice and theoretical critique. In addition, there is the notion of the 'analytic attitude': a balanced rational consciousness, free from unconscious distortions, enabling one to free oneself from what Rieff (1966) terms the 'ecstatic' attitude of affiliation to some salvational community or idea, and to judge and appraise its worth. The analytic attitude is an ideal, I grant, but at least, as an ideal, it exists. It is supposedly the attitude held by the analyst during therapy; it is also the attitude to be directed towards all intellectual systems, including psychoanalysis itself. Freud criticized 'therapeutic zeal' but demonstrated theoretical zeal himself; distancing oneself from the latter is, however, part of the analytic attitude to which psychoanalysis aspires. Mystical belief may make one feel better, but psychoanalysts would not recognize it as a sign of mental health – even if it is mystical belief in psychoanalysis itself.

Professor Gellner is quite detailed on all this, so here are a few comments on his specific accusations regarding de-proceduralization, operationalization and therapeutic change.

De-proceduralization

'Anything, including . . . doubts and feelings about the process itself and the practitioner, must be investigated and related to [the analysand's] deeper motives . . . *within* the investigation by its own peculiar rules.' This is a correct description of therapeutic activity, but it is not reasonable to extend it as a criticism of theory. The two tasks are different and it is important not to conflate the therapeutic encounter with the investigative procedures and theoretical complexities of psychoanalysis. At the therapeutic level, if one chooses to enter psychoanalysis as a therapeutic exercise, then that is what one is doing: the psychoanalytic approach entails focusing on the unconscious meanings and determinants of actions, that is its sole method, technique and aim. That has to be allowed within the therapeutic encounter, because it is the way psychoanalytic therapy works. Even here, however, people do evaluate therapy: the analyst might interpret their criticisms or, indeed, their praise, in terms of underlying motives, but people who go through analysis do nevertheless usually feel free to make some kind of personal evaluation of it – of whether it was any use, made any sense, helped them at all. Inside the psychoanalytic whale, its rules obtain; outside, rational evaluation is possible.

So, too, at the theoretical level. In addition to the point concerning the ideal 'analytic attitude' mentioned above, the whole psychoanalytic enterprise is not as monolithic as Professor Gellner suggests. The dissensions between different psychoanalytic schools are magnificent: Freudians and

Kleinians, object-relations theorists and ego psychologists, Lacanians and everyone else. Even though all these schools espouse some version of the dynamic unconscious (that is what defines them all as psychoanalytic), the content, form and developmental history of unconscious functioning is theorized radically differently in each case. From Jung to Kohut, Klein to Irigaray, it has never been possible for psychoanalysis to keep its dissidents quiet – despite its over-liberal use of *ad hominem* arguments. Some of these dissensions may be just more mysticism, but many relate to the detail of work with clients and others are resonant of the huge cultural concerns of modern times. Still others, it should be noted, relate to the findings of mainstream psychology – for example, evidence concerning the cognitive capacities and social orientation of infants (see Frosh 1989). My point here is that psychoanalysis has never been able to take its own truth for granted; it has never been as closed a system as Professor Gellner suggests.

Operationalization

Professor Gellner correctly notes that 'operationalization' is an important strategy in scientific research, however difficult it can often be to achieve. He suggests that the concept of the unconscious makes operationalization unavailable within psychoanalysis, because the unconscious subverts every-thing, is 'constantly shuffling the "meaning" of observable data'. Moreover, 'the linkage of data to concepts is being ever revised by the practitioner: impersonal operationalization is impossible'.

Once again, there is justice in this complaint: psychoanalysis often throws up vague and illimitable concepts, switching their meaning whenever one tries to pin them down. However, once again, it goes too far and is in some senses at the wrong level. For example, Professor Gellner points out that the meaning of 'data' derived from individuals is variable, making the psycho-analytic approach idiographic. This is true: there is no simple dictionary of symbols available to psychoanalytic practitioners. However, while specific interpretations and meanings might vary from case to case, in the light of the particular personal context of the individual concerned, the processes and procedures of psychoanalysis do not. Thus, in principle at least, the great Freudian organizing processes of unconscious, primary process thinking – those of displacement and condensation – can be operationalized even if the content of different dreams or symptoms might vary. So, it is possible to predict that a specific symptom might refer metonymically to a range of emotionally loaded material, or might be a metaphoric condensa-tion of a whole class of ideas or impulses. Similarly, repression, projection and transference are predictable processes the operations of which might be (and in some cases have been) investigated, even though what each individual analysand says during analysis is likely to be different. Professor Gellner is looking at too low a level for the operationalizable points in psychoanalysis: they are to be found in the characteristic activities of unconscious thought, not in the particular symbolic contents.

Therapeutic change

Professor Gellner raises an extremely embarrassing difficulty for psycho-analysis when he draws attention to the circularity of the common assess-ments of outcome. If someone does not change, it is because they have not been analysed enough; as there are no objective grounds for knowing whether someone has received the 'full treatment', it is not possible to evaluate independently what is offered and what impact it has. More generally, the 'de-proceduralization of the practice, the insistence that everything of im-portance must be "looked through" *within* the therapeutic relationship, precludes any appeal to outside validation or quality control'. I have two responses to this complaint. The first acknowledges its justice: even friends of psychoanalysis often find it galling to encounter its refusal to take re-sponsibility for its therapeutic failures. My second response is 'Well, what is so different about psychoanalysis here?' Evaluating any system by refer-ence only to the views of its practitioners is a dodgy empirical procedure: try asking behaviour therapists about cases in which their approach has failed and you are likely to get answers which focus on errors in applying the procedure, or the difficulty of identifying all the controlling contingencies in this specific case, or external interferences – but rarely a statement that this case comprises a refutation of behavioural theory. With any type of work in which people have substantial investments (and psychoanalysts do have such investments, given the demands of their training and the fact that psychoanalytic therapy is likely to be their livelihood), it is necessary to have outside scrutiny, an external point of view, to assess its efficacy. This is a point well recognized by researchers into the comparative effectiveness of different forms of therapy.

To conclude: Professor Gellner's 'discontent' is of the constructive kind. If taken too much to heart, it is true, it might bring despair to those of us who think psychoanalysis offers more than a system of mystical consola-tion and lead us either to throw the whole thing up or to take refuge in its apparent certainties. But if treated rationally, in moderation, what he points to is the importance of developing modes of psychoanalytic thought which can deal with the personal and subjective – because that is what psycho-analysis is about, and where it is an advance on many other psychological approaches – but which can also be scrutinized and exposed to critical doubt. One thing, however, psychoanalysis should not be made to apologize for: its transformative nature. Both as a body of knowledge and as a thera-peutic method, psychoanalysis is an approach that induces emotion, that challenges us to change; this is exactly how it should be.

References

Freud, S. (1917/1974) *Introductory Lectures on Psychoanalysis*. Harmondsworth: Penguin.

Freud, S. (1930) *Civilisation and its Discontents*. London: Hogarth Press.
Frosh, S. (1987) *The Politics of Psychoanalysis*. London: Macmillan.
Frosh, S. (1989) *Psychoanalysis and Psychology*. London: Macmillan.
Jacoby, R. (1975) *Social Amnesia*. Sussex: Harvester.
Jacoby, R. (1983) *The Repression of Psychoanalysis*. New York: Basic Books.
Marcuse, H. (1955) *Eros and Civilisation*. Boston, Mass: Beacon Press.
Richards, B. (1989) *Images of Freud*. London: Dent.
Rieff, P. (1959) *Freud: The Mind of the Moralist*. Chicago: University of Chicago Press.
Rieff, P. (1966) *The Triumph of the Therapeutic*. Harmondsworth: Penguin.

REBUTTAL – Ernest Gellner

Stephen Frosh's essay is elegant, perceptive and, above all, exceedingly generous. His comments on my views are probably kinder than I deserve and certainly gentler than I am used to. Moreover, his description of the actual practice and current intellectual climate of psychoanalysis is of great value both as a document and as an implicit recommendation. His suggestion that my criticisms should be used constructively, but that their importance should not be exaggerated, is so gracious that it would seem churlish not to endorse it.

If one is treated with such a mixture of elegance, kindness and charm, one's instinctive reaction – mine at any rate – is to try to respond in kind. Yet the logic of the situation does not allow me to indulge this impulse to the full. The obligation of intellectual honesty prevails over those of courtesy and reciprocity.

Frosh's defence of psychoanalysis hinges on the contention not only that it is what I say it is, but also that it is something else, something which can claim objective validity. Very flatteringly, he compares its status to that of my own rhetoric, and says this about the problem of evaluating it: 'There are no purely external criteria for evaluating Professor Gellner's contribution; on the other hand, it is not a completely mystical phenomenon, there are some points on which we might take hold. As with psychoanalysis, I would say.'

I must leave it to others to judge whether this Janus-like account of my own style (half self-sustaining facade, half publicly testable claims) is correct. But I accept it entirely as an account of psychoanalysis. It is not one thing but at least two distinct things. The duality invoked by Frosh as a defence of it is in fact part of my critique of it. The theoretical propositions of psychoanalysis, when so to speak chemically isolated, cleaned up and seen on their own (in an unnatural state of purity which is not their normal condition) clearly are specimens of the hypothetico-deductive method, in other words of science. They consist of striking assertions about human behaviour and psychic life, assertions which are intuitively endowed with very interesting meaning, and which, given a bit of careful definition and serious operationalization of the terms used, can be made to confront the reality which they purport to describe and explain. These affirmations are made in the public domain, as sentences in articles and books, and are subject to public controversy deploying argument and evidence. This *is* science, if anything is. Moreover, were this not so, psychoanalysis would never have made the impact which in fact it has. Its appeal hinges in part on being part of medicine which is part of science, the most prestigious form of cognition. This distinguishes it from self-confessed, open forms of mysticism and therapy hinging on the possession of private, secret, incommunicable powers, or, on the other hand, from a merely literary expression of similar ideas in writers such as Schopenhauer or Nietzsche.

But – and this is a very *big* but – what distinguishes psychoanalysis from other clusters of ideas whose claim to scientific status is more robust is precisely the intimate fusion of its ideas with another set of practices. Within this other set, evidence and argument are no longer King. The vision of psychoanalytical therapy hinges on a powerful notion of the Unconscious and its capacity to disinform us all, a vision which leads to the overriding of mere 'surface' evidence by a hierarchy of authority, legitimized by that vision itself. The rules of psychoanalytical clinical inquiry are a kind of Martial Law of knowledge, justified by the requirements of combating so powerful and cunning an enemy. With such an opponent, special Enabling Powers must be granted to our champion. It is precisely this duality, this bifocal vision, the inseparable fusion of hypothetico-deductive method with something quite different and alien to it, which bothers me. It is not the coexistence of intense personal experience with more tepid, or positively cold, external evidence – which is a bit the way Frosh presents the situation – which is at issue: it is the authority of an entrenched vision, linked all at once to a circle of self-sustaining ideas *and* to intense experience which is slotted into that circle and claims to validate it, which creates the problem. (This rather abstract diagnosis – the Dual Monarchy of Evidence *and* an Entrenched Vision – applies, in my view, to most of the intellectual activities which are to be found in human history. I have argued this in greater detail in Gellner (1988) *Plough, Sword and Book*.)

It is only science proper which escapes this model: this is what makes it unique, and presumably explains its unrivalled power. Scientific practice distinguishes between a database – a database independent of society and its values and hierarchy and of the capacity of doctrine-linked ritual to induce intense emotion purporting to confirm this doctrine – and, on the other hand, a system of interpretations which may never be absolutized and which in the final, but not too distant or ever-deferred analysis, must be subjected to the verdict of that database.

Frosh quite rightly expresses some doubts concerning whether this idealized account of science is to be taken entirely at face value. He wonders whether 'what goes on in the institutions of "objective" science' really lives up to this ideal, or whether, on the contrary, it does not resemble in great measure the habits I attribute to psychoanalysis and to pre-scientific thought generally.

In supporting these doubts, Frosh might well invoke a great deal of currently fashionable philosophy of science. The idea of an independent database has been much undermined by the plausible claim that data are always inevitably 'theory-saturated'. The claim that, in science, no theoretical interpretation may be absolutized, but must always live under the sovereign judgement of data, has been contradicted by the widely used notion of a 'paradigm', denoting, precisely, dictator-like ideas within science. The author who coined this term (Kuhn 1962) delights in insisting that such doctrinal dictatorship, far from being a disgrace to science, is a condition of its very existence.

I do not wish to dispute the partial truth, and relevance, of these insights. But it is all a matter of degree. The idea of an entirely pure and independent database, existing prior to the theories treated by it, is no doubt a myth. And presumably there are indeed theoretical constructions which effectively dominate entire schools of science. None the less, the domination exercised by powerful theories over the collection and interpretation of data, seems to me mild indeed compared to the manner in which key Freudian ideas govern the psychoanalytical acquisition of data in the course of clinical practice.

This fusion of empirical inquiry with the dominance of a set of ideas and associated institutions and ecstatic ritual confirmation, must be so to speak organic, natural, plausible, intuitively persuasive, if it is to persuade. I could easily invent any number of Janus-like systems, saying, in effect, that in a given domain free inquiry is in order, but the deep structure of that domain is such that the findings of inquiry can always be overruled by the Top Boss of the Domain. The identification of that Top Boss would be a corollary of some of the key attributes of its deep structure, which would also require well-orchestrated rituals confirming the authority of the Boss. Logically, such a system could work impeccably. But who would accept it? If the logical scaffolding is too obvious, it betrays the working of the mechanism and discourages credulity. In fact, certain institutions and belief systems inherited from the pre-scientific age have precisely this structure, but they only perpetuate it, at any rate in modern societies, with a sense of unease and awkwardness. They tend to try to escape from their embarrassment by saying something like, two quite different kinds of truth are involved, functioning at quite distinct levels, and so the two cognitive sovereigns, Evidence and Top Boss, do not really get in each other's way. The ironic consequence of this version of the Dual Sovereignty doctrine is that it no longer provides what it offered in the past, a cosy world in which fact and value dovetail, in which Nature and Social Hierarchy support each other. They offer only their own version of a bifurcated world, with a deep chasm between truth and value.

Freud's great achievement was to erect a new realm under dual Sovereignty, but one which is seamless, without fissure, without alienation. Truth and salvation are one. It is its therapeutic power, its capacity to make whole the individual, which makes truth exciting; it is its linkage with science which legitimizes the therapy. This marvellous unity is the corollary of the entirely naturalistic conception of the Unconscious. If endowed with the properties with which it is plausibly credited, it follows that the methods of both inquiry and therapy must adjust themselves to the fact that the main activity of the Unconscious is Sustained Disinformation. This automatically devalues a large class of data, and disqualifies a large class of observers, and establishes the authority of another group and of their findings. The identification of either group is in the hands of one of them. But this reintroduction of authority and hierarchy has a natural and plausible feel. It does not offend, because it is not affirmed directly, but simply appears to be the natural corollary of the central and plausible ideas of the system.

Frosh sees the point of this worry, but attempts to cope with it by separating theoretical investigative validity from therapy. 'The two tasks are different and it is important not to conflate the therapeutic encounter with the investigative procedure'. I concur wholeheartedly with the proscription of conflation, but suspect that it is inherent in psychoanalysis, rather than being, as Frosh hopes, an eliminable weakness.

My doubts on this score are based on reflection both on therapy and on investigation. Take therapy. Patients are entitled to Consumer Protection. They are entitled to ask, *outside* the framework of the therapeutic encounter – what are the grounds for accepting the claims concerning therapeutic effectiveness? Are they not entitled to ask this at any time? But the rules of the encounter eventually preclude them from asking the question. The rules themselves transform the terms of reference. They require that everything, including doubts about the therapy and therapist, be interpreted not in terms of their validity, but in terms of their role in the patient's own psychic functioning and its manifestation in the therapeutic relationship. This is reinforced further by the ambiguity of the therapeutic promise, by what I am inclined to call the Stoic Tautology. I say unto you, I am your salvation, and my teaching is, Accept Reality! This recipe for cure cannot fail, for those who complain that the therapy has not worked, have automatically betrayed the fact that they have failed to carry out its conditions. So the rules of therapy preclude both the testing of those alleged levers which are to work within us, and the checking of the delivery of the goods.

Equally, one may well worry about the separability of the investigative side. If the attribution of motive in theoretical debate were really a minor phenomenon, not so very much more prominent than in other fields, one might be satisfied. But Frosh could hardly claim that, in the history of psychoanalytic thought, this element had been a minor one. Once again, this seems to me not an eliminable weakness, but a corollary of certain basic ideas of the system. Its theory of knowledge conceives discovery and validation not in terms of testing independent truths, but in terms of removing inner obstacles to something immediately visible, to an intuitively obvious and accessible truth. If that is so, then motive is indeed far more relevant than evidence.

However, while not persuaded by his defence, I am most impressed by the civilized, humane, tolerant and open tone of his argument. In this mode, perhaps the investigation will make advances. In the meantime, some concessions: unquestionably the idiom of psychoanalysis offers a phenomenology of our inner life and of our relationships which is far closer to reality than any other available psychology. This is so notwithstanding the fact that specific propositions, when benefiting from the Dual Regime, are too elusive to have precise meaning and to be tested. Moreover, in an affluent, mobile, competitive, atomized society, devoid of any firm faith, the vast amount of personal anguish cries out for pastoral care. So far, only Freudianism and its multiform offshoots seem able to supply this, at any rate at what might be called a respectable intellectual level. Our Delphic oracles can only consult the individual psychic deep in the pursuit of solace and direction, because there is nothing else, because the transcendent has been pensioned off, and communal ritual can hardly work when the communities are eroded.

In a crisis, we must use flawed tools if we have no others. Whether the humane liberalism practised by Frosh will strengthen or weaken the appeal of those tools, only time can tell. It may advance investigation, but diminish therapeutic appeal: the prospects of the two may be inversely related. Other faiths have suffered by liberalizing themselves. We have yet to see whether psychoanalysis can practise such Glasnost with impunity.

References

Gellner, E. (1988) *Plough, Sword and Book*. London: Collins Harvill.
Kuhn, T. (1962) *The Structure of Scientific Revolutions*. Chicago: University of Chicago Press.

Dryden. W. (1992) Psychotherapy & Its
Feltham. C.   Discontents. O.U.

FOUR

Problems of methodology in studies of psychotherapy

PAUL KLINE

Introduction

There is a very large number of studies of the outcome and process of
psychotherapy yet the findings from these, whether positive or negative,
have to be treated with considerable caution, on account of the considerable
methodological problems in this work. Indeed some research is rendered
valueless on account of flaws in the research design.

In this chapter I shall examine these methodological difficulties in order
that readers may be able to assess for themselves the value of any research
in this field. At the outset it must be stated that I am restricting myself to
the quantitative study of the outcome of psychotherapy since it is quantitative
research that is usually used to give a scientific basis to psychotherapy. This
is not to say that the more qualitative, subjective analysis of psychotherapy
is without value but I shall not be discussing research of this type.

To simplify the task I shall list the most important of these methodological problems and discuss them separately. Then I shall examine one of the
best recent studies of the outcome of psychotherapy in the light of these
difficulties. Only at the end shall I attempt to draw some conclusions from
what is, inevitably, a depressing catalogue of problems which have not been
entirely overcome.

Important problems

1 The meaning of recovery
2 Variance among therapists

These problems will now be discussed in turn.

The meaning of recovery

The problem here lies in the fact that it is difficult to define what is meant by recovery. For example, is recovery a remission of symptoms, or feeling more cheerful, or a complete change in the way clients view their lives? Although this is a serious difficulty in the study of psychotherapy, I shall not deal at length with this, because Eysenck covers similar ground in Chapter 5 of this volume.

Actually, it conceals a more formidable conceptual difficulty in the investigation of psychotherapy. What is deemed to constitute recovery must depend upon how psychotherapy is conceived. This varies from the simple (behaviour therapy) to the complex (psychoanalytic therapies) and to its virtual denial (Smail 1984). Thus behaviour therapy (Eysenck and Rachman 1965) regards neurosis as nothing more than maladaptive responses, say fear of spiders. For therapists of this persuasion, remission of symptoms is recovery. Psychoanalysts consider that a more harmonious balance of aspects of the mind (ego, id and superego) has to be attained before a client may be deemed recovered. Smail (1984), however, has argued that much psychological distress is not abnormal but is a reasonable response to a wretched life. Clearly what constitutes recovery is no simple matter to decide. This certainly makes for difficulties in trying to compare the results from different kinds of treatments.

Even if we accept that it is meaningful to investigate recovery there are numerous problems in the design of any such investigations, as are set out below.

Variance among therapists

There must be individual differences in therapeutic skill among therapists, of whatever school. See, for example, the study by Shapiro *et al.* (1989) where one outstanding therapist was identified. This means that if different therapies are compared it is necessary to have a good sample of therapists from each type of therapy.

Personal qualities of therapists

It could be the case that it is advantageous for therapists to be empathic and non-judgemental (Truax 1963) and it is these characteristics that effect therapeutic change rather than the type of therapy which they practise. Thus even the demonstration that a type of therapy produced good results may be misleading, if this is regarded as proof that the therapy is efficient.

Patient–therapist interaction

Again, as Truax (1963) argued, there may be an interaction between the personal characteristics of a client and therapist that makes for therapeutic success. Some clients may do better with some psychotherapists than with others. If this is the case, the results of assessing therapy without taking this interaction into account are likely to be misleading.

Some psychotherapies attract certain therapists

Although I have no experimental evidence to support this assertion I feel confident that Jungian therapists, for example, are not similar to behaviour therapists on a variety of dimensions. Thus some types of therapy might be successful simply because of the type of therapist who practises them.

Logical difficulties

Even if a particular type of therapy shows itself to be consistently inferior to others, this failure cannot be attributed logically to the deficiencies of the therapy, as Cheshire (1975) has argued. The therapy may have been badly applied.

Need for control groups

In all studies of outcome there is the need for at least one control group in order to overcome the placebo effect treated at such length by Grunbaum (1984). The placebo effect is seen in the evaluation of all treatments, for example in medicine with drugs, even in educational procedures, as well as psychotherapy, where it has been found that the fact of receiving treatment at all, regardless of what it is, produces improvements.

Spontaneous remission

In many cases psychological symptoms disappear for no apparent reason, the phenomenon known as spontaneous remission. In the evaluation of psychotherapy this needs to be taken into account: an untreated control group is required for this purpose.

Life events

The effects of other events in the patient's life, during the time of psychotherapy, should be studied. This is simply because the best therapy in the world could be completely thrown by the death of the patient's spouse, the loss of her job, her being charged with serious fraud and the discovery that she had cancer. Conversely, good events can drastically change symptoms.

Problems of patient diagnosis

This is known to be unreliable but is clearly important (Beck 1962) since there may be interactions with types of therapy and therapists. Thus it could be the case that depressives do best with psychoanalytically oriented therapists while phobics are best suited to behaviour therapy. This could not be discovered if clinical diagnosis is poor.

Variance among patients

It is important to choose representative samples of patients in studies of the effectiveness of psychotherapy. If this is not done the results may not be generalizable to other samples of apparently similar patients.

If these problems of design have been dealt with successfully or sufficiently to make the study worthwhile, there arise considerable problems of measurement, although these are common to all scientific investigations.

Validity of the psychological tests

It is a truism to argue that all tests must be valid. Yet it is noteworthy that well-known psychological tests have poor evidence for their validity. Indeed some have none, as is clear from scrutiny of the *Mental Measurement Yearbooks* (e.g. Buros 1979). In the study of the outcome of psychotherapy, tests of recovery are used, yet in many cases these are of dubious validity, as for example the MMPI (Hathaway and McKinley 1951).

Reliability of the psychological tests

As Cronbach (1976) demonstrates, where change scores are to be used, as is often the case, in the study of psychotherapy, whether of outcome or process, it is essential that reliable tests are used. Yet this is often not so.

Length of follow-up studies

To be convincing, follow-up studies should show improvement or main-tenance of recovery, for at least six months after treatment. This is an experimental demand which is more usually met than are many others in our list. However, it must be pointed out that six months is a minimum figure.

Symptom substitution

The difficulty of establishing whether or not symptom substitution has occurred arises from the fact that the whole range of a subject's feelings, anxieties and behaviour has to be studied before one can be confident that there is no symptom substitution.

Base-line measurements

To estimate change and symptom substitution it is necessary to know what individuals were like before the onset of their disorder.

Sex differences

These should be investigated. Although this is an example of the personal qualities of therapists, it is so important it should always be studied; thus it is treated separately.

Variance in effects of psychotherapy

It is possible that psychotherapy makes some clients better but others worse, as is found with certain drug treatments. When this occurs mean differences between treated and untreated groups would be reduced although for some individuals the therapy was successful. For this reason it is always valuable to investigate means and variances of outcome scores. In this instance the variance of the treatment groups would be larger than that of the untreated.

The research design

There are obvious difficulties in developing a research design that can deal with all the problems which have been described above. Thus in evaluating the effects of psychotherapy, to take just a few of the problems which we have discussed above, we have to take into account variance among patients and therapists, intervening life events in the patients' lives, set up untreated control groups and ensure that, with different therapies, the measures of outcome are fair and comparable, not to say reliable and valid. How this may be done will be discussed throughout the remainder of this chapter but it should be stated here that to design sound experiments is no easy matter.

Most of these problems apply equally to outcome and process studies of psychotherapy, although obviously variance among patients (problem 11) is not relevant to the latter. In process studies part of the research is concerned with outcome at a particular point in psychotherapy; in some cases, the process measures, for example, of client and therapist interaction, are related to measures of outcome.

On account of the problems in the study of the outcome of psychotherapy (which were succinctly described by Kiesler 1966) many researchers believed that the only sound approach to evaluation, especially of dynamic therapies, was to study the process itself, as advocated for example by Bellack (1985). However, to do this presupposes, as Eysenck (1960) argued, that there is some value in psychotherapy.

These are the most important problems of methodology which can weaken the findings from the investigation of psychotherapy. As can be seen from this list these are so numerous and severe as to render worthless any meta-analytic studies of psychotherapy. As I have argued (Kline 1983) it is beyond comprehension how the enumeration of dozens of studies, the majority, if not all, with severe methodological inadequacies, can be held to demonstrate anything other than the inadequacy of meta-analysis. What count are studies which are not flawed by errors of methodology and one such cannot be overturned by poorly designed research.

The main part of this chapter will be concerned with solutions to these problems. Since there is a vast literature on the evaluation of psychotherapy which is far too large to summarize in a chapter of this length and of which, in any case, many good summaries already exist (e.g. Orlinsky and Howard 1986) I shall examine in detail, as a basis for the discussion, an excellent paper by Shapiro *et al.* (1990). In this paper, as will become clear when it is discussed, they describe the results of a study where a large number of clients were treated by one of five psychotherapists using four different psychotherapeutic procedures. Both the process of psychotherapy and the outcome were evaluated.

Shapiro and his colleagues at Sheffield are rightly well known for their work in the study of the effectiveness of psychotherapy and an analysis of their paper, which makes about as good an effort to deal with many of the problems that I have listed as can be found, is useful in clarifying the solutions to these difficulties. In seeing how they attempted to deal with these problems the full extent of the difficulties is revealed.

Solutions to the problems

Shapiro and colleagues (1990) point out that to carry out the controlled outcome studies that are necessary to evaluate psychotherapy is costly, to such an extent that some compromise is inevitable and that their work is limited by the need for cost-effectiveness.

There are two points here. First, in practice this is perfectly true. However, my discussion will not be thus limited by the demand for cheapness, for compromised research is still not effective if the compromise has allowed error, and ultimately flawed research is never cost-effective.

The questions asked in this research included: the differences in effectiveness of two kinds of therapy (exploratory and prescriptive); the effects of length of therapy (eight or sixteen sessions); the effects of different therapists; the effects of different samples of patients. Thus some of the major questions in outcome studies were asked.

There were also some process questions investigated. These included: expectancy effects after the first and later sessions and the effects of the impact on the patient and the psychotherapist of particular sessions and their relationship to outcomes. Again, therefore, some important questions were investigated.

Design of the experiment by Shapiro et al. *(1990)*

This research is about as good as can be done in the inevitable economic restraint of a relatively small research project. I shall describe their design and then discuss how it overcomes the problems which I have listed. In discussing the solutions I shall refer to them by the numbers in the list rather than deal with them in order, which would be repetitious.

Shapiro *et al.* investigated 120 clients. Each of five therapists treated twenty-four clients, of whom six were assigned at random to the four treatments (long and short exploratory and long and short prescriptive therapy). In all thirty clients were assigned to the four treatments. As far as was possible each of the six in each therapist × treatment cell were equally divided by sex and by three levels of initial severity of symptoms. No control group was used because of the interest in comparing treatments, and because they argued that research pointed to the overall efficacy of psychotherapy (Shapiro and Firth 1987).

Analysis of the design

This is statistically a highly sophisticated analysis of variance design which takes account of variance of therapists (problem 2), sex differences (17) and patient diagnosis (10). However, by virtue of its design it cannot deal with the problems of placebo effects, spontaneous remission, effects of the patients' life events and having no control group (7, 8, 9). Nevertheless, despite its statistical sophistication this design is far from adequate, even to achieve the limited aims of the authors.

Variance of therapists *(problems 2, 3, 4, 5)*

In this design there are five therapists. It has to be said that five therapists cannot be a representative sample. Furthermore since each therapist carries out each treatment it is easily possible that each is more suited to one type of treatment than the others. Even five therapists per treatment would not be sufficient. There is a severe sampling difficulty with this design.

Indeed examination of the training of the therapists shows that these sampling difficulties are important. Three of the therapists were newly qualified, while the other two had six and sixteen years' post-qualification experience. Thus whatever statistical findings are reported from this study generalization is difficult, given the sample of therapists.

In brief a much larger number of therapists is required so that the variance of therapists may be taken into account. Furthermore these ought to be sampled from a pool of therapists of each type. The problem of one therapist carrying out different kinds of treatment is discussed below.

Lack of control group (problems 7, 8)

Shapiro *et al.* claim that this is not important since they are interested in treatment differences. However, even if they show treatment differences it is valuable to have a control group to see whether the improvements are as great or greater with a no-treatment group or a group having a placebo treatment. If these differences were placed into the analysis of variance, *post hoc* comparisons via the Scheffe test might well be non-significant.

I think that these arguments need a little elaboration. Suppose that in this study one of the treatments shows itself to be better than the others. Even if the results could be taken at their face value (which, as we shall see, is not possible) the absence of any control group makes the results difficult to interpret. Three control groups are needed, one receiving no treatment and two which have the same amount of time spent with them as each of the therapies – a long and a short treatment – the placebo groups.

Suppose, for example, the long therapy groups were superior to the short groups. The interpretation of this finding would surely be different if it turned out that the long placebo group were better than the short placebo group. This argument destroys the claim that there is no need for control groups. This claim is true if we are attempting to establish whether there are differences between treatments. It is not true if any attempt is made to interpret the results. Of course this latter is always attempted and a control group is, therefore, essential.

The no-treatment group is, perhaps, when therapies are being compared, of no less interest since it would again affect the interpretation of the findings if the no-treatment group did better than some therapies.

It is often assumed that a no-treatment group is a control against the effects of spontaneous remission. However, as Malan (1959) freely admits, changes in symptomatology can occur due to changes in circumstances, although it might be argued that spontaneous remission embraces such events. Unless all these changes are monitored, and this is rarely done, these changes can affect the results and destroy the validity of the findings. An example was given by Malan (1959) of a case of a homosexual client whose problems disappeared when the homosexual temptation was removed (the individual moved away). This change, however, could hardly be attributed to the therapy. This is where the no-treatment control can be useful. In a sufficiently large sample the number of good and bad changes in circumstances and their consequent effects on the outcome scores should be the same in control and experimental groups. Thus their effects should not confuse the results.

Sex of therapist (problems 17, 3, 4)

In this design the effects of the sex of the therapist on the outcome and process of the therapy cannot be examined. This is a pity since, on a number of a priori grounds, the psychoanalytic theory of transference (Freud 1916), the effects of the sex of the tester on test results (e.g. Jensen 1980) and one's own experience, which is, admittedly, not generally permitted as evidence in scientific discourse, the interaction of the sex of therapist and patient deserves investigation.

There is another point about this experimental design which deserves comment. As often occurs in academic, scientific psychology (see Kline 1988 for examples) the demands of scientific rigour result in a design which reflects nothing in the real world. In psychotherapy it is highly unlikely that one therapist would use one of four therapies. If she did she would not choose the one she used at random (at least, one hopes not) but would attempt to fit it to the client. Given this, one must ask the question as to what psychotherapeutic context does this experiment pertain?

In brief the small number of therapists limits what may be inferred from the design, which itself does not reflect what normally occurs in psychotherapy. In this respect the statistical sophistication of the research may be misleading. It is capable of yielding results which to unsophisticated readers look impressive.

Selection of clients (problems 4, 10, 11)

Some clients were referred by general practitioners, psychiatrists and occupational health services, who had been mailed information concerning the clinic. Others came of their own accord having seen the publicity. This offered psychotherapy to 'professional, managerial and white-collar workers suffering from depression and/or anxiety'.

Initial screening excluded people not complaining that their work was affected by their problems, those with a continuous history of psychiatric disorders extending over more than two years, and those who during the last five years had had similar treatments to those being investigated. In addition those who had recently changed psychotropic drugs were excluded. This is the initial selection of the pool of clients, who then underwent further testing to determine whether they suffered from major depressive disorder. I shall comment first on these initial selection procedures.

The fact that there were any screening procedures at all indicates that the sample of clients cannot reflect the general population of clients, for the screening was not designed to produce a stratified sample. At best this sample could represent a middle-class population. Since psychiatric disorders are unfortunately not thus restricted to the middle classes a practitioner might well decide that the findings were simply not relevant to her practice or certainly only to a small part of it. This seems to be a severe limitation of this research.

However, this sample does not represent even middle-class clients. It excludes those who have had a history of psychiatric disorder. Given the nature of depressive disorders (Mayer-Gross *et al.* 1967) which do not usually strike suddenly (although, obviously, there is a first time of onset) this is far from a representative sample of even middle-class depressive clients. Indeed it is almost as restricted as the sample on which early psychoanalytic theory was based.

Conclusions concerning the sample of clients

Again, as was the case with the sample of therapists, the sample of clients chosen for this study means that the conclusions to be drawn from it are strictly limited. At this point, having been critical of the sampling of both clients and therapists and about certain features of the design, I want to stress that this is a good study and that the Sheffield Project is designed by psychologists who understand the principles of scientific investigation. That there are problems in generalizing from the results simply indicates how difficult it is to design good research in this area.

Meaning of recovery (problem 1)

Before the validity and effectiveness of the tests used to assess outcome and process can be evaluated it is necessary to discuss the meaning of recovery for this will have an important bearing upon the criteria for therapeutic success and hence outcome measures.

It is obvious that psychoanalysts and behaviour therapists, to take two extremes, have quite different objectives. To the former, the balance between ego, id and superego has to be modified – 'where id was there shall ego be' (Freud 1933) – and remission of symptoms is regarded as but a flight into health (Fenichel 1945). In behaviour therapy, on the other hand, symptoms are the problem and their disappearance represents therapeutic success (Eysenck and Rachman 1965). Any study of psychotherapeutic outcome, therefore, which compared clients treated by these two kinds of regime, could not use the same measures. This means that, in this instance, they would have to be measured in terms of their own aims.

Of course one argument could be used to overcome these difficulties, namely that all therapies aim to make the client feel better, and that, therefore, a common assessment is possible – some measure of happiness of the patient. This might be combined, the argument runs, with measures of clients' work efficiency and assessments by their family.

This argument makes several assumptions about the nature of psycho-therapy and of human life itself (the latter topic almost certainly out of bounds in respectable academic psychology!). Thus I see no necessary reason why a client should be happy. As Freud (1923) put it, the aim of psychoanalytic therapy is to make neurotic unhappiness into normal un-happiness. It seems to me a quite respectable argument, as Smail (1984) has eloquently shown, to admit that the lives of many people are unhappy and that to assert otherwise or to attempt to persuade clients that there is something wrong with them because they are unhappy, is distasteful and ultimately propping up a society that is better changed. With such a view, the aim of psychotherapy becomes one of helping clients to accept their feelings. In fact political rather than psychological change is implied in such a viewpoint.

It is not my intention here to support or attack any of these notions concerning the nature of psychotherapy, psychoanalytic, behavioural or, for want of a better term, political. My point is simply that implicit within the aims of psychotherapy and the consequent outcome measures lie such fundamental viewpoints or values. The problem, from the standpoint of research into psychotherapy, is that research results are unlikely to be relevant to all these views. Thus the fact that aversion therapy reduces the intake of alcohol (or does not) is literally irrelevant to practitioners whose theoretical concept of alcoholism entwines drinking with a multitude of other problems.

Base-line levels (problem 16)

One of the problems of assessing therapeutic outcome is to know with what to compare the outcome scores. The ideal would be the base-line of the clients, as they were before they became ill. This, however, is difficult to attain since in most cases no such data exist. Clients are seen only after the onset of their symptoms. Thus the best that can be done is to compare clients, after-treatment scores with those obtained at the start.

The outcome process measures (problems 1, 12, 13)

In measuring the outcome of psychotherapy and the process itself there are some fundamental difficulties associated with the problem of the different meanings of recovery within different psychotherapeutic viewpoints. This affects the variables to be measured and the reliability and validity of such measures.

Variables to be measured in outcome studies

Symptom change

If reduction in symptomatology is the aim of the therapy, or at least one aim, some kind of symptom checklist administered at various stages of the therapy will be one useful measure. It is not difficult to construct such lists and the reliability of these measures is usually satisfactory. Shapiro and colleagues (1990) used a number of such tests and if scores are reduced at the end of therapy, so much the better. Some of these measures of symptoms are based upon psychiatric interviews and if the symptoms are clearly defined these can also be reliable.

Reasonably reliable measures of these symptoms, which were used in the Sheffield Project, included, among others, the Present State Examination (Wing *et al.* 1974), the SCL-90R (Derogatis *et al.* 1973), the Beck Depression Inventory (Beck *et al.* 1961), which, of course, deals only with depressive symptoms, and the Spielberger State Trait Anxiety Scale (Spielberger 1983), which is concerned with anxiety. These may be regarded as satisfactory outcome measures in terms of symptoms.

However, mention of this last test touches upon a real problem with symptom measurement in the evaluation of psychotherapy, a problem implicit in the meaning of the term. We pointed out (earlier in this chapter) that psychoanalysis is not interested, *per se*, in the removal of symptoms. However, many other therapies regard it as part of their task to help clients deal better with the problems which they face in their lives and this involves not only symptom change but also personality change, for example being, perhaps, more confident or having better self-esteem.

This, then, opens up the whole field of personality measurement. If psychotherapy has had any effect, we should expect personality changes but on what variables?

Measurement of personality change in psychotherapy

The whole work of Cattell (e.g. Cattell 1973; Cattell and Kline 1977) in personality, spanning over half a century of psychology, stemming from Spearman and Burt, has aimed to establish what are the important factors in the field of personality both normal and abnormal. Bolton (1986) has a succinct summary of these findings in a chapter devoted to their relevance to the assessment of psychotherapy and their use in clinical psychology. The point of this work, which is still not widely understood, has been to establish through factor analysis the largest personality dimensions, i.e. those which account for the most variance in personality.

There have been disputes among factorists as to what these dimensions are but Kline and Barrett (1983) summarizing research up to that date with personality questionnaires among normal subjects showed that there were three clear factors: neuroticism (or anxiety), extraversion and obsessional traits (or authoritarianism). A factor of tough-mindedness also appeared to be important and this would include Eysenck's P factor (Eysenck and Eysenck 1976).

This study by Kline and Barrett (1983) was interesting from the viewpoint of this chapter because first it indicated that there was little basic disagreement between the work of Eysenck, with the three-factor EPQ (Eysenck and Eysenck 1975) and Cattell with sixteen factors (Cattell *et al.* 1970). Furthermore it was shown that many other of the most well-known factored personality questionnaires, such as the Comrey Personality Inventory (Comrey 1970) and the Guilford–Zimmerman Temperament Survey (Guilford *et al.* 1976) measured essentially the same variables.

Second, it was pointed out that there was remarkable agreement between the factors of questionnaires and those emerging from modern and comprehensive studies of the ratings of personality (actually the original basis of Cattell's work: Cattell 1946). These, for example McRae and Costa (1987), are known as the big five and are labelled: extraversion, anxiety, openness to experience, tough mindedness and conventionality. Kline and Lapham (1990; 1991) have recently studied these variables, together with the EPQ, and shown that they form five correlated scales and at the second order load on two factors only: anxiety (which included extraversion) and obsessionality. They have a brief test of these big five, the PPQ (Kline and Lapham 1991), which could prove useful in the assessment of psychotherapy.

From this discussion of the factor analysis of <u>normal personality</u> it would appear that the five main factors should be included in the assessment of psychotherapeutic outcome, along with symptom measures.

Measures of abnormal personality

Although the original factor analyses of Cattell were assumed to be comprehensive it became clear that there were abnormal factors in addition to those found among normal subjects. The most important of these are measured by the Clinical Analysis Test CAQ (Krug 1980). One of the most interesting aspects of the list of these abnormal factors is that there are seven depression factors: hypochondriasis, suicidal depression, agitation, anxious depression, low energy depression, guilt and resentment, and boredom and withdrawal. It would be useful to see if there were differential effects of different therapies or therapists on changes in these factors or whether certain factors were more resistant to change than others, just for example. In the final section of this chapter I shall suggest how these factored scales, normal and abnormal, might be used in psychotherapeutic studies.

Other measures

For analytic and dynamic psychotherapies other measures are needed than any so far discussed. I cannot discuss here all the possible tests for psychoanalytic concepts which have been developed. These have been fully described in Kline (1973; 1981). Furthermore the validity of these measures is truly a matter of dispute and it would be difficult to advocate their use in studies of psychotherapy except on a truly experimental basis, rather than in the hope of obtaining substantive information.

As is well known, many projective tests claim to be able to measure underlying dynamics. Thus, if they were valid, they would be useful for assessing some of the variables of interest to some psychotherapists. However, as is equally well known (e.g. Eysenck 1959) they are not valid. Yet this gloomy condemnation may yet be unfair. Research by Holley (1973) with the Rorschach Test and by Hampson and Kline (1977) with the House Tree Person (HTP) Test (Buck 1970) indicated that projective tests – objectively and hence reliably scored into dichotomous variables, and subjected to multivariate analysis – could yield powerfully discriminating variables. Thus Holley (1973) showed complete separation (not just significant mean differences) between schizophrenics and depressives on certain Rorschach variables. Hampson and Kline (1977) found that the HTP Test was effective in discriminating among different categories of abnormal offenders. In both these cases, it should be pointed out, other personality tests had not been able thus to discriminate.

The statistical analysis to which these projective tests were subjected was G analysis, which has been fully described by Holley (1973) and Kline (1986). Briefly, the dichotomous test variables (indicating the presence or absence of any feature in the test protocols) were correlated using the G index (Holley and Guilford 1964) and these coefficients were then Q factored. Q factor analysis reveals groups of people and is thus particularly useful in psychotherapy where the emphasis is on clients rather than measures. What measures contributed to the group separation are then discovered by the calculation of D estimates.

Although the G analysis of projective tests is still far from proven it is a promising form of analysis which could well make using projective test data a real possibility. This would be an excellent thing if only because projective test data are unique in that they cannot be obtained from any other type of test.

This discussion can be summarized thus: in addition to symptom lists, measures of the fundamental dimensions of normal personality, and measures of abnormal personality factors, together with objectively scored projective tests, could all prove valuable and greatly extend the scope of measurement in the assessment of psychotherapy. The use of these tests would enable different types of therapies (which aimed at more than the alleviation of symptoms) to be compared. For example, in the work of Shapiro it could well be that the longer therapeutic sessions were producing changes on the personality variables while the shorter psychotherapies were not.

So far all these tests could be used in studies of the outcome and the processes of psychotherapy. However, there are some variables that are exclusive to the study of process and these will now be considered.

Exclusive process measures

These measures used by Shapiro *et al.* (1990) are largely tailor-made for the research, measuring variables such as the impact of session, intentions of session and helpfulness of session. Clients also completed, at various points in the treatment, therapy review forms, indicating how helpful the therapy had been. The moods of clients were also measured for the session about to begin and for the previous session.

I do not want to comment on these particular measures for it would not be of general interest. Rather I shall make some general points about tests in general which will apply to these and the previous outcome measures.

Reliability of tests

Classical test theory (Nunnally 1978) stresses the importance of tests being reliable especially if the scores are to be used with individuals. The point here is that it can be shown that the reliable variance is true score variance, the true score being defined as the subject's score on all possible items in the relevant universe of items of which any test is a random sample. An obtained test score consists of error and true score variance.

From the viewpoint of the practical tester the important concept is the standard error of measurement; 68 per cent of obtained scores, for any subject, fall between the obtained score and plus and minus one standard error, 95 per cent within two standard errors. It is, therefore, important to know the standard error of measurement, for individuals on a test, when interpreting changes in their scores as in therapeutic outcome. It is for this reason that it is essential that all measures used in studies of psychotherapy, where changes are important have a high reliability, since the higher this is, the lower the standard error. The formula for calculating the standard error of measurement is set out in Formula 1.

Formula 1
$$SE_{meas} = SD_t \sqrt{(1 - r_{tt})}$$
where SE_{meas} = the standard error of measurement
SD_t = the standard deviation of the test
r_{tt} = the reliability of the test.

From this classical test theory it can also be shown that the longer a test is, the more reliable it is. This is the Spearman-Brown prophecy formula. Test items are each notoriously unreliable as they are one-item tests. Indeed, depending on the homogeneity of the items it can be shown that a twenty-item test is highly reliable and that it is possible to go as low as ten items and maintain a reasonable reliability, although if the items are homogeneous this must be a highly specific test. Thus tests with fewer than ten items are suspect and fifteen or more should be used. It is noteworthy, in parenthesis, that one of the tests used by Shapiro, that for self-esteem, had only eight items.

The work of Shapiro *et al.* (1990), which as I indicated was a good study, uses tests of reasonable reliability. However, as I pointed out at the beginning of this chapter this is not always the case in studies of psychotherapy. The MMPI and projective tests, scored normally, are highly unreliable.

Validity of tests

Tests are said to be valid if they measure what they claim to measure. However, to establish the validity of many psychological tests, especially in the field of personality, is no simple matter. This is particularly true of many of the process measures used in the research by Shapiro. This is in contradistinction to a variable such as extraversion of which the construct validity and its relationship to other tests has been well established (Kline and Barrett 1983). There is no doubt what the variable, extraversion, as measured by the EPQ or the 16PF, is.

If we take a variable such as helpfulness of session, as used in the study by Shapiro *et al.* (1990), it is difficult to see how its validity could be established. It means little more than the extent to which clients found the session helpful: they might as well be asked. It is hard to see how there could be any other independent verification of this variable. Thus the validity of such scales is essentially face validity.

This is not to say that these scales do not assess such variables. Rather it is to say there is no special magic in the results or the numbers derived from them.

It must be realized that tests can be reliable but not valid. This in no way counteracts the claim that reliable variance is true score variance. Thus a test which is highly homogeneous, where most of the items are paraphrases of each other, is highly reliable. But the true variance is narrow and specific to the items. In Cattellian terms (Cattell 1973) this is a bloated specific. It is a simple matter, given a good computer and time, to construct reliable tests, with the items loading on just one factor. This, however, may well be a bloated specific and it is always necessary to demonstrate in further studies what this factor is.

This is the problem which besets many tests constructed for a specific purpose such as the evaluation of psychotherapy. The tests are reliable and load a factor yet the further step of demonstrating their construct validity is not undertaken, often because, as has been pointed out, this is so difficult to do. In social psychology, as I have previously argued (Kline 1988), this has resulted in sets of factored and face valid items, which do little more than would a simple question. For example it has been shown that the lengthy Strong Vocational Interest Blank (Strong *et al.* 1971), with more than 600 items, predicts enjoyment at a job less well than asking subjects whether they think they would enjoy it.

From all these arguments concerning the validity of tests I think it is wise for researchers not to kid themselves as to what they are measuring. In the field of ability and personality there is a small number of clearly established and well-validated factors with psychological meanings beyond the set of items which measure the constructs. Fluid ability, anxiety and obsessionality would be examples of these, which have been set out and described in Kline (1979; in press). Beyond these there are many tests which are reliable but whose validity is little more than face validity. Some of the measures used by Shapiro *et al.* (1990) are of this kind: the session-evaluation question-naire, the client post-session questionnaire, session evaluation question-naire (pre-session), and the client–therapist relationship scale. There is a final set of tests which are neither reliable nor valid. In assessing results from tests it is necessary to know to which group the test belongs.

Experimental design

Given all the difficulties and problems which have been described, clearly a complex experimental design would appear to be a necessity if sense is to be made of any resulting differences between clients before and after treatment, clients treated by different psychotherapies and untreated controls.

Kiesler (1966), in a classic paper, laid down what seemed to be the minimum requirements for a satisfactory experimental study of psychotherapy. He proposed an analysis of variance design: the main factors would be types of patient and schools of therapy. However, account would be taken of individual differences between therapists within schools and between patients. This design allows, of course, observations of the interactions between types of therapy and types of patient.

Such a design needs adequate sampling of patients of each type and of therapists of each type. In addition two types of control are required: one receiving no treatment and those receiving placebo treatments, similar to the real psychotherapies in time spent with therapists. These controls present ethical problems (since to deny useful treatment could be regarded as un-ethical) as well as practical problems – obtaining samples and controls. However, even if these design constraints are overcome, reliable and valid measures must be used. The difficulty here is, as I have discussed, that there is no common outcome measure which would be equally suitable for different types of therapy. This difficulty might, perhaps, be overcome by carrying out several different studies in which only similar therapies were compared.

As Kiesler (1966) indicated, the practical problems of carrying out such a design are so great that at that time it had never been executed. I think it is fair to say that this is still true. I think it is also fair to say that the work of Shapiro and colleagues on the Sheffield Project is a practical, cost-effective realization of this design. However, as I have pointed out, unfortunately, in cutting costs, the effectiveness of the design has been reduced. As with all analysis of variance designs, the power depends on good sampling of clients, therapists and the establishment of control groups. Without these, the results have an elegance that is misleading. The Sheffield Project cannot lead to definitive results.

An alternative design

Even if the practical problems of the analysis of variance design are ignored and it is scrutinized in its ideal form, I believe that there are severe defects in it and that it is possible to design research into psychotherapy more effectively. The essence of the problem is that the outcome of psycho-therapy is determined by a multiplicity of variables, some more influential than others. Although analysis of variance can deal with a number of vari-ables, it is a small number unless interactions are to become uninterpretable and the difficulties of obtaining equal numbers in all the cells insuperable.

In such a multivariate context a true multivariate design would be more appropriate. As Nunnally (1978) has shown, essentially there is little dif-ference between multivariate techniques such as multiple regression, factor analysis and discriminant functions, since they all make use of linear, additive models. Obviously each is more suited to particular purposes than others and I shall outline, in this section of the chapter, a factor analytic design which has certain clear advantages over the analysis of variance approach. For some questions, as will be seen, multiple regression could also be used.

Advantages of the factor analytic design

In this discussion the numbers in parentheses refer to the problems men-tioned in the first section of the chapter. The main advantage of the factor analytic design in the evaluation of psychotherapy is that it enables the effects of a large number of variables to be examined. I shall take the example of events in the client's life (9), which might affect the course of the neurosis. In the analysis of variance design it is hoped that these will randomize themselves out between the groups. However, in small samples this may not be so, and in any case, such randomization means that their effects will never be known. That is why analysis of variance is such a strange research method in a field where so much is unknown.

Spontaneous remission (8) is another example of a variable whose effects can be gauged by the use of a control group in the analysis of variance, but it can never be understood in such a design. Spontaneous remission means recovery through causes unknown. The factor analytic approach could re-veal its determinants.

Thus in the factor analytic design many of the problems outlined in the first section of the chapter can be dealt with. The meaning of recovery (1) is accounted for by using a variety of different measures in the analysis. Variance of therapists, patients and their interaction (2, 3, 4, 5) will also be teased out in the design. All variables that load on the recovery factor will contribute to or militate against (negative loadings) recovery. Variables are set up to indicate which type of therapy or which therapist each patient had and if these load on the recovery factor the efficacy of the therapy or the fact that controls do as well will be indicated (7). How this is done is described below.

The factor analytic design

Variables

Let us suppose that we are attempting to answer the same questions as the workers in the Sheffield Project: which of several therapies is the most effective? The first point to notice is that all the same outcome measures could be used. There are no special data that have to be obtained. In fact, as has been argued, it would be useful to include the main personality factors as well as more specialized personality tests. However, in addition we would obtain a history of the life events of each client and these could go into the analysis. For example, death of spouse would be scored 1 or 0. We could insert as many of these variables as seemed desirable: money difficulties, house sale, marital problems, children's difficulties and so on. Personal characteristics which seemed important could be put into the analysis: whether the subject was religious, the number of friends just for example. This deals with 8 and 9.

From this it is clear that we can use far more variables than is the case with analysis of variance. Generally in factor analyses the more the better.

Subjects

In factor analyses twice the number of subjects to variables is required for replicable analyses: this is a minimum (Barrett and Kline 1988). Furthermore a sample of 100 is a minimum statistically to reduce the standard error of the correlations, which would otherwise render the factor analysis dubious. We would want good samples of each kind of client by diagnosis, and of controls, untreated and treated, and these would be allocated randomly to each therapist within each type of treatment. In this design each therapist would utilize only one treatment, which resembles real-life psychotherapy, although if one therapist gave several treatments this could be fitted in.

As was pointed out previously, we want to use as many therapists of each type as possible and these would preferably be experienced practitioners.

Dummy variables

A dummy variable is set up when membership of a category (e.g. being a control or a depressive) has to be quantified for factor analysis. Thus if being a control is scored 1 and this variable loads on a measure of recovery it indicates that controls recover as well as treated patients. For each subject a number of dichotomous dummy variables would be set up for the factor analysis. These would accommodate: diagnosis (e.g. a depressive client would receive 1 for depression and 0 for all the other nosological categories); treatment (1 if treated by therapy A and 0 for all the other therapies); therapist (1 if treated by therapist W and 0 for all the other therapist variables).

Interpretation of results

A rotated, simple structure factor analysis of all these variables would be carried out. To test the efficacy of psychotherapy the relevant factor would be that on which the variables showing recovery or therapeutic success loaded. What would be important would be the other variables significantly loading this factor. Thus if we found that the depressive variable, and the therapy B variable and therapists X, Y, Z loaded the factor, the meaning is obvious: that depressives tend to recover if treated by these three therapists, who used therapy B. If type of therapy did not load, it would mean that the therapist, not the type of therapy, was important. If regular church attendance loaded negatively, then this meaning is equally obvious. There might be more than one success factor and that could tell us that there were different determinants of success, perhaps for different groups of subjects, or for controls.

Clearly the eventualities are endless but there can be no doubt, as this illustration shows, that a factor analytic design could be extremely powerful in elucidating the questions posed in psychotherapeutic research. It should be pointed out, at this juncture, that process measures, of the kind used in the Sheffield Project, could also be inserted into the factor analysis. If any of these loaded on the success factor their importance would be obvious.

Variants of the design

A multiple regression could be carried out to predict high scores on the recovery variable or variables. If there were sufficient subjects, the sample, in the regression, could be restricted to depressives and then to anxious subjects. I should be surprised if these two approaches, the multiple regression and the factor analytic, yielded different results.

Conclusions

From this discussion of nineteen important problems in the assessment of psychotherapy it is quite clear that for adequate research large samples of patients, controls and therapists of various types are required. Whether the neater but more restricted analysis of variance model is preferred to the true multivariate design, or not, in both cases great resources are required for proper research. This assumes, which is far from the case, that adequate outcome measures can be found. The study of processes which is valuable only if the outcome of psychotherapy is found to be positive, can be tacked on to the multivariate designs, as a set of further variables, although measurement here is a severe problem.

Given all these difficulties it can be seen that the ideal research, with proper sampling and valid measures, constitutes a massive practical problem demanding enormous resources. It is hardly surprising, therefore, that researchers depart from this ideal. However, as I have shown, when reductions are made, as in the case of the Sheffield Project, it is difficult to generalize from the results, because the sampling of patients and psychotherapists is insufficient.

In brief, in the context of all these problems I am forced to the conclusion that the case for the effects of psychotherapy remains to be made. This is not to say that it is ineffectual, simply that it remains unproven, despite the weight of research findings (from experiments which have not overcome these problems) in its favour. I should like to see determined researchers demanding and putting in the necessary resources, so that definitive, or more definitive, answers could be obtained.

References

Barrett, P. and Kline, P. (1988) The observation to variable ratio in factor analysis. *Personality Study and Group Behaviour* **1**: 23–33.

Beck, A.T. (1962) Reliability of psychiatric diagnoses: a critique of systematic studies. *American Journal of Psychiatry* **119**: 210–15.

Beck, A.T., Ward, C.H., Mendelson, M., Mock, J. and Erbauch, J. (1961) An inventory for measuring depression. *Archives of General Psychiatry* **4**: 561–71.

Bellack, L. (1985) Studying the psychoanalytic process of the method of short-range prediction and judgment. *British Journal of Medical Psychology* **31**: 249–52.

Bolton, L.S. (1986) Clinical diagnosis and psychotherapeutic monitoring, in R.B. Cattell and R.B. Johnson (eds) (1976) *Functional Psychological Testing*. New York: Brunner/Mazel.

Buck, J.N. (1970) *The House Tree Person Technique: Revised Manual*. Los Angeles: Western Psychological Services.

Buros, O.K. (ed.) (1979) *VIIIth Mental Measurement Yearbook*. Highland Park, NJ: Gryphon Press.

Cattell, R.B. (1946) *Description and Measurement of Personality*. London: Harrap.

Cattell, R.B. (1973) *Personality and Mood by Questionnaire*. New York: Jossey Bass.

Cattell, R.B. (1978) *The Scientific Use of Factor Analysis in Behavioural and Life Sciences*. New York: Plenum.

Cattell, R.B. and Kline, P. (1977) *The Scientific Study of Personality and Motivation*. London: Academic Press.

Cattell, R.B., Eber, H.W. and Tatsuoka, M.M. (1970) *The 16PF Test*. Champaign, Ill: Institute for Personality and Ability Testing.

Cheshire, N. (1975) *On the Nature of Psychodynamic Interpretation*. Chichester: Wiley.

Comrey, A.L. (1970) *The Comrey Personality Scales*. San Diego, Calif: Edits.

Cronbach, L.J. (1976) *Essentials of Psychological Testing*. New York: Harper & Row.

Derogatis, L.R., Lipman, R.S. and Covi, M.D. (1973) SCL-90, an outpatient rating scale: preliminary report. *Psychopharmacology Bulletin* **9**: 13–20.

Eysenck, H.J. (1959) The Rorschach Test, in O.K. Buros (ed.) *Vth Mental Measurement Yearbook*. Highland Park, NJ: Gryphon Press.

Eysenck, H.J. (1960) *Handbook of Abnormal Psychology*. New York: Basic Books.

Eysenck, H.J. and Eysenck, S.B.G. (1975) *The E.P.Q.* London: Hodder & Stoughton.

Eysenck, H.J. and Eysenck, S.B.G. (1976) *Psychoticism as a Dimension of Personality*. London: Hodder & Stoughton.

Eysenck, H.J. and Rachman, S. (1965) *The Causes and Cure of Neurosis*. London: Routledge & Kegan Paul.

Fenichel, O. (1945) *The Psychoanalytic Theory of Neurosis*. London: Routledge & Kegan Paul.

Freud, S. (1916) *Introductory Lectures on Psychoanalysis*, vols 15–16 in (1960)

Standard Edition of the Complete Psychological Works of Sigmund Freud. London: Hogarth Press and the Institute of Psychoanalysis.

Freud, S. (1923) *The Ego and the Id,* vol. 19 in (1960) *Standard Edition of the Complete Psychological Works of Sigmund Freud.* London: Hogarth Press and the Institute of Psychoanalysis.

Freud, S. (1933) *New Introductory Lectures in Psychoanalysis,* vol. 22 in (1960) *Standard Edition of the Complete Psychological Works of Sigmund Freud.* London: Hogarth Press and the Institute of Psychoanalysis.

Grunbaum, A. (1984) *The Foundations of Psychoanalysis.* Berkeley, Calif: University of California Press.

Guilford, J.S., Zimmerman, W.S. and Guilford, J.P. (1976) *The Guilford–Zimmerman Temperament Survey Handbook.* San Diego, Calif: Edits.

Hampson, S. and Kline, P. (1977) Personality dimensions differentiating certain groups of abnormal offenders from non-offenders. *British Journal of Criminology* **17**: 310–31.

Hathaway, S.R. and McKinley, J.C. (1951) *The Minnesota Multiphasic Personality Inventory.* New York: Psychological Corporation.

Holley, J.W. (1973) Rorschach analysis, in P. Kline (ed.) *New Approaches in Psychological Measurement.* Chichester: Wiley.

Holley, J.W. and Guilford, J.P. (1964) A note on the G index of agreement. *Educational and Psychological Measurement* **24**: 749–53.

Jensen, A. (1980) *Bias in Mental Testing.* New York: Free Press.

Kiesler, D.J. (1966) Some myths of psychotherapy research and the search for a paradigm. *Psychological Bulletin* **65**: 110–36.

Kline, P. (ed.) (1973) *New Approaches in Psychological Measurement.* Chichester: Wiley.

Kline, P. (1979) *Psychometrics and Psychology.* London: Academic Press.

Kline, P. (1981) *Fact and Fantasy in Freudian Theory,* 2nd edn. London: Methuen.

Kline, P. (1983) Meta-analysis, measurement and methodological problems in the study of psychotherapy. *Behaviour and Brain Sciences* **6**: 296–7.

Kline, P. (1986) *Handbook of Test Construction.* London: Methuen.

Kline, P. (1988) *Psychology Exposed: The Emperor's New Clothes.* London: Routledge.

Kline, P. (in press) *Handbook of Psychological Testing.* London: Routledge.

Kline, P. and Barrett, P. (1983) The factors in personality questionnaires among normal subjects. *Advances in Behaviour Research and Therapy* **5**: 141–202.

Kline, P. and Lapham, S. (1990) *The PPQ.* London: Psychometric Systems.

Kline, P. and Lapham, S. (1991) The validity of the PPQ. *Personality and Individual Differences* **12**(6): 631–5.

Krug, S. (1980) *The CAQ.* Champaign, Ill: Institute for Personality and Ability Testing.

McRae, R.B. and Costa, P.T. (1987) Validation of the five-factor model of personality across instruments and observers. *Journal of Personality and Social Psychology* **52**: 81–90.

Malan, D. (1959) On assessing the results in psychotherapy. *British Journal of Medical Psychology* **32**: 86–105.

Mayer-Gross, W., Slater, E. and Roth, M. (1967) *Clinical Psychiatry.* London: Cassell.

Nunnally, J.O. (1978) *Psychometric Theory.* New York: McGraw-Hill.

Orlinsky, D.E. and Howard, K.I. (1986) Process and outcome in psychotherapy, in S.L. Garfield and E. Bergin (eds) *Handbook of Psychotherapy and Behaviour Change.* New York: Wiley.

Shapiro, D.A. and Firth, J.A. (1987) Prescriptive vs. exploratory psychotherapy: outcomes of the Sheffield psychotherapy project. *British Journal of Psychiatry* **151**: 790–9.

Shapiro, D.A., Firth-Cozens, J. and Stiles, W.B. (1989) The question of the therapist's differential effectiveness: a Sheffield Psychotherapy Project Addendum. *British Journal of Psychiatry* **154**: 383–5.

Shapiro, D.A., Barkham, M., Hardy, G.E. and Morrison, L.A. (1990) The second Sheffield psychotherapy project: rationale, design and preliminary outcome data. *British Journal of Medical Psychiatry* **63**: 97–108.

Smail, D. (1984) *Illusion and Reality*. London: Dent.

Spielberger, C.D. (1983) *Manual for the State Trait Anxiety Inventory: STAI*. Palo Alto, Calif: Consulting Psychologists Press.

Strong, E.K., Campbell, D.P., Berdie, R.E. and Clerk, K.E. (1971) *Strong Vocational Interest Blank*. Stanford, Calif: Stanford University Press.

Truax, C.R. (1963) Effective ingredients in psychotherapy: an approach to unravelling the patient–therapist interactions. *Journal of Consulting Psychology* **10**: 256–63.

Wing, J.K., Cooper, J.E. and Sartorius, N. (1974) *The Measurement and Classification of Psychiatric Symptoms*. Cambridge: Cambridge University Press.

RESPONSE – Michael Barkham and David Shapiro

Overview

Kline's critique of the Second Sheffield Psychotherapy Project (SPP2: Shapiro *et al.* 1990) is prefaced by an account of nineteen 'important problems' in the methodology of psychotherapy outcome research. These problems are indeed important and are extensively treated in the literature (e.g. Basham 1986: Kazdin 1986: Stiles *et al.* 1986). Our purpose in designing SPP2 was to make a defensible contribution to the cumulative body of knowledge concerning the effectiveness and change mechanisms of individual psychotherapy for depression; we understood all too well the nature of the creative compromises required in such an endeavour. Our approach differs fundamentally from that adopted by Kline and initially we present three arguments against his approach. First, we challenge the argument, implicit in Kline's critique, that a single study can satisfy all validity threats. We consider it inconceivable that any one study could meet all possible objections and thereby stand above criticism. This becomes clear when the range of possible validity threats faced by psychotherapy studies is considered. Second, we question the goal of designing an ideal study when psychotherapy research addresses a wide and diverse audience. There are considerable differences of opinion both within and between the groups of methodologists, theoreticians and practitioners who read – and hopefully are influenced by – psychotherapy research reports. Kline's chapter reflects some of these diverse views and shows that not only are the desiderata in conflict with one another, but also there are discrepant views as to the best way to resolve these conflicts. Third, we are cognizant of resource limitations. Resources of time, expertise and money available to psychotherapy research are strictly limited. The decision to support the field's closest approximation so far to such an ideal, the multi-million dollar National Institute of Mental Health Treatment of Depression Collaborative Research Project (Elkin *et al.* 1985; 1989) aroused concern at the high proportion of the available funds consumed by the one study. Since first, independent replication is a fundamental requirement of believable scientific findings, second, there are so many psychotherapeutic methods, populations and settings requiring investigation, and third, even the most costly study has to make design choices between incompatible requirements, there is a strong case for distributing resources among a larger number of methodologically diverse studies rather than relying upon a handful of purportedly 'ideal' ones.

Against this background, our response to Kline's specific points will be organized in terms of the four validity types (internal, external, construct and statistical conclusion) described by Cook and Campbell (1979) and Shapiro (1990). Following this, we shall address issues of design and analysis. Before doing so, we wish to amplify Kline's statement that Shapiro *et al.* (1990) 'describe the results of a study where a large number of clients were treated by one of five psychotherapists using four different psychotherapeutic procedures'. The paper actually presents the rationale, design and preliminary outcome data on forty-eight clients seen by five therapists divided equally between the four contrasting treatment conditions. The data presented were analysed in order to address initial ethical considerations about the delivery of the four conditions prior to implementation of the study proper. The paper outlined the full design involving 120 clients to be seen by five therapists with clients assigned randomly to the four treatment conditions.

Validity threats

Internal validity

Threats to internal validity refer to the validity with which statements can be made about whether there is a causal relationship from independent to dependent variables. Kline argues that no-treatment control groups are required (7, 8) because 'it is valuable to have a control group to see whether the improvements are as great or greater with a no-treatment group or a group having a placebo treatment'. Our decision not to include such groups was taken for three main reasons: first, the scientific and practical questions addressed in the study did not require them, second, data obtained under such conditions are difficult to interpret, and third, collection of such data has substantial ethical and practical costs that would threaten the viability of the study. A review of these reasons follows.

First, whether or not no-treatment or placebo conditions are desirable depends upon the specific scientific questions addressed in the study. SPP2 is a comparative process and outcome study, designed to identify similarities and differences in the outcomes and change mechanisms of the four treatment conditions. The study does not address the question of whether any of these conditions is more effective than a further set of placebo or no-treatment conditions, however those might be defined. To date, no psychotherapy study has reported clients in a control group achieving better outcomes than in a treatment group. The order of effectiveness between conditions has been almost constant: active treatments do better than placebo conditions which in turn do better than no-treatment control conditions. Changes recorded by clients in such studies presumably include those due to life events, 'spontaneous remission' (whatever mechanisms that vague term encompasses) and other extra-therapeutic influences that may befall members of treated and untreated groups alike. It is unclear what scientific yield there would be in another study showing the same trend.

Second, control groups raise their own scientific problems of interpretation. In theory, the purpose of a no-treatment control group is to evaluate the contribution of competing variables in accounting for change. This assumes that there are no *unique* factors present in the control group which might be causally related to change. While most factors can be controlled through standard procedures, expectancy artifacts relating to the experimental situation itself present a validity threat. Clients randomly assigned to either a delay or no-treatment condition will develop expectancies specific to that particular condition (e.g. disappointment, rejection, etc.) and these are likely to differ from those developed by clients assigned to an active treatment condition. Similarly, Kline does not acknowledge the severe methodological and conceptual difficulties with placebo controls. The placebo concept originated in drug research, in which context it simply denotes psychological as opposed to pharmacological pathways to therapeutic response. Pharmacological factors are isolated by the use of the 'double blind' control in which neither patient nor doctor knows whether the drug is active or inert. In contrast, use of the placebo concept in psychotherapy research requires a much more problematic distinction among psychological pathways. It has proved well-nigh impossible to devise a placebo psychotherapy that can be delivered double-blind so that neither therapist nor client knows whether the treatment is active or inert. To achieve a satisfactory psychotherapy placebo requires a clear conceptual and operational isolation of the active or specific elements of the psychotherapy under test. Limited progress has been made in this direction, by measuring common factors that could contribute to placebo effects in psychotherapy, ranging from credibility or expectancy effects, to the quality of the therapeutic relationship and the therapist's general therapeutic skills. Critical to the logic of a placebo condition is the requirement that factors comprising that condition be a subset of the factors applied to the treatment group. However, Shapiro and Shapiro (1983) found only fifteen out of seventy-three placebo studies to have employed a component control condition.

Third, there are also ethical and practical difficulties in securing informed client and referrer participation in a study including no-treatment or purportedly ineffective placebo conditions, whose outcomes are generally inferior, when this involves clients being excluded from what are known to be more effective treatment conditions. Accordingly, in consideration of these three issues, SPP2 therefore follows Basham (1986) in contrasting two active treatments with sharply differing rationales and procedural contents, and incorporating within the study process measures of a range of common and specific components. We also monitor life events (9) at intake and outcome assessments and via weekly checklists throughout treatment. In contrast to a no-treatment condition, which *might* control for life events, this strategy can *inform* us about the relationship between specific life events and the process of psychotherapy outcome.

External validity

Threats to external validity refer to the validity with which conclusions can be drawn about the generalizability of a causal relationship to and across populations. On the basis of the constraints placed upon the design in order to meet threats to internal validity (e.g. randomization), Kline then proceeds to raise questions about the external validity of the design. One example of this is his criticism that 'the demands of scientific rigour result in a design which reflects nothing in the real world'. This criticism is naive with respect to the trade-off between internal and external validity that necessitates creative compromise in outcome research design. The aim of *experimental* studies is not to devise studies replicating the course of events in the outside world: this is the realm of *naturalistic* studies which are equally important for their own contribution and have a valuable contribution under the rubric of methodological pluralism. The purpose of controlled outcome studies is to address issues which can become confounded in naturalistic studies. Accordingly, the purpose of SPP2 was to protect against threats to internal validity whilst maintaining equally credible treatment conditions. The design suggested by Kline calls for clients to be randomly assigned to no-treatment, placebo and active conditions: does *this* reflect actual clinical practice in the real world more than is the case where all clients receive active, albeit different, treatments? Once the aims of a study are made clear, this restricts both the claims to be made on its behalf and the grounds upon which it may be appropriately critiqued.

Kline argues that the N of therapists cannot be a representative sample (2), noting that as therapists carry out all treatments, there may be possible bias. Several points are relevant here. The logical response is that SPP2 is not a study of therapists but of differential treatment effects. If the aim of the study *were* primarily to focus on therapist effects, then Kline is correct. However, the design would differ fundamentally from that of SPP2 in that a large pool of therapists would need to take part with each therapist perhaps treating just two or four clients. In general, we readily acknowledge the spirit of the argument which calls for testing the generalizability of research findings and we therefore implemented a parallel study, the Collaborative Psychotherapy Project (CPP: Halstead *et al.* 1990) in which an additional forty-eight clients are being seen by four NHS therapists following a modified design. The constraint of clients being in employment was dropped for the CPP so that no employment or status criterion is used to screen clients. However, they are still required to meet other research desiderata. Still addressing the issue of therapists, Kline is right to point to the importance of therapist effects (2). The finding by Shapiro *et al.* (1989) of a Therapist x Treatment interaction (not, as reported by Kline, 'one outstanding therapist', but a pattern whereby a treatment effect was largely confined to one of two principal therapists) impressed upon us the importance of having several therapists treat equal numbers of clients in all conditions. Therapist effects have recently assumed great importance in the literature (Crits-Cristoph and Mintz 1991); careful training and monitoring of treatment delivery, as incorporated within SPP2, may eliminate them but this must be ascertained by data analysis; if therapist effects are suspected (reflected in a p value less than 0.25) then analysis of treatment effects must take account of therapist effects. Failure to do this means that any treatment effects reported cannot be generalized beyond the sample of therapists in question. A final point regarding therapists: Kline is mistaken in stating that the effects of the sex of therapist on the outcome and process of therapy cannot be examined in the SPP2 study (3, 4, 17). The design calls for equal numbers of male and female clients to be seen by three male and two female therapists in each of four (treatment conditions) x three (severity levels) conditions, thereby enabling the effects of gender of therapist to be investigated.

Regarding the selection of clients (4, 10, 11), a requirement for internal validity is that the client sample is homogeneous with respect to, for example, diagnosis or some background variable. A heterogeneous sample of clients (e.g. including those with a history of psychiatric disorder) introduces another variable into the matrix. The question of whether the sample is 'representative of even middle-class depressive clients' arises because this research question was not the priority in designing the project. The priority was to determine the differential effectiveness of contrasting therapies within a specific client population. It would be the aim of *subsequent* studies to address the question of generalizability. If no differential effect is found between contrasting treatments holding constant as many other variables as possible, then it is unlikely that any differential effects would be obtained where other factors (e.g. client characteristics) were not held constant. These decisions reflect the stage-wise process of carrying out psychotherapy research.

Construct validity

Construct validity refers to the validity with which generalizations can be made about higher order constructs from research operations. Kline's discussion of 'the meaning of recovery' (1, 15) neglects the literature's distinction between 'effects' and 'effectiveness' of treatment (Shoham-Salomon and

Hannah 1991). From a practical viewpoint, interest may focus upon the effectiveness of treatment in terms of the proportions of clients who 're-cover' as judged by some clinically based criterion of improvement. From the more theoretical viewpoint of the investigator interested in the change process, interest focuses upon the nature of the effects associated with different interventions. SPP2 attempts to meet both these interests, via first, a battery of outcome instruments which, taken together, offer a state of the art index of effectiveness as currently understood (12, 13); and second, specific instruments within that battery that measure change domains or effects predicted by the theoretical rationales of the two treatment models examined in the study. This comprehensive battery enables us to investigate the process of recovery as well as tapping the potential for symptom substitution (15).

A further issue raised by Kline (3) concerns therapists carrying out different treatments (i.e. crossed with treatments). One clear advantage, providing all therapists receive training to a criterion level, is that the delivery of common factors as the competing account for change can be systematically investigated holding therapists constant (i.e. the therapists contribute equally to all treatment conditions). Indeed if therapists are crossed with treatments (i.e. all therapists deliver all types of therapies being studied), therapists can be investigated as a main or interaction effect (i.e. with treatment). That is, the effectiveness of therapists may be a function of what therapy they are delivering. If therapists are nested as a factor (i.e. each therapist delivers only one of the therapy orientations), therapists and therapy are confounded. There is general agreement among researchers that crossing therapists with treatments is the preferred strategy (Kazdin 1986). Being able to evaluate the contribution of common factors to therapeutic outcome is critical to the construct validity of the research.

Kline acknowledges the multiplicity of definitions and meanings of improvement espoused by different theoretical orientations within psychotherapy, but suggests that 'research results are unlikely to be relevant to all these views'. He also recognizes some superordinate level where a common assessment across therapies might be possible. The researcher's task is to incorporate both these elements through first, the adoption of a 'core outcome battery' (Waskow 1975), and second, adopting multiple levels and perspectives of the change process. The first component (i.e. a core outcome battery), facilitates comparisons across studies using similar measures, while the second (i.e. multiple levels and perspectives) enables validation of change both within the client and as assessed by other parties (e.g. clinical assessor, partner, work colleague, etc.).

Kline is correct in noting the need for additional measures for analytic and dynamic psychotherapies. We are particularly interested in the recent development of the Inventory of Interpersonal Problems (IIP: Barkham *et al.* 1991: Horowitz *et al.* 1988) which shows promise in tapping clients' interpersonal difficulties, a core focus of more dynamically oriented therapies. However, we disagree with Kline's position that 'if psychotherapy has had any effect, we should expect personality changes but on what variables?' It is not immediately apparent that the benefits from psychotherapy must *necessarily* lead to personality change. Within SPP2 we have measured personality disorders via an early and shortened version of the Personality Disorders Examination (PDE: Loranger *et al.* 1987). Importantly, any measure, be it of personality or symptoms, must be sufficiently sensitive to detect change. The question is whether measures of personality *other* than the PDE, which has not been used as a change measure in SPP2, would be sufficiently sensitive to detect small changes in dimensions in which larger changes might not be expected.

Statistical conclusion validity

Statistical conclusion validity refers to the extent to which a study permits statements about the causal relationship between independent and dependent variables. The issue of treatment delivery (6) is important in this respect (i.e. introducing unsystematic error) and the recent advances, adopted in SPP2, regarding both standardizing therapies through manualization (e.g. Shapiro and Firth 1985) as well as monitoring adherence (e.g. Shapiro and Startup 1990) have enabled us to be more confident about the delivery of the therapy. With regard to clinical diagnosis (10), our use of trained clinical assessors working under supervision via the use of audiorecordings of assessments as well as employing both the DSM-III (American Psychiatric Association 1980) and the PSE-ID-CATEGO system (Wing *et al.* 1974) provides us with as secure a procedure for making a diagnosis as is reasonable.

A central concern for statistical conclusion validity, not mentioned by Kline but one which we would wish to stress, is the need for adequate statistical power (Cohen 1977). This refers to the ability of a study to detect differences between treatments should they actually exist and is a function of the size of effect an experimenter is seeking to detect as well as the numbers of clients in each group. Kazdin and Bass (1989) found only 45.3 per cent of studies they sampled to have sufficient power at post-treatment when comparing two or more active treatments. Because insufficient power will result in an increased probability of making a Type II error, adequate power is critical in any psychotherapy outcome study.

However, drawing statistical conclusions need not necessarily be the primary aim: there is intense interest now in making statements about clinical significance. In this respect, while access to baseline data (16) is valuable, there is normative data available on core outcome measures which can be used in order to evaluate the clinical significance of psychotherapy outcomes employing social comparisons (Nietzel *et al.* 1987). We would espouse the adoption of these procedures, in particular those in which the probability of change being attributable to the standard error of measurement is taken into account when evaluating *reliable and clinically significant change* (Jacobson and Truax 1991).

Design and analysis

Kline concludes by proposing a factor-analytic design. We have addressed this issue last for two reasons. First, much of the reasoning for it derives from suggested shortcomings addressed under previous headings. Our rebuttal of many of these will influence the appeal, or not, of the factor-analytic design. Second, as Kline notes, it is also an issue of analysis, with the factor-analytic procedures being, at least in principle, possible on existing data. Essentially, a factor analysis is based upon a correlation matrix and addresses the relationship between items; it is not designed to determine the causal relationship between events at Time 1 and a situation at Time 2 or 3. As outlined by Kline, a factor-analytic design raises a number of issues which are always present when using this approach.

1 There are questions of the appropriateness of exploratory factor analytic techniques given the accrued knowledge base – many questions would be more concerned with model testing via confirmatory factor-analytic techniques.
2 There is the issue of the number of factors to elicit – our experience of attempts such as the Autoscree Test (Barrett and Kline 1982) to provide a quantitative basis for this decision have not been wholly satisfactory (Barkham *et al.* 1991).
3 There is the problem of the relevance of elicited factors – it might be, for example, that all outcome measures (i.e. recovery) load on to a single factor to the exclusion of any other item because they correlate more highly with each other than with any other variable (e.g. therapist).
4 There is the problem of eliciting too few factors and producing complex composites which are uninterpretable (perhaps like four-way interactions).
5 There is the issue, which Kline alludes to, of the observation-to-variables ratio – Kline refers to needing 'good samples', but it is likely that the sample size required would be large.

Our own interest in factor-analytic techniques focuses on first, testing the validity of the measures used (12), and second, in the potential for evaluating qualitative changes in the nature of clients' worlds via procedures akin to a structural equation approach (e.g. Millsap and Hartog 1988). However, this is but one analytical 'tool'. For example, the multiplicity of procedures available enables us to seek aptitude-treatment interactions (3, 4, 5), thereby helping us to identify differential change processes (Shoham-Salomon and Hannah 1991). We are also interested in modelling individual client growth curves in which change is conceptualized as a process rather than as simply incremental. This approach is of increasing interest in clinical and psychotherapy research (Francis *et al.* 1991), reflecting the view that simple pre- and post-therapy differences (i.e. a linear model of change) is not necessarily the most informative model summarizing the change process.

Conclusion

While Kline may well be able to address the points raised here to the same extent as we have addressed the issues raised by him, the difference appears to be that we recognize difficulties in *all* research strategies while at the same time espousing methodological pluralism. By contrast, Kline presents his strategy as somehow resolving all problems without presenting any of their own. The bottom line is that no *single* methodology is adequate in and of itself to address the complexities inherent in psychotherapy research. As active psychotherapy researchers (Shapiro *et al.* 1991), we look forward to Kline testing, empirically, his propositions both at the practical (i.e. logistic) and scientific level.

References

American Psychiatric Association (1980) *Diagnostic and Statistical Manual of Mental Disorders*, 3rd edn. Washington, DC: American Psychiatric Association.

Barkham, M., Hardy, G.E. and Startup, M.J. (1991) The validity and reliability of the Inventory of Interpersonal Problems. Paper submitted for publication.

Barrett, P. and Kline, P. (1982) An item and radial parcel factor analysis of the 16PF questionnaire. *Personality and Individual Differences* 3: 259–70.

Basham, R.B. (1986) Scientific and practical advantages of comparative design in psychotherapy outcome research. *Journal of Consulting and Clinical Psychology* 54: 88–94.

Cohen, J. (1977) *Statistical Power Analysis for the Behavioral Sciences*, 2nd edn. New York: Academic Press.

Cook, T.D. and Campbell, D.T. (1979) *Quasi-experimentation: Design and Analysis for Field Settings*. Chicago: Rand McNally.

Crits-Cristoph, P. and Mintz, J. (1991) Implications of therapist effects for the design and analysis of comparative studies of psychotherapies. *Journal of Consulting and Clinical Psychology* 59: 20–6.

Elkin, I., Parloff, M.B., Hadley, S.W. and Autry, J.H. (1985) National Institute of Mental Health Treatment of Depression Collaborative Research Program: background and research plan. *Archives of General Psychiatry* 42: 305–16.

Elkin, I., Shea, M.T., Watkins, J.T., Imber, S.D., Sotsky, S.M., Collins, J.F., Glass, D.R., Pilkonis, P.A., Leber, W.R., Docherty, J.P., Fiester, S.J. and Parloff, M.B. (1989) National Institute of Mental Health Treatment of Depression Collaborative Research Program: general effectiveness of treatment. *Archives of General Psychiatry* 46: 971–82.

Francis, D.J., Fletcher, J.M., Stuebing, K.K., Davidson, K.C. and Thompson, N.M. (1991) Analysis of change: modeling individual growth. *Journal of Consulting and Clinical Psychology* 59: 27–37.

Halstead, J.E., Agnew, R.M., Barkham, M., Harrington, V.M.G., Culverwell, A.M. and Shapiro, D.A. (1990) The MRC/NHS Collaborative Psychotherapy Project: intensive psychotherapy research in normal clinical practice. *Clinical Psychology Forum* 26: 30–2.

Horowitz, L.M., Rosenberg, S.E., Baer, B.A., Ureno, G. and Villasenor, V.S. (1988)

Inventory of Interpersonal Problems: psychometric properties and clinical applications. *Journal of Consulting and Clinical Psychology* **56**: 885–92.
Jacobson, N.S. and Truax, P. (1991) Clinical significance: a statistical approach to defining meaningful change in psychotherapy research. *Journal of Consulting and Clinical Psychology* **59**: 12–19.
Kazdin, A.E. (1986) Comparative outcome studies of psychotherapy: methodological issues and strategies. *Journal of Consulting and Clinical Psychology* **54**: 95–105.
Kazdin, A.E. and Bass, D. (1989) Power to detect differences between alternative treatments in comparative psychotherapy outcome research. *Journal of Consulting and Clinical Psychology* **57**: 138–47.
Loranger, A.W., Susman, V.L., Oldham, J.M. and Russakoff, L.M. (1987) The personality disorder examination: a preliminary report. *Journal of Personality Disorders* **1**: 1–13.
Millsap, R.E. and Hartog, S.B. (1988) Alpha, beta, and gamma change in evaluation research: a structural equation approach. *Journal of Applied Psychology* **73**: 574–84.
Nietzel, M.T., Russell, R.L., Hemmings, K.A. and Gretter, M.L. (1987) Clinical significance of psychotherapy for unipolar depression: a meta-analytic approach to social comparison. *Journal of Consulting and Clinical Psychology* **55**: 156–61.
Shapiro, D.A. (1990) Outcome research, in G. Parry and F.N. Watts (eds) *Behavioural and Mental Health Research: A Handbook of Skills and Methods*. Hove: Lawrence Erlbaum Associates.
Shapiro, D.A. and Firth, J. (1985) Exploratory therapy manual for the Sheffield Psychotherapy Project. SAPU Memo 733, Department of Psychology, University of Sheffield.
Shapiro, D.A. and Shapiro, D. (1983) Comparative therapy outcome research: methodological implications of meta-analysis. *Journal of Consulting and Clinical Psychology* **51**: 42–53.
Shapiro, D.A. and Startup, M.J. (1990) The Sheffield Psychotherapies Rating Schedule. SAPU Memo 1154, Department of Psychology, University of Sheffield.
Shapiro, D.A., Firth-Cozens, J. and Stiles, W.B. (1989) Therapists' differential effectiveness: a Sheffield Psychotherapy Project addendum. *British Journal of Psychiatry* **154**: 383–5.
Shapiro, D.A., Barkham, M., Hardy, G.E. and Morrison, L.A. (1990) The Second Sheffield Psychotherapy Project: rationale, design and preliminary outcome data. *British Journal of Medical Psychology* **63**: 97–108.
Shapiro, D.A., Barkham, M., Hardy, G.E., Morrison, L.A., Reynolds, S., Startup, M. and Harper, H. (1991) University of Sheffield Psychotherapy Research Program: Medical Research Council/Economic and Social Research Council Social and Applied Psychology Unit, in L.E. Beutler and M. Crago (eds) *Psychotherapy Research: An International Review of Programmatic Studies*. Washington, DC: American Psychological Association.
Shoham-Salomon, V. and Hannah, M.T. (1991) Client–treatment interaction in the study of differential change processes. *Journal of Consulting and Clinical Psychology* **59**: 217–25.
Stiles, W.B., Shapiro, D.A. and Elliott, R.K. (1986) 'Are all psychotherapies equivalent?' *American Psychologist* **41**: 165–80.
Waskow, I.E. (1975) Selection of a core battery, in I.E. Waskow and M.B. Parloff (eds) *Psychotherapy Change Measures*. Rockville, Md: National Institute of Mental Health.

Wing, J.K., Cooper, J.E. and Sartorius, N. (1974) *The Measurement and Classification of Psychiatric Symptoms*. Cambridge: Cambridge University Press.

REBUTTAL – Paul Kline

In my reply to the response by Barkham and Shapiro I shall not go into the technical matters of experimental design in this field which are contentious and matters of dispute even among putative experts. Instead I shall try to answer the more general points which they raise and which, ultimately, are the important ones in the study of psychotherapy.

In the first place I made it clear that my criticisms of the Sheffield Project were not directed at its authors but were made simply to illustrate the virtually insuperable problems of carrying out watertight research into the effects of psychotherapy. My list of problems was to alert readers to the difficulties involved and to enable them to assess reports of psychotherapeutic success or failure.

Thus the first point raised by Barkham and Shapiro that it is inconceivable that any study could meet all possible objections is one that I agree with. It was not implicit in my paper that a single study could meet all validity threats. What was implicit, however, was the argument that if a study was not free from fault, it was difficult to know what value could be attached to it. It is this argument, indeed, that makes questionable all meta-analytic studies of psychotherapy.

Barkham and Shapiro argue that the nature and meaning of a control group is difficult to specify in psychotherapy as distinct from a drug trial in organic medicine and that this is a good reason for not utilizing one. It is true that specification is difficult but this is a further example of the problems in psychotherapy. I might well have added this to my list. However, the fact that it is a severe difficulty does not mean that it should be ignored. On simple logical grounds controls, no matter how difficult to instantiate in practice, should be used.

The issue of the degree to which an experiment reflects the real world is indeed important, as I have argued in respect of experimental psychology in general (Kline 1988). Their argument is that my design where clients receive either placebo, no treatments or active treatment, is no more realistic than theirs where all clients receive active but different treatments. This may well be the case but my purpose, in my chapter, was not to find fault with the study by Barkham and Shapiro but to point out the problem that experimental rigour could render a research valueless because it ceased to resemble what it was intended to investigate in the real world. As a matter of fact I believe that the decision to have therapists carrying out different treatments is an example of this problem. It is, undeniably, statistically the most elegant solution to the difficulty that the effectiveness of therapists may be a function of the therapy which they are using. However, it may have rendered the experiment quite unlike any therapy which goes on outside the experiment.

One of the greatest difficulties in assessing the effects of psychotherapy is to disentangle the therapist and therapy variance. The only way to do this is to have a large sample of therapists of each type, although I accept fully the impracticality of such an endeavour. Thus the counter-argument used by Barkham and Shapiro, namely that if they had been studying therapists, then a large sample of therapists would have been required, will not do. Certainly, in a study of therapists a large sample is required but so it is in the study of therapy, for the reasons which I have stated above.

I had questioned the representativeness of the client sample used in the Sheffield study. The reply to this point is that the aim of the study was to examine the effectiveness of psychotherapy within a specific population. It would be the aim of subsequent studies to address the question of generalizability. I regard this response as disingenuous. A research study is of little interest if the results are specific to the sample used. Furthermore many readers of research reports, especially in the applied field, may not be well acquainted with the problems of sampling and may make impermissible generalizations.

I was rash enough in my concluding discussion of the problems in assessing the effectiveness of psychotherapy to propose a factor analytic design in an attempt to overcome some of the difficulties. However, I did not suggest that such a design overcame all the problems in research into psychotherapy. This appears to be a fantasy of Barkham and Shapiro. I simply claimed that it appeared to have certain advantages over the more common approaches. Indeed, I would like to put it to the empirical test, as Barkham and Shapiro advise.

Although factor analysis can be discussed incomprehensibly (and often is) I want to discuss briefly some of the objections raised to this design by Barkham and Shapiro. They propose that confirmatory rather than exploratory factor analysis should be used. In confirmatory analysis, essentially a target set of factors is proposed and it is possible to test statistically how closely the solution has reached the target. In exploratory analysis, on the other hand, the simplest solution is obtained and this has to be interpreted by the researcher. However, there are severe problems with confirmatory analysis. Unless, on the basis of previous research one can precisely specify the factor loadings (and knowledge in the field of psychotherapy renders this impossible) the specification has to be general, e.g. high negative or positive and zero loadings. In these cases, especially with large samples, it is hard to reject the hypothesis. Thus there is apparent confirmation. I think that the preference for confirmatory analysis over exploratory analysis lies in its statistical rigour rather than its practical advantages in research.

Barkham and Shapiro are right to argue that there is an unresolved problem over the correct number of factors to rotate in the solution and that if too few are chosen they will be composites. However, it should not be beyond the wits of researchers to compare several solutions and choose the one which seems to fit the data best. These are exploratory factors and they should form a basis for further research. As Cattell (1978) demonstrates, simple structure factors are replicable. Thus if factor solutions are good they will yield replicable factors.

Barkham and Shapiro attempt to argue that elicited factors might not be relevant. There is a problem here over the meaning of relevance. Their example is an illustration of this – namely that all outcome measures loaded on a single factor because they were more highly correlated with each other than with any other variable, e.g. therapist. This does not mean that no therapist could load on the factor. This would be the case only if there were *no* correlation between therapist and outcome. In any case if a wide variety of outcome measures were selected they would not intercorrelate more highly among themselves than with the therapist, if this variable were correlated at all. The fact is that if no therapists load on an outcome variable then it means that they have no effect on the outcome. This is the logic of factor analysis and, of course, this is reflected in the correlations.

Finally, it is true that fairly large samples would be necessary. However, a further study of the observation to variable ratio by Arrindel and Ende (1985) showed that a ratio of 2:1 was not strictly necessary for simple structure. What was important was the expected number of factors and five times more subjects than this was what was required, although the N should be sufficient to reduce the standard errors of the correlations. This is a useful finding for research in which, as in the case of psychotherapy, a large number of variables is required.

Conclusions

I think that, in fact, there is little fundamental disagreement between Barkham and Shapiro and me. We both agree that it is impossible to design and execute a single study which overcomes all the problems which await the researcher in psychotherapy. We agree concerning the nature of the problems. Where we differ is in the response to them. Barkham and Shapiro, in the Sheffield Project and elsewhere, as was made clear in my chapter, have carried out about as good research as it is possible to do given the constraints of time and funding. However, excellent as this work is, it still has considerable problems, as the authors fairly admit.

I believe that, given these difficulties, it is exceedingly difficult to draw any conclusions concerning the effectiveness of psychotherapy. Even if we put together a number of different studies they will all be flawed in some way. How important these flaws are must be a matter of judgement. The purpose of my chapter was to make readers sensitive to the problems. Whether they be optimists, as Barkham and Shapiro, or pessimists, is perhaps a matter of personality rather than logic.

References

Arrindel, W.A. and Ende, J. van der (1985) An empirical test of the utility of the observation to variables ratio in factor and components analysis. *Applied Psychological Measurement* **9**: 165–78.

Cattell, R.B. (1978) *The Scientific Use of Factor Analysis*. New York: Plenum.

Kline, P. (1988) *Psychology Exposed: The Emperor's New Clothes*. London: Routledge.

FIVE

The outcome problem in psychotherapy

HANS EYSENCK

Introduction

As I have pointed out in two autobiographical sketches (Eysenck 1990a; 1990b), my connection with psychotherapy has been along three main lines. The first was an initiation of the debate, still continuing, concerning the efficacy of psychotherapy; the second was playing a part in the establishment of behaviour therapy, and writing its first textbook (Eysenck and Rachman 1965); and the third was the setting up of clinical psychology as a profession in the United Kingdom. These three contributions are not of course independent. The first step in the sequence was my being given the task of setting up clinical psychology as a profession in the United Kingdom; as a result I got interested in the degree to which psychotherapy might be considered to be useful in the treatment of neurosis, and as a consequence of my discovery that there was no evidence to support the view that psychotherapy had any beneficial consequences, as opposed to no treatment, or placebo treatment, I was led to investigate the possibilities of behaviour therapy, originally adumbrated by Watson and Rayner (1920), Jones (1924) and others, as discussed by Kazdin (1978) and Schorr (1984). Thus in my connection with clinical psychology the outcome problem was absolutely crucial, and my feeling was and is that this problem has never been properly addressed by clinical psychologists, and forms the weakest part of our argument to be a socially useful profession.

In the late 1940s and early 1950s, when I became involved in this field, certain things were generally taken for granted. It was widely believed and taught that psychoanalysis was the only acceptable method of treatment for neurotic patients, being the only method that concerned itself with *causes* rather than merely with *symptoms*; that symptomatic treatment might be superficially successful, but that it would soon be followed by a recurrence of symptoms, or symptom substitution; that 'deep', 'psychodynamic' and long-lasting investigations by trained psychoanalysts were required to produce stable and long-lasting cures; and that such cures could be effected only by analysts who had themselves been psychoanalysed. Diagnoses and cures might be helped by psychodynamically oriented projection tests, like the Rorschach or the Thematic Apperception Test (TAT); the emphasis of both tests and treatment were unconscious causes, transference phenomena, and early childhood experiences reconstructed through analysis of dreams and other types of 'dynamic' evidence.

Few knowledgeable psychologists or psychiatrists would now deny that there was no objective evidence for any of these beliefs. There were no clinical studies comparing the progress of neurotic patients under psychoanalysis with that of similar patients receiving no treatment, or placebo treatment; it was often suggested that it would be unethical to withhold such obviously beneficial treatment as psychoanalysis from patients, disregarding the fact that of all the people suffering from severe neurotic illness in the United States, less than 0.01 per cent would in fact receive psychoanalytic treatment! The superiority of psychoanalysis was simply assumed on the basis of pseudo-scientific arguments, without there being any evidence in its favour. It was often suggested that the cases treated and described by Freud provided such evidence, but apart from the obvious point that there were no controls involved in his work, and no follow-ups, it is now well known that Freud was very economical with the truth, as far as description of his famous cases is concerned, and that the alleged 'cures' in fact were not cures at all (Eysenck 1985b). Thus the famous 'Wolf Man' was not in fact cured as claimed, but continued with the self-same symptoms from which Freud claimed to have relieved him for the next sixty years of his life, being under constant treatment during this time (Obholzer 1982). Similarly, the famous 'cure' of Anna O. by Breuer, which was supposed to constitute the beginnings of psychoanalytic treatment, was shown by historians to have been a misdiagnosis and the 'cure' a fraud (Thornton 1983). Anna O. was not a hysteric, but suffered from tuberculous meningitis: she was not cured, but lived for many years with the self-same symptoms in a hospital (Hirschmuller 1989). The 'Rat Man' was far from a therapeutic success as claimed, and Freud's process notes deviate notably from his final account (Mahony 1986). It would be difficult to adduce these and other cases treated by Freud as evidence of psychoanalytic successes (Eysenck 1985b).

The outcome problem, then, was being completely disregarded, and the only kind of clinical studies to be done were concerned with problems internal to the analytic process, it being assumed that psychoanalysis was not only the best, but also the only method of treatment. It seemed to me from the beginning that this was entirely the wrong way to look at the whole problem of psychotherapy. Both from the theoretical and the practical points of view, the outcome problem was the most important and critical of all; if psychoanalysis, or psychotherapy in general, which was then as it is now, largely based on Freudian assumptions, did not in fact do better than placebo treatments or no treatment at all, then clearly the theory on which it is based was wrong. Similarly, if there were no positive effects of psychoanalysis as a therapy, then it would be completely unethical to apply this method to patients, to charge them money for such treatment, or to train therapists in these unsuccessful methods. The practical importance of the issue will be clear without any great discussion, but the theoretical implications have been debated for a long time; it has been asserted that even if the therapy itself did not work, the theory might nevertheless be correct. I took it for granted that if a treatment method based on theory does not work, then this suggests that the theory itself must be mistaken. Grunbaum (1984) has argued the case in considerable detail, and has come to a very similar conclusion. I shall return to this point presently.

Effectiveness of psychoanalysis

In order to satisfy myself concerning the alleged efficacy of psychoanalysis, I carried out an analysis of all the published material concerning recovery from neurotic illness after psychoanalysis, after psychotherapy, and after no treatment of a psychiatric nature at all; the results were published in an article which has been referred to as 'the most influential critical evaluation of psychotherapy' (Kazdin 1978: 33). In this article (Eysenck 1952) I examined a number of outcome studies that primarily evaluated treatment of neurotic patients. I attempted to assess the effects of psychotherapy by comparing its outcome with an estimate of improvements in patients that occurred in the absence of therapy. I concluded that approximately 67 per cent of seriously ill neurotic patients recover within two years, even in the absence of formal psychotherapy. If we regard this as an approximate baseline against which treatment can be evaluated, then we can compare therapy outcome with it, and I found a cure rate of approximately the same magnitude. Thus remissions with no treatment ('spontaneous remission') appear to be as effective as psychotherapy and psychoanalysis. The dissatisfaction with psychotherapy expressed in this conclusion was shared by many others who published similar articles around the same time (e.g. Denker 1946; Landis 1937; Salter 1952; Wilder 1945; Zubin 1953), all of whom came to very similar conclusions, although they tended to express them less definitively and perhaps less clearly than I had done.

The paper produced a plethora of replies, all of which, interestingly enough, criticized me for saying something I had not said, namely that the evidence proved psychoanalysis and psychotherapy to be ineffective. The quality of the papers surveyed, it was stated, was too poor to allow such a conclusion to be substantiated. This, of course, is true; the evidence is methodologically and statistically inadequate, but my conclusion had been rather different, namely that the evidence was *not sufficient to prove that psychoanalysis and psychotherapy were instrumental in mediating recovery*. The poorer the evidence, the stronger this conclusion is; if the studies surveyed are so poor that no conclusions can be drawn, then they cannot be used to support the idea that psychoanalysis and psychotherapy have a positive effect!

In case it might be thought that I am making a special case for my own view, or that the issue is not a serious and important one, readers are recommended to read an article by Erwin (1980) who, as a trained philosopher, has exhaustively looked at the argument (also treated in his previous book: Erwin 1978). His conclusion agrees with me that the issue is important, and that the critics of my original thesis were mistaken.

It is interesting, in view of other criticisms that I have to make, that the critics of my paper had to resort to misrepresentation in order to enable them to put up some kind of argument. It is also interesting that neither the referees nor the editors of the journals concerned noted this misrepresentation.

I took up the topic again in 1960 and in 1965, summarizing the large number of articles that had appeared, partly as a consequence of the stress on the importance of the outcome problem which we had insisted on. The results were not very dissimilar, as the following quotation from my 1960 paper will illustrate:

1 When untreated neurotic control groups are compared with experimental groups of neurotic patients treated by means of psychotherapy, both groups recover to approximately the same extent.

2 When soldiers who have suffered a neurotic breakdown and have not received psychotherapy are compared with soldiers who have received psychotherapy, the chances of the two groups returning to duty are approximately equal.

3 When neurotic soldiers are separated from the service, their chances of recovery are not affected by their receiving or not receiving psychotherapy.

4 Civilian neurotics who are treated by psychotherapy recover or improve to approximately the same extent as similar neurotics receiving no psychotherapy.

5 Children suffering from emotional disorders and treated by psychotherapy recover or improve to approximately the same extent as similar children not receiving psychotherapy.

6 Neurotic patients treated by means of psychotherapeutic procedures based on learning theory improve significantly more quickly than do patients treated by means of psychoanalytic or eclectic psychotherapy, or not treated by psychotherapy at all.

7 Neurotic patients treated by psychoanalytic psychotherapy do not improve more quickly than patients treated by means of eclectic psychotherapy and may improve less quickly when account is taken of the large proportion of patients breaking off treatment.

8 With the single exception of the psychotherapeutic methods based

on learning theory, results of published research with military and
civilian neurotics, and with both adults and children, suggest that
the therapeutic effects of psychotherapy are small or non-existent
and do not in any demonstrable way add to the non-specific effects
of routine medical treatment, or to such events as occur in the
patients' everyday experience.

(Eysenck 1960: 719–20)

In these writings I made a number of other points, which have not always
been considered by critics. Thus I emphasized the need for carefully controlled
therapy research that not only took into account spontaneous remission,
but also controlled for non-specific treatment effects, that is the inclusion
of placebo treatment in assessment. I also pointed out that showing that
therapy is superior to no treatment is not sufficient to demonstrate that any
particular technique or ingredient of therapy is effective; non-specific treatment effects such as attending treatment and meeting with the therapist
would still have to be ruled out to argue for specific benefits of treatment
(Eysenck 1966). Arguments for and against were taken up by many contributors whose points of view are summarized by Kazdin (1978) and Schorr
(1984). It would not be useful to take up these arguments here again, but it
may be worthwhile to look at more recent surveys of the burgeoning literature, and try and see to what extent more recent studies have validated or
invalidated my original conclusions.

Before turning to this task, however, let us consider the degree to which
psychoanalysts have responded to the widespread criticism voiced concerning the efficacy of their treatment. Following the principle that criticism
should be directed at what is regarded the best, rather than the worst project
in the area, we may look at the Menninger Clinic project (Kernberg 1972;
1973), a lavishly financed study published after eighteen years of work. The
aim of the project was to 'explore changes brought about in patients by
psychoanalytically oriented psychotherapies and psychoanalysis' (Kernberg
1972: 3). Forty-two adult neurotic patients were studied, those in psychoanalytic therapy receiving an average of 835 hours of treatment, and those
in psychoanalytically oriented psychotherapy receiving an average of 289
hours. A detailed criticism of the project has been made by Rachman and
Wilson (1980). Listing such obvious faults as contamination, non-random
allocation, absence of any control, and so on, we find that the authors of the
Menninger report themselves admit that the most severe limitation of their
study was its 'lack of formal experimental design' (Kernberg 1972: 76). They
point out that it was not possible:

(i)   To list the variables needed to test the theories;
(ii) To have methods of quantification of the variables, preferably
      existing scales which would have adequate reliability and validity;
(iii) To be able to choose and provide controlled conditions which
      would rule out alternative explanations for the results.

(iv) To state the hypothesis to be tested; or finally,
(v) To conduct the research according to the design.

(Kernberg 1972: 75)

As Rachman and Wilson correctly point out,

> This astonishing conclusion can have few equals . . . one is left with a study that is so flawed as to preclude any conclusions whatsoever. Whilst the honesty of this self-appraisal is highly commendable, one cannot help wondering how the authors succeeded in persuading large and reputable foundations to provide them with financial support extending over many years. How does one persuade a foundation to uphold research which, in the words of the authors themselves, lacks a formal experimental design, or methods of quantification, or hypotheses? And which cannot be conducted 'according to the design'?

(Rachman and Wilson 1980: 73)

(Over $1 million was spent on the project, at a time when this was a considerable amount of money.)

Did this waste of time and money induce in the authors of the report a suitable feeling of humility? Malan (1976: 21) states: 'When I met Dr. Kernberg at the meeting of the Society for Psychotherapy Research in Philadelphia, in 1973, he said that the problem of measuring outcome on psychodynamic criteria was essentially solved, and I could only agree with him.' It is difficult not to resort to a quotation: 'Quem Jupiter vult perdere dementat prius' (Whom Jupiter wants to destroy, he first renders mad). Clearly psychoanalysts have learned nothing and forgotten nothing! They have no intention of submitting their beliefs to any kind of empirical proof: they prefer assertion to demonstration. Anyone seriously interested in this topic ought to read the detailed critique of Rachman and Wilson (1980) to discover how far intellectual vacuity can go.

It is sometimes said that no proper clinical trial of psychoanalytic therapy has been carried out because of the expense involved. This is not true. The Menninger study failed because of incompetence, complacency and a daunting lack of elementary methodological sophistication, not because of lack of funding. Or consider another example. Many years ago a large grant-giving body offered Sir Aubrey Lewis $1 million to organize a clinical trial to compare psychoanalytic treatment and behaviour therapy. He asked the Tavistock Clinic, the leading psychoanalytic institution in Britain, to take part, offering them a leading role in the design and organization of the clinical trials, and the evaluation process. (Sir Aubrey was quite neutral between the rival claims made at the time for these methods of treatment.) The Tavistock Clinic turned down the offer, presumably because they feared the outcome would be unfavourable to their claims. My colleagues and I welcomed it, but of course the offer was contingent on both sides agreeing, and was withdrawn when no psychoanalysts could be found to take up the challenge.

Am I being too hard in my interpretation? As Anthony Storr, one of the best known psychoanalysts in Britain, wrote in 1966:

The American Psychoanalytic Association, who might be supposed to be prejudiced in favour of their own speciality, undertook a survey to test the efficacy of psychoanalysis. The results obtained were so disappointing that they were withheld from publication. . . . The evidence that psychoanalysis cures anyone of anything is so shaky as to be practically non-existent.

(quoted by Wood 1990)

If a soi-disant 'scientific' organization can behave in this fashion to prevent the public from knowing that their 'science' was worthless, we should not be surprised at anything done by psychoanalysts to protect their religion.

Rachman and Wilson (1980) provide us with so far the best and most honest survey of the literature, and it is reassuring that their verdict is not very different from that I arrived at thirty years before. A quotation makes clear their overall evaluation:

The need for strict evaluations of the effects of various forms of therapy arises from several observations. In the first place, there is clear evidence of a substantial remission; as a result any therapeutic procedure must be shown to be superior to 'non-professional' processes of change. Closely allied to this point is the wide range of therapeutic procedures currently on offer and the competing and often exclusive claims for effectiveness. The lengthy business of separating the wheat from the chaff can only be accomplished by the introduction of strict and rational forms of evaluation. One important function of strict evaluation would be to root out those ineffective or even harmful methods that are being recommended. The availability of incisive methods of evaluation might have averted the sorry episode during which coma treatment was given to a large number of hopeful but undiscriminating patients.

The occurrence of spontaneous remissions of neurotic disorders provided a foundation stone for Eysenck's (1952) sceptical evaluation of the case for psychotherapy. His analysis of the admittedly insufficient data at the time led Eysenck to accept as the best available estimate the figure that roughly two-thirds of all neurotic disorders will remit spontaneously within 2 years of onset. Our review of the evidence that has accumulated during the past 25 years does not put us in a position to revise Eysenck's original estimate, but there is a strong case for refining his estimate for each of a group of different neurotic disorders; the early assumption of uniformity of spontaneous remission rates among different disorders is increasingly difficult to defend.

Given the widespread occurrence of spontaneous remissions, and it is difficult to see how they can any longer be denied, the claims made for the specific value of particular forms of psychotherapy begin to look exaggerated. It comes as a surprise to find how meagre is the evidence to support the wide-ranging claims made or implied by psychoanalytic therapists. The lengthy descriptions of spectacular improvements achieved in particular cases are outnumbered by the descriptions of patients whose analyses appear to be interminable. More important, however, is the rarity of any form of controlled evaluation of the effects of psychoanalysis. We are unaware of any methodical study of this kind which has taken adequate account of spontaneous changes or, more importantly, of the contribution of non-specific therapeutic influences such as placebo effects, expectancy, and so on. In view of the ambitiousness, scope, and influence of psychoanalysis, one might be inclined to recommend to one's scientific colleagues an attitude of continuing patience, but for the fact that insufficient progress has been made in either acknowledging the need for stringent scientific evaluations or in establishing criteria of outcome that are even half-way satisfactory. One suspects, however, that consumer groups will prove to be far less patient when they finally undertake an examination of the evidence on which the claims of psychoanalytic effectiveness now rest.

(Rachman and Wilson 1980: 259)

The rather negative evaluation of psychoanalysis, and indeed other forms of psychotherapy, to which Rachman and Wilson are finally forced contrasts spectacularly with conclusions arrived at by authors like Bergin (1971), Bergin and Lambert (1978) and Luborsky *et al.* (1975). The latter, in a memorable phrase, summarized their comparative studies of psychotherapies in the quotation that 'Everyone has won, and all must have prizes'. This will illustrate the *Alice's Adventures in Wonderland* atmosphere of this whole field, as do the equally optimistic conclusions of Bergin and his colleagues.

Let us first consider the argument advanced by Luborsky and his colleagues, which is also put forward by Smith *et al.* (1980) in a meta-analysis of all published data, to the effect that all types of therapy are equally effective, and that this proves the correctness of the views of those who support the effectiveness of psychotherapeutic research, and the theories on which this is based. Let us assume that it is true that different methods of psychotherapy (let us call them $T_1, T_2, T_3 \ldots T_n$) have indeed been shown to be equally effective in reducing or abolishing the neurotic illnesses for which they have been recommended. It should be obvious that such an outcome would not support the hypotheses or theories on which the treatments were based (let us call them $H_1, H_2, H_3 \ldots H_n$), but would completely disprove them. Let us consider psychoanalysis as T_1. This is based on H_1, which asserts, as we have seen, that only psychoanalytic methods can produce a proper cure, and that all other methods must inevitably fail to do so. But according to Luborsky, $T_2, T_3 \ldots T_n$ are equally successful as T_1; this clearly demonstrates that H_1 is incorrect, because it predicted the opposite, namely that T_2, $T_3 \ldots T_n$ would have no effect, or at most, a markedly weaker effect, than T_1.

Much the same can be said for all the other types of treatment – client-centred, Gestalt, 'primal therapy', etc. They are all based on specific hypotheses which would assert that the respective methods of treatment should be superior to all others; if they are not, then surely the theories themselves cannot be correct. If it can also be shown, as we shall see, that placebo treatments are as effective as genuine treatments, then it should become plain that the outcome of all these studies must be that it is non-specific factors, such as discussing one's troubles with a friendly person, receiving advice, relieving one's tensions through receiving positive reactions, etc. which are effective in mediating therapeutic success, rather than the specific methods derived from the various theories in question. If indeed all have won, and all must have prizes, then that surely spells the definite rebuttal to all the theories psychotherapists have fought so earnestly to elaborate and establish.

As far as Bergin and Lambert (1978) are concerned, their main argument rests on the assertion that Eysenck's original suggestion of a spontaneous remission rate of about two-thirds is incorrect, and that this figure should be very much lower. As they say, '*It can be noted that the two-thirds estimate is not only unrepresentative but is actually the most unrealistic figure for describing the spontaneous remission rate or even rates for minimal treatment outcomes*' (Bergin and Lambert 1978: 147, original emphasis).

Eysenck's estimate had been based on data published by Landis (1937) and Denker (1946), which gave an estimate of spontaneous remission effects of something like two-thirds; Bergin (1971) compiled a table containing fourteen studies, and provided percentage improvement rates for each. The rates vary from 0 per cent to 56 per cent and 'the median rate appears to be in the vicinity of 30 per cent!' Although his figures 'have their weaknesses', Bergin nevertheless felt that 'they are the best available to date' and rest 'upon a much more solid base' than the Landis–Denker data. In the face of such a large discrepancy, which is obviously vital in coming to any conclusions, it is essential to study the figures and arguments in detail. This has been done very carefully by Rachman and Wilson (1980), and the reader is referred to their discussion. We shall quote only brief excerpts to illustrate the essential dishonesty of the Bergin and Lambert argument:

> Before commencing the close examination of what Bergin presents as the best available data, two points should be borne in mind. In the first place it seems to be a curious procedure in which one rediscovers data and then calculates a median rate of improvement, while ignoring the data on which the original argument was based. The new data (actually some of them are chronologically older than those of Landis–Denker) should have been considered in conjunction with, or at least in the light of, the existing information. The second point is that although Bergin considered some new evidence, he missed a number of more satisfactory, and indeed more recent, studies which are more pertinent to the question of spontaneous recovery rates. His estimate of a 30% spontaneous recovery rate is based on the fourteen studies which are incorporated in Table 8 of his work. It will be noticed that the list omits some of the studies discussed earlier in this chapter, which antedate Bergin's review.

> (Rachman and Wilson 1980: 41)

Rachman and Wilson now give a list of the fourteen studies cited in Bergin's review, and then go on to a detailed discussion of each. Let us consider as an example the spontaneous remission rate of 0 per cent given by Bergin for a study by Cappon (1964). Here is what Rachman and Wilson have to say about this study:

> The first surprise is its title – 'Results of psychotherapy'. Cappon reports on a population consisting of 201 consecutive private patients 'who underwent therapy between 1955 and 1960'. Their diagnoses were: psychoneurosis 56%, psychopathic personality 25%, psychosomatic reactions 8%, and others 3%. As 163 had ended their therapy in 1960, 'this was the operative sample'. Cappon describes his treatment as being 'applied Jungian'. The results of the treatment were 'admittedly modest', and the follow-up was conducted by mail. Unfortunately, only 53% of the patients returned their forms, and the follow-up period varied from 4 to 68 months. In addition, the follow-up sample 'was biased in that these patients did twice as well at the end of therapy, as rated by the therapist, as those who did not return the forms'. It was also noted that 'the operative patient sample (n = 158) was still different (sicker) from a controlled normal sample, at the time of the follow-up. Patients showed more than 4 times the symptoms of normals. This ensured the fact that the sample was indeed composed of patients'.
>
> Cappon states that 'the intention of this work was not so much to prove that results were actually due to psychotherapy as to show some of the relationships results. Consequently, there was no obsessive preoccupation with "controls" as the sine qua non dictate of science.' We seem in the midst of all this to have strayed from the subject of spontaneous remissions. In fact, Cappon did make some brief comments on the subject. He argued that 'if worsening rather than improvement were rated, 4 to 15 times as many patients changed (got worse) in the follow-up (control) period combined with the therapeutic (experimental) period, depending on the index used'. As the follow-up period averaged some 20 months and the therapeutic period some $6\frac{1}{2}$ months, 'this fact alone casts great doubt on Eysenck's data on spontaneous remission which led him to the false conclusion that patients did better without treatment than with treatment'. Leaving aside the fact that Cappon unfortunately lost approximately half of his sample between termination of treatment and follow-up, we can perhaps leave uncontested his conclusion that many of the patients got worse after treatment. Cappon's report adds slender support to the belief that some patients get worse after psychotherapy. It tells us nothing at all about spontaneous remission rates, and far from giving a spontaneous remission rate of 0%, Cappon does not provide *any figures* on which to calculate a rate of spontaneous remission.

Bergin's figure of a 0% spontaneous remission rate appears to be drawn from Cappon's introductory description of his patients, in which he says that they 'had their presenting or main problem or dysfunction for an *average of 15 years* before the treatment' (original italics). Clearly, one cannot use this single-sentence description in attempting to trace the course of neurotic disorders or to determine their spontaneous remission rate. Nearly half of Cappon's patients apparently had disorders other than neurotic; we are not aware that they had been untreated prior to attending Cappon; we cannot assume that their diagnosis at the beginning of treatment would correspond with their condition in the years prior to treatment; we do not know whether the 201 patients constitute 90% of the relevant population or even 0.00001% of that population. Without labouring the point, this incidental sentence cannot be taken as evidence for or against the occurrence of spontaneous remissions. Bergin's use of the information is unjustified. His introduction of Cappon's report, coming from someone who complains of the 'irrelevance' and 'inadequacy' of the studies by Landis, Shepherd, and others, is baffling. In any event, the occurrence of therapeutic failures, and of a large minority (33%?) of unremitting neuroses, are consistent with the Eysenckian argument. A special collection of therapeutic failures no more demonstrates a spontaneous remission of 0% than a similar collection of patients who have recovered without treatment (easy to compile) would demonstrate a spontaneous remission rate of 100%. The matter rests on the proportion of neurotic patients who show marked improvements within 2 years of the onset of their disorder – or if one prefers a longer or shorter period of study, then a modified hypothesis can be put forward.

(Rachman and Wilson 1980: 41)

Rachman and Wilson continue:

Bergin also gives a 0% spontaneous remission rate for the paper by O'Connor *et al.* (1964). Once again, the title – 'The effects of psychotherapy on the course of ulcerative colitis' – is surprising as the subject under discussion is the spontaneous remission rate in neurotic disorders. Ulcerative colitis is defined by O'Connor and his co-authors as 'a chronic non-specific disease characterized by inflammation and ulceration of the colon and accompanied by systemic manifestations'.

(Rachman and Wilson 1980: 42)

According to O'Connor *et al.* (1964)

'its course is marked by remissions and exacerbations, its aetiology is considered multifactorial, and it has been variously attributed to infections, genetic, vascular, allergic and psychological phenomena'.

(quoted in Rachman and Wilson 1980: 42)

Rachman and Wilson further note the following:

It will not pass unnoticed that 'psychological phenomena' are only one in a list of five types of attribution, nor indeed, that the course of the disease is 'marked by remissions'. The observation that patients who have ulcerative colitis can show remissions is of interest to gastro-enterologists. The study compares the progress made by fifty-seven patients with colitis who received psychotherapy and fifty-seven patients who received no such treatment. The patients in both groups continued to receive medical and even surgical treatment, and those who had psychotherapy are said to have progressed better. In the treated group, '19 patients were diagnosed as schizophrenic, 3 were psycho-neurotic, 34 were diagnosed as having personality disorders, and 1 received no diagnosis'. In the control group, however, '3 of the patients were diagnosed as schizophrenic, 3 as psychoneurotic, and 14 as having personality disorders. The remaining 37 control patients were not di-agnosed because of the lack of overt psychiatric symptoms'. As only three of the control group were diagnosed as psychoneurotic, the spon-taneous remission rate over the fifteen-year period would have to be expressed as the number of spontaneous remissions for a group with an N of 3. Bergin's use of the data in this report also raises a methodo-logical point. He quotes the spontaneous remission rate for colitis patients as 0 per cent over fifteen years. In fact no percentage rate can be obtained from the report as all the results are given as group means – it is possible, and indeed likely, that numbers of patients experienced remission even though the *group* mean showed little change. The study leaves us in no position to determine the spontaneous remission rate in three neurotic patients with ulcerative colitis.

(Rachman and Wilson 1980: 42–3)

Another report quoted by Bergin is equally irrelevant as Rachman and Wilson report thus:

Orgel's (1958) report on fifteen *treated* cases of peptic ulcer is quoted as showing a 0% remission rate. Bergin appears to argue that because the patients had suffered from stomach ulcers for 4 to 15 years prior to entering treatment, this indicates a remission rate of 0. Factually, Bergin is incorrect in stating that the peptic ulcers 'had persisted from 4 to 15 years without change'. Several of the patients had experienced remissions prior to entering psychoanalytic treatment. Furthermore, some of them experienced remissions and recurrences *during* the treatment. Far more serious, however, is Bergin's assumption that these fifteen ulcer cases are representative of the relevant population. More-over, the introduction of material on the 'natural history' of patients with peptic ulcer into a discussion on spontaneous remissions in neu-rotic disorders is not justified.

(Rachman and Wilson 1980: 43)

The remaining studies examined by Rachman and Wilson (1980) are equally irrelevant to the issue in question:

For reasons that are not explicit, neither Bergin nor Lambert (separ-ately or jointly) appear to be willing to confine their analyses to the question in hand, i.e. the rate of spontaneous remission in neuroses. They repeatedly introduce irrelevant information – on the effects of treatment, on recovery rates in surgical patients, on remissions in schizophrenia, on the fate of delinquents, and so on. Lambert (1976: 116) took this inexplicable process one step further and objected to analyses that are confined to untreated neurotic disorders. Contrary to the drift of his argument, the inclusion of studies should not be dictated by caprice, but rather should be an exercise in applying firm standards of selection. It is, after all, simple – if you wish to determine the rate of remission in neurotic disorders, then study data on neurotic disorders.

(Rachman and Wilson 1980: 48)

Above all else, however, the evidence gathered since the original estimate was attempted, emphasizes the need for more refined studies and more accurate statistics. In particular, one can now postulate that the gross spontaneous remission rate is not constant across different types of neurotic disorders. For example, obsessional disorders probably have a lower rate of spontaneous remission than anxiety conditions. Future investigators would be well advised to analyse the spontaneous remission rates of the various neuroses within, rather than across, diagnostic groupings. If we proceed in this manner it will be possible to make more accurate estimates of the likelihood of spontaneous remission occurring in a particular type of disorder and, indeed, for a particular group of patients.

Although the gross spontaneous remission rate has thus far been based on a two-year period of observation (and this serves well for many purposes), attempts to understand the nature of the process will be facilitated by an extension of the periods of observation. The collection of reliable observations on the *course* of spontaneous remissions will, among other things, greatly assist in making prognoses.

Readers will be able to form their own opinion on whether these excursions by Bergin and Lambert into the higher realms of imagination constitute an honest appraisal of the evidence; Rachman and Wilson (1980) leave little doubt on the point. Unfortunately, it has to be said that most writers on the topic prefer the conclusions provided by Luborsky, by Bergin and by Lambert to the much more realistic appraisal offered by Rachman and Wilson; the reasons for this preference are not far to seek in people whose professional advancement and livelihood depend on the popular acceptance of the kinds of psychotherapy they provide. Whether such a procedure is ethically defensible, and scientifically meaningful is of course another question.

The relevance of meta-analysis

Where Luborsky, Bergin and Lambert at least pretend to some kind of scientific objectivity, a much praised book by Smith *et al.* (1980) provides the seeds of destruction within itself, without requiring any aid from outside critics. The contents of this book, which essentially aims at a meta-analysis of all published studies to date, amount to an essential contradiction of the conclusions I drew in 1952, and which have been virtually unchanged in the review by Rachman and Wilson (1980). To illustrate this conclusion, let me quote first of all the general conclusions drawn by the authors from their data. They assert that

> *Psychotherapy is beneficial, consistently so and in many different ways. Its benefits are on a par with other expensive ambitious interventions, such as schooling and medicine. The benefits of psychotherapy are not permanent, but then little is.*
>
> (Smith *et al.* 1980: 183, original emphasis)

They go on to say that

> The evidence overwhelmingly supports the efficacy of psychotherapy ... psychotherapy benefits people of all ages as reliably as schooling educated them, medicine cures them, or business turns a profit.
>
> (Smith *et al.* 1980: 183)

Apparently psychotherapy sometimes seeks the same goals as education and medicine, and when it does, psychotherapy performs commendably well:

> We are suggesting no less than that psychotherapists have a legitimate, though not exclusive, claim, substantiated by controlled research, of those roles in society, whether privately or publicly endowed, whose responsibility is to restore to health the sick, the suffering, the alienated, and the disaffected.
>
> (Smith *et al.* 1980: 183)

Smith *et al.* then go on to repeat the Luborsky view that

> Different types of psychotherapy (verbal or behavioural; psychodynamic, client-centred, or systematic desensitization) do not produce different types or degrees of benefit.
>
> (Smith *et al.* 1980: 184)

Allied to this odd conclusion is another one, to wit that

> *differences in how psychotherapy is conducted (whether in groups or individually, by experienced or novice therapists, for long or short periods of time, and the like) make very little difference in how beneficial it is.*
>
> (Smith *et al.* 1980: 188, original emphasis)

As we have already noted, if indeed all different methods of psychotherapy give pretty much the same results, then this disproves conclusively all the theories on which the different methods of therapy are based. Actually of course the data presented in their Table 5.1 completely contradict their own conclusions; they found average effect sizes of 0.28 for undifferentiated counselling, for instance, and of 0.14 for reality therapy, with figures like 1.82 for hypnotherapy and 2.38 for cognitive therapies. This does not suggest equality of outcome! They also fail to note a very important conclusion from the same table that placebo treatment (effect size 0.56) is as effective as Gestalt therapy (0.64), client-centred therapy (0.62) or psychodynamic therapy (0.69). Clearly, their own conclusions force us to argue that all the vaunted effects of psychotherapy are simply placebo effects, a conclusion also arrived at by the much more meaningful analysis carried out by Prioleau *et al.* (1983). It is curious that almost none of the reviewers of the book saw this obvious contradiction between data and conclusions, or commented on the devastating effects this must have on the claims for efficacy of psychotherapy.

Much the same must be said about the final conclusion of the book quoted above, to the effect that for the effectiveness of therapy it makes very little difference if it is done by an experienced or an inexperienced therapist, or for long or short periods of time. If that is true, then clearly claims by psychoanalysts that their discipline requires a lengthy training, and a lengthy time to establish and then resolve transference relations, are completely unjustified. Obviously what we should do is to train therapists for just one hour, and restrict treatment to one hour's duration; clearly, if we can rely on Smith, Glass and Miller, this should make no difference to the outcome! To keep up with our *Alice's Adventures in Wonderland* story, we should apparently have followed the practice of the Red Queen to believe as many as six impossible things before breakfast. To believe the conclusions of Smith *et al.* (1980) would certainly constitute good practice for that.

Smith *et al.* curiously enough do discover that behaviour therapy is more effective than psychotherapy, but they try to argue this conclusion out of existence by a rather specious argument which this is not the place to discuss. Eysenck and Martin (1987) have discussed this question in some detail, and have come to the conclusion that not only is a learning theory of neurosis the only scientific theory available at present, but also the methods of treatment to which it gives rise are the only ones which show a significant improvement over no treatment or placebo treatment. Thus the 'spontaneous remission' objection does not apply to behaviour therapy; Rachman and Hodgson's (1980) book presents an excellent example. The failure of psychotherapy to achieve a similar status, alas, does not seem to have reduced the ardour with which many therapists still proclaim its virtues, and foist it on innocent victims.

Have more recent studies suggested that my estimate was wrong? Garfield and Bergin (1986) have reviewed the field, but I still do not see a single study which would meet what I consider minimum requirements of a meaningful comparison between no treatment, placebo treatment of an acceptable kind, psychoanalysis or closely specified psychotherapy, and behaviour therapy carried out by a properly qualified behaviour therapist, using appropriate methods. If we are dealing with obsessive handwashing, for instance, flooding with response prevention works very well, while desensitization, in our experience, does not (Rachman and Hodgson 1980); it would be easy to make behaviour therapy do no better than psychotherapy by choosing the wrong method. Also, many people call themselves behaviour therapists without any proper training; one would need to be assured on this point. Ideally studies should be set up by a supervisory group comprised of leading exponents of the methods under comparison, free to select the therapists using their type of treatment. Alas, no such study is familiar to me.

Two objections are often made to the claims of psychotherapeutic lack of effectiveness. The first is that clients often report satisfaction with the outcome of the treatment, even if symptom-removal failed to occur. Cognitive dissonance theory would lead us to expect precisely this; patients who have spent four years or more in treatment, and spent upwards of $100,000 on fees, would not be human if they willingly acknowledged that it was all for nothing. There is also the suggestion constantly reiterated by analysts that if the patients are no better it is all their own fault –'resistance' and all that! Finally, there is the hello-and-goodbye phenomenon; all mental disorders have their ups and downs, and therapy is usually entered in a down phase, and left in an up phase. Anyone making claims of this kind would have to make a proper study of the proportions of satisfied customers, then eliminate possible causes like those mentioned, and finally set the results against the number of dissatisfied customers. Nothing of the kind has yet been done.

The other argument concerns 'market forces' – why, if behaviour therapy is so much more successful, do people not choose it in preference to the discredited psychotherapy? Such an argument is clearly disingenuous. There are still very few properly qualified behaviour therapists, so there can be no proper choice. Few people have heard of the alternatives, so can hardly make a choice. They are not told of the evidence favouring behaviour therapy, so cannot make a *meaningful* choice. 'Market forces' require an open market where buyers and sellers know what the conditions governing the sale are; this is demonstrably not so in the psychiatric field. Patients are sent to the hospital by a general practitioner who has probably never beard of behaviour therapy, and are seen by a psychiatrist who has been brought up in the psychotherapeutic tradition, and regards the psychologists who use behaviour therapy as rivals whose lack of a medical background disqualifies them from treating patients altogether.

But above all there is the Semmelweiss effect. Semmelweiss was a Hungarian physician in Vienna who reduced the mortality of women giving birth in hospital from something like 30 per cent to something like 2 per cent by asking his colleagues to wash their hands when going from one woman to another, thus avoiding the infections which were the killers. The effect was obvious, and so huge, that no argument would seem necessary. However, his colleagues laughed him out of court, refused to follow his advice, and finally forced him to go back to Budapest in disgrace. I recall giving a lecture on behaviour therapy in the university there which bears his name – honoured centuries after the event. New methods make their way slowly in medicine; there is an immense resistance to change, and arguments concerning facts, experiments and clinical trials tend to fall on deaf ears. Psychologists should know better than anyone that human beings are seldom motivated by rational considerations; in the long run psychoanalytic notions will be recognized as the oddities they are, but this time is not yet (Eysenck 1985b). When that happens, behaviour therapy will be the universal method of choice, and historians will wonder about our medieval superstitions.

Negative effects of psychoanalysis

It should not be assumed that the term 'victims' has been chosen inadvisedly in any of the preceding paragraphs. There is ample evidence that psychoanalysis is not an innocent, if ineffective, method of talking to people. As Mays and Franks (1985) have shown, there is frequently a negative outcome in psychotherapy, so that instead of improving the neurotic disorders from which patients suffer, it actually makes them worse. Not only is there good evidence that this is true, but also I have suggested a mechanism, derived from the general theory of neurotic illness in terms of learning theory, which explains why this is so, and why it would have been expected on a theoretical basis (Eysenck 1976a; 1976b; 1977; 1982; 1985a). Those who praise the wonderful effects of psychotherapy customarily disregard or dismiss the negative effects, the evidence for which is much more impressive. This is completely irresponsible of course; the essence of the Hippocratic Oath enjoins us not to harm our patients.

The suggestion that some of the psychological effects of psychoanalysis may be negative, and harm the patients rather than cure them is often rejected as being relatively unimportant, the assumption being that negative consequences cannot be very serious. However, recent work has suggested that not only are they serious psychologically, but also they may involve psychoanalysis as a risk factor in cancer and coronary heart disease (Grossarth-Maticek and Eysenck 1990). These data, as well as those suggesting that behaviour therapy is a very powerful prophylactic aid in avoiding cancer and coronary heart disease, may not be known to all readers, and hence may deserve a special mention, illustrating the wide generality of the positive effects of behaviour therapy, and the negative effects of psychoanalysis.

The work of Eysenck (1987a; 1987b; 1988b; 1989) and of Grossarth-Maticek and Eysenck (1989) and Grossarth-Maticek *et al.* (1988) has demonstrated very clearly two things. The first is that in large-scale prospective studies, in which healthy probands were tested for personality, smoking, drinking, cholesterol levels, blood sugar and blood pressure at the beginning of the study, and were then followed up for ten years or more, specific personality reactions to stress were found to be highly predictive of cancer, while other types of reactions were found to be highly predictive of coronary heart disease. Personality/stress reactions were six times as predictive of these diseases as were smoking, cholesterol level and the other medical predictors, and deaths from cancer and coronary heart disease were very significantly more frequent in people who were stressed than in people who were not stressed.

It was also demonstrated that a special type of behaviour therapy used in changing the behavioural pattern of cancer-prone and coronary heart disease-prone probands was highly effective in preventing death from cancer or coronary heart disease thirteen years later. When therapy groups were compared with carefully matched control groups, it was found that out of fifty controls, sixteen died of cancer, while in the therapy group none died of cancer. Similarly, out of forty-six controls, sixteen died of coronary heart disease, while in the therapy group only three died of coronary heart disease. These results were obtained with thirty hours of individual therapy; similar results were obtained with group therapy, and with bibliotherapy accompanied by short-term individual therapy (Grossarth-Maticek and Eysenck 1991; Eysenck and Grossarth-Maticek 1991).

In another study an attempt was made to see whether psychoanalysis, which is generally regarded as a very stressful procedure, would add to the stress suffered by cancer-prone and coronary heart disease-prone healthy probands, and would be associated with an increase in mortality from these causes. Studies were made of some 7,000 inhabitants of Heidelberg who were first interviewed in 1973. In 1977 probands were asked whether they had been under any form of psychotherapy, and notes were made at the time concerning duration and type of treatment. In 1986 the participants were followed up, and death and cause of death established by reference to the death certificates of those who had died.

Two groups of physically healthy probands who were under psychoanalytic treatment of an orthodox kind, for mild psychiatric disorders in the main, constituted our therapy groups. One group had been treated for between one and two years, and had then discontinued treatment. Group 2 had been in treatment for two years or more, and had not broken off treatment. Two control groups were created from a large pool of probands so that they could be matched closely with the two treatment groups on age, sex, personality type and cigarette consumption. Matching was person-to-person, thus guaranteeing equality of means and SDs (a measure of variability). A final control group was created to match the two groups together overall.

Table 5.1 shows the final results of our study. The results make certain conclusions very clear (at a high level of statistical significance). Cancer, as expected, is the most frequent cause of death in Type 1 (cancer-prone) persons, coronary heart disease in Type 2 (CHD-prone) persons. Cancer and coronary heart disease are most frequent in the group that had psychoanalysis for over two years, less frequent in those who had psychoanalysis for less than two years, and least in the control groups whose members were not treated by psychoanalysis. There is thus in this table clear evidence that psychoanalysis acts as a stressor, and is a strong risk factor for cancer and coronary heart disease.

Table 5.1 Mortality from cancer, coronary heart disease and other causes for controls and probands treated by psychoanalysis for psychiatric complaints

Therapy	Status	Type 1		Type 2		Type 3		Type 4	
			%		%		%		%
(1) Up to two years	Cancer	11	7.1	4	4.6	5	4.8	1	100.0
of psychoanalysis,	CHD	7	4.5	5	5.8	6	5.7	0	0
then terminated	Other	7	4.5	5	5.8	6	5.7	0	0
	Living	129	83.7	72	83.7	87	83.6	0	0
	Omitted	8	4.9	4	4.4	5	4.5	0	0
	Total	162		90		109		1	
			%		%		%		%
(2) Psychoanalysis for	Cancer	9	9.3	3	6.5	8	7.7	1	33.3
longer than two years,	CHD	8	8.2	6	13.0	8	7.7	1	33.3
not terminated	Other	8	8.2	5	10.8	7	6.7	1	33.3
	Living	72	74.2	32	69.5	81	77.8	0	0
	Omitted	5	14.9	0	0	4	3.7	0	0
	Total	102		46		108		3	
			%		%		%		%
(3) Control group for	Cancer	2	1.3	1	1.2	0	0	0	0
Group 1, matched on	CHD	1	0.6	2	2.4	0	0	0	0
age, sex, type and	Other	3	1.9	2	2.4	3	2.7	0	0
amount of smoking	Living	149	96.1	80	94.1	100	95.2	1	100.0
	Omitted	7	4.3	5	5.5	5	4.6	0	0
	Total	162		90		108		1	
			%		%		%		%
(4) Control group for	Cancer	1	1	1	2.2	0	0	0	0
Group 2, matched on	CHD	1	1	1	2.2	1	0.9	0	0
age, sex, type and	Other	1	1	3	6.6	5	4.6	0	0
amount of smoking	Living	94	96.9	40	88.8	98	95.1	3	100.0
	Omitted	5	4.9	1	2.1	5	4.6	0	0
	Total	102		46		109		3	
			%		%		%		%
(5) Control group for	Cancer	1	0.6	1	0.5	0	0	1	0.9
Groups 1 and 2	CHD	2	1.2	2	1.0	1	0.9	0	0
combined, matched	Other	5	2.9	5	2.7	2	1.8	2	1.8
on age, sex,	Living	166	95.4	180	95.7	107	96.4	107	97.3
and cigarette	Omitted	13	6.9	9	46.6	10	8.3	6	5.2
consumption	Total	187		197		120		116	

These results ought to give pause to those who still advocate the use of psychoanalysis as a treatment for neurotic disorders; not only does the literature suggest that negative consequences of a psychological kind may often follow, but also as we have seen there is now evidence that quite serious health consequences may also follow. Conversely not only is behaviour therapy superior in curing neurotic patients, but also it can be used as a prophylactic aid in preventing cancer and coronary heart disease. These facts ought to, but probably will not, be instrumental in making therapists think twice about using the discredited methods introduced by Freud and his colleagues so many years ago.

Psychoanalysts reply

What is the reaction of advocates of psychoanalytic treatment to these rather grave charges? Their major reaction has been one of disregarding all criticisms, and discrediting the critics by appealing to the concept of 'resistance'; critics cannot and should not be taken seriously because their criticisms are based on neurotic motivations of a very subtle kind which only a psychoanalyst is capable of understanding. It hardly needs a philosopher of science to see through this attempt at side-tracking criticism; it is not the motivation of the critics that is at issue, but the truth or otherwise of the criticisms made. These require to be answered, regardless of the motives of the critics. Furthermore of course the psychoanalyst's answer to the critic presupposes what has to be proved, namely the correctness of psychoanalytic theories, including that of 'resistance'. As we know, there is no such evidence (Grunbaum 1984; Eysenck and Wilson 1973).

Another argument frequently adduced, following Freud, is that neurotic states are so complicated that it is impossible for any matching to be made between therapy and control groups, so that statistical comparisons and clinical trials become meaningless and impossible. This argument leaves out the essential feature of all clinical trials, namely the power of random assignment to eliminate differences between groups. Psychoanalysts have made no attempt to answer this counter-argument and thus their research has resulted in such absurd and meaningless studies as the Menninger one cited previously.

A third argument often propounded is that critics assess the success or failure of treatment merely by looking at the elimination or persistence of symptoms, while psychoanalysis aims at a complete restructuring of personality. As Erwin (1978) and Grunbaum (1984) have pointed out, there are two counter-arguments. In the first place, the elimination of symptoms is *necessary*, although it may not be a *sufficient* criterion for success of treatments. Second, there is no evidence at all for the success of psychoanalysts in 'restructuring' personalities, and no proper criteria are offered for testing this alleged change. Until and unless this is provided, there clearly is no answer to the criticism that psychoanalysts have no evidence to offer supporting their claims.

It is also frequently adduced that these matters are too complex and difficult to allow any natural science approach or answer; this argument is often produced by those who would turn psychoanalysis into a hermeneutic discipline. However difficult it may be to prove the efficacy of psychoanalysis, claims have been made in that direction, and require proof. If this proof is too difficult to obtain, then the claim should be withdrawn until methods have been elaborated to substantiate it. All scientific advances are difficult and require complex reasoning and experimentation; claims for success are not made until such success can be substantiated and replicated.

The final argument originally proposed by Freud, and enthusiastically adopted by his followers, is what Grunbaum (1979; 1980) has called the 'Tally Argument'. This argument is based on the premise that 'clinical data', that is findings coming from *within* the psychoanalytic treatment sessions, substantiate all the claims of psychoanalysis. Grunbaum (1984) suggests that this argument is the basis for five claims made by psychoanalysts, each of which is of the first importance for the legitimation of the central parts of Freud's theory. These five claims are the following:

1 Denial of an irremediable epistemic contamination of clinical data by suggestion.
2 Affirmation of a crucial difference, in regard to the *dynamics* of therapy, between psychoanalytic treatment and all rival therapies that actually operate entirely by suggestion.
3 Assertion that the psychoanalytic method is able to validate its major causal claims – such as its specific sexual aetiologies of the various psychoneuroses – by essentially *retrospective methods* without vitiation by *post hoc ergo propter hoc*, and without the burdens of prospective studies employing the controls of experimental inquiries.
4 Contention that favourable therapeutic outcome can be warrantedly attributed to psychoanalytic intervention *without* statistical comparisons pertaining to the results from untreated control groups.
5 Avowal that, once the patient's motivations are no longer distorted or hidden by repressed conflicts, credence can rightly be given to his or her introspective self-observations, because these data then do supply probatively significant information.

It is Grunbaum's (1984) very detailed and competent destruction of this argument which forms the basis of his book, and his argument has not been refuted by any philosophers or psychoanalysts, as far as I know. I will not try to undertake a detailed discussion here as this would obviously be out of place.

Summary and conclusions

We may now try to see what conclusions can be drawn from this lengthy discussion. It is sometimes suggested by historians of behaviour therapy like Kazdin (1978) and Schorr (1984) that the major contribution of behaviour therapy has been an insistence on the importance of the outcome problem, and an attempt to investigate it in relation to the different methods of behaviour therapy. This is no doubt true in part, but it would seem that many, too many, behaviour therapists have followed the temptations of Lazarus (1967; 1971) to go along the primrose path of 'eclectic' therapy – in other words, to indulge in an arbitrary and subjective mish-mash of theories, practices and therapies without regard to strict outcome measures, empirical guidance or experimental control. This, taken together with the unscientific and arbitrary handling of data by writers such as Luborsky, Bergin, Lambert, Smith, Glass and Miller, has tended to hide the truth behind the veil of inaccurate and tendentious assertions and claims.

Rachman and Wilson have made it only too clear that there is still no good evidence that psychotherapy is any more effective than any reasonable placebo treatment. As the latest publication by the National Institute of Mental Health Treatment of Depression Collaborative Research Program (Elkin *et al.* 1989) makes clear, even after all this time, we are still faced with a virtual equivalence of lauded programmes of psychotherapy and placebo treatments. No doubt this study, like all the others showing negative effects, will be silently consigned to the oubliette where so many other negative reports are secreted, and there will be no slowing down of claims for the wonders that psychotherapy can perform! The people suffering from neurotic symptoms whom we are supposed to help will not thank us for disregarding all the evidence, in continuing to claim successes where no successes exist. Only behaviour therapy can be exempted from this accusation; as even Smith *et al.* (1980) are forced to admit, as a result of their meta-analysis:

> In those studies in which behavioral therapies were compared directly with developmental therapies, the former were vastly superior. In the direct comparison of verbal and behavioral therapies, behavioral therapy has produced reliably larger effects.
>
> (Smith *et al.* 1980: 107)

Perhaps future generations will pay more attention to empirical facts than has been customary over the past half-century; this certainly is a consummation devoutly to be wished.

References

Bergin, A.E. (1971) The evaluation of therapeutic outcomes, in A.E. Bergin and S.L. Garfield (eds) *Handbook of Psychotherapy and Behavior Change: An Empirical Analysis.* New York: Wiley.

Bergin, A.E. and Lambert, M.J. (1978) The evaluation of therapeutic outcomes, in S.L. Garfield and A.E. Bergin (eds) *Handbook of Psychotherapy and Behavior Change: An Empirical Analysis*, 2nd edn. New York: Wiley.

Cappon, D. (1964) Results of psychotherapy. *British Journal of Psychiatry* **110**: 34–45.

Denker, P.G. (1946) Results of treatment of psychoneurosis by the general practitioner: a follow-up study of 500 cases. *New York State Journal of Medicine* **46**: 2,164–6.

Elkin, I., Shea, M.T., Watkins, J.T., Imber, S., Sotsky, S.M., Collins, J.F., Glass, D.R., Pilkonis, P.A., Leber, W.R., Docherty, J.P., Fiester, S.J. and Parloff, M.B. (1989) National Institute of Mental Health Treatment of Depression Collaborative Research Program: general effectiveness of treatment. *Archives of General Psychiatry* **46**: 971–82.

Erwin E. (1978) *Behavior Therapy: Scientific, Philosophical and Moral Foundations.* New York: Cambridge University Press.

Erwin, E. (1980) Psychoanalytic therapy: the Eysenck argument. *American Psychologist* **35**: 435–43.

Eysenck, H.J. (1952) The effects of psychotherapy: an evaluation. *Journal of Consulting Psychology* **16**: 319–24.

Eysenck, H.J. (1960) The effects of psychotherapy, in H.J. Eysenck (ed.) *Handbook of Abnormal Psychology: An Experimental Approach.* London: Pitman Medical Publishing.

Eysenck, H.J. (1965) The effects of psychotherapy. *International Journal of Psychiatry* **1**: 99–144.

Eysenck, H.J. (1966) *The Effects of Psychotherapy.* New York: International Science Press.

Eysenck, H.J. (1976a) Behaviour therapy – dogma or applied science?, in M.P. Feldman and A. Broadbent (eds) *The Theoretical and Experimental Foundations of Behaviour Therapy.* London: Wiley.

Eysenck, H.J. (1976b) The learning theory model of neurosis – a new approach. *Behavior, Research and Therapy* **14**: 251–67.

Eysenck, H.J. (1977) *You and Neurosis.* London: Maurice Temple Smith.

Eysenck, H.J. (1982) Neobehavioristic (S-R) theory, in G.T. Wilson and C.M. Franks (eds) *Contemporary Behavior Therapy.* New York: Guilford.

Eysenck, H.J. (1985a) Negative outcome in psychotherapy: the need for a theoretical framework, in D.T. Mays and C.M. Franks (eds) *Negative Outcome in Psychotherapy.* New York: Springer.

Eysenck, H.J. (1985b) *The Decline and Fall of the Freudian Empire.* London: Viking Press.

Eysenck, H.J. (1987a) Anxiety, 'learned helplessness', and cancer – a causal theory. *Journal of Anxiety Disorders* **1**: 87–104.

Eysenck, H.J. (1987b) Personality as a predictor of cancer and cardiovascular disease, and the application of behaviour therapy in prophylaxis. *European Journal of Psychiatry* **1**: 29–41.

Eysenck, H.J. (1988a) Psychotherapy to behavior therapy: a paradigm shift, in D.B. Fishman, F. Rotgers and C.M. Franks (eds) *Paradigms in Behavior Therapy: Present and Promise.* New York: Springer.

Eysenck, H.J. (1988b) The respective importance of personality, cigarette smoking and interaction effects for the genesis of cancer and coronary heart disease. *Personality and Individual Differences* **9**: 453–64.

Eysenck, H.J. (1989) Prevention of cancer and coronary heart disease, and reduction in the cost of the National Health Service. *Journal of Social, Political and Economic Studies* **14**: 25–47.

Eysenck, H.J. (1990a) *Rebel With a Cause* (autobiography). London: W.H. Allen.

Eysenck, H.J. (1990b) Maverick psychologist, in E. Walker (ed.) *History of Clinical Psychology in Autobiography*. Pacific Grove, Calif: Brooks-Cole.

Eysenck, H.J. and Grossarth-Maticek, R. (1991) Creative novation behaviour therapy as a prophylactic treatment for cancer and coronary heart disease. II. Effects of treatment. *Behavior, Research and Therapy* **29**: 17–31.

Eysenck, H.J. and Martin, I. (eds) (1987) *Theoretical Foundations of Behavior Therapy*. New York: Plenum.

Eysenck, H.J. and Rachman, S. (1965) *Causes and Cures of Neurosis*. London: Routledge & Kegan Paul.

Eysenck, H.J. and Wilson, G.D. (1973) *The Experimental Study of Freudian Theories*. London: Methuen.

Garfield, S. and Bergin, A. (1986) *Handbook of Psychotherapy and Behavior Change*, 3rd edn. New York: Wiley.

Grossarth-Maticek, R. and Eysenck, H.J. (1989) Length of survival and lymphocyte percentage in women with mammary cancer as a function of psychotherapy. *Psychological Reports* **65**: 315–21.

Grossarth-Maticek, R. and Eysenck, H.J. (1990) Prophylactic effects of psychoanalysis of cancer-prone and coronary heart disease-prone probands, as compared with control groups and behaviour therapy groups. *Journal of Behaviour Therapy and Experimental Psychiatry* **21**: 91–9.

Grossarth-Maticek, R. and Eysenck, H.J. (1991) Creative novation behaviour therapy as a prophylactic treatment for cancer and coronary heart disease: I. Description of treatment. *Behavior, Research and Therapy* **29**: 1–16.

Grossarth-Maticek, R., Eysenck, H.J. and Vetter, H. (1988) Personality type, smoking habit and their interaction as predictors of cancer and coronary heart disease. *Personality and Individual Differences* **9**: 479–95.

Grunbaum, A. (1979) Epistemological liabilities of the clinical appraisal of psychoanalytic theory. *Psychoanalysis and Contemporary Thought* **2**: 451–526.

Grunbaum, A. (1980) Epistemological liabilities of the clinical appraisal of psychoanalytic theory. *Nous* 307–85.

Grunbaum, A. (1984) *The Foundations of Psychoanalysis: A Philosophical Critique*. London: University of California Press.

Hirschmuller, A. (1989) *The Life and Work of Josef Breuer*. New York: University Press.

Jones, M.C. (1924) The elimination of children's fears. *Journal of Experimental Psychology* **7**: 382–90.

Kazdin, A.E. (1978) *History of Behavior Modification*. Baltimore, Md: University Park Press.

Kernberg, O. (1972) Psychotherapy and psychoanalysis: final report of the Menninger psychotherapy research project. *Bulletin of the Menninger Clinic* **36**: 1 and 2.

Kernberg, O. (1973) Summary and conclusions of 'Psychotherapy and Psychoanalysis', final report of the Menninger Foundation's psychotherapy research project. *International Journal of Psychobiology* **11**: 62–77.

Lambert, M. (1976) Spontaneous remission in adult neurotic disorders. *Psychological Bulletin* **83**: 107–19.

Landis, C. (1937) A statistical evaluation of psychotherapeutic methods, in L.E. Hinsie (ed.) *Concepts and Problems of Psychotherapy*. New York: Columbia University Press.

Lazarus, A.A. (1967) In support of technical eclecticism. *Psychological Reports* **21**: 415–16.

Lazarus, A.A. (1971) *Behavior Therapy and Beyond*. New York: Wiley.

Luborsky, L., Singer, B. and Luborsky, L. (1975) Comparative studies of psychotherapies: is it true that 'everyone has won and all must have prizes'? *Archives of General Psychiatry* **32**: 995–1,008.

Mahony, P.J. (1986) *Freud and the Rat Man*. New Haven, Conn: Yale University Press.

Malan, D.W. (1976) *Toward the Validation of Dynamic Psychotherapy*. New York: Plenum.

Mays, D.T. and Franks, C.M. (1985) *Negative Outcome in Psychotherapy*. New York: Springer.

Obholzer, K. (1982) *The Wolf-Man: Sixty Years Later*. London: Routledge & Kegan Paul.

O'Connor, J., Daniels, G., Narsh, A., Mores, L., Flood, C. and Stern, L. (1964) The effects of psychotherapy as the cause of ulcerative colitis. *American Journal of Psychiatry* **120**: 738–42.

Orgel, S. (1958) Effects of psychoanalysis on the course of peptic ulcer. *Psychosomatic Medicine* **20**: 117–25.

Prioleau, L., Murdoch, M. and Brody, N. (1983) An analysis of psychotherapy versus placebo. *Behaviour and Brain Science* **6**: 275–85.

Rachman, S. and Hodgson, R. (1980) *Obsessions and Compulsions*. Englewood Cliffs, NJ: Prentice-Hall.

Rachman, S.J. and Wilson, G.T. (1980) *The Effects of Psychological Therapy*. London: Pergamon.

Salter, A. (1952) *The Case Against Psychoanalysis*. New York: Holt.

Schorr, A. (1984) *Die Verhaltenstherapie*. Weinkeim: Beltz.

Smith, M.L., Glass, G.V. and Miller, T.I. (1980) *The Benefits of Psychotherapy*. Baltimore, Md: Johns Hopkins University Press.

Thornton, E.N. (1983) *Freud and Cocaine: The Freudian Fallacy*. London: Bland & Briggs.

Watson, J.B. and Rayner, R. (1920) Conditioned emotional reaction. *Journal of Experimental Psychology* **3**: 1–14.

Wilder, J. (1945) Facts and figures on psychotherapy. *Journal of Clinical Psychotherapy* **7**: 311–47.

Wood, J. (1990) The naked truth. *Weekend Guardian* 25–26 August.

Zubin, J. (1953) Evaluation of therapeutic outcome in mental disorders. *Journal of Nervous and Mental Diseases* **117**: 95–111.

RESPONSE – *Sol Garfield*

There is little question that Hans Eysenck was, and remains, the staunchest and foremost critic of psychotherapy, and of psychoanalysis in particular. Despite the rather significant increase in research on outcome in psychotherapy in the past thirty years, the results secured haven't caused Eysenck to change the view he first espoused in 1952, namely that the effectiveness of psychotherapy has not yet been demonstrated. Thus he exhibits an amazing consistency in his point of view. In what follows, I shall offer my appraisal of Eysenck's consistently critical view of the outcome problem in psychotherapy.

Earlier responses to Eysenck

There is no question that Eysenck's 1952 article in the *Journal of Consulting Psychology*, 'The effects of psychotherapy: an evaluation', created quite a stir among clinical psychologists, a number of whom hastened to publish critiques of the article (DeCharms *et al.* 1954; Luborsky 1954; Rosenzweig 1954). Not only has this article become the most frequently cited article on outcome in psychotherapy, but also Eysenck kept the controversy alive by additional publications in which he continued to maintain, and even to increase, his critical evaluation of psychotherapy. (Eysenck 1961; 1966).

My own response to Eysenck's 1952 article was much more positive than was true of the responses of most of the clinical psychologists I knew. Even though I could see the important limitations in the 'control groups' used by Eysenck in his appraisal and in his subsequent estimate of the spontaneous remission rate of neurotic individuals, I responded positively to his emphasis on the need to evaluate the effects of psychotherapy. To me, this was an important and needed emphasis. However, the data presented by Eysenck did not provide a truly adequate basis upon which to rest his case. Conceivably, he might have pointed to the need for research in a way which did not alienate clinicians and that would not be viewed as 'overkill'.

In my 1957 text on clinical psychology, for example, I had a section entitled 'Evaluation of psychotherapy'. In this section I mentioned the need for research on outcome and the limitations in the existing research at that time. I also referred to Eysenck's paper, gave a brief summary of it, and made the following comment:

> At first glance the material presented by Eysenck appears quite damaging to the entire field of psychotherapy, and, indeed, it is so presented. However, before accepting such a drastic conclusion, it is worth discussing at greater length the problems encountered in the evaluation of therapy.
>
> (Garfield 1957: 334)

In my view, and in the view of many others, Eysenck did not fully evaluate the limitations in the research reviewed and in the assumptions made for the two so-called control groups. Once he reached his conclusion about the effects of psychotherapy, it seemed as if he were reluctant to consider other alternatives. Certainly, serious questions could be raised about the comparability of the patients treated in the various studies, the suitability of the control groups, and the criteria of improvement used. The classification of patients into the broad classification of 'Neurosis' is an overly broad and unreliable one on which to base serious conclusions.

Despite the various critiques offered of Eysenck's 1952 article, he continued to hold to his original conclusions in his later presentations (Eysenck 1961; 1966) and in the present chapter. As I have already indicated, I believe that Eysenck was fully justified in asserting in his earlier work that the efficacy of psychotherapy had not been demonstrated. Clearly, the existing research was of poor quality and the rates of improvement reported ranged rather widely, from 39 per cent to 67 per cent for psychoanalysis and from 41 per cent to 77 per cent for so-called eclectic therapy. However, both the quantity and quality of research on psychotherapy has increased since the mid-1950s, and there is a much larger body of data available at present to be evaluated and from which at least tentative conclusions can be drawn that do not necessarily agree with those of Eysenck. However, before discussing this material a few other comments can be offered.

Eysenck's critical pronouncements on psychotherapy did appear to stimulate a greater awareness on the part of others to conduct research and to present evidence in response to his critiques. Meltzoff and Kornreich (1970) and Bergin (1971) published reviews that included studies not mentioned by Eysenck and that presented a more favourable view of outcome in psychotherapy. Bergin, in particular, responded to Eysenck's interpretations and included a re-analysis of some of the data on psychoanalysis that had been modified and reinterpreted by Eysenck. This led him to offer very different interpretations. In turn, Bergin was rather strongly criticized by Eysenck's colleague, Rachman (1973), and by Eysenck in the present chapter. There is little question that such heated controversies tend to create polarization and at times to diminish objectivity. As I have pointed out elsewhere, 'Whereas Eysenck (1952) came up with a 39 per cent improvement rate for the Berlin Institute, Bergin (1971) came up with a 91 per cent rate of improvement! Clearly, no scientific conclusions are possible from such data' (Garfield 1974: 388).

Since the early 1970s, additional comprehensive and critical reviews of research on outcome have appeared which are based on a larger number of studies than those reviewed earlier by Eysenck and that are not alluded to in his current chapter. Rather than list a series of such references, I shall simply refer to the review by Lambert et al. (1986) which not only evaluates the recent literature but also includes a table that summarizes all or practically all of the meta-analytic reviews that have dealt with outcome in psychotherapy. Although one can criticize some of the studies included in the individual meta-analyses, the overall pattern is relatively clear, and clearly positive. There is a median effect size of 0.82 which does indicate a positive effect for the psychotherapies evaluated. Interpretations of this effect size may vary (Rosenthal 1983; Smith et al. 1980), but the direction is clear.

Since Eysenck has questioned this type of finding and its interpretation, some elaboration is required. According to Smith, Glass and Miller an effect size of 0.85 signifies that the average treated patient at the end of treatment is better off than 80 per cent of untreated controls. This is considered to be a large effect according to Cohen (1977) and such results 'suggest that the assignment to treatment versus control conditions accounts for some 10 per cent of the variation in outcome assessed in a typical study' (Lambert et al. 1986: 159). My own interpretation based on a variety of clinical reports and studies is that about 65 per cent of patients who receive psychotherapy show some improvement and that perhaps 10–20 per cent of this group show marked improvement. Since Eysenck himself has reported an improvement rate of about 65 per cent for psychotherapy, we agree on this estimate. However, the interpretation of this estimate is another matter, and, therefore, I want to discuss several areas where we definitely disagree.

The placebo response

One basic disagreement concerns the interpretation of the placebo response and the role of the placebo as a control in psychotherapy research. Eysenck believes it is a desirable control whereas I and some others see placebos as by no means 'inert' or comparable to a no-treatment group. Although a placebo may be appropriate for studies of pharmacological agents, it is not a meaningful control for psychotherapy. People do respond to a placebo for a variety of reasons and thus it would appear to have 'psychological' properties. It mirrors certain general features that probably constitute some of the components of the psychotherapeutic process such as the generation of hope, the support received from the placebo therapist, the feeling that one is doing something about one's problem, and the like. Thus, in my view it is not an appropriate control for evaluating psychotherapy outcome *per se* and some individuals have referred to it as the 'powerful placebo'. When some forms of psychotherapy perform little better than some placebos, it may be that the former rely on the same general factors as the placebo without offering much in addition. It is well to remember that the placebos used in the different studies have varied widely (Garfield 1983a). In any event, although some studies may not show statistically significant differences between a form of psychotherapy and a placebo, in most of them psychotherapy secures a visibly larger number who show positive gains.

The recently completed collaborative study of the treatment of depression co-ordinated by our National Institute of Mental Health is also worth referring to here (Elkin *et al*. 1985; 1989). In this study, 239 patients in three medical centres were assigned randomly to one of four treatment groups: Cognitive-Behaviour Therapy (CBT), Interpersonal Psychotherapy (IPT), Imipramine plus Clinical Management (IMI-CM) and a Pill Placebo plus Clinical Management (PLA-CM). Although the placebo group was selected to be a control for the Imipramine group, comparisons were made with all groups. The patients studied all met specific criteria of unipolar depression, therapy manuals were used for training the therapists to ensure the integrity of the therapies, the therapy sessions were monitored and were conducted in centres not associated with the developers of the therapies studied, and a variety of standard measures were used.

The results obtained at the end of treatment are quite similar to those obtained in many studies (Elkin *et al*. 1989) – no significant differences were obtained between the two forms of psychotherapy. Actually, there were few significant differences among the four treatment groups although the patients in all groups showed significant improvement over the course of treatment. In terms of the patients considered 'recovered' at the end of treatment on the basis of securing a score of six or less on the Hamilton Rating Scale of Depression, the percentage reaching this level ranged from 51 per cent to 57 per cent for the three treatment conditions and was 29 per cent for the PLA-CM condition. These findings were for those patients who completed treatment. Although there was a trend toward a statistically significant difference, the group findings were not statistically significant. Nevertheless, the pattern obtained is quite comparable to the pattern secured by Smith *et al.* (1980) in their meta-analysis of 475 studies on outcome and deserves some additional comment.

In the Smith *et al.* review, the overall effect size (ES) for psychotherapy was 0.85 whereas the ES for placebos was 0.56. Thus, the ES for the placebo treatments was somewhat more than half the ES secured for psychotherapy. In the NIMH study, the ratio of the 'recovery' rate for the pill placebo plus clinical management to the rate for the two psychotherapies is approximately the same. In other words, as indicated previously, the so-called placebo used in many studies is not an inert stimulus, but conceivably contains a number of the factors that are common to most of the psychotherapies. In the NIMH study, for example, each of the patients in the pill-placebo plus clinical management condition received an intensive diagnostic appraisal and were seen by a psychiatrist for twenty to thirty minutes throughout the sixteen weeks designated for the study. Without question, this experience was beneficial for a certain percentage of patients, but the number was clearly less than the number helped by the two psychotherapies or Imipramine.

Psychotherapy and behaviour therapy

It is quite evident that Eysenck sharply differentiates behaviour therapy from psychotherapy, or, preferably, from all other forms of psychotherapy. He believes firmly that behaviour therapy is effective, and that psychotherapy is not. I do not know if this is a widely held view in Britain or not, but I believe most of us in the United States tend to view behaviour therapy as one form of psychotherapy, and there is currently an organized movement to attempt some integration of various forms of psychotherapy (Goldfried and Newman 1986). Be that as it may, there is considerable interaction among behaviourally oriented clinical psychologists and clinical psychologists of other theoretical persuasions.

Of more importance, however, is the fact that there have been studies that compared behaviour therapy with other forms of psychotherapy. Eysenck does not mention the very well-known study of Sloane *et al.* (1975) that compared behaviour therapy and brief psychoanalytically oriented psychotherapy. This study was distinguished by the fact that the therapists used were for the most part very experienced and well-known therapists. Joseph

Wolpe and Arnold Lazarus, for example, were two of the three behaviour therapists employed in the study and the analytically oriented therapists were of comparable experience and distinction. Overall, in terms of most of the group comparisons, there were no important differences among the two forms of psychotherapy. In terms of the primary criteria of change, the target symptoms of each patient, both therapies secured significantly better results than a wait-list control group, and were not significantly different from each other. Furthermore, of particular interest was the finding that at the end of therapy, 'The successful patients in both therapies placed primary importance on more or less the same items' (Sloane *et al.* 1975: 206).

As I have noted elsewhere, 'The Society for Psychotherapy Research in 1980 awarded Sloane and his colleagues its first award for an outstanding research study in the area of psychotherapy' (Garfield 1981: 39). Although the study was criticized by several behavioural psychologists (Bandura 1978; Kazdin and Wilson 1978; Rachman and Wilson 1980), similar findings have been reported by others (Berman *et al.* 1985; Thompson *et al.* 1987; Zeiss *et al.* 1979). Space limitations preclude additional elaboration.

Concluding comments

As I indicated previously, despite inadequacies in the evaluation made by Eysenck in his 1952 article, I responded very positively to his emphasis on the need to evaluate the effects of psychotherapy. 'There is little question that this was an important event historically and helped focus attention on the need to evaluate the effectiveness of psychotherapy' (Garfield 1983b: 35). I also felt his criticisms of psychoanalysis had justification and I, too, offered a strong criticism of the eighteen-year Menninger study (Garfield 1981). However, my current view of the research on outcome in psychotherapy diverges from that of Eysenck. His view has remained unchanged since 1952 and apparently the accumulated research over forty years has had little impact on him. In my opinion, Eysenck has adhered too fixedly to his views concerning spontaneous remission, the placebo response and the complete superiority of behaviour therapy over all other forms of therapy. Because of this, he has not been able to accept the fact that even if neurotic patients recover in two years without treatment, they may be helped more rapidly by means of psychotherapy. In a similar fashion, although behaviour therapy may be the most effective for such disorders as phobias, compulsions and infantile autism, there is considerable comparability in outcomes for behaviour therapy and other forms of therapy for a variety of other problems and this does suggest the possibility of important common factors among the psychotherapies (Garfield 1980; Lambert *et al.* 1986). We shall not settle our differences here and both of us most likely won't be around when these issues may be settled more conclusively on the basis of better research in the future.

130   *Hans Eysenck*

References

Bandura, A. (1978) On paradigms and recycled ideologies. *Cognitive Therapy and Research* 2: 79–104.
Bergin, A.E. (1971) The evaluation of therapeutic outcomes, in A.E. Bergin and S.L. Garfield (eds) *Handbook of Psychotherapy and Behavior Change: An Empirical Analysis*. New York: Wiley.
Bergin, A.E. and Lambert, M.J. (1978) The evaluation of therapeutic outcomes, in S.L. Garfield and A.E. Bergin (eds) *Handbook of Psychotherapy and Behavior Change: An Empirical Analysis*, 2nd edn. New York: Wiley.
Berman, J.S., Miller, R.C. and Massman, P.J. (1985) Cognitive therapy versus systematic desensitization: is one treatment superior? *Psychological Bulletin* 97: 451–61.
Cohen, J. (1977) *Statistical Power Analysis for the Behavioural Sciences*. New York: Academic Press.
DeCharms, R., Levy, J. and Wertheimer, M. (1954) A note on attempted evaluations of psychotherapy. *Journal of Clinical Psychology* 10: 233–5.
Elkin, I., Parloff, M.B., Hadley, S.W. and Autry, J.H. (1985) National Institute of Mental Health Treatment of Depression Collaborative Research Program: background and research plan. *Archives of General Psychiatry* 42: 305–16.
Elkin, I., Shea, M.T., Watkins, J.T., Imber, S.D., Sotsky, S.M., Collins, J.F., Glass, D.R., Pilkonis, P.A., Leber, W.R., Docherty, J.P., Fiester, S.J. and Parloff, M.B. (1989) National Institute of Mental Health Treatment of Depression Collaborative Research Program: general effectiveness of treatments. *Archives of General Psychiatry* 46: 971–82.
Eysenck, H.J. (1952) The effects of psychotherapy: an evaluation. *Journal of Consulting Psychology* 16: 319–24.
Eysenck, H.J. (1961) The effects of psychotherapy, in H.J. Eysenck (ed.) *Handbook of Abnormal Psychology*. New York: Basic Books.
Eysenck, H.J. (1966) *The Effects of Psychotherapy*. New York: International Science Press.
Garfield, S.L. (1957) *Introductory Clinical Psychology*. New York: Macmillan.
Garfield, S.L. (1974) *Clinical Psychology: The Study of Personality and Behavior*. Chicago: Aldine.
Garfield, S.L. (1980) *Psychotherapy: An Eclectic Approach*. New York: Wiley.
Garfield, S.L. (1981) Psychotherapy: a 40-year appraisal. *American Psychologist* 36: 174–83.
Garfield, S.L. (1983a) Commentary. Does psychotherapy work? Yes, No, Maybe? *Behavioral and Brain Sciences* 6: 292–3.
Garfield, S.L. (1983b) The effectiveness of psychotherapy: the perennial controversy. *Professional Psychology* 14: 35–43.
Goldfried, M.R. and Newman, C. (1986) Psychotherapy integration: an historical perspective, in J.C. Norcross (ed.) *Handbook of Eclectic Psychotherapy*. New York: Brunner/Mazel.
Kazdin, A.E. and Wilson, G.T. (1978) *Evaluation of Behavior Therapy: Issues, Evidence, and Research Studies*. Cambridge, Mass: Ballinger.
Lambert, M.J., Shapiro, D.A. and Bergin, A.E. (1986) The effectiveness of psychotherapy, in S.L. Garfield and A.E. Bergin (eds) *Handbook of Psychotherapy and Behavior Change*, 3rd edn. New York: Wiley.
Luborsky, L. (1954) A note on Eysenck's article, 'The effects of psychotherapy: an evaluation'. *British Journal of Psychology* 45: 129–31.

Meltzoff, J. and Kornreich, M. (1970) *Research in Psychotherapy.* New York: Atherton Press.

Rachman, S. (1973) The effects of psychological treatment, in H.J. Eysenck (ed.) *Handbook of Abnormal Psychology.* New York: Basic Books.

Rachman, S.J. and Wilson, G.T. (1980) *The Effects of Psychological Therapy: Second enlarged edition.* New York: Pergamon.

Rosenthal, R. (1983) Assessing the statistical importance of the effects of psychotherapy. *Journal of Consulting and Clinical Psychology* 51: 4–13.

Rosenzweig, S. (1954) A transvaluation of psychotherapy: a reply to Hans Eysenck. *Journal of Abnormal and Social Psychology* 49: 298–304.

Sloane, R.B., Staples, F.R., Cristol, A.H., Yorkston, N.J. and Whipple, K. (1975) *Psychotherapy versus Behavior Therapy.* Cambridge, Mass: Harvard University Press.

Smith, M.L., Glass, G.V. and Miller, T.I. (1980) *The Benefits of Psychotherapy.* Baltimore, Md: Johns Hopkins University Press.

Thompson, L.W., Gallagher, D. and Breckenridge, J.S. (1987) Comparative effectiveness of psychotherapies for depressed elders. *Journal of Consulting and Clinical Psychology* 55: 385–90.

Zeiss, A., Lewinsohn, P. and Munoz, R. (1979) Nonspecific improvement effects in depression using interpersonal skills training, pleasant activities schedules, or cognitive training. *Journal of Consulting and Clinical Psychology* 47: 427–39.

REBUTTAL – Hans Eysenck

I am not at all convinced that Garfield and I differ all that much with respect to *answers*; we may well differ with respect to *questions*.

This may mirror our respective major commitments to therapy and science. Garfield sees large numbers of people suffering from neurotic disorders; his major interest is in what may help them. I see a scientific problem of discovering *why* neurotics fall prey to neurotic disorders, why they seem to recover without treatment, or with placebo treatment, whether any of the treatments based on some form of theory does better than placebo treatment, or any alternative form of treatment, and to what extent results bear out theoretical preconceptions. My emphasis thus has been to build a model which would incorporate the major empirical findings. On these findings Garfield and I seem to agree for the most part, but there is a curious lack of response by Garfield to my interpretation of these findings.

I have tried to show that if 'all have won, and all must have prizes' is really true; that is if different forms of treatment based on different theories have the same effect, then all these theories must be wrong. Each theory predicts that the treatment based on it will be significantly more successful than treatments based on other (false) theories; if that prediction fails, then the theory fails. The result would seem to be that *all* theories concerning psychotherapy are wrong (I am here sharply divorcing psychotherapy from behaviour therapy). Garfield does not tell us whether he agrees with this conclusion, but it seems to me incontrovertible, and highly damaging to the whole enterprise seen as a scientific endeavour to build a proper *model* of therapeutic effectiveness.

The placebo response, I believe, is particularly important in this discussion. I fully agree with Garfield that placebos are by no means inert, but have 'psychological' properties. I would go even further than that and say that what a 'non-treatment control' does to alleviate a person's suffering (consult a priest, discuss his or her problems with a friend, talk over worries and anxieties with a family member) has the same psychological properties, and explains the 'spontaneous remission' which has been found so successful.

If there is a grading from 'spontaneous remission' through placebo treatment to psychotherapy and finally to behaviour therapy, I would explain this in terms of a model which makes desensitization and other methods of behaviour therapy the fundamental ingredients in successful treatment (Eysenck 1980). The differential effectiveness of their methods would be explained in terms of the deliberate use of these methods, least for spontaneous remission, most for behaviour therapy. It should be remembered that nearly all these encounters contain some personal interaction between patient and therapist – friend–priest–relative, in which friendly acceptance facilitates desensitization. The only exception would be psychoanalysis along classical lines in which such sympathetic aid and friendly interaction is neglected in favour of dogmatic neutrality and 'interpretation' (Sutherland 1976). It is this that probably accounts for the 'negative outcome in psychotherapy' (Mays and Franks 1985) that Garfield fails to mention.

Garfield is right in thinking that I make a firm distinction between behaviour therapy and psychotherapy, and he is also right in saying that in the United States there is some attempt to produce some integration between them. Seeing how different the theories are on which behaviour therapy and psychotherapy are based, it will be interesting to see how such reconciliation is produced. My own interpretation would be that what is sought is simply an eclectic mish-mash of theories (Eysenck 1970) signifying nothing, and completely untestable scientifically. I am certainly unaware of any demonstration that a treatment based on such a confabulation has been shown significantly superior to behaviour therapy. To some this may read like dogma; I have elsewhere argued that behaviour therapy is applied science, not dogma, and that science is not well served by eclectic committee decisions, but only by firm theorizing and experimental testing of deductions (Eysenck 1976).

It is sometimes suggested that behaviour therapy, based on deductions from learning theory, has been displaced by cognitive behaviour therapy, which admits cognitive elements. This, it is suggested, brings behaviour therapy and psychotherapy closer together.

This argument is completely fallacious (Eysenck and Martin 1987). Learning theory from Pavlov onwards has always included cognitive elements, and these are absolutely fundamental (Mackintosh 1984). Criticisms based on the aberrations of Watson or Skinner are irrelevant; in my definition of behaviour therapy as being based on modern learning theory, I laid special emphasis on the relevant theories being *modern*, not anchored in the early 1920s. The term 'cognitive behaviour therapy' is either an oxymoron or a tautology, and it should be eliminated from meaningful scientific discourse. One final comment. Garfield cites some meta-analyses which at times seem to contradict my conclusions based on other meta-analyses. But disagreements between meta-analysts are no less frequent than those between reviewers prior to the advent of this particular type of analysis. Wittman and Matt (1986), for instance, in a meta-analysis of the large body of German studies, found, contrary to Smith *et al.* (1980) that quality of study did make a large difference, and that the effects of different types of psychotherapy did differ with therapies of behavioural orientation showing the highest effects. (Riedel and Schneider-Duker (1991) criticize and extend this discussion.) What all this suggests to me is that in the presence (still!) of gross disagreement between experts (Rachman vs Bergin; Wittman and Matt vs Smith, Glass and Miller; Wolpe vs Lambert), it would be premature to dismiss my original conclusion that the superiority of psychoanalytic treatment or psychotherapy over (credible) placebo treatment had not been proved beyond reasonable doubt. (The average effect size of placebo treatment is badly affected by placebos which lack credibility.) For behaviour therapy I would claim a more positive conclusion; such advances as those demonstrated by Rachman and Hodgson (1980) over all previous therapeutic interventions in the treatment of obsessive-compulsive disorders show what can be done when we take theories seriously, and base our methods of treatment on modern learning theory. But above all I agree with Garfield on the need for better research in the future; this alone will settle any differences.

References

Eysenck, H.J. (1970) A mish-mash of theories. *International Journal of Psychiatry* 9: 140–6.

Eysenck, H.J. (1976) Behaviour therapy – dogma or applied science?, in M.P. Feldman and A. Broadhurst (eds) *The Theoretical and Experimental Foundations of Behaviour Therapy*. London: Wiley.

Eysenck, H.J. (1980) A unified theory of psychotherapy, behaviour therapy and spontaneous remission. *Zeitschrift für Psychologie* **188**: 43–56.

Eysenck, H.J. and Martin, I. (eds) (1987) *Theoretical Foundation of Behaviour Therapy*. New York: Plenum.

Mackintosh, N.J. (1984) *Conditioning and Associative Learning*. Oxford: Clarendon.

Mays, D.T. and Franks, C.M. (1985) *Negative Outcome in Psychotherapy*. New York: Springer.

Rachman, S. and Hodgson, R. (1980) *Obsessions and Compulsions*. Englewood Cliffs, NJ: Prentice-Hall.

Riedel, H. and Schneider-Duker, M. (1991) Kontextbedingungen 'Kontrollierter' und 'Unkontrollierter' Psychotherapieforschung. *Psychologische Rundschau* **42**: 19–28.

Smith, M.L., Glass, G.V. and Miller, T.I. (1980) *The Benefits of Psychotherapy*. Baltimore, Md: Johns Hopkins University Press.

Sutherland, S. (1976) *Breakdown*. London: Weidenfeld & Nicolson.
Wittman, W.W. and Matt, G.E. (1986) Meta-Analyse als Integration von Forschungsergebnissen am Beispiel deutschsprachiger Arbeiten zur Effektivität von Psychotherapie. *Psychologische Rundschau* 37: 20–40.

Dryden. W. + Feltham. C. (1992)
Psychotherapy and Its Discontents.
Open University Press.

SIX

The myth of therapist expertise

KATHARINE MAIR

Psychotherapists of the 1990s are in many ways in a similar position to the physicians of eighty years ago. Their patients have faith in their expertise and expect them to say what is wrong and how to put it right. Psychotherapists' understanding of patients' problems, and knowledge about how they can be remedied is, however, very much less than they imagine. It is also less than therapists imagine. They have been through a training which claims to give them a model by which to understand their patients, and methods by which to treat them. Physician and psychotherapist alike believe in their models and methods because they see them work. I hope to demonstrate that, although psychotherapy can be a valuable means of helping people, its efficacy is not due primarily to the models and methods that it uses (which may be as irrelevant to the patient's problems as the application of leeches was to the curing of a fever eighty years ago), and that too blind a faith in them may actually interfere with therapists' ability to help their patients. George Bernard Shaw voiced his scepticism of the doctors of his day in his preface to *The Doctor's Dilemma* in 1911. His comments seem appropriate to this argument.

The expert healer

> *I presume nobody will question the existence of a widely spread popular delusion that every doctor is a man of science.*
>
> (Shaw 1911)

Throughout history communities have had their designated experts in heal-ing. They have been turned to for cure and for counsel in the face of affliction, and their authority has been accepted without question. Perhaps this is because people in distress need relief, not debate. Healing techniques have ranged from the dramatic and public rituals of exorcism to the confidential prescription of a few tablets, or the 'talking cure' of psychotherapy, and always there has been an expectation that the healer will be able to do something that will be effective.

Psychotherapists depend upon this expectation, even when they claim that they are merely enabling their patients to help themselves. They ex-ploit the mystique of the expert healer, often to good effect, but they also assert that their achievements are due to their understanding of how people function and their skill in bringing about specified changes. Psychotherapy, like medicine, is said to be based on knowledge. Perhaps, like the medicine of eighty years ago, its true foundation is on the myth of knowledge.

There may always have been a few sceptics who, like Shaw, have said that they do not believe in doctors. This has been a minority view, despite the fact that, until well into the twentieth century, nearly all of the physical remedies prescribed by these respected authorities are now thought to have been, in themselves, at best useless and at worst damaging to the patient. It has been pointed out that almost every known organic and inorganic sub-stance, including most human and animal secretions, have been prescribed at some time as a cure for some ailment. People have also been immobilized, purged and bled without apparent complaint or question (Shapiro and Morris 1978). Faith in the medical profession never seems to have been seriously dented by the individual failures of some of its practitioners or by the implausibility of some of its theories.

An illustration of the way in which ordinary people will trust experts, and experts will defend their body of knowledge to the end is provided in Thomas's account of changing beliefs in seventeenth-century Britain (Thomas 1971). At that time astrology was widely accepted as an explanatory system for most of the vagaries of human and natural behaviour. This belief in astrology was not at first dented by the discoveries of Copernicus and Newton or by new information about the vastness and immutability of the heavens that resulted from the invention of the telescope. Astrologers struggled to reform their system rather than abandon it, and the general public were at first as undeterred by astrology's growing implausibility as they had been by its occasional practical disappointments. An orthodox system does not have to produce results every time and trust in a body of expertise can outlive trust in its individual practitioners:

> The paradox was that the mistakes of any one astrologer only served to buttress the system as a whole, since the client's reaction was to turn to another practitioner to get better advice. . . . The notorious internal disputes among the astrological fraternity . . . did not discredit astrology as such, any more than did religious controversy make men

atheists. They merely stimulated the public desire to know which side was right. By concentrating on each other's errors, the astrologers thus diverted attention from their art as a whole.

(Thomas 1971: 338)

Doctors used astrology during the middle of the seventeenth century, and quietly let it drop as its basis became undermined. They never bothered to refute it, but aligned themselves with the spirit of scientific inquiry that made its dogma unfashionable. Thomas points out that it was this new ability to admit ignorance and search for knowledge that led to the abandonment of many magical beliefs, not any evidence that they did not work. There was a new faith in human initiative that made magic unnecessary.

Science and the healer

The doctor learns that if he gets ahead of the superstitions of his patient he is a ruined man.

(Shaw 1911)

Science is usually assumed to be rational, objective, value-free and open to disproof. Yet individuals who earn their living by healing must serve the needs of their community, and must be believed. They must deal with the problems that people bring them in a way that fits in with their expectations and their values, and they must also be authoritative. When the psychiatrist of a hundred years ago declared that masturbation was a major cause of insanity, he reflected the attitudes of those around him. He also invoked the authority of science. No one asked him to test his hypothesis and it has probably still never been scientifically tested, but because our attitudes have now changed we are certain that it was wrong.

Doctors are generally expected to know what is wrong and to be able to do something about it; they are expected to cure rather than just to care for their patients. A general practitioner recently decided to see whether an honest admission of uncertainty would have any effect on the progress of his patients (Thomas 1987). He gave two different types of consultations to those patients who came to him with mild, self-limiting symptoms for which no diagnosis was appropriate. He truthfully told half of them that he was not certain what was wrong with them. He gave the rest a firm but fraudulent diagnosis and told them confidently that they would get better in a few days. Immediately afterwards those with the diagnosis expressed greater satisfaction; they felt that the doctor had understood their problem and that they had been helped. Two weeks later, 64 per cent of them said that they were now better. Only 39 per cent of those who had had the honest consultation said that they were better after two weeks. The doctor concluded that his honest doubt had actually prolonged some of his patients' symptoms, since they would normally be expected to clear up within the two weeks.

Scientists must admit, however reluctantly, to uncertainty. Their theories are only hypotheses, to be modified or discarded in the light of new evidence. Healers must inspire confidence, and to do this they have to appear certain. People go to the doctor for help; they do not expect to have hypotheses tested on them. This puts those healers who claim that their remedies are based on science in a difficult position. Perhaps they must be prepared, like the general practitioner above, to forgo their scientific principles at times in the interests of their patients' recovery. In doing this they are pretending to a bogus, but nevertheless effective, expertise.

Psychotherapists today vary in the extent to which they invoke science as a justification for their activities, but few seem to be prepared to see themselves simply as faith healers. Science enjoys prestige and power, and many psychotherapists have themselves had lengthy scientific educations. They want their efficacy to be based on their ability to relate the complaints of their clients to a body of scientific knowledge, which enables them to understand mental processes and make interventions which bring about change in a predictable way. Above all, they want to understand what is going on.

In their attempts to buttress their work with science, psychotherapists may ignore the findings of the sciences of psychology or medicine in which many of them were educated: for example, that verbal agreement between people may mask divergent thoughts, that memories and even perceptions can be distorted by wishes and expectations, and that these may be further altered in order to agree with other people's judgements; also that apparently inert substances can produce mental and physical changes in people who consume them: the well-known placebo effect. Thus psychotherapists ignore the fact that we do not really know what goes on in anyone else's mind, that people are very suggestible and that we do not understand how some of them manage to get better. These facts are disguised by a variety of elaborate conjectures about mental processes which are presented as hard data.

The rhetoric of the pseudo scientist

Science becomes dangerous when it imagines it has reached its goal. What is wrong with priests and popes is that instead of being apostles and saints, they are nothing but empirics who say 'I know' instead of 'I am learning' and pray for credulity and inertia as wise men pray for scepticism and activity.

(Shaw 1911)

In presenting themselves as learned experts, psychotherapists stress that the methods they use relate to a theory of human functioning. Although some psychotherapists may sample a variety of theories, searching for the best fit with the story each patient is relating, others will ruthlessly adapt their patients' stories to fit the one particular theory that they believe in. What is the basis for this belief? Theories of psychotherapy are often based on useful observations of the way people think and act. However, as a school of psychotherapy emerges and is promoted, these observations and conjectures can become extended and elaborated into a self-serving dogma which, as the following five examples show, owes nothing to scientific inquiry.

A visionary design

The most elaborate and inclusive modern theory of mental functioning must be that developed by Sigmund Freud. Like the magical and astrological theories of the past, it was born of conjecture rather than observation or experiment, but was presented as science. For Freud, psychoanalysis was more than just a method of treatment:

> As a depth psychology, a theory of the mental unconscious, it can become indispensable to all the sciences which are concerned with the evolution of human civilisation and its major instruments such as art, religion and the social order. It has already, in my opinion, afforded these sciences considerable help in solving their problems.
>
> (Freud 1926: 162)

However, it also needed to work as a form of treatment in order to be credible. Thus Freud's 'discovery' that neurotic symptoms were the result of repressed memories of childhood traumas rested on his assertion that when these repressions were lifted during analysis the symptoms disappeared.

The elevation of conjecture to science on the basis of a series of reported cures seems to be a common feature of most psychotherapeutic theories. However, understanding psychological functioning is not necessarily related to change. 'There is no a priori reason to assume that the better one understands a person, the easier it is to exert a therapeutic influence on him' (Strupp 1973: 769). There is also, perhaps, no reason to assume that because one has exerted a therapeutic influence on someone, one has necessarily understood that person.

A strategy that worked

Sometimes the therapeutic success seems to come first, followed by a theory which claims to explain it. Aaron Beck's cognitive therapy developed out of his disenchantment with psychoanalysis and attempts to find a more effective way to help depressed people. He discovered that they benefited from having their ideas challenged and also from 'a graded series of successes in attaining a tangible goal' (Beck *et al.* 1979). He developed a directive, structured approach, in which patients were encouraged to test out their gloomy assumptions and to place themselves in potentially rewarding situations, and found that this was more successful than the non-directive approach he had used before.

Beck's therapy emerged from his observations of depressed people's attitudes. From these observations he postulated 'three specific concepts to explain the psychological substrate of depression':

1 A 'cognitive triad' of negative views about the self, the world and the future.
2 'Schemas' that were presumed to dispose depressed people towards these views.
3 'Faulty information processing' that maintained them.

In other words, people were depressed because of their attitudes and their thoughts. He thus passed off his description of the thinking of depressed people (beefed up with a lot of jargon) as an explanation for depression, which had been validated by 'systematic research'. Even as a description, its validity has been questioned. There is a wealth of experimental data which suggests that depressed people do not have distorted perceptions, and that they may indeed be rather more accurate than the rest of us in many of their judgements. (For a comprehensive review of these findings, see Taylor and Brown 1988.)

Beck can be seen as a good therapist who wants to be a scientist. Like Freud, he has claimed that the efficacy of his therapy will validate his theory:

> Cognitive therapy is derived from this formulation: The source of the depression is a hypervalent set of negative concepts; therefore, the correction and damping down of these schemas may be expected to alleviate the depressive symptomatology. . . . Studies of the efficacy of cognitive therapy offer an indirect test of the cognitive model.
>
> (Beck *et al.* 1979: 386)

Unlike Freud, he has tested his therapy exhaustively and it does seem to work rather well, because in practice it offers rather more than his meagre model would suggest. This has enabled him to promote it for use with problems far removed from depression without apparently needing to adjust his model in any way at all. The treatment that was said to stem from an understanding of one specific disorder is now applied to many, unhampered by any backward glances at its theoretical base.

Science to the rescue

Behaviour therapy was another treatment born out of disagreement with the ideas of Freud and his followers, and one which made even stronger claims to be a science: 'There is reason for confidence in the practice of behaviour therapy. It is founded in biology and its principles and practices are determined by the rules of science' (Wolpe 1973: 10). Joseph Wolpe, in partnership with Arnold Lazarus, devised a new treatment for neurotic symptoms which was based on a theory firmly backed by experimental evidence. 'Behaviour therapy could not enter the world of science before there was a sufficient foundation for it in the basic studies of the experimental laboratory' (Wolpe and Lazarus

1966). The experiments were indeed carefully and systematically carried out and they seemed to demonstrate that neuroses could be seen as conditioned responses, caused by prior exposure to frightening stimuli. Therefore it was logical to suppose that they could be cured by the deconditioning techniques of behaviour therapy.

The subjects of the experiments were all animals, mostly cats and dogs. They were kept in laboratory cages and given carefully controlled electric shocks. The subjects of the therapy were all humans, living freely. On finding that the therapy did indeed work, Wolpe proclaimed:

> Before the advent of behaviour therapy, psychological medicine was a medley of speculative systems and intuitive methods. Behaviour therapy is an applied science, in every way parallel to other modern technologies, and in particular those that constitute modern medical therapeutics. Therapeutic possibilities radiate from the uncovering of the lawful relations of lawful organismal processes.
>
> (Wolpe 1973: xi)

Few behaviour therapists would now believe that the client that they are successfully treating must have been exposed to a frightening stimulus which was then associated with other, previously neutral stimuli, producing a generalized conditioned response. Like the seventeenth-century doctors, who used astrology as a justification until it became unfashionable, and then quietly let it drop, today's behaviour therapist keeps quiet about the traumatized cats and dogs and just gets on with the therapy because it seems to work.

Roles into ego states

Most promoters of new psychotherapies do not seem to feel the need for experimental verification. They get an idea, usually from careful observation of the way people act, and proceed to develop this into a way to help people change. However, if their original idea relates only to a limited aspect of behaviour, they will need to extend and dignify it; a new jargon and hints of organic underpinnings can help in this endeavour.

Eric Berne noticed that when we interact with others we behave sometimes as though we are children and sometimes as though we are adults. This was a useful observation: it made sense to a lot of people and could be used to help them understand and change their behaviour. It formed the lynchpin of his therapy, transactional analysis. But Berne too wanted to be more than just an observant therapist; he tells us how he made the journey from behavioural observation to the discovery of two new organs:

> What actually happened was that patients could be observed, or observed themselves, shifting from one state of mind to another and from one behaviour pattern to another. Typically there was one ego state characterised by . . . reality testing . . . another archaic and autistic

... this led to the assumption of two psychic organs, a neopsyche and an archeopsyche. It seemed appropriate, and was generally acceptable to all concerned, to call the phenomenological and operational manifestations of these two organs the adult and the child respectively.

(Berne 1975: 75)

When Berne noticed that people sometimes adopt a parental role, a third organ was added, and we got three ego states:

Technically these are called, respectively, exteropsychic, neopsychic, and archeopsychic ego states. Colloquially their exhibitions are called Parent, Adult and Child, and these simple terms serve for all but the most formal discussions.

(Berne 1964: 23)

The world within

A common feature of most psychotherapies is that they encourage individuals to look at what is behind their immediate feelings or actions, that is to look into their minds. Even the most behavioural of therapists usually aims to tell clients something about themselves that they did not know before. Many people seem to believe that the psychotherapist can read their minds and may hope that their therapist will act as a kind of spirit guide, leading them into previously uncharted territory within themselves.

Therapists who are willing to play this role may insist that they only enable clients to discover for themselves what is already there, but therapists are often prepared to give clients helpful suggestions along the way, and then to use their responses to reinforce the theoretical system the therapists originally had in mind. In this way something that starts out as a useful analogy can gradually become an article of faith. Thus John Rowan observes in 1976:

One of the characteristic methods used by psychosynthesis is the use of a fantasy which leads to the discovery of one or more subselves or subpersonalities. It is often found that strange habits or quirks, sometimes quite destructive, make a lot of sense if seen as a kind of subsystem which 'takes over' at certain times and dominates the whole self. And quite often it makes sense to give this subsystem a name, and to concretize it by seeing it in fantasy as a real person with an appearance and history of her own.

(Rowan 1976: 67)

By 1989 he is able to be far less tentative about the subpersonality, which he defines as 'a semi-permanent and semi-autonomous region of the personality capable of acting as a person', and he claims 'a given person probably has from four to nine subpersonalities, coming from at least six different origins' (Rowan 1989: 279).

Rowan may feel vindicated by the inclusion in the tenth edition of the

International Classification of Diseases (WHO 1987) of a new category: Multiple Personality Disorder, defined as a 'dissociative disorder of memory, awareness and identity'. When therapists believe in the existence of multiple personalities, their patients are likely to share these beliefs. Spanos (1989) reports that 60 per cent of patients in one United States clinic were found to suffer from this disorder. However, it seems to be extremely rare outside the United States. Its appearance seems to be associated with therapists' attempts to uncover the past, often using hypnosis. Patients are led to believe that by contacting the repressed aspects of themselves and 'working through' whatever they may encounter, they will be enabled to recover. The shared fantasies of patient and therapist thus become reinforced in therapy.

The unconscious mind is fertile territory for many psychotherapists. Jung extended the rather crude terrain uncovered by Freud, and made it more attractive for explorers. The idea of a hidden self, or selves, in tune with the essential, instinctive forces which drive us all and holding the key to our well-being, is common to many present-day therapies. It has been adopted also by many who work outside the conventional psychotherapeutic framework, who may find the emphasis on irrationality helpful.

> When magic is practised, the principal aim of the magus is to sidetrack the conscious mind, which is conditioned with preconceived ideas and limited by conventional personality patterns, and contact the subconscious . . . a very powerful agent which, when released from captivity and *controlled* can cause changes in environmental patterns. By doing this the practitioner of candle burning can bring into manifestation his desires and wishes, gain the love of others, heal the sick, secure financial aid and progress along the path towards psychic and physical attainment.
>
> (Howard 1980: 2)

The search for active ingredients

> *Even trained statisticians often fail to appreciate the extent to which statistics are vitiated by the unrecorded assumptions of their interpreters.*
>
> (Shaw 1911)

The evaluation of psychotherapy is notoriously difficult and many psychotherapists seem to find it quite unnecessary. However, as a result of a vast amount of work done over more than forty years, evidence has accumulated of its tendency to be beneficial (Luborsky *et al.* 1975; Smith *et al.* 1980), and of some aspects of it being more important than others in bringing this about. Orlinsky and Howard (1986) review 1,100 outcome studies, spanning thirty-five years, in an attempt to link the various processes in psychotherapy to its outcome. They have been able to point to five factors that seem to be related to a successful outcome of therapy:

1 The therapeutic contract: whether the patient was seen promptly and attended all sessions.
2 Patient participation: whether the patient was encouraged to take an active role in the therapy.
3 The therapeutic bond: whether patient and therapist both felt committed to their roles, were empathic and mutually affirmative.
4 The patient's self-relatedness: whether the patient was open rather than defensive.
5 Therapeutic realizations: whether some sort of catharsis or insight occurred during therapy.

None of these factors relates to any of the theories behind the therapy. The most crucial factor, according to Orlinsky and Howard, is the bond that therapists form with their patients, which they find more important than the therapist's interventions, since they can work only if the patient is able to be open rather than defensive. They thus support the earlier finding of Rogers, that the most important determinant for successful therapy is that patients should be able to experience the warmth, empathy and genuineness of their therapists (Rogers 1957); but unlike Rogers, they do not suggest that these qualities are always both necessary and sufficient for successful therapy.

Some of the assumptions behind Orlinsky and Howard's review have been criticized (Stiles and Shapiro 1988). Psychotherapy is a lengthy interaction in which it is difficult to separate process from outcome. A patient's active participation and self-relatedness may be seen as outcomes as much as processes, though they may influence further outcomes. More importantly, if therapists gauge their interventions to the patient's need of them (for example, prescribing only as many behavioural tasks as the patient seems to need) then a zero, or even negative correlation with outcome may mask the effectiveness of these interventions when they are used. Stiles and Shapiro argue that most of the many process-outcome studies, including Orlinsky and Howard's, try to evaluate psychotherapy as they would a drug treatment, assuming that it is possible to isolate and measure the active ingredients and that there is a linear dose–response curve (if it is any good then more should automatically be better). None of these assumptions is valid: the components of psychotherapy are interdependent and patients are not passive recipients of them; patients determine what and how much they get.

The comparison with drug trials is interesting and suggests a wish to establish psychotherapy as a technology, capable of competing on equal terms with anything the medical profession has to offer. Certainly that was what Freud, Beck and Wolpe seemed to have in mind. They also each suggested that their own brand of psychotherapy was particularly effective because of its sound theoretical basis. However, Orlinsky and Howard's review shows, like so many before them, that the theoretical orientation of the therapist bears no relation to the success of the psychotherapy. This seems to be true, not only when general measures of well-being are used to measure outcome, but also when outcome is measured by questionnaires that are designed to tap the specific changes aimed at in each therapy (Imber *et al.* 1990). Patients seem to benefit from a wide range of procedures, some of them even designed to be 'inert'. So what do psychotherapists, armed with their theory of mental functioning and their carefully worked-out techniques, actually do? And do they really understand what is going on?

The placebo problem

When men die of disease they are said to die from natural causes. When they recover (and they mostly do) the doctor gets the credit for curing them.

(Shaw 1911)

It has often been pointed out that people go to psychotherapists when they feel bad and stay until they feel better. Psychotherapists then assume that they have cured their patients. In this respect they are just like any other healer; overlooking the fact that the patients would probably have got better anyway, and enjoying an unwarranted feeling of power. Like other healers, however, psychotherapists probably also overlook the fact that any effect they do have may result not from their actions directly, but from the patient's expectations that their actions will be effective. In other words, the patient's improvement may be due to the placebo effect.

This improvement is sometimes referred to as a non-specific treatment effect, which is misleading, as Grunbaum (1989) has pointed out, because the effect itself may be highly specific. It will usually mimic the expected effects of the treatment and can produce comparable mental and physical changes. For example, placebos (i.e. supposedly inert substances) have been known to produce side-effects and even be addictive when substituted for drugs which are known to have these properties (Vinar 1969; Shapiro and Morris 1978). When we call a change a placebo effect what we usually mean is that it was brought about by some means other than that intended in a particular treatment.

It is important to distinguish between intentional and inadvertent placebos. An intentional placebo is a treatment that is designed to have no effect, in itself, on a particular disorder. An inadvertent placebo is a treatment that is intended to have an effect on a particular disorder by a specified means, but which is then found to produce its effect in some other way, for which we have no explanation. A frequently cited example of this is the surgical treatment for angina, which was carried out in the United States during the 1950s (Beecher 1961, quoted by Grunbaum 1989). Proponents of this treatment attributed the marked improvements in their patients to the effects of redirecting the mammary artery, so increasing blood flow to the heart muscle. It was later discovered that merely making an incision in the skin, so that patients believed that the artery had been relocated, produced the same 'dramatic and sustained' benefits. Here an intentional placebo was used to reveal that the surgical treatment had been an inadvertent placebo. It now seems likely that most medical and surgical procedures before this century were in fact inadvertent placebos, and some of them may have been highly effective. Whether or not a given treatment is a placebo depends both on what it is treating and on the therapeutic rationale being employed.

The use of intentional placebos to test the efficacy of psychotherapy is another example of the misapplication of drug trial methods, noted by Stiles and Shapiro (1988). In testing a drug, it is quite appropriate to try to cancel out placebo effects, which may account for an appreciable part of its action. In psychotherapy, however, the expectancy is part of the treatment. The whole point of the placebo controlled trial is that patients do not know which treatment is supposed to be active. Therefore they have to be persuaded to engage in an 'inert' therapy in the belief that it may help them. Critelli and Neumann (1984) point out that most of the inane procedures that have so far been adopted as psychotherapy placebos would not fool anyone. They suggest:

> At a minimum, placebo controls should be equivalent to test proce-
> dures on all major recognized common factors. These might include
> induced expectancy of improvement; credibility of rationale; credibil-
> ity of procedures; demand for improvement; and therapist attention,
> enthusiasm, effort, perceived belief in treatment procedures, and com-
> mitment to client improvement.
>
> (Critelli and Neumann 1984: 38)

Once one has achieved all that, one has created a new psychotherapy!

How does psychotherapy work?

> *Nobody seems yet to discount the effect of substituting attention for*
> *neglect in drawing conclusions from the health statistics.*
>
> (Shaw 1911)

There are thought to be hundreds of different versions of psychotherapy, and many of them seem to work equally well. Does this debase the concept of psychotherapy? Is it any more than an inadvertent placebo, and does that matter? Frank (1989) neatly turns the question around by suggesting that the placebo is psychotherapy:

> As a symbolic communication that combats demoralisation by inspir-
> ing the patient's hopes for relief, administration of a placebo is a form
> of psychotherapy. It is therefore not surprising that placebos can pro-
> vide marked relief in patients who seek psychotherapy.
>
> (Frank 1989: 97)

As long ago as 1961, when evidence of the similar effectiveness of different therapies was already accumulating, Frank first turned his attention to those factors that they all seemed to have in common (Frank 1973). He listed four components:

1 Patients feel that the therapist, whom they respect, cares about them.
2 The setting for therapy is designated as a place of healing.
3 Therapy is based on a rationale or myth which includes an explanation of illness, deviancy and normality.
4 A task or procedure is prescribed by the therapy.

Frank pointed out that these components were shared, not only by all psychotherapies, but also by all the healing arts, both magical and scientific. Compared to medicine, psychotherapy relied more on learning and was essentially a form of persuasion. The therapeutic rationale was therefore extremely important:

> The rationale of each school of psychotherapy explains the cause of the sufferer's distress, specifies desirable goals for him, and prescribes procedures for attaining them. To be effective, the therapeutic myth must be compatible with the cultural world view shared by the patient and the therapist.
>
> (Frank 1973: 327)

Frank used the word 'myth' because the rationale for the therapy was not usually subject to disproof by therapeutic failures. This was necessary to protect therapists' self-esteem, and hence patients' confidence in them. For Frank the importance of the various rationales and techniques lay not in their specific contents, but in their function.

Psychotherapy works, according to Frank, as follows:

1 It gives the patient new opportunities for learning, problem solving and reality testing.
2 It gives the patient hope of relief.
3 It gives the patient experience of success; therapy is structured to give a sense of progress.
4 It helps the patient to overcome a sense of alienation through interaction with the therapist.
5 It involves emotional arousal which leads to psychotherapeutic change.

For those psychotherapists who might, as a result of Frank's rather cavalier attitude to their various creeds, feel tempted to forsake them, he has a warning and a consolation:

> The therapist's ability to help his patient depends partly on his self confidence, and this in turn depends on mastery of a particular conceptual scheme and its accompanying techniques. Since the leading theories of psychotherapy represent alternative rather than incompatible formulations, it is unlikely that any one of them is completely wrong.
>
> (Frank 1973: 342)

/ *Integrationism.*

Frank's formulation of the five healing properties in psychotherapy helps explain some of the findings of comparative studies. When different therapies are found to be differentially effective, it is often the more active, structured therapy that works best (e.g. Marks 1978; Rachman *et al.* 1979). Perhaps that is because these therapies give the patient more opportunity to experience success and have a structured sense of progress. The effectiveness of cognitive therapy is more easily explained along these lines than as a vindication of the powers of rational argument. Likewise, behaviour therapy, which will often also involve intense emotional arousal, changes by challenging patients to succeed rather than by systematically desensitizing them.

Psychoanalysis, as traditionally practised, seems to handicap itself, not only by its lack of structure, but also by its denial of the warm patient–therapist bond. It requires that the therapist be neutral, so that patients can transfer on to them an uncontaminated image of someone else. Freud did notice that patients displayed 'a degree of affectionate feeling' towards their therapists but insisted that it was 'based on no real relation between them', but was a transference of fantasies that had become unconscious (Freud 1977). However, the transference becomes the means whereby the patient is healed and the patient's attention is repeatedly focused on it, so that in fact Freud paradoxically exploited the patient–therapist relationship while seeming to deny it, and so gave his therapy a chance of being effective *despite* its theory.

Therapists emerge, in all evaluations of psychotherapy, as crucial to its success. Therapists are not a vehicle for valuable theories of human functioning, rather the theories are a vehicle for them. Theories bring therapists to their patients, confident that they have the expertise to help patients, prepared to invade their privacy and willing to offer themselves as model, guide and friend.

Psychotherapy as a profession

> *There would never be any public agreement among doctors if they did not agree to agree on the main point of the doctor being always in the right.*
>
> (Shaw 1911)

Twenty years ago, as a result of anxiety about the effects of scientology, a committee appointed by the British government recommended that there should be a statutory register of psychotherapists, and that they should all undergo an agreed form of training (Foster 1971). A working party was duly set up, representing seven professional organizations associated with psychotherapy and with observers from several other professions. It met for three years but was unable to produce a unanimous report (Sieghart 1978). The government tried again in 1981, this time with more than thirty interested organizations, with similar results. Ever since then, people from many different professions, all claiming to be psychotherapists, have met once a year to try to decide what sort of people should be allowed to call themselves psychotherapists. In 1990 it was decided to call this annual meeting the United Kingdom Standing Conference for Psychotherapy. The number of organizations represented had now grown to sixty-eight and government representatives no longer bothered to attend. One delegate has sadly observed, 'For any Government action to take place they are waiting for the profession to get its act together' (Pedder 1989).

Healing has always been an entrepreneurial activity, though it also has to serve the needs of its community. Individual healers will submerge their rivalries and 'get their act together' only when it is in their interests to do so. The twenty-year campaign to create a recognized profession of psychotherapy in the United Kingdom has been based on the assumption that only 'properly qualified' people can be trusted not to harm the public. Members of established professions (psychiatry, clinical psychology and social work) and others working outside these professions have been invited to pronounce upon just what the proper qualifications for psychotherapy were. They have failed to agree because their own qualifications and interests are all so different. As the number of organizations represented grows to reflect something of the diversity of those who now call themselves psychotherapists, the possibility of agreement dwindles to extinction.

The protection of the public has always been a useful front from behind which members of professional organizations can work to protect their own interests. They can advise the public to consult a list of 'reputable dealers' if it wants to be safe; knowing that the prestige of those who are on this list will rise in proportion to the number of people who are excluded (a principle Groucho Marx recognized when he wanted to join a club). If they encourage the customer to look more carefully at the product itself or to question whether he really needs it, they are in danger of protecting him from themselves.

Training and psychotherapy

> *Bone setters make fortunes under the very noses of our greatest surgeons from educated and wealthy patients, and some of the most successful doctors on the register use quite heretical methods, and have qualified themselves solely for convenience.*
>
> (Shaw 1911)

The methods by which people train to become psychotherapists are as varied as the therapies that they practise, and seem to range from flipping through a treatment manual to undergoing years of study, supervision and one's own therapy. There are, however, common features in most psychotherapy trainings:

1 *Instruction*   Indoctrination in the theories and rationales of a particular therapy or range of therapies.
2 *Practice*   Opportunity to learn treatment techniques and practise using them under supervision.
3 *Initiation*   A rite of passage, leading to loyal identification with a professional group.

Training thus imparts expertise. Trained therapists have a model by which they hope to make sense out of what their patients tell them. Trained therapists also have a justification for attempting certain procedures, skill in using them and an expectation that they will work. More importantly, they feel qualified to intervene in other people's lives because they are now members of an exclusive club of professionals.

The implication behind the United Kingdom Standing Conference for Psychotherapy seems to be that this expertise is helpful. Hattie *et al.* (1984) reviewed forty-three studies in which 'professionals', defined as those who had undergone a formal clinical training in psychology, psychiatry, social work or nursing, were compared with 'paraprofessionals', educated people with no clinical training, for effectiveness in carrying out a variety of psychotherapeutic treatments. They came to the unpalatable conclusion that the paraprofessionals were, on average, rather more effective.

This review was later criticized by Berman and Norton (1985) because it included studies in which the designation of therapists into the two groups was somewhat arbitrary: some of the people labelled professional had no training in psychology, and some labelled paraprofessional had an academic training which could be considered relevant to psychotherapy. They considered that eleven out of the forty-three studies were invalid for these and other methodological reasons. They then re-analysed the data from the remaining thirty-two studies and found that the advantage of the paraprofessionals was no longer apparent. However, there was no advantage for the professionals either: both groups were judged to be equally effective, both at the end of treatment and at follow-up. Differential treatment effects failed to emerge when the various problems treated and methods of treatment were considered separately, and the only variables that distinguished the two groups were the age of the patient (professionals doing better with older and paraprofessionals with younger patients) and the length of the treatment (professionals doing better in shorter and paraprofessionals in longer treatments).

The success of those without professional expertise raises awkward questions about the nature of this expertise. Training gives the therapist a theory, some techniques and a professional status, but how valuable are these when it comes to helping people?

The 'paraprofessionals' in the studies reviewed above seem to have been intelligent people, given permission to try to help others with their problems. They may have had some simple instructions or guidelines, but were not trained to believe in a theory of human functioning and behaviour change: they had no model to guide them. A model simplifies the baffling complexity of all the information coming from an individual and often gives a helpful analogy: it is *as if* he has regressed to an anal level, is suffering primal pain, has learnt faulty habits, has more than one personality or has misconstrued his experiences. Part of the appeal of psychotherapy may lie in its claim to explain behaviour by a model. This has been called a 'higher order framework' (Mahrer 1989), which is assumed to 'go beyond' or 'delve beneath' the surface confusion. Well-trained therapists may be discouraged from naively addressing themselves to the problem that appears to be staring them in the face: 'We believe the tendency of many psychotherapists to ignore the traditional nosological categories and to concentrate simply on the patient's problems is restrictive and may lead to unfortunate consequences' (Beck *et al.* 1979: 23). However, the framework itself is restrictive; it always simplifies, and may at times provide blinkers rather than illumination. Those without training may sometimes be at an advantage in having rather more to look at.

The techniques acquired by training may also be double edged. Recently there seems to have been a proliferation of manuals and 'workbooks' (e.g. Langs 1985; Beck *et al.* 1979; Luborsky 1984) in which verbatim extracts of therapy sessions play a large part and readers are encouraged to model their responses on those demonstrated. Rogers's claim (1957) about the importance of the therapist's personal qualities of warmth, empathy and genuineness had earlier generated training methods in which students were coached to increase their 'response repertoires' and to simulate these qualities (Truax *et al.* 1964). Therapy sessions were observed through one-way screens or taped, so that students could learn, not about patients, but about therapists. This assumption that the therapist needs to be told how to respond at every turn continues to be prevalent. Mahrer (1989) insists that detailed operating instructions have always been an essential component of any theory of psychotherapy: 'The theory provided a working manual of conditions-operations-consequences. If a theory did not include this component, the therapist would not know what to do, or when to do what, or what to try to do it for' (Mahrer 1989: 50).

Perhaps this rehearsal of responses can be another handicap to the trained therapist. Individual psychotherapy is a personal encounter between two people, one of whom has the task of helping the other. An untrained person will draw on a host of perceptions and skills for this task, will adjust instinctively to the individual in front of her and proceed by a hit-or-miss approach until she finds something that seems to work. This strategy seems to be denied to well-trained therapists, who are expected to follow instructions and model themselves on the masters, rather than to risk being themselves. In addition to this, they have laboriously learnt how to express genuineness, empathy and warmth, only to be left with the embarrassing knowledge that their patients value these qualities only because they assume that they are spontaneous.

Theory and practice

> *The truth is, hardly any of us have ethical energy enough for more than one really inflexible point of honour.*
>
> (Shaw 1911)

Psychotherapists do seem to be able to help people; perhaps because they often manage to outgrow the handicaps imposed by their training. Wherever two or three psychotherapists are gathered together, confessions gradually emerge about their deviations from orthodoxy. Occasionally these confessions even reach the literature.

A psychoanalyst tells us of his lapses:

> The proper attitude for the practice of psychotherapy is, as Freud termed it, one of benevolent neutrality. But when I reflected how I actually functioned from session to session, it was evident that I actually deviated from this ideal on numerous occasions. My attitude varied from patient to patient, and even within the same session could shift from the empathic to the confrontational and back again. Most disturbing was the recognition that with some patients I was often inclined to be challenging, while with others it was difficult not to be empathic . . . both states seemed a long way from the dispassionate objectivity required of the analyst, yet both the 'healer' and the 'exorcist' proved on occasion to be therapeutically effective. . . . I began to reconsider whether what I had feared were serious lapses from good practice might, in fact, be time honoured therapeutic responses appropriate to the patient at that time.
>
> (Field 1990: 274)

A 'scientist practitioner' wrestles with the conflict between his actions and the theory that is supposed to underpin them:

> I found myself drawn toward particular methods of listening to what patients said, toward attractive directions of therapeutic change, toward explicit principles of therapeutic change, and especially toward what seemed to be effective therapeutic stratagems – yet none of these seemed to connect too well to existential-humanistic notions about human beings and even seemed to conflict at too many points. The choice was to continue to muddle around in arriving at some way of doing therapy, to try to ignore the jarring disconnections . . . or to revise the existential humanistic theory of human beings.
>
> (Mahrer 1989: 54)

As usual, theory gave way to practical expediency and was adjusted to give 'a reasonably high goodness of fit' with therapy (Mahrer 1989: 54).

The need for theoretical adjustment can have serious consequences. Richard Wessler was for several years a director of training and staff supervisor at the Institute for Rational Emotive Therapy (RET); he also edited the RET journal, *Rational Living*. He was identified with, and financially dependent on, one particular school of therapy, but gradually discovered that what worked with his patients did not fit the dogma. He tells Windy Dryden (1985) how this led him, with regret, to bite the hand that fed him and suffer excommunication:

> I found myself becoming increasingly dissatisfied and began to make what many people thought were innovative interventions. . . . So as I was developing my practical ideas about how best to work with clients, I began to face the dilemma which arose from my actual therapy work becoming increasingly at variance with my position as a spokesman for RET. My conscience began to trouble me. Somebody who is a spokesman for a particular point of view I think ought to practise what he teaches . . . if we are going to teach other people a set of techniques or procedures or a point of view, I think we are obliged to follow those ourselves. . . . I have had the experience of novice therapists saying to me: 'Why doesn't this work? I'm doing exactly what Albert Ellis did. Why isn't it working?' And what can I say, except to tell them that . . . he doesn't do what he says he does all the time. In fact the RET that he demonstrates and people so eagerly try to duplicate when they become enthusiastic about RET is something he almost never does. . . . Now, at the Institute for Rational Emotive Therapy I know that none of the supervisors and none of the therapists there practise rational-emotive therapy in a pure sense, I don't know why they don't acknowledge this.
>
> (Wessler, in Dryden 1985: 82–5)

Accommodating psychotherapy

Most people fall back on the old rule that if you cannot have what you believe in you must believe in what you have.

(Shaw 1911)

The proclamations of such heretics, together with the embarrassing multiplicity of therapeutic faiths, have given strength to an ecumenical movement. This allows therapists respectably to declare themselves 'eclectic' or 'multimodal', and thus widen the options that are open to them and their patients. There are no practical problems with this approach, which follows logically from Frank's (1973) demonstration of the commonalities between therapies; but for many it is distasteful because it loosens the connection between the therapist's actions and his ideology, and therefore threatens his status as scientist. Eclecticism must be legitimized by some unifying theoretical structure (Prochaska and DiClemente 1985; Mahrer 1989).

Mahrer addresses himself to the problems of achieving this integration and urges that all practices be related to some 'theory about human beings'. He hopes that this will limit the 'mushrooming proliferation' of therapies, which he deplores, and that, as the result of integration

We will become much more sophisticated in spelling out our theories
of psychotherapy, in locating and strengthening areas of looseness, in
evaluating the soundness of our theories, and in knowing how to improve the inner conceptual structure of our theories.

(Mahrer 1989: 178)

His fear is that the urge to integrate will simply lead to a further proliferation, this time of the 'integrative super-frameworks' that are superimposed
on the original therapies. This would have the consequence foreseen by
Frank:

levelling out most psychotherapies, accepting that most therapies are
essentially similar to each other, masking genuine differences and
highlighting commonalities, and therefore justifying each therapist doing
that individual's brand of therapy.

(Mahrer 1989: 180)

Frank (1973) punctuated *Persuasion and Healing* with quotations from *Alice's
Adventures in Wonderland* and *Through the Looking Glass*. When the Dodo
was asked who had won the Caucus race, he replied 'Everybody has won
and all must have prizes'. This was Frank's assessment of the current research
findings of equivalent efficacy of different therapies. Luborsky *et al.* (1975)
later picked up the quote to make the same point in their review and we
now have the 'Dodo' view repeatedly debated. Many seem to share Mahrer's
aversion to it, but their arguments seem to owe more to professional self-
interest than to logic.

Stultifying consequences for psychotherapy research can be foreseen if
scientific curiosity is blunted by acceptance of the Dodo view. . . . We
end up with the same advice for everyone – 'Regardless of the nature
of your problem, seek *any* form of psychotherapy'. This is absurd. We
doubt whether even the strongest advocates of the Dodo bird argument
dispense this advice. If they begin to do so, they (and the profession as
a whole) will quickly earn the deserved contempt of their clients.

(Rachman and Wilson 1980: 257)

Psychotherapy in the market-place

*Private medical practice is governed not by science but by supply and
demand; and however scientific a treatment may be, it cannot hold
its place in the market place if there is no demand for it; nor can the
grossest quackery be kept off the market if there is a demand for it.*

(Shaw 1911)

Psychotherapy is both a personal encounter and a business. As a business it
is thriving, despite the worries of the theoreticians. Those who offer psychotherapy within the British National Health Service usually have long waiting lists and those who offer it privately are prospering.

To the chagrin of the United Kingdom Standing Conference for Psychotherapy, anyone in Britain can call himself a psychotherapist and offer his services. However, most people who wish to do so recognize the importance of qualifications, since people seeking help will look for an expert, especially if they know that the help will cost them money. Training courses therefore abound; they do not always fulfil all the functions of instruction, practice and initiation, but what they do usually promise successful students is a diploma or certificate with which they will be able to impress their future clients.

The growing interest in magical or 'paranormal' ideas is reflected both in the variety of courses offered (for example, 'Psychic counselling', 'The use of Tarot'), and the treatments given, by these private-sector therapists. There seems to be a merging of superstition, fortune-telling, religion and psychotherapy; with clairvoyants, spiritualists and priests all offering 'counselling', and psychotherapists drawing on a variety of magical systems in addition to those that are reputed to be scientific. Astrology is once again being used, as it was before the eighteenth century, as a framework to help the healer. 'Alternative' medicine challenges today's knowledge with its 'ancient wisdom', and doubtless succeeds in much the same way as the medicine of eighty years ago.

Two psychologists, Greene and Sasportas (1987) somehow manage to combine a system which explains behaviour in terms of genetic and environmental influences, with one which claims it is influenced by the position that certain stars and planets occupied in the sky at the moment when that individual was born. They organize seminars in 'psychological astrology' and welcome the fact that astrologists' clients are now turning to them not only for prediction but also for personal help: 'The consultant astrologer has arrived as a counsellor . . . for the most part astrology has responded to this new role by accepting the psychological dimension of the study and . . . astrology is taking its place among the helping professions' (Greene and Sasportas 1987: xii). Greene and Sasportas use astrology in the same way that other psychotherapists use their theoretical frameworks:

> Astrology gives meaning to people's lives. A man experiencing a difficult marriage, with Venus square Pluto, can be helped if he can find some meaning or relevance in his relationship troubles. . . . Psychological astrology can . . . provide a surgical scalpel which cuts through to the underlying motives, complexes and family inheritance which lie behind the manifest problems and difficulties which the individual faces.
>
> (Greene and Sasportas 1987: xiii)

Psychotherapy and magic share a similar appeal, they both offer the hope of transformation. They are both likely to flourish when people feel emotionally needy and are looking for some meaning to their lives (Smail 1987; 1988). They also make use of similar processes, as Frank (1973) pointed out, and depend upon belief in some rationale. This rationale usually finds expression in some form of healing ritual in which the subject is encouraged to have complete faith.

The psychotherapist's dilemma

There is no harder scientific fact in the world than the fact that belief can be produced in practically unlimited quantity and intensity, without observation or reasoning, and even in defiance of both, by the simple desire to believe, founded on a strong interest in believing.

(Shaw 1911)

Psychotherapists' stance as scientific experts makes them reluctant to use methods that work in ways they do not understand. Perhaps this explains the marginal position of hypnosis as a therapeutic technique, despite its acknowledged power to enable therapists to influence their patients.

Freud used hypnosis before he developed psychoanalysis. He later discarded it because he believed that if the patient lost his symptoms simply by suggestion, rather than by uncovering and working through the trauma that had led to their development, any improvement must be short lived and illusory. Hypnosis bypassed his theoretical framework and was therefore an illegitimate short cut. Similar scruples seem to prevent its widespread use by psychotherapists today. It is thought to be cheating to use persuasion on its own, unsubstantiated by any therapeutic rationale. Thus the use of hypnosis is rarely included in the lengthier training courses for psychotherapists. As well as lacking an ideology, it has the disadvantage of requiring the therapist to adopt the posture of a faith healer in relation to his patient, whom he might prefer to engage as a collaborator or pupil.

At a time when a growing band of astrologers, spiritualists and 'new age' magicians are capitalizing on the demand for guidance and enlightenment, most professionally trained psychotherapists vehemently distance themselves from anything that smacks of charlatanism, ignoring the possibility that unscientific practices may actually help a lot of people. There is a horror of any treatment that is 'just a placebo', however well it works. Thus psychotherapists, unwilling to resort to trickery, must either restrict their practices to those that they believe to be theoretically sound, or must try to persuade themselves that they understand the mechanism behind those that seem to work.

In trying to maintain their position as scientific experts, psychotherapists are in danger of losing sight of their patients and the world that they live in. Psychotherapy is sometimes spoken of as though it were an end in itself rather than a way of helping people. Patients are used for demonstration purposes and treated according to therapists' needs to prove themselves. There are institutions (e.g. Centre for Cognitive Therapy, Institute for Rational-Emotive Therapy, Centre for Personal Construct Psychology) for the promotion of 'own brands' of therapy, where any deviation from the true design is frowned upon. Despite the movement towards integration, reputations are still built, and fortunes made, on distinctiveness. Workshops foster this, as one performer notes: 'Why would anyone come to a workshop in which I get up and say I'm doing what everybody else is doing?' (Wessler, in Dryden 1985: 83).

Therapists may try to convince themselves that what they are doing is in their patients' interests, but when patients fail to improve, they are more likely to try another technique or blame their original formulation than to question whether psychotherapy is what this person really needs. Turning to friends, going to church, getting a job or simply having a rest may be far better solutions for some people. Because of this there are dangers in any ideology, whether based on science or frankly magical, that claims to provide solutions to the difficult business of living.

The only things people can ever hope fully to understand are those they have made themselves. Perhaps this is why, as Smail (1987) points out, most models of human behaviour are analogies with manmade objects.

> Even those 'humanistic' therapies which loudly disavow a mechanistic approach, in fact almost without exception treat human beings as if they were mechanically constructed and understandable in terms of analogies with (depending on the history of the particular theory) steam engines, telephone exchanges or digital computers. In order to belong to the 'scientific' club it is virtually out of the question for psychological theorists to characterise people in any other way, and it is impossible to belong to any other club while expecting at the same time to gain professional 'credibility'.
>
> (Smail 1987: 39)

Doctors have the advantage of being able to observe, to some extent, the workings of the body. They have therefore made some progress since Shaw's day. The workings of the mind will never be open to the same inspection. Psychiatrists (and, regrettably, some psychologists) attempt to understand the mind in terms of its neurological correlates, thus giving themselves a medical model to justify their interventions. Like psychotherapists, they are apt to mistake description for explanation and to reify hypothetical concepts. They thus forget that the 'mental illnesses' that they successfully treat are useful analogies rather than scientific facts. Kendall's (1975) admission – 'In spite of numerous casual claims to the contrary, we have not yet established the existence of any disease entities within our territory' – seems likely to remain true, but will not deter psychiatrists from their activities. Both psychiatrist and psychotherapist are able to use their imperfect and grossly simplified models to good effect, but can become dangerous when they imagine that they have a complete understanding of their patients, and can repair them as they would a faulty engine.

If psychotherapy is seen as just one way of helping troubled people, options are increased for both therapist and patient. The challenge for psychotherapists must be to see whether it is possible to abandon some of their pretensions and still be of use to their patients. Patients and therapists alike are prey to mythical systems. Magical beliefs abound because they impose order and hope on incomprehensible and uncontrollable reality, and psychotherapy can seduce its participants into a collaboration which relieves feelings of helplessness on both sides. There are times when people can be served best by being encouraged to have less faith in experts and more in themselves. The problem is that the advice is more likely to be accepted, and less likely to be given, if it comes from someone whom they consider to be an expert.

> *The true doctor is inspired by a hatred of ill-health, and a divine impatience with any waste of vital forces ... his motives in choosing the career of a healer are clearly generous.*
>
> (Shaw 1911)

References

Beck, A.T., Rush, A.J., Shaw, B.F. and Emery, G. (1979) *Cognitive Therapy of Depression*. New York: Guilford.

Beecher, H.K. (1961) Surgery as placebo. *Journal of the American Medical Association* **176**: 1102–7.

Berman, J.S. and Norton, N.C. (1985) Does professional training make a therapist more effective? *Psychological Bulletin* **98**: 401–7.

Berne, E. (1964) *Games People Play*. Harmondsworth: Penguin.

Berne, E. (1975) *Transactional Analysis in Psychotherapy*. London: Souvenir Press.

Critelli, J.W. and Neumann, K.F. (1984) The placebo: a conceptual analysis of a concept in transition. *American Psychologist* **39**: 32–9.

Dryden, W. (1985) *Therapists' Dilemmas*. London: Harper & Row.

Field, N. (1990) Healing, exorcism and object relations theory. *British Journal of Psychotherapy* **6**: 274–84.

Foster, J. (1971) *Enquiry into the Practice and Effects of Scientology*. London: HMSO.

Frank, J.D. (1973) *Persuasion and Healing*, 2nd edn. Baltimore, Md: Johns Hopkins University Press.

Frank, J.D. (1989) Non-specific aspects of treatment: the view of a psychotherapist, in M. Shepherd and N. Sartorius (eds) *Non-Specific Aspects of Treatment*, Toronto: Hans Huber.

Freud, S. (1977) *Two Short Accounts of Psychoanalysis*. Harmondsworth: Penguin.

Greene, L. and Sasportas, H. (1987) *The Development of the Personality: Seminars in Psychological Astrology*. London: Routledge & Kegan Paul.

Grunbaum, A. (1989) The placebo concept in medicine and psychiatry, in M. Shepherd and N. Sartorius (eds) *Non-Specific Aspects of Treatment*. Toronto: Hans Huber.

Hattie, J.A., Sharpley, C.F. and Rogers, H.J. (1984) Comparative effectiveness of professional and paraprofessional helpers. *Psychological Bulletin* **95**: 534–41.

Howard, M. (1980) *Candle Burning: Its Occult Significance*. Wellingborough, Northants: Aquarian.

Imber, S.D. *et al.* (1990) Mood specific effects among three treatments for depression. *Journal of Consulting and Clinical Psychology* **58**: 352–9.

Kendall, R.E. (1975) *The Role of Diagnosis in Psychiatry*. Oxford: Basil Blackwell.

Langs, R. (1985) *Workbooks for Psychotherapists*. Emerson, NJ: Newconcept Press.

Luborsky, L. (1984) *Principles of Psychoanalytic Psychotherapy: A Manual for Supportive Expressive Treatment (SE)*. New York: Basic Books.

Luborsky, L., Singer, B. and Luborsky, L. (1975) Comparative studies of psychotherapies: is it true that everyone has won and all must have prizes? *Archives of General Psychiatry* 32: 995–1,008.

Mahrer, A.R. (1989) *The Integration of Psychotherapies*. New York: Human Sciences Press.

Marks, I.M. (1978) Behavioural psychotherapy of adult neuroses, in S.L. Garfield and A.E. Bergin (eds) *Handbook of Psychotherapy and Behaviour Change*, 2nd edn. New York: Wiley.

Orlinsky, D.E. and Howard, K.I. (1986) Process and outcome in psychotherapy, in S.L. Garfield and A.E. Bergin (eds) *Handbook of Psychotherapy and Behaviour Change*, 3rd edn. New York: Wiley.

Pedder, J.R. (1989) Courses in psychotherapy: evolution and current trends. *British Journal of Psychotherapy* 6: 203–21.

Prochaska, J.O. and DiClemente, C.C. (1985) Transtheoretical therapy: toward a more integrative model of change. *Psychotherapy: Theory and Practice* 19: 276–88.

Rachman, S.J. and Wilson, G.T. (1980) *The Effects of Psychological Therapy*, 2nd edn. Oxford: Pergamon.

Rachman, S.J., Cobb, J., Grey, S., *et al.* (1979) The behavioural treatment of obsessional-compulsive disorders, with and without clomiprimine. *Behaviour Research and Therapy* 17: 467–78.

Rogers, C.R. (1957) The necessary and sufficient conditions of therapeutic personality change. *Journal of Consulting Psychology* 21: 95–103.

Rowan, J. (1976) *Ordinary Ecstasy*. London: Routledge & Kegan Paul.

Rowan, J. (1989) The self: one or many? *The Psychologist* 2: 279–81.

Shapiro, A.K. and Morris, L.A. (1978) The placebo effect in medical and psychological therapies, in S.L. Garfield and A.E. Bergin (eds) *Handbook of Psychotherapy and Behaviour Change*, 2nd edn. New York: Wiley.

Shaw, G.B. (1911) Preface on Doctors, *The Doctor's Dilemma*, standard edn (1932). London: Constable.

Sieghart, P. (1978) *Statutory Registration of Psychotherapists: Report of a Professions' Joint Working Party*. Cambridge: Plumbridge.

Smail, D. (1987) Psychotherapy and 'change': some ethical considerations, in S. Fairbairn and G. Fairbairn (eds) *Psychology, Ethics and Change*. London: Routledge & Kegan Paul.

Smail, D. (1988) Magic, manipulation and clinical psychology. *Changes* 6: 76–80.

Smith, M.L., Glass, G.V. and Miller, T.I. (1980) *The Benefits of Psychotherapy*. Baltimore, Md: Johns Hopkins University Press.

Spanos, N.S. (1989) Hypnosis, demonic possession and multiple personality, in C.A. Ward (ed.) *Altered States of Consciousness and Mental Health: A Cross Cultural Perspective*. Newbury Park, Calif: Sage.

Stiles, W.B. and Shapiro, D.A. (1988) Abuse of the drug metaphor in psychotherapy process-outcome research. *Clinical Psychology Review* 58: 352–9.

Strupp, H.H. (1973) *Psychotherapy: Clinical Research and Theoretical Issues*. New York: Jason Aronson.

Taylor, S.E. and Brown, J.D. (1988) Illusion and well-being: a social psychological perspective on mental health. *Psychological Bulletin* 103: 193–210.

Thomas, K. (1971) *Religion and the Decline of Magic*. London: Weidenfeld & Nicolson.

Thomas, K.B. (1987) General practice consultations: is there any point in being positive? *British Medical Journal* **294**: 1,200–2.

Truax, C.B., Carkhuff, R.R. and Douds, J. (1964) Toward an integration of the didactic and experiential approaches to training in counselling and psychotherapy. *Journal of Counselling Psychology* **11**: 240–7.

Vinar, O. (1969) Dependence on a placebo: a case report. *British Journal of Psychiatry* **115**: 1,189–90.

Wolpe, J. (1973) *The Practice of Behaviour Therapy*. Elmsford, NY: Pergamon.

Wolpe, J. and Lazarus, A.A. (1966) *Behaviour Therapy Techniques: A Guide to the Treatment of Neuroses*. Oxford: Pergamon.

WHO (World Health Organization) (1987) I.C.D. 10 1986: Draft of ch. 5. Geneva: WHO.

RESPONSE – *John Rowan*

There is a story told in some places that psychotherapy is carried out by scientist practitioners. This is put forward as an ideal and believed to be a reality, at least in most cases. It doesn't have a lot of evidence to support it, however, and the sceptic might be forgiven for doubting whether it really amounts to a row of beans. But it is this story which Katharine Mair refers to constantly through her argument, usually to accuse psychotherapists of pretensions beyond their station in life.

The reason why psychotherapy is not conducted by scientist practitioners is that the scientists (that is, the people who try to conduct research into psychotherapy) have become remote from the practitioners. Greenberg tells us:

> After decades of research the amount of well established knowledge about what affects therapeutic outcomes is disappointingly meagre. Research of the sort done in the last decade, although approaching clinical relevance, still has not offered much to practising clinicians.
>
> (Greenberg 1981)

More recently, Mahrer (1985) has told us that such research has very little effect on actual therapeutic practice, and that he would rather read transcripts and listen to tapes of other psychotherapists. Perhaps most therapists would say that in addition to these sources, the main way in which they have learned about what works and what does not work are first of all from their own therapy (whether individual or group) and from their clients. Of course both of these are very limited, and no one would claim that they amount to being scientific about it.

It is difficult for the ordinary person to realize just how irrelevant most of the research actually is. In the Beutler *et al.* chapter (1986) which we shall mention later on, the authors even say at one point that precision and relevance are opposed, as though that were a well-known fact, instead of an unacceptable contradiction.

Mair does not appear to know about this gap between scientists and practitioners. Her key paragraph reads like this:

> Psychotherapists today vary in the extent to which they invoke science as a justification for their activities, but few seem to be prepared to see themselves simply as faith healers. Science enjoys prestige and power, and many psychotherapists have themselves had lengthy scientific educations. They want their efficacy to be based on their ability to relate the complaints of their clients to a body of scientific knowledge, which enables them to understand mental processes and make interventions which bring about change in a predictable way. Above all, they want to understand what is going on.

This does not agree with my experience, nor with the experience of those with whom I have talked in depth. First there are more possibilities than just *either* scientist *or* faith healer. What seems very common is for psychotherapists to have several theories (some more scientific, others less), and to find one useful in one situation, another useful in another situation. This is a kind of post-modern attitude to their work, which they adopted long before the expression 'post-modern' was invented. It entails a denial of the idea that there is or should be just one 'body of scientific knowledge' to which all questions can be referred, and answers given. As for the 'lengthy scientific educations' which psychotherapists are supposed to have (some do, some do not), ask any practitioner how much use the scientific education actually is in daily practice, and you will get a pretty dusty answer. The usable part is generally less than 10 per cent of what was actually offered, and sometimes less than 1 per cent.

So what Mair is doing, when you look at it clearly, is to say that either psychotherapists are scientists basing their work on proven fact, or else they are nothing more than faith healers or purveyors of placebos. They are not scientists, though they may be pseudo-scientists, so they must be con artists, deceiving the public through their rhetoric, but really having nothing to offer other than a place to huddle together waiting for improvements to appear. I am arguing that both sides of this dichotomy are wrong.

Let us have a closer look at this business of being a scientist, in case anyone is convinced that this is what psychotherapists ought to aim at. Let us look at what the genuine scientists actually do.

Outcome research

Mair goes mainly to outcome research in her attempt to show that therapists of all persuasions, trained or untrained, get much the same results. This is a point which has often been made before, so much so that I think it has become part of the received wisdom. Why I think it is dubious is that it relies on outcome research, which is perhaps about the weakest area in the whole field of psychological research.

If we take as our exemplar the standard work on outcome research, Garfield and Bergin (1986), and look at the chapter on therapist variables in outcome research, we find a very interesting state of affairs. The chapter is neatly divided into four sections, according to whether the research was about matters external or internal to the therapist, and external or internal to psychotherapy as such. But the interesting thing is – and I didn't believe this myself until I went through it line by line – that every single piece of research turns out to be minimally revealing. In each case, whatever variable one looks at, the answer seems to be the same – either there is no effect, or the effect is very small, or the answers are confused in some way. No clear results emerge at all. And the best-controlled studies tell us virtually nothing about psychotherapy as ordinarily practised. What conclusions do our authors come to themselves? Here is one quotation from the section marked 'Conclusions':

> With the awareness that unidirectional studies have produced largely weak and inconclusive results, increasing attention is being directed to understanding complex interactions between the therapist, the intervention, the patient and the nature of outcome.
>
> (Beutler *et al.* 1986: 298)

This seems to be saying that we can't do something relatively easy, so let's try something more difficult instead. These are really very unimpressive results indeed, and I can only believe in the end that this kind of research is fundamentally flawed.

So when Mair quotes these studies, to show how unimportant the differences are between different psychotherapies, this does not impress me much, because they do not in fact show very much at all, one way or another. It is not just me who says this. We have already seen some conclusions from people who have examined this work, and the way in which these researchers do not even seem very perturbed about the gap between precision and relevance.

This calm acceptance of the unacceptable becomes quite unbelievable at times. A recent large volume on process research (Greenberg and Pinsof 1986) makes the excellent and totally valid point that process research and outcome research are mutually necessary. Basing outcome research on ascribed or alleged orientations without actual verification is equivalent to giving blue and green pills to patients in a drug study without knowing the content of the pills. Similarly, process research which pays no attention to outcome is inadequate and one-sided in its complementary way: for instance, to know that certain behaviour therapists convey high levels of warmth and support to their patients during desensitization is interesting, but did their high level of warmth and support make any kind of meaningful difference?

Well, that all makes sense and leads in to the rest of the book, with its detailed examinations of many different systems of measuring or describing the process of psychotherapy. But 720 pages later, Greenberg is saying this:

A study of the relationship between the three variables therapist intervention (T), client process (C) and outcome (O), however, poses a difficult 'three-variable' problem for traditional experimental designs. Although it is possible to study the relationship between any two in both correlational and experimental designs, the task of relating all three at the same time is difficult . . . unless T is shown to cause C and cause O at the same time, the nature of the *direction* of the causal relationship between T and C always remains in doubt and one never knows whether it is T or C which leads to O. [To research this problem adequately] appears beyond the capabilities of current research procedures.

(Greenberg and Pinsof 1986: 726)

So after all the work has been done, and all the research surveyed, all that the authors can do in the end is to throw up their hands, and say in effect – let the next generation do it.

Most of what Mair says about 'active ingredients' and the 'placebo problem' has to be looked at in this light. Like most other writers, she takes outcome research at face value, but this is just what I am suggesting we cannot do.

Now this kind of research has been going on for over a hundred years now, and the old paradigm is wearing thin and running out of excuses. I think we have to move to a new paradigm of research which does not even attempt to talk about variables, but which talks instead about people, and to people, and with people. This is not the place to go into all that, which has been fully described and discussed elsewhere (Reason and Rowan 1981; Lincoln and Guba 1985; Mahrer 1985).

But the final conclusion must be that the kind of research which is being relied on by Mair for many of her conclusions is arid, sterile, and unlikely to bring results in the next hundred years. She, and we, and all of us had better just give it up.

Mair's five examples

Coming back now to Mair's argument, what we are now saying is that it is not OK to say that all therapists are equal: it is much more true to say that we do not know whether they are or not. In fact we really know extraordinarily little about how psychotherapy works. It is only the research of Mahrer and people like him which may eventually tell us.

One of the things which has happened in recent years is that there has been more adoption of the point of view of holistic health, which says that the patient makes a contribution to the success or otherwise of the treatment. Mair actually quotes this work, and makes much of it. But of course, if this is true even in ordinary medicine, it is much more obviously true in the case of psychotherapy. It is the work of the client which produces the results: all that the therapist can do is to facilitate that, to make it more possible, to help with the unhindering process.

A psychotherapist who takes on the job of curing the client, and feels committed to that, and disappointed if it does not happen, is deeply into counter-transference, and needs to be confronted, perhaps by a good supervisor or other trusted friend. A real psychotherapist has to be genuinely with the client, not with some future projection of what the client *should* be like. Mair continually makes comparisons with medicine, as if psychotherapy were like mending a broken leg, or giving an antibiotic for an infection. The holistic approach says that even ordinary medicine does not have to be like this, never mind psychotherapy.

In order to clinch the matter, Mair gives us five examples of how some quite genuine observations and conjectures can become extended and elaborated into a self-serving dogma which owes nothing to scientific inquiry. The first one is Freud and psychoanalysis. I don't like the way in which Mair sets this one up, as if psychoanalysts went gung-ho for cure and kept on quoting success figures and claiming to be scientific. In my experience psychoanalysts are not like this, even as an ideal, never mind as a general practice. And Freud himself was certainly very reticent about the idea of selling psychoanalysis as a cure for anything.

The second one is Aaron Beck and cognitive therapy. Here she seems to have a better case, that something which originally was specifically about depression was just extended without any great justification to other forms of mental distress.

The third example is behaviour therapy. Here we definitely do have people claiming to be scientific, and I think Mair is quite right to throw some cold water on this claim, though I think she does it much too briefly. There is some doubt in my mind as to whether behaviour therapy should be counted as psychotherapy at all, if it denies the existence of the psyche.

The fourth example is transactional analysis. Eric Berne was of course a maverick, a fascinating character, who I think tried to be quite precise, but not exactly scientific. He was more interested in making his ideas accessible than bombproof. So I don't think there is too much wrong here.

The fifth and final example is a more general point about the world within, and here Mair kindly quotes my work on subpersonalities as demonstrating this. Unfortunately she mixes this up with the psychiatric category of multiple personality, which is both qualitatively and quantitatively different. So I don't think we can make much of this one. Also it is a pity that she didn't notice that this concept is now in use among psychologists and philosophers, not just by psychotherapists, as was mentioned in the article she quotes, and is made clear in my book (Rowan 1990).

At the end of this examination, then, we come to the conclusion that there certainly are examples to be found of psychotherapies which start out with a great deal of scientific baggage, and then gradually lose it or forget about it. But she does not show, and I do not believe, that the model of the scientist-practitioner is very common (though lip-service is paid to it from time to time when funds are needed for research).

How does psychotherapy work?

I quite like Mair's approach to this final question, and think her points quoted from Frank make a lot of sense. However, where I think she goes wrong is in regarding training in spontaneity as not really spontaneous. This is one of the great paradoxes, like the parallel paradox in meditation, that you have to try very hard to give up trying hard. The reason why most people are not spontaneous is that they have never really considered the matter, and if they have, have probably confused it with being impulsive. They may also have internal reservations or conflicts about being spontaneous, which have to do with problems about control. This is why therapy for the therapist is so important, and why therapies which steer clear of that tend to talk so much about science and control.

Mair seems to misunderstand training at many levels. Her picture of well-trained therapists following instructions and modelling themselves on the masters, and laboriously expressing genuineness, and never risking being themselves, may be true at early stages in the learning process, just as a learner driver may laboriously work at being in the right gear or making a hill start. But as learning proceeds, the driver speeds up and driving becomes, as we say, second nature. Similarly with psychotherapy and most other skills – once the skills are mastered, the personality of the therapist shines through.

I think Mair is unnecessarily cavalier about professionalism and the United Kingdom Standing Conference for Psychotherapy (UKSCP), which has done a tremendous job under enormously difficult conditions. To hold together in one regular meeting all the various tendencies within psychotherapy, to enable dialogue and mutual understanding to take place, and to find a growing mutual respect emerging, is no mean achievement. Why she thinks that this record of increasing success means that the possibility of agreement dwindles to extinction I do not know. In any case, it is not agreement on theory which is being attempted, but agreement on staying together so that the UKSCP can be recognized by the European Community as the only competent authority in the UK which can speak for all psychotherapists: hopefully thus preventing the atrocious oppression which has taken place in most countries of Europe, where only such psychotherapy as is approved and controlled by the psychiatric establishment is allowed to take place. Those countries where strict control is also exercised by the psychological establishment are regarded on the Continent as liberal. The UKSCP stands for a system by which free organizations freely combine into groupings with explicit criteria of membership, which can be scrutinized and modified by mutual criticism. This exists nowhere outside the UK, and it is a credit to all of us who have been involved since its inception. It is the best approach to professionalism I have ever seen, and I don't want Mair or anyone else slagging it off.

Conclusion

Psychotherapists are much more honest with themselves than Mair suggests. Recent books such as Kutash and Wolf (1986), Dryden and Spurling (1989) and Mearns and Dryden (1990) are full of excellent material about this. Few of them regard themselves as 'scientific experts', a phrase which Mair throws around again and again. The whole idea of being a scientific expert has received many knocks in recent years, and even physicists and chemists are a bit reluctant to make such claims nowadays. It is more fashionable, and actually makes more sense, to point to the elegance of a theory or the fruitfulness of a model, and abandon claims for fundamental truth or finality. To keep on calling psychotherapists 'scientific experts' does rather smack of setting something up in order to be able to knock it down. The scientist practitioner is in practice vanishingly rare.

I would go along with her notion that psychotherapy is just one way of helping troubled people. Psychotherapy can abandon all its false pretensions and still be of use to people in need. People can be served best by being encouraged to have less faith in experts and more in themselves. And this is just what happens when psychotherapy is successful.

References

Beutler, L.E. *et al.* (1986) Therapist variables in psychotherapy process and outcome, in S.L. Garfield and A.E. Bergin (eds) *Handbook of Psychotherapy and Behaviour Change*, 3rd edn. New York: Wiley.

Dryden, W. and Spurling, L. (1989) *On Becoming a Psychotherapist*. London: Routledge.

Garfield, S.L. and Bergin, L.E. (eds) (1986) *Handbook of Psychotherapy and Behaviour Change*, 3rd edn. New York: Wiley.

Greenberg, L.G. (1981) Advances in clinical intervention research: a decade review. *Canadian Psychology* 22(1): 25–34.

Greenberg, L.S. and Pinsof, W.M. (1986) *The Psychotherapeutic Process: A Research Handbook*. New York: Guilford.

Kutash, I.L. and Wolf, A. (eds) (1986) *Psychotherapist's Casebook*. San Francisco: Jossey Bass.

Lincoln, Y.S. and Guba, E.G. (1985) *Naturalistic Inquiry*. Beverly Hills, Calif: Sage.

Mahrer, A.R. (1985) *Psychotherapeutic Change*. New York: W.W. Norton.

Mearns, D. and Dryden, W. (1990) *Experiences of Counselling in Action*. London: Sage.

Reason, P. and Rowan, J. (1981) *Human Inquiry: A Sourcebook of New Paradigm Research*. Chichester: Wiley.

Rowan, J. (1990) *Subpersonalities*. London: Routledge.

REBUTTAL – Katharine Mair

There are many definitions of science, but most of them include the notions of knowledge and of study: science is knowledge acquired through study. This study involves observation, classification and measurement; it is sys-

tematic and will generate theories which can be tested. Rowan seems to disapprove of science and claims that 'even physicists and chemists' are today
reluctant to call themselves scientific experts, relating this to the abandonment of claims to fundamental truth or finality. I thought science had
always involved the testing of hypotheses rather than the pronouncement of
truths and that, especially in these post-Popperian days, the subjectivity and
impermanence of scientific theories were well recognized.

I make the point in my chapter that psychotherapists cannot be scientists
because they have to convince their patients that they possess the knowledge and skills that will help them, and they need to convey certainty rather
than doubt. They are thus not in the business of testing hypotheses to
destruction, yet they often invoke the vocabulary and the rhetoric of science
to bolster their credibility as experts. I agree with Rowan that the 'scientist
practitioner' is vanishingly rare, and doubt if he ever really did exist, but in
the practice of psychotherapy Rowan himself demonstrates that the pseudo-
scientist is still with us.

The distinction between science and psuedo-science is an important one
and relates to the distinction between psychotherapy research, which does
attempt to be scientific, and the practice of psychotherapy, which does not.
Rowan wrongly assumes that I am unaware of this distinction and casti-
gates the researchers for becoming remote from the practitioners. I would
regard this distancing as inevitable: the more the researchers appreciate the
complexity of what they are studying, the less they are able to give the clear
answers that the practitioners are asking for. Rowan disapproves of Beutler
et al.'s recognition that any understanding of what actually happens in
psychotherapy will involve trying to untangle the complex interactions of
many different variables and he seems to be blaming the researchers for the
inconclusive results which arise partly from their painstaking attempts to
be scientific. He can legitimately complain that the research is unhelpful,
since it does not produce the results that he would like, or irrelevant, since
psychotherapists seem content to ignore independent evaluations of their
work, but he cannot claim that 'this kind of research is fundamentally
flawed' simply because he is disappointed with its results.

Rowan suggests that I am saying that if psychotherapists are not scientists then they must be 'con artists', deliberately deceiving the public and
having nothing of value to offer them. I am sorry that he should misunderstand me in this way. I think that most psychotherapists believe in what
they do and have a beneficial effect on their patients. In order to do this they
may deceive *themselves* by attributing their effect to an untested theory,
but the value of what they do does not appear to be related to the scientific
merit of its rationale. Belief seems to be a key factor, on the part of both
therapist and patient. When this brings beneficial results, in the absence
of any mechanism that we fully understand, this should be a cause of
celebration, not dismissal as 'only' a placebo effect or 'only' faith healing;
as Frank says: 'Placebos are psychotherapy' and are worthy of respect and
study in their own right.

I agree with Rowan that there is a refreshing lack of dogma in much that has recently been written about psychotherapy, and that the post-modern eclecticism that he advocates may be preferable to former purism. What worries me is that the retreat from dogma seems to be leading us into an 'anything goes' position, where we can fill the gap uncritically with anything as long as it works. So we get psychotherapists talking of astral projections, energy fields and auras, and gradually losing their critical judgement as they see their patients improve. When the discipline of science is rejected along with some of its discarded theories, no ideas will seem to be too outlandish, and scepticism will always be replaced with belief.

Rowan seems to be in the thick of this with his belief in subpersonalities, which he presents, not as useful metaphors, but as facts. He gently reprimands me for confusing subpersonalities with multiple personalities, claiming that these are 'both qualitatively and *quantitatively* different'. I wish he would tell me just what the numerical difference is between sub- and multiple personalities! His dogmatic yet fanciful approach demonstrates that the pseudo-scientist is not a strawman of my construction, but is alive and well, and propagating untestable theories.

Rowan misses my point that these phenomena, like so many others, seem to reveal themselves only to those therapists who specifically look for them. They may be therapeutically useful, but that does not mean that they have an independent existence. He indulges in more pseudo-science when he states that therapists who are disappointed when their clients fail to get better are 'deeply into counter-transference', another dogmatic statement that obfuscates rather than clarifies.

The quandary for psychotherapists is how to maintain their confidence in the absence of a dogma that explains and justifies what they are doing. Can they afford scepticism and will they still be effective if they share their doubts with their patients? If this were possible, psychotherapists might, if they wanted, be able to start calling themselves scientists.

SEVEN

What goes wrong in the care and treatment of the mentally ill

STUART SUTHERLAND

Introduction

The treatment of the mentally ill still depends mainly on common sense, with the exception of the administration of drugs most of which were discovered by serendipity. Even the more effective therapies are largely based on what has come to be known as folk psychology rather than on rigorous scientific ideas. If confronted with a depressive, the natural thing to do is surely to try to make him take a more optimistic view of the world: in this respect cognitive therapy differs from common sense only in that it is more systematized and in that some of its techniques have been validated. The points I have to make may also be regarded as common sense, but they may be none the worse for that. After Adler had given a lecture, a member of the audience approached him saying, 'That was a very interesting lecture, but wasn't it just common sense?' to which Adler replied, 'Yes. It's a pity more psychiatrists don't give lectures like that.'

I shall concentrate not on the treatment of the mentally disordered, but on their maltreatment. This includes the ways in which psychiatrists, psychotherapists and nurses respond to their patients in their contacts with them. Much has been written on this topic, particularly in the 1960s when several novels vilifying psychiatrists appeared, usually with bizarre titles like *One Flew Over the Rose Garden* or *I Never Promised You a Cuckoo's Nest* (sic). There were also books of a more serious but equally hysterical nature, by authors like Laing and Szasz, that took an exaggeratedly antipsychiatric stance. What I have to say differs from such onslaughts in three ways. First it is based on what happens in the best mental hospitals in Britain and in some of the best in the United States. Second, I shall try to make explicit the mistakes which for the most part have previously been only implicitly delineated. Third, I shall point to some of the dilemmas that face psychiatrists and psychotherapists. Their lot is not an easy one, for mental patients can be very demanding people. As I shall show, they have to take very difficult decisions, including whether to commit: if they do so unnecessarily, they lose the patient's co-operation; if they wrongly fail to commit, they may have a suicide on their hands and be summoned before the courts for negligence.

Much of the material I shall use comes from my own experience of psychiatrists and psychotherapists, which I gained over a protracted period of bipolar manic-depressive illness, involving two spells in mental hospitals each of about six weeks. When I was first admitted, I was deeply depressed and extremely agitated, but I had in no sense lost touch with reality and I am certain my observations were accurate. I will support my own observations with those obtained by pseudo-patients, who are rapidly becoming the psychiatrist's greatest occupational hazard. As we shall see, their experiences bear a remarkable similarity to my own.

The best known psuedo-patient study is that of Rosenhan (1973), who had himself and seven of his students admitted to different mental hospitals: each claimed he had heard voices and was given a diagnosis of schizophrenia. Perhaps the most thorough pseudo-patient investigation was conducted by David Reynolds (Reynolds and Farberow 1976). He gave himself a false identity, pretending to be a down-and-out veteran of the US Navy. He was admitted to a Veterans' Hospital, by claiming he had made a suicide attempt and by shamming extreme depression. 'Shamming' is perhaps not the right word, for he claims that in pretending to be depressed, he became genuinely depressed: on several occasions he burst into tears. Of all the pseudo-patients, then, his experiences presumably most resemble those of the genuine article. As a potential suicide, he spent over a week on a locked ward and about a further week on an open one. He had arranged to telephone a friend to come to his rescue, if he could not stand the hospital any longer. The other studies from which I will quote are as follows (a description of the people acting as pseudo-patients and their length of stay in hospital are added): Barry (1971) – journalist, one week; Caudill (1952) – an anthropologist, two months; Deane (1961) – sociologist, one week; Goldman (1970) – a social psychologist and a clinical psychologist, about a fortnight; Mueller and Sherman (1969) – nurses, one day; Rockwell (1973) – psychiatric registrar, three weeks; Weitz (1972) – clinical psychologist, one day.

The reports of all these pseudo-patients are remarkably similar, but I shall use mainly material from Reynolds and myself: my own experiences are written up in more detail in Sutherland (1987). The first edition of that book was published in the same year as Reynolds and Farberow, so that neither of us had read the other's account: moreover neither I nor Reynolds had read any of the reports by other pseudo-patients.

In order to understand why the failings in treatment that I shall list have such serious effects on the mentally ill, it is necessary to understand how such patients feel. I therefore give a brief sketch of the feelings engendered by my own depressions. For much of my waking hours, I was in a state of panic. If you are driving a car and just manage to avoid a serious accident, there is a few seconds' delay and then the bottom of your stomach falls out. I had that feeling day in day out for weeks on end. Like all depressives, I suffered extreme guilt and shame: I thought – wrongly as it turned out – that I had broken down as a result of a particularly loathsome emotion: sexual jealousy. Much of my shame was caused by the feeling that I should have been able to control myself and that the breakdown was my own fault. So obsessed and harrowed was I by my jealous thoughts and images that I could not concentrate sufficiently to read. I simply could not keep one sentence in mind long enough to connect it with the next. An even more significant indicator of my inability to concentrate was that I could not watch television, despite the mindlessness of its outpourings. Because I could not concentrate, I was bored beyond belief: even my own harrowing thoughts became boring but would not go away.

Most depressives suffer from several of these symptoms, but all suffer a further one: the feeling of sheer hopelessness, of having nothing in life to look forward to. When I was depressed, I found no pleasure in eating, in drinking, in shaping clay into hideous bowls in the Occupational Therapy Unit or indeed in anything else in life. Above all, I felt I would never recover: indeed had someone assured me I would recover in a year's time, I believe I would have recovered on the spot. I went through ten depressions, not all of them as severe as the first but none the less nasty enough: despite the fact that I had recovered from the previous nine, I was convinced during the tenth that I would never emerge from it. Some psychiatrists maintain that depression is on a continuum with misery or unhappiness. They can never have been depressed. Subjectively, it is a totally different condition, marked by a complete inability to do anything to help oneself. Sadness can be ennobling; depression is degrading.

Most but not all of what follows is about the treatment of depression (the commonest form of mental illness), but I believe the points I make apply to almost all other forms of mental disorder. The one exception is mania or hypomania: I have experienced that too. Such is the overweening self-confidence of the hypomanic that none of the errors made by psychotherapists can have the least effect on him: he cannot be ruffled, let alone upset.

Sensitivity

Anyone lacking self-confidence is vulnerable to slights whether real or imagined. The depressive lacks confidence to an abnormal degree, so does the agoraphobic. All psychotherapists must realize this if they stop to think: but even if they do, it is not easy to make allowances for the extreme sensitivity of the mentally ill. Here are a few examples of therapists' failure to take account of the patient's sensitivity: some of them are outrageous, others are seemingly trivial but still upsetting for the patient.

Before I was admitted to hospital I was persuaded by my general practitioner (GP) to consult an analyst: he directed me to one of the best known in Britain. The analyst told me in no uncertain terms that I must change and become more sensitive to my feelings. His insistence that I could emerge from depression only by making radical changes in myself, which I felt I could not possibly achieve, only plunged me into a deeper depression: there was no hope. Just as I was becoming dependent on him, he went on holiday (a habit of almost all analysts), having referred me to a much younger analyst.

One always tells therapists what they want to hear, so I told him that when I was about four years old I used to have night fears and my father would come to my bedroom to comfort me. He replied by asserting that I was a latent homosexual. Now, had I been mentally well, I would of course have realized that according to Freud the only people who are not latent homosexuals are practising homosexuals and I would have greeted the remark with a light laugh. As it was I was deeply upset, for although I felt there should be no stigma attached to being a homosexual, as the saying goes, 'I'd rather see than be one'. The analyst subsequently told me that I must have wanted to be 'fucked by my father until the shit ran out'. It should be remembered that he was making these helpful remarks to someone already in a state of extreme panic, agitation and hopelessness. He also told me that I 'had missed out on all the best things in life'. Finally he let me know that I would have to get worse before getting better, a standard psychoanalytic ploy which one cannot help thinking is designed to keep the patient in analysis even though he knows very well, as I did, that the treatment is making him worse rather than better. He told me he had been trained at the British Mecca of psychoanalysis, the Tavistock Clinic. Whether his own lack of sensitivity is typical of those trained there I cannot say.

I eventually gained the courage to have myself admitted to a mental hospital, despite dire warnings from both analysts that they were terrible places from which I might never emerge. With few exceptions, the staff in my mental hospitals were much more aware than the analysts of their patients' sensitivities. But depressives are very easily upset. I had become quite friendly with a black woman nurse, who at one point told me that I should go out and play tennis. I said that I was on such a dose of drugs that it was quite impossible, my co-ordination was too bad. She replied, 'Oh, you're always blaming your troubles on something else'. She may have been right, but this trivial remark rankled with me for a long time. Again, in a normal mood one would just brush it aside.

Although all the pseudo-patients were upset, most of them severely, by their treatment, they were not of course over-sensitive if only because they were not mentally ill. A typical remark is that of one of the nurses (Mueller and Sherman 1969): 'I had the feeling of being a prisoner, as we walked through the tramway in single file'. Further evidence that the pseudo-patients were usually upset by their treatment will be provided in later sections. The sensitivity of genuine patients is borne out by Steven Hughes (1990), a surgeon who had been in the Falklands War. He was subsequently admitted to hospital with post-traumatic stress disorder. Unfortunately, he does not give sufficient details of his treatment, but he does complain of being taken from one hospital to another without notice and of 'never seeing the same person twice'. He writes 'all that [had] happened so far [in hospital] had served only to destabilise me'. His report is marred by the fact that he seems to have expected special treatment because he was a doctor: doctors 'need special efforts to engender reassurance, comfort and stability'. He fails to specify what these special efforts should be, but they were clearly not made. From the other side of the fence, a psychiatrist (Beck 1967) writes that 'the depressed patient is prone to read insults, ridicule or disparagement into what other people say to him. He often interprets neutral remarks as directed against him in some way'.

There can be no excuse for the crass remarks made by my second analyst, but one can ask whether psychotherapists and others should try to avoid upsetting patients by taking their extreme sensitivity into account. For three reasons, I believe they should. First, on humanitarian grounds one should try not to make people who are already desperately upset even more upset. Second, there is usually a suicide risk with severely depressed patients and it is foolish to do anything that might drive them over the brink. Third, the rapidly expanding literature on cognitive therapy suggests that building up patients' self-confidence may alleviate their depression. Upsetting them is likely to have the opposite effect. My own clinical psychologist in the first hospital tried to undo some of the damage done by the analysts by saying 'Your trouble at the moment is not that you are too insensitive to your feelings: you are far too sensitive'. This was a very helpful remark.

Therapists do, however, face a dilemma over their patients' sensitivity. Both analysts set me impossible and rather vague goals, such as becoming more sensitive to my feelings. Setting an impossible goal can only make patients feel worse, since they know they cannot attain it. On the other hand, if they are to recover they must change in some way. It must be extremely difficult for therapists to judge how much change they can realistically ask for at any time. As a matter of fact the clinical psychologist in my first hospital got this right: he persuaded me to construct a card index of all the reprints belonging to another member of staff, a task that I could just carry out because it was episodic: I could write the authors' names on a card, brood for a bit, and then write the title and so on. Tackling this job every morning for several weeks and finding I could do it gave me a little confidence.

Dependence

A second characteristic of mental patients is that they are prone to become dependent on those looking after them. Whenever a doctor (or therapist) walked through my ward, one or more of his patients would approach and ask, 'When are you going to see me?' Often the doctor would say without thinking, 'I'll see you later today' or 'Tomorrow morning'. Usually such casual promises were not kept. The patient – and this often happened to me – would sit waiting for the summons to the doctor's room and would become more and more upset with the passage of time until he eventually despaired of the appointment being kept. Reynolds was equally upset by broken appointments, even though he was only a pseudo-patient.

I encountered other instances of broken promises. My first analyst asked me whether I had cried since the onset of my depression. When I told him I had not, he said darkly 'Ah, there must be some deep underlying conflict. We must get to the bottom of that'. Subsequently I raised the topic of crying several times, but he made no attempt to get to the bottom of it. Again, when I told a clinical psychologist about my obsessive thoughts, he said he would treat them by desensitization. In preparation for this, I learned to relax at will in the classes that were held every morning, but when I asked him to fulfil his promise he would change the subject.

Broken promises may not seem so terrible to the sane, but in deep depression one is clutching at any straw and the breaking of promises by therapists takes away even the faint hope engendered by the promise and deepens one's misery. All the patients on the ward felt the same way. They were visibly envious of anyone seen by a doctor and longed for the time when they would be seen themselves, even though the longing was misplaced, since for the most part the doctors could do little to help them. Despite the fact that she was in hospital for only a day, one of the nurses in Mueller and Sherman's study commented 'The doctor made rounds and spoke to me. I was still cherishing every bit of attention I could get'.

Handling patients' dependence creates a problem for therapists. If a doctor walks through a ward, he cannot stop to speak to all the patients who besiege him, though that is no excuse for making promises he has no intention of keeping. Perhaps of more importance, the therapist has to give the patient hope but not false hope, and the line between the two is thin. When I asked my analysts whether I would recover, they became very cagey, saying that about one in three recovered. This was upsetting for me: it was also false. My psychiatrist was more familiar with the relevant statistics: on our first meeting, he told me firmly that he had encountered many patients like myself who after a successful career had suffered depression in middle age and that he was certain I would recover.

Promises that instil hope have to be made with care, but the casual failure to keep other types of promise is all the more extraordinary in that it is known that trust in one's therapist augurs well for recovery. A broken promise not only causes pain, but also is bad therapy.

The artificial nature of therapy

Not all therapy is artificial: cognitive therapy and behaviour therapy are exceptions in that they address themselves directly to the patient's needs. However, in my experience and that of Reynolds many therapists do not begin to speak to the needs of the patients. Unless you have been treated by a dynamic therapist, you can have little idea how dotty many of them are. Here are some examples.

When I complained to my first psychoanalyst that I could not radically change myself at the age of 45, he said he had just had a marvellous break-through with a woman of 65 after several years of intensive therapy. He told me that she had seen a flower for what it was for the first time in her life and had burst into tears. I am not belittling the woman: that may have been an entirely appropriate response for her. But I was not then nor ever will be the sort of person in whom a marigold produces floods of tears. The therapist simply had not understood how irrelevant his story was to my own life.

A more extreme example occurred when I had recovered from my first depression and my wife and I were having marital therapy. Admittedly the marital therapist was having a hard time, since whenever he asked us to do something – like posing towards one another in a way that would reveal our respective attitudes – my wife, being a sensible woman, would say 'I'm not doing that: it's silly', and I would say 'Give me five references to show that that helps'. But this hardly excuses his next move. He drew on the black-board my wife's family tree. Having placed her father and his parents, he added my wife's mother and the mother's mother. When my wife told him that the identity of her mother's father was unknown, he looked at her and said meaningfully, 'Ah, so your maternal grandfather is just a faceless penis to you'. Since my wife and I were both, as these things go, mentally normal at the time, we passed the remark off as a piece of idiocy on his part, but being told that one has a faceless penis as an ancestor could well both puzzle and perturb anyone who was depressed.

Another example of lunatic therapy, to coin a phrase, occurred in the second hospital. The clinical psychologist there was well intentioned but did not have the wisdom of the one in the other hospital. I told him I was preoccupied with the thought that my wife was having an affair. The psychologist pondered and eventually said,

> What we'll do is to get the social worker to find out. If she really is having an affair, we'll try to get your wife to let you watch her making love. It won't take long: sex never goes on for more than an hour or so. Of course we'll have to get the chap's permission too.

Voyeurism even in cold blood did not make much appeal to me, but maybe he thought he had invented a novel form of flooding.

Reynolds gives instances of other daft approaches.

> One patient's problem seemed to centre on his guilt at sending his mother to a nursing home and his dissatisfaction with their subse-quent relationship. I wondered why he didn't try to make amends and

straighten out the relationship with her rather than trying to learn, in the group, how to handle his guilt more constructively.

Or again, he describes how in psychodrama a patient was asked to re-enact a telephone conversation with his ex-wife in which she had asked for money to furnish the living-room. Afterwards there was a discussion among all the patients about the problem, in which a young black patient asked, 'Does he have the money to buy the furniture?' The psychiatrist responded in a somewhat deprecating manner that the question raised 'a reality problem'. 'We aren't concerned with that here but with emotional problems that usually have their roots in early childhood' . . . blah, blah, blah. In fact the solution of practical problems should be an important aspect of psycho-therapy, since there is evidence that if any facet of a depressed person's life improves, other aspects also tend to improve.

Both of Reynolds's examples come from group therapy, of which my own experiences were no better. In my second hospital there was a group therapy session at which nobody spoke for about fifteen minutes. I started to talk and then burst into tears. Although this might have pleased my first analyst, it greatly displeased the woman registrar who was running the group and I was severely told off for being selfish. Most of the sessions at that hospital took place in almost complete silence. I had the impression that the psychiatrists had no idea what group therapy was for or indeed whether it had any point at all. Often there would be a sudden burst of conversation just before the hour was up, whereupon the psychiatrist would say 'Time's up' and march out.

Sessions at the first hospital were more dramatic, since the registrar there, again a woman, attempted to stir up false emotions. We all knew that it was the custom of one woman to leave the group after half an hour and run round the grounds of the hospital. The registrar was new to the group and when the woman left, said excitedly, 'Why do none of you go after Sue?' A comparatively new patient did so and returned, having had her face slapped by the escapee. The registrar folded her in her arms uttering, 'Oh, what a brave girl you are'. The attempt to whip up false emotion and to see signifi-cance in things that have no significance seems characteristic of group therapy.

There is no real dilemma about giving artificial therapy. Therapists prob-ably do so because they like to think that they have access to a body of knowledge and techniques, such as those of psychoanalysis, Rogerian therapy, or Gestalt therapy, that are not known to the non-expert and whose use therefore renders them in some sense professionals. None of the dynamic approaches has been validated, though it is possible that a therapist who combines their use with common sense may do better than a placebo control.

Not being taken seriously

One of my fellow inmates at the first hospital was a rather amiable con-man, who had been in prison. He went on alcoholic binges and was at present drying out. He told me that he would 'rather do two years in Dart-moor than two weeks in this place'. When I asked him why, he said 'There you can at least get at the screws. Here there's nobody to get at'.

Most of the remarks made by the patients on my wards were quite sensible, with the exception of those of a florid schizophrenic: they, therefore, deserved to be taken seriously. Nevertheless, one had the feeling that the staff (with the exception of my own psychiatrist and my first clinical psychologist, both of whom treated my remarks with appropriate gravity) simply disregarded what the patients had to say. I knew exactly what tablets I was supposed to receive: when, as quite frequently happened, I was given the wrong ones, I would complain. The error was never put right: instead, I pictured the nurse going to the day book and writing, 'Patient paranoid about his tablets'. Rockwell (1973) makes a similar comment: the patient 'is herded by the staff from place to place, his leisure and privacy are constantly intruded upon by the staff, and his objections to any of these intrusions are interpreted to him as evidence of his pathology'. Caudill *et al.* (1952) quote one of his fellow inmates as saying that a hospital nurse 'had treated us like seven-year-olds'.

This ground has been well worked over. One of Rosenhan's patients went up to his doctor and asked 'When do I get my discharge?' This is a perfectly reasonable question, but instead of replying the doctor looked over the pseudo-patient's head and said, 'Oh good morning, Dave, and how are you today?' Rosenhan also found that when a patient and a psychiatrist met casually, the psychiatrist would make eye contact on only 29 per cent of occasions. For comparison, he studied meetings of strangers where one was asking for directions: eye contact always occurred.

It is so damaging to be completely ignored as a person that when someone in the hospital responds normally, it can be very helpful. In both my hospitals the occupational therapists took some of the edge off my misery. They looked me in the eye and spoke to me as they would do to any normal person. Reynolds had exactly the same experience. When I was beginning to recover, I was on my way home from the hospital alone one weekend when I happened to meet a woman registrar with whom I had had several sharp arguments. She stopped her car and said, 'Are you going home for the weekend?' I said I was and she wished me well. I found this event immensely cheering. Reynolds had a similar experience: while walking in the grounds of the hospital, he met a nurse from his ward, who took his arm and conducted a perfectly normal conversation with him. He comments, 'This completely fortuitous encounter was a memorable experience'. Again, one of the nurses in Mueller and Sherman's study comments on receiving a smile from a hospital nurse, 'It was at this moment that I realized how important a smile can be to a new patient'.

In Gotkin and Gotkin (1977) Janet Gotkin recounts her terrifying experiences as a schizophrenic in American mental hospitals. She writes, 'Nobody takes you seriously and that's the most demoralising experience in the world'. She felt that the use of psychiatric jargon was dehumanizing. Wanting to know your diagnosis is 'morbid curiosity'. 'Sad? No. You're depressed. Angry at your shrink? Resisting therapy. Like your doctor? Positive transference. Make a joke your doctor can't understand? Thought processes disturbed.'

Although it is apparent that for the most part nurses, therapists and psychiatrists make a poor job of treating their patients as people, there are real difficulties. As I have already remarked, psychiatrists cannot stop to pass the time of day with everyone on their wards. Moreover, mental illness is an agonizing affliction not merely for the patient but for those who look after the patient: they may feel, often rightly, that there is little they can do to help. In these circumstances therapists may without knowing it keep the patient at a distance in order to protect themselves from involvement. In this respect Freud wrought great harm. According to him, nothing the patient says should be taken at face value, because it merely reflects unconscious drives or conflicts and it is to these that therapists must address themselves, not to the superficial problems that the patient presents: although these may be preoccupying the patient, the therapist is encouraged to ignore them, that is not to take them seriously. Freud's view of humankind (especially the female of the species) is the most degrading ever presented: he encouraged generations of therapists not to take the patient seriously.

Lack of information

When psychiatrists preach to physicians, which they are prone to do, they adjure them to give their patients full information: unfortunately, they rarely follow this admirable precept themselves. I first saw my consultant as an outpatient. He spent three continuous hours with me and I came to trust him. It was on his advice that I admitted myself to hospital, largely to break the *folie à deux* into which my wife and I had entered. I had, perhaps naively, expected to be treated by him in the hospital, but after the first few days I was dismayed to discover from other patients that I would be treated only by his registrars. Reynolds (and several of the other pseudo-patients) complained that they were given no information about the running of the ward when they first came on to it; nor was any forthcoming subsequently except by chance. He managed to discover how to get clean sheets after nine days: it took me three weeks. He had no idea that there was a clothes drier in the hospital.

Of more consequence, the drugs I was taking made me extremely constipated: a visit to the lavatory was torture. I saw doctors so rarely that it did not occur to me to waste time discussing a complaint that no matter how painful seemed trivial by comparison with my state of mind. It was, therefore, three weeks before I raised the problem. The doctor was surprised that I did not know that laxatives were available on demand from the nurses. Mental patients cannot look after themselves very well, and it still seems extraordinary that given the extremely costive effects of my drugs, no steps had been taken to provide laxatives if needed. At least I was told what all of the four drugs I was taking were for and what were their likely effects (excluding constipation); Reynolds complains with some heat that he was never given this information. An even more serious omission was made when a bricklayer on my ward was taken to another hospital to record his EEG. When he returned, he told me that it had been a terrible experience: the electrodes had caused unimaginably searing pains throughout his head. Neither the registrar who had ordered the assay nor the nurse who accompanied him nor the operator of the electroencephalogram had thought to explain that the whole procedure was completely painless since no electric shocks were to be applied.

One of the worst aspects of the lack of information is being unable to discover what one's privileges are. In my second spell in a mental hospital, I became paranoid (and I do not use the word lightly) about the possibility that the hospital would prevent visits from my wife and stop me going home at weekends. This fear arose because the clinical psychologist (not the same as the one in the first hospital) had told me that the whole point of my being in hospital was to separate me permanently from her. I agonized about this problem for several weeks, but none of the hospital staff would put my mind at rest. I eventually telephoned a knowledgeable friend who assured me that the hospital did not have the power to do this, but as I shall show later, she was only half right.

Reynolds complains that he learned only by accident that he could discharge himself AMA (Against Medical Advice) at any time. Until then he 'had naively believed that he could leave only when the staff gave permission': he was also unable to find out under what conditions he would be removed from the special status locked ward, on to which he had been admitted as a potential suicide, and placed on an open ward.

There have been numerous studies (see Fallowfield 1990) on the benefits of giving information in physical medicine. For example, in a study by Egbert *et al.* (1964) patients admitted to hospital for abdominal surgery were randomly assigned to two groups: before the operation took place, the patients in one group were given full information about how long it would last, the circumstances under which they would regain consciousness, the nature of the pain they were likely to experience and so on. This information was not supplied to the second group, who went through the standard hospital procedures. The patients who were thoroughly briefed about the operation subsequently complained less about pain, needed fewer sedatives and recovered more quickly: on average they were discharged from hospital three days earlier than the other group. There is surely no problem in providing patients with more information both about their medication and about the workings of the ward. One can conclude only that the lack of it stems from pure thoughtlessness on the part of psychiatrists. I shall return to the question of information about rights in the section on Powerlessness (pp. 181–3).

Boredom

Had I been questioned before my breakdown about what to expect, I would probably have listed most of the symptoms of depression: the one experience that surprised me was the unmitigated boredom that accompanied it. Boredom is a concomitant of depression, but it is exacerbated by being in a mental hospital. Several of the nurse pseudo-patients comment on it despite the fact that they spent only one day in the hospital and were all mentally normal. Here are quotations from five of them. 'The thing that impressed me most about the whole day was the lack of something to do.' 'I decided, I can't take this, I am going to ask to leave. I looked at the clock and much to my amazement I had been there exactly fifteen minutes.' 'I felt uncomfortable at having no purpose except to sit and exist.' 'I kept watch on the clock and it seemed to stand still.' 'I kept checking my watch. . . . First I checked my watch, then the clock, then read a little. Time just stood still.' The sociologist (Deane 1961) writes, 'I became aware of a huge boredom. The day dragged endlessly.' Similar quotations could be given from all the accounts of pseudo-patients. The most excruciating boredom I suffered was on the first weekend at the second hospital. Almost all the other patients had gone home and given that I could not read or watch television, I did not know how I could get through the day. At 4.30 p.m. I sat with my back to a clock, thinking that it was only an hour until supper, which would provide a slight break in the monotony. I would wait until I thought at least five minutes had elapsed, then turn to check the time on the clock: on each occasion less than a minute had gone by.

The period from 10 a.m. to 4 p.m. was slightly more tolerable than the evening since one could go to OT, where the heroic band of occupational therapists would strive to engage one's attention in something. My own boredom was also alleviated slightly in the first hospital by the psychologist's ingenious idea of having me fill out index cards. At this hospital, the nurses attempted to relieve patients' boredom by offering to play table tennis or Scrabble or by persuading them to take advantage of the outdoor sports facilities. But supper was at 5.30 p.m. and after that there was a complete void until bedtime, with few nurses and no other staff on the ward.

Some boredom is likely to accompany a protracted stay in any kind of hospital, particularly if one has no idea when or whether one will emerge into the outside world. Moreover, to ameliorate boredom in mental hospitals would be expensive. I would certainly have gone to occupational therapy in the evening had it been available. Perhaps more could be done to find jobs in which patients could be employed, including gardening, cooking and cleaning: such tasks may not sound very exciting, but they could provide the patient with some sense of being useful, of having a purpose, instead of slowly drifting through the endless day.

Common mould

On this point I am on less sure ground, for there is less evidence to offer. Nevertheless, when I was being treated by psychoanalysts, I had the strong impression that they believed there was only one right way to live which they summed up in the phrase 'You must be more sensitive to your feelings'. This may be a panacea for some, even though spending too much time dwelling on oneself savours of self-indulgence. But there are some people, commonly known as extroverts, for whom the outside world is more important than the internal. Who can say whether the great physicist living in a fantasy world of quarks and pi-mesons is more or less happy or even more or less useful to society than the man who devotes his life to caring for his family?

Many modern psychotherapies seem to prescribe how people should live. Gestalt therapy takes an aggressive approach and can foster selfishness and hostility in its patients: two of its mottos are 'Do your own thing', and 'Live in the here and now': it is violently anti-intellectual. It fails to take the clients' remarks seriously, challenging them with phrases like 'Stop mind fucking'.

As for Maslow, he strove to turn his clients into priggish saints fulfilling their 'metaneeds', which include 'enjoying doing good', 'delight in bringing about justice', 'avoiding flattery, applause, popularity, status, prestige, money, honours, etc.', 'being attracted by mystery', 'helping self-actualization of others', and so on and on. These ideals may or may not represent a portrait of himself, though the number of references he makes to his own articles (no fewer than thirty, for example, in Maslow 1971) suggests that he failed to avoid seeking status. No ordinary mortal could possibly aspire to his standards. He fails to recognize that it is impossible to instruct people to take delight in doing good: many people have to fight with themselves in order to do good, and it can be argued that they are in some sense nobler than those who take a priggish delight in it.

In summary, there are many different kinds of people and many different ways to live well. Although it is hard to prove, it seems likely that many conventional psychotherapists have fixed ideas on how people should live, which they impose inappropriately on their patients. Maybe it is too much to expect a therapist to encompass the full range of human diversity, but the behaviour therapist overcomes this problem by establishing before treatment begins what changes the patients would like to make in themselves.

Powerlessness

I make the patients' feelings of powerlessness the penultimate point, partly because of its importance and generality, and partly because it is a result of many of the factors already discussed, such as the failure to take patients seriously or to give sufficient information.

Many of the pseudo-patients felt a sense of powerlessness simply through being subjected to the hospital regime. All the nurses

> commented on the admissions shower, saying they were taken to shower rooms and their clothes removed and they didn't know what was happening. I think this situation impressed upon me the fact [*sic*] of having activities in which patients can have some voice instead of already being planned for them.
>
> (Mueller and Sherman 1969)

Weitz writes

> I found the loss of control over my own life to be the greatest threat; ... traditional ward situations do not permit patients to have much control over their eventual fate. ... Suddenly tremendous feelings of anger overwhelmed me as I sensed a loss of personal control over my life ... I was jealous of those staff people who could come and go on the ward, those individuals with a sense of their own freedom.
>
> (Weitz 1972)

According to Rosenhan, 'Powerlessness was evident everywhere'.

The pseudo-patients also complain about the lack of privacy. Reynolds was particularly upset when he was moved to a different room that contained no lockers: he had felt that the locker in his previous room represented his private space. Oddly enough, submission to the hospital regime did not bother me nor did the lack of privacy, despite the fact that in the second hospital I slept in a tiny ward with eleven other men whose beds were placed back to back and were separated laterally by only three feet. In both my hospitals, there was as little regimentation as was consistent with life in any institution. We were not ordered to go to OT or to play games, we were merely encouraged. It may be that I was in such a state of depression that the hospital regime and the lack of privacy seemed trivial by comparison, whereas they loomed large for the pseudo-patients.

I did, however, feel powerless in other ways, for example, about whether I would be allowed visits by my wife, as I have already described. I also went through nasty periods towards the end of my stay in each hospital. I did not know and could not find out whether I could freely discharge myself or whether if I attempted to do so I could be committed: this was foolish of me but I was mentally disordered at the time. I was not the only person to worry about being 'sectioned' (that is, committed) and relegated to a closed ward. The subject came up repeatedly among my fellow inmates and always induced dread. The stories about the closed ward were doubtless apocryphal: one that I can remember was that patients there became extremely thirsty because they could get a glass of water only by asking a nurse and were sometimes made to wait for hours. Apart from fretting about committal, I would, more realistically, worry about whether if I did discharge myself, the hospital would prescribe the cocktail of drugs that I was taking. I felt, probably rightly, that I was dependent on them. Towards the end of my stay in the first hospital, the woman registrar told me I must not discharge myself, though the clinical psychologist disagreed with her. In the second, I was persuaded to remain for three extra agonizing days for that *coup de théâtre*, the ward round, in which the consultant surrounded by his minions plays God, though in this case he did so in a most affable manner. Hughes (1990), the surgeon who was a genuine patient, was also upset that he had to wait for discharge for the once-a-week ward round. He comments, 'Psychiatrists do not share the same time scale as other clinicians'. The necessity to await a ward round before discharge is a puzzle. No matter how wise, consultants are unlikely to know more about the patient's condition than their registrars, who are in more immediate contact.

There are more ways of keeping someone in a psychiatric hospital than commital, refusing to issue drugs, or awaiting the ward round. I visited one of my students when he had been admitted to hospital with what appeared to be a schizophrenic episode. He could not have discharged himself because his shoes and some of his clothes had been removed. What were his rights? He was never told and I met with evasive replies.

My own feelings of powerlessness induced a form of paranoia both over my wife's visits and over the problem of discharge. Most of the pseudo-patients also developed such feelings. The two psychologists (Goldman 1970) 'experienced a fear that they had been betrayed by their colleagues. Each was remarkably concerned about whether he would be left in the hospital indefinitely, only to be forgotten by friends and relatives', while the journalist Anne Barry (1971) writes 'Because I was acting out paranoia, I began to feel somewhat paranoid'.

The feeling of powerlessness and the resulting paranoia cannot possibly be conducive to improved mental health. The powerlessness about the hospital regimen could surely be alleviated: in the case of the nurses who were upset about the shower on admission, a simple explanation would have helped. Moreover, there seems little point in detaining patients in hospital by ruses or by not explaining their rights. Such tricks are hardly likely to gain their trust. Mental hospitals have four functions. First, to prevent patients inflicting damage on themselves or others. Second, patients may be too disordered to look after themselves and have nobody else who will. Third, it may be desirable to observe a person with a mental disorder over a period of time in order to reach a diagnosis and determine treatment. Fourth, as in my case, the hospital may provide a temporary refuge from a stressful situation, with which the patient is too disordered to cope. Only the first function justifies the detention of patients against their will. There seems to be little dilemma here, though in cases where commital is not possible some psychiatrists may resort to ruses because they believe it is for the patient's own good. It seems likely that most patients would react better to a more honest approach. The lack of information or reassurance over one's right to discharge oneself or over receiving visitors or even over the almost certainly mythical stories of what happens on the closed ward suggests that hospital staff have little idea what goes on in patients' minds. Many patients become dependent on the hospital and they need reassurance that this dependence will not be abused.

Stigma

There is still considerable stigma attached to being mentally ill. The reader might think that I was lucky since it is well known that academics are liberal people. Unfortunately this is not entirely true, for shortly after emerging from the first hospital, I attended a committee meeting, at which someone said, 'I really don't think we have to listen to Professor Sutherland's views: after all he's just come out of a loony bin'. Many of the other patients were more unlucky. One woman with anorexia nervosa went home as usual for a weekend. She attended a church service with her next-door neighbour, who said to her, 'Where are you going to live when you come out of that place?' It took her a moment to realize the implication, which was 'You can't go on living in our nice middle-class road after being in a mental hospital'.

It is likely that schizophrenia and bipolar manic-depressive psychosis have a physical basis, though life events may trigger an episode. Nobody should be blamed for such illnesses. There is no good evidence that a person's way of life or character traits make him or her prone to mental disorders, though they may determine the form the disorder takes. Almost everyone has their breaking point. Few of the British aircrews who survived a tour of twenty-five bombing missions over Germany came back as 'normal' as they started. Some believe that depression is associated with creativity. Although this is unproven, it is certainly true that many powerful and famous people have suffered from depression, including Churchill, Newton, Dickens, John Donne, Coleridge, Sylvia Plath, Byron, van Gogh, Dr Johnson, Wittgenstein, Stephen Spender, and John Ogdon, not to mention our very own Spike Milligan. These people had no reason to feel shame about their achievements.

Although the failure of medical staff to take patients seriously is a form of stigma that could be avoided, there is a real problem in overcoming stigma. No matter how big an attempt is made to educate the public, the fact remains that the mentally ill are often frightening: depressed patients may be hard to reach and it is difficult to deal with the incoherence of the florid schizophrenic. It is, moreover, unfortunately true that people who have been mentally ill are at greater risk of further episodes than others. Hence, they may have difficulty finding employment. Stigma is, therefore, likely to remain a problem, but more effort should be made to remove the guilt that attaches to many forms of mental illness. Psychiatrists could set an example by treating patients as people.

Conclusion

I end with three points.

First, most of what I have written about mental hospitals applies to other institutions – to general hospitals, to schools, to golf clubs, to universities, and perhaps above all to prisons. Yet for two reasons it does not apply with quite so much force. The mentally ill are much more sensitive than normal people and the staff of these other institutions (with the exception of prisons) cannot exert so much power over their members' lives. That is not to imply that the mistakes to which I have drawn attention (where applicable) should not be avoided in other institutions: most doctors in physical medicine have a lot to learn about their patients' dependency and about giving information.

Second, psychiatrists, clinical psychologists and nurses are as imperfect as anyone else. They are, for example, bound sometimes to tread by accident on the extreme sensitivities of the mentally ill. It is hard for them to deal with the dependence of mental patients even if they have the time, which often they do not. Inevitably, they may fail to foresee what information is needed and a real effort to alleviate patients' boredom would be expensive in terms of extra staff.

Third, if the staff of psychiatric hospitals are themselves imperfect, what is the point of listing systematically the mistakes they make? The answer is that drawing these points to their attention provides something to aim at. There is considerable room for improvement, even if it falls short of perfection.

References

Barry, A. (1971) *Bellevue is a State of Mind*. New York: Berkley.

Beck, A.T. (1967) *Depression*. New York: Harper & Row.

Caudill, W. *et al.* (1952) Social structure and interaction processes on a psychiatric ward. *American Journal of Orthopsychiatry* 22: 314–34.

Deane, W.N. (1961) Reactions of a non-patient to a stay on a mental hospital ward. *Psychiatry* 24: 61–8.

Egbert, L. *et al.* (1964) Reduction of post-operative pain by encouragement and instruction of patients. *New England Journal of Medicine* 270: 825.

Fallowfield, L. (1990) *The Quality of Life*. London: Souvenir Press.

Goldman, A.R. (1970) On posing as mental patients: Reminiscences and recommendations. *Professional Psychology* 1: 427–34.

Gotkin, J. and Gotkin, P. (1977) *Too Much Anger, Too Many Tears*. London: Jonathan Cape.

Hughes, S. (1990) Inside madness. *British Medical Journal* 301: 1,476–8.

Maslow, A. (1971) *The Farther Reaches of Human Nature*. Harmondsworth: Penguin.

Mueller, B.S. and Sherman, C.C. (1969) Nurses' experiences as psychiatric patients. *Hospital and Community Psychiatry* 20(1): 40–1.

Reynolds, D.K. and Farberow, N.L. (1976) *Suicide Inside and Out*. Berkeley: University of California Press.

Rockwell, D.A. (1971) Some observations on 'living in'. *Psychiatry* 34: 214–23.

Rosenhan, D.L. (1973) On being sane in insane places. *Science* 179: 250–8.

Sutherland, N.S. (1987) *Breakdown: A Personal Crisis and a Medical Dilemma*, 2nd edn. London: Weidenfeld & Nicolson.

Weitz, W.A. (1972) Experiencing the role of a hospitalized psychiatric patient: a professional's view from the other side. *Professional Psychology* **3**: 151–4.

RESPONSE – *Jeff Roberts*

I take care to believe what my patients tell me until proved otherwise. In order to do this, at times I need to suspend my critical faculties or at least to compartmentalize and render inoperative my disbelief. None the less whenever I hear a hard-luck story I tend to conclude that finding or experiencing persecution is a personality trait of the unlucky client. Professor Sutherland had, as a result of his depressive breakdown, an experience of a broad spectrum of psychiatric treatment and sampled from a range of psychotherapies. He was discontented with almost everything he found. In the following brief response to his chapter, I shall be looking at his experiences of these various psychotherapies. First, however, I would like to clarify what I understand by the psychotherapies.

Sir William Sargant, one of the most staunch antagonists of the psychological approaches to psychological disorder, put forward his views in a book called *Battle for the Mind* (Sargant 1957). This battle at times seems to be fought between various disciplines as to who is entitled to claim sole possession of this territory, as their province for therapeutic effectiveness. Indeed one of the less fortunate experiences of Professor Sutherland was that his mind got caught in the crossfire of this battle and he was offered a bewildering array of different approaches to his problem. It has to be admitted that psychiatry's various treatment approaches are derived from as yet crude and unproven ideas about how mind works. The most widely used of these are

1 gross anatomical
2 biochemical/pharmacological
3 neurophysiological[1]
4 behavioural (conditioned reflexes and operant conditioning): the behaviourists would say that you cannot objectively measure mind, ergo you cannot study it
5 cognitive psychology
6 psychoanalytic theories (subtly incorporating both cognitive and behavioural ideas): psychoanalytic theories make the important contribution of introducing ideas of development and maturation; none the less, psychoanalysis gives an incomplete view of mind, since it is primarily the science of the intimate relationship
7 models of group and family psychology (some would regard mind as a group or even social phenomenon)
8 models of social and community psychology
9 racial and ethnic psychology.

From these various models a variety of 'physical', 'chemical' and 'psychological' approaches to the healing of mental disorder have been developed. We are here interested in the psychological models of mind and the psychological treatments developed out of them. There are in fact a large number of definitions of psychotherapy (Wolberg 1977). Of these the most straightforward and inclusive is as follows:

> Psychotherapy is the psychological, as opposed to physical or chemical, approach to the treatment of psychological disorder involving primarily verbal interaction between two or more individuals.

The following is a schema for the classification of the most important of the psychotherapies:

1 psychoanalysis and psychoanalytically oriented psychotherapy
2 other individual therapies
   - client centred (Carl Rogers)
   - transactional analysis (Eric Berne)
   - Gestalt psychotherapy (Fritz Perls)
   - existential analysis/psychotherapy
3 group psychotherapies
4 various individual and group approaches to counselling
5 social therapy
6 cognitive and behavioural psychotherapies
7 psychodrama
8 art therapy and psychotherapy
9 family and couple therapies.

Most of these approaches can be accessed by patients in the United Kingdom and the professor had experience of approximately half of them. He was apparently extremely unlucky in his encounters with the mental health professionals, who practised examples of these psychotherapeutic approaches and even fell foul of a therapist who used common sense to harm rather than help him. He presents us with a series of anecdotes which include a number of apparently foolish and unjustified statements, promises, prognostications and comments, taken incidentally out of context but none the less made by mental health experts. I would agree with him that these statements appear unempathic and at times profoundly unhelpful and indeed even destructive. My contention would be that his essay is more an expression of personal discontent than a legitimate critique of the psychotherapies. However, it would be churlish to discount the whole of his story. He undoubtedly encountered poor quality care and treatment. Indeed I would suggest that his experience was of bad psychotherapy, poorly executed psychology, inferior psychiatry and typical but generally agreed poor institutional practice. I shall point out ways in which appropriate psychotherapeutic expertise could have eased his experience and do the best I can to comment on some of the experiences he had. Not all of the interventions were as bad as he believes them to have been. He undoubtedly suffered a great deal but also bravely and honestly acknowledges that he was not an easy patient. Difficult patients do not always bring out the best in their therapists. In his various encounters with mental health professionals Professor Sutherland appears to have experienced quite sadistic counter-transference responses, and by no means to have brought out the best in his therapists.

I find myself at odds with the professor's method, which is to assemble a collection of anecdotes and unsupported opinion to attack the whole of psychiatric practice. This unscientific approach is no doubt excellent journalism but is not in any sense an argument that psychotherapy is either harmless or harmful. My overall response is to suggest that Professor Sutherland would have benefited greatly if he had encountered greater psychotherapeutic skill and awareness along his sad and painful journey.

More diagnostic skill from his GP, and an awareness of what psychotherapy can and cannot help would perhaps have enabled him to meet a general psychiatrist before his unfortunate encounters with psychoanalysis. It is an axiom of most psychotherapists that severe depression, with endogenous or biological features, rarely if ever responds to psychotherapy alone. Once such a diagnosis is unequivocally made, systematic treatment with antidepressant medication is the first course of action. This treatment is underpinned by a predominantly supportive psychotherapeutic approach, if necessary in the safe context provided by a well-run (non-institutionalizing) residential setting. Usually this is a psychiatric hospital ward. Treatment is thus undertaken with an awareness that the patient in these circumstances may need protecting from self-destructive impulses arising as an irrational consequence of the depressed state.

Neither psychoanalyst shines, as described by the professor, and both seem lacking in basic psychotherapeutic skills and awareness. Neither appears to have reached a convincing diagnostic formulation. Both seem overly ready to hand out narcissistic wounds and the younger one appears to practise what I believe most well-trained and sensible analysts would call 'wild analysis'. Wild psychoanalysis is defined in the respected *Language of Psychoanalysis* (Laplanche and Pontalis 1973) as follows:

> Broadly understood, this expression refers to the procedure of amateur or inexperienced 'analysts' who attempt to interpret symptoms, dreams, utterances, actions, etc., on the basis of psychoanalytic notions which they have as often as not misunderstood. In a more technical sense, an interpretation is deemed 'wild' if a specific analytic situation is misapprehended in its current dynamics and its particularity – and especially if the repressed content is simply imparted to the patient with no heed to the resistances and to the transference.
>
> (Laplanche and Pontalis 1973: 480–1)

This definition would be agreed by the vast majority of psychoanalysts, who would I am sure also agree that the interpretations offered to Professor

Sutherland by the young analyst were 'wild'. The analysts here were at
fault, *not* psychoanalysis or psychotherapy.

His junior doctors seem as they so often are overly busy, unsophisticated
and under-trained. He describes events of some twenty years ago so I suspect some improvement in the personal and interpersonal awareness of
many junior doctors may have by now occurred. The Royal College of Psychiatrists makes it clear that all trainee psychiatrists are expected to have
experience and systematic training in the psychotherapies. It is not impossible
to be in touch with the inner world of disturbed patients and use basic
psychotherapeutic skills to attenuate their suffering a little. It should have
been possible to regularly provide reassurance that recovery from depression
will occur. I remember myself as a junior psychiatrist, twenty years ago,
being very aware of the intensity of suffering of the severely biologically
depressed patient. Such individuals need initially a sensitive supportive
relationship which is almost continuously reassuring. I was able to say to
my patients in this condition that it was as if they were in a waking night-
mare from which they would inevitably emerge, within two to eight weeks.
This was usually helpful but only for five or ten minutes. I believe that my
ability patiently to reiterate this reassurance was made possible with the
help of our regular psychotherapy supervision, conducted by a psychoanalyst. He also encouraged us to offer regular appointments to our inpatients,
to keep our promises, to listen carefully and to empathize as best we could
with all of the patients under our care.

The psychologists in this story come across in a rather mixed way. One
or two sensible and helpful remarks were made; there were also some rather
silly comments together with thoughtless ill-considered promises.

The professor didn't very much enjoy his dose of common sense, handed
out by the 'black woman nurse' he became friendly with. I believe that psychiatry and the psychotherapies are quite powerful in their healing capacity
but undoubtedly need careful articulation and sensible management. It is a
gross distortion to write off the work of hundreds of thoughtful and scientifically minded people in the way that the professor does in his opening
remarks, giving no supporting evidence for these statements. Common sense
is just not enough, and as a patient he did not find it very helpful.

In my opinion what Professor Sutherland needed was first, good diagnosis;
second, psychiatric treatment, which entailed initially supportive psychotherapy and medication, given with greater sensitivity than he experienced;
and third, attention to the precipitating factors of his illness. Depression is
often caused by experiences of loss, most obviously of a loved one through
death. The loss in this case appears to have been the loss of a loved one (and
self-esteem) as the result of real or fantasized marital infidelity. I suspect
sensitive and gentle exploration of feelings of hurt, betrayal and loss during
the recovery period from the depression would have been helpful. Maybe
this was done? Couple therapy also seems sensible and the professor was
offered this opportunity. His motivation and belief in the form of therapy
offered were apparently quite low so that his chances of gaining would have

been also quite low. I'm not sure about the 'faceless penis' remark: a little literary maybe and quite imaginative. If anything it probably indicates that the therapist was either a poor judge of his patients or in some way trying to take them off balance by being rather shocking.

All in all then, I think that Professor Sutherland has bravely written subjectively and in so doing abdicated his professorship. I am inclined to think he complains too much. I also believe he may have brought down on his own head some of what happened to him. None the less there is no arguing with the fact that he was subject to poor psychotherapeutic practice at all levels and from many of the people he encountered. This does not amount in any way to an indictment of psychotherapy. It is an indictment of the quality of personnel he encountered, the supervision they were having and a lack of simple psychotherapy training. It is also an indication of the lack of coherence of the psychiatric teams which treated him. There was and is in the so-called multidisciplinary team a tendency for all the members to work independently without sufficient reference to each other and team co-ordinators, so that there is a pulling in different directions rather than together.

There is good evidence that skilled, supervised psychotherapeutic practice is helpful to correctly diagnosed and selected patients. On the other hand, unskilled, untrained and unsupervised practitioners with poorly selected patients, using implicit personality theory and common sense can be unhelpful and often harmful. I do not think therefore that we should respond to the professor's tirade by stopping doing therapy or abandoning psychotherapy to the purveyors of common sense. We should note his criticisms, evaluate them, and improve our own practice where necessary.

Note

1 There are elements of neurophysiological processes which resemble both analog and digital computers. Recent work on artificial intelligence moreover makes use of networks not unlike those found in the nervous system (of humans and other animals), in the development of 'expert systems'.

References

Laplanche, J. and Pontalis, J.-B. (1973) *The Language of Psychoanalysis*. London: Hogarth Press.

Sargant, W. (1957) *Battle for the Mind*. London: Heinemann and Pan.

Wolberg, L.R. (1977) *The Technique of Psychotherapy*, vol. 1, ch. 1. New York: Grune & Stratton.

REBUTTAL – *Stuart Sutherland*

I had expected that in his commentary Dr Roberts would consider some or all of the nine areas in which I claim treatment of the mentally ill sometimes falls short and would discuss whether it is important for psychotherapists to pay attention to them. He might also have thrown further light on the unavoidable difficulties that psychotherapists experience in dealing with patients. Instead of examining the validity of my points, he dismisses them, partly by alleging that my anecdotes are inaccurate and partly by claiming that the mistakes I list would be made only by bad therapists: it would appear that there must be a lot of those around. I start by rebutting some of his points, classifying them, as all good psychotherapists should, under the different Freudian defence mechanisms he has unconsciously used.

1 *Repression* He writes that my 'method is to assemble a collection of anecdotes and *unsupported* opinion' (my italics). He has completely repressed the fact that I was at pains to support all but one of my points by the experiences of pseudo-patients, including three psychiatrists.
2 *Denial* He implies that I was in rather bad mental hospitals. In fact, I was privileged to be in two of the best known psychiatric hospitals in the country. Both had a very high ratio of staff to patients; patients were never chivvied and the general atmosphere was as good as I can imagine it being in such places. The staff consistently worked as a 'multidisciplinary team' and were not in the least 'incoherent'. Moreover, far from being maverick analysts, my first was one of the three best known in the country and the second had trained at the Tavistock Clinic.
3 *Displacement* He writes that I brought my problems on myself, thus displacing the fault from therapist to patient. Perhaps I should have added another heading to my chapter, namely 'It's all the fault of the patient', a common but disgraceful attitude among psychotherapists. In fact, I was a difficult patient only when hypomanic. It is, moreover, a poor psychotherapist who has not learned how to deal with difficult patients. What would one think of a dentist who refused to make a difficult extraction?
4 *Projection* Roberts engages in a standard psychotherapeutic manoeuvre when he writes 'experiencing persecution is a personality trait of the unlucky client'. Here, he projects his own feelings of persecution on to me, thus allowing him to dismiss the points I make. To support his allegation, he claims that I am complaining. This is of course irrelevant: all that matters is whether my points are valid.
5 *Reaction formation* Roberts is mistaken in thinking that I believe all treatment of the mentally ill is uniformly bad, as a glance at my book, *Breakdown*, will show. I have nothing but praise for my consultant psychiatrist who was always courteous, supportive and reassuring. I regard my first clinical psychologist as a model therapist. And the occupational therapists did a difficult job superbly well: it was a relief to meet people who looked you in the eye and treated you as a person. Roberts must surely realize that even psychotherapists are not perfect: I was merely pointing to areas in which their behaviour – or that of some of them – might be improved.
6 *Intellectualization* He attempts to dismiss my account by writing that

the remarks of psychotherapists reported in my chapter were 'taken incidentally out of context'. He gives no examples to support this generalization, but on rereading my chapter I find the context is almost always given and some of the therapists' remarks were so foolish that it is irrelevant.

7 *Acting out*   A final instance of his dismissive technique is that he writes of my wife's 'real or fantasized infidelity', another example of not taking the patient seriously. I was careful to explain that I never lost touch with reality and the implication that Dr Roberts might know more about my wife than I do myself exemplifies the presumptuous attitudes to which some psychotherapists are prone.

I now turn to a more substantive issue. Roberts repeatedly remarks that my chapter does not use the scientific approach; this puzzles me for several reasons. It suggests that there is something wrong with making and recording careful observations. As I pointed out, there are many 'scientists', starting with Rosenhan, who as pseudo-patients have recorded their observations of psychiatric wards. Their findings are surely valuable and it is curious that a psychotherapist should want to dismiss them as unscientific rather than attempting to learn from them. In fact, because I was genuinely mentally ill I was in a better position to know where the shoe pinched than the pseudo-patients. Nevertheless, although none of them encountered the full range of psychotherapeutic folly that I did, all but one of my points is supported by at least one of them. Unfortunately, Roberts does not tell us how to discover 'scientifically' the ways in which the practices of individual therapists harm patients. His attitude to psychotherapy is curious, for according to him 'it is a gross distortion to write off the work of hundreds of thoughtful and scientifically minded people in the way that Professor Sutherland does' (I had no intention of doing any such thing). Now science has three aspects: carefully designed methods for making observations, the recording and analysis of those observations (usually employing mathematical techniques), and the construction of rigorous theories. As far as I know – with one exception – none of these has been attempted by any psychotherapist from Freud to Maslow, Rogers or Perls. They have all simply used subjective clinical observations that were heavily biased by their own vague theories.

The exception is that scientific method can be brought to bear on testing the success of different kinds of psychotherapy, though this work has mainly been undertaken by psychologists rather than by psychotherapists. What is the outcome? There are several published papers, each of which puts together the results of over 100 studies comparing the efficacy of different treatments. Using a cunning statistical technique, known as meta-analysis, they all present very similar findings. In the first such paper, Smith and Glass (1977) showed that dynamic therapy and client-centred therapy (the two commonest forms of psychotherapy) are no more successful than a placebo treatment (in which a sham therapist listens to the patient but says as little as possible), while Shapiro and Shapiro (1982) reported that dynamic psychotherapy actually did worse than a placebo treatment. So psychotherapy does no better than or actually worse than having a sympathetic listener. Since these studies are undoubtedly 'scientific' and since Roberts has such faith in science, he might perhaps reconsider the value of psychotherapy. Instead, he will doubtless argue that these studies included many bad therapists, whereas he is a good one, a claim he appears to make but for which he fails to provide any evidence, scientific or otherwise. One problem with this approach is that the wretched patient or client cannot possibly know in advance who is a good therapist and who is a bad one. Finally, Roberts insists that all psychotherapists should be properly trained: but there is no evidence whatsoever that training improves their performance, whereas there is evidence that experienced therapists are no better than inexperienced ones (Orlinsky and Howard 1987).

So where does that leave us? Psychotherapy is not a science: it is an art. Moreover, it seems likely that the closer to common sense is the approach, the more successful it is likely to be. Despite the window-dressing of science, the two forms of therapy that achieve much the greatest success – behaviour therapy and cognitive therapy – are both simply glorified common sense.

To summarize, I feel that Roberts, perhaps threatened by my chapter, has misrepresented me. I was at pains to point out the problems and dilemmas that therapists face, but of these he makes no mention. Nor was I attacking a whole profession: I was merely pointing out some of the ways in which some of its members err, often unknowingly and with the best intentions. My chapter is based on a talk that I have given to psychiatrists all over the world. I think it is true to say that on every occasion one or more psychiatrists came up to me at the end to tell me that they had unintentionally committed within the last few days one or other of the sins I listed. They were prepared to learn from their mistakes. But to learn from mistakes one has to acknowledge that one makes them, which, it would appear, some psychotherapists are not prepared to do.

References

Orlinsky, D.E. and Howard, K.I. (1987) Process and outcome in psychotherapy, in S.L. Garfield and A.E. Bergin (eds) *Handbook of Psychotherapy and Behaviour Change*, 3rd edn. New York: Wiley.

Shapiro, D.A. and Shapiro, D. (1982) Meta-analysis of comparative therapy outcome studies: a replication and refinement. *Psychological Bulletin* **92**: 581–604.

Smith, M.L. and Glass, G.V. (1977) Meta-analysis of psychotherapy outcome studies. *American Psychologist* **32**: 752–60.

EIGHT

Does psychotherapy need a soul?

GILL EDWARDS

As we approach the twenty-first century, almost every field of human endeavour – from physics and biology to economics and medicine – seems to be perched on the brink of a paradigm shift. As Fritjof Capra (1983) puts it, we are at a 'turning point' in history, and there must be few people who do not sense that, at a global level, massive changes are afoot. In *The Awakening Earth*, Peter Russell (1988: vii) suggests that the coming evolutionary leap will be as profound, as significant, as that which produced life on earth. 'And the changes leading to this leap are taking place right before our eyes, or rather right behind them – within our own minds.'

Curiously, despite the many portents of a quantum leap in consciousness, a transformation of the way in which we perceive reality, psychology has seemed slow to respond to the coming shift. Many therapists are still clinging to the scientific tradition of empirical data, logical positivism and Cartesian-Newtonian assumptions, and refusing to open their eyes. Will psychology be caught slumbering when every other branch of science – not to mention the general public – has woken up to a new vision of reality?

In this chapter, I explore the old and new paradigms, their impact upon psychotherapy, and how 'new paradigm' psychotherapy might be characterized. Inevitably, much of this is speculative – but my intention is to challenge and stimulate, not to provide definitive answers. (As will become apparent, dogma lies firmly within the 'old' psychology!)

So what is the old Cartesian-Newtonian paradigm which we must now abandon? For the past three hundred years, we have been brainwashed into seeing life as a random, meaningless accident which somehow emerged from the primordial broth. According to this mundane world view, spiritual beliefs are merely a pathetic, self-deluding attempt to breathe meaning and significance into a cold, harsh, empty, clockwork universe. The 'reality' is that – since the universe comprises *material* building blocks – death marks the end of our existence, and our only 'function' is to perpetuate the species.

Like any orthodoxy, science has claimed a monopoly on truth, seeing the scientific method as the only valid path towards knowledge. Descartes viewed rational analysis, observation, measurement and quantification as revealing 'certain, evident knowledge' – a belief still shared by most scientists today. Whether we want to find out more about a steam engine, a viral disease or a panic attack, scientific reductionism says that analysing it into its component parts will reveal all there is to know.

Since whatever does not fit this paradigm tends to be dismissed or ignored, the scientific model is self-perpetuating. The French Academy once announced that it would accept no further reports of meteorites, since it was quite 'impossible' for rocks to fall from the sky. Shortly after this, a shower of meteorites nearly broke the windows of the Academy (Ferguson 1982: 163). Scientists who rock the boat with challenging new ideas are not treated as heroes, but as either traitors or idiots.

Science has debased and devalued alternative visions of reality – such as those of mystics, shamans, poets or artists – which are based upon intuitive knowledge or subjective experience. Obligingly, people have generally assumed that science is 'correct', that it somehow has privileged access to the one-and-only 'objective' reality, and that it will (eventually) solve all our problems. We have been seduced by science, just as other eras and cultures have been mesmerized by religious dogma. We have mistaken the limited metaphors of science for reality. Yet as physicist Paul Davies (1984) notes,

> to say that a human being is nothing but a collection of cells, which are themselves nothing but bits of DNA and so forth, which in turn are nothing but strings of atoms, and therefore to conclude that life has no significance, is muddle-headed nonsense.
>
> (Davies 1984: 63)

The mechanistic, reductionist, determinist assumptions of the Cartesian-Newtonian world view have gradually permeated every aspect of our lives – from ecology and politics to health care and psychology – with consequences as wide-ranging as 'hurry sickness' and anomie to the destruction of the rainforests. The clockwork universe seems to have become overwound.

As Stan Gooch (1980) graphically observes

> the society which recognises only objective reality is a barren desert, a nightmare world 'peopled' by soulless zombies and lifeless machines. It is the land of King Midas, at whose touch all living creatures, all that loves and breathes, turn to lifeless metal. It is the psychotic

universe of Joey, the mechanical boy, from which all animate life, all warmth and compassion, has been excluded.

(Gooch 1980: 119)

A new vision of reality

Paradoxically, the 'common sense' reality of the Cartesian-Newtonian world view is now several decades out of date, and since the mid-1970s a steady stream of books has suggested that physics is moving towards a world view which looks remarkably mystical (e.g. Capra 1976; Bohm 1980; Zukav 1980; Talbot 1988).

As long ago as 1930, Sir James Jeans noted that

the universe begins to look more like a great thought than a great machine. Mind no longer appears as an accidental intruder into the realm of matter; we are beginning to suspect that we ought rather to hail it as the creator and governor of the realm of matter.

(quoted in Talbot 1988: 16)

Although traditional physicists still dispute such claims, David Bohm (1987: 7) suggests they have yet to realize how truly radical the implications of quantum mechanics are.

Like ancient mysticism, the new physics suggests that the world of separate objects is just a superficial appearance, 'maya', illusion. At the quantum level, everything and everyone is interconnected. Everything is an interwoven pattern of dancing energy. We are all aspects of the same whole. What is more, quantum physics shows that consciousness not only has *impact* upon physical reality; it might even *create* physical reality (e.g. Davies 1982: 13; Talbot 1988: 180–2).

On the cutting edge of biology, similar dramatic changes are afoot. The new biology is exploring the oneness of living things, and the apparently 'magical' ways in which members of a species – whether people, monkeys, rats or crystals – seem to communicate with each other. Rupert Sheldrake (1987), a pioneer in this field, suggests that molecular biology is not 'wrong'; it merely takes a limited perspective. He compares it to understanding how a television works. Molecular biology examines the 'hardware' of the TV set in trying to see how the picture is formed, but ignores the invisible wave transmissions, the 'software'.

Many people assume, as if it were self-evident, that matter is the 'real stuff' of the universe – that consciousness is a curious emergent property of matter, which somehow evolved because it had survival value. The old paradigm assumes that we live in a material universe, that we are bodies which happen to have minds. Within the new world view, the universe comprises energy and consciousness which *can* express itself in the form of 'matter' – so we are likely to be conscious *minds* which happen to be *embodied* at present. If so, perhaps the 'software' of our minds can exist without the 'hardware' of our brains?

Targ and Puthoff (1978) offer remarkable experimental evidence that consciousness is indeed 'mobile' in this way, in living people. And psychologist Alan Gauld (1983) carefully reviews the evidence for survival after death and concludes that, although much of the evidence can be explained in ordinary ways, or even as a form of 'super-ESP', such theories cannot account for all of the evidence. He concludes that the likeliest explanation is that we do indeed survive death – that life is merely a part of our journey as conscious, evolving beings.

Mystics have always said that enlightenment requires turning one's perceptions inside-out or upside-down. ('What is isn't, and what isn't is,' as it states in *The Upanishads*.) Within a mystical world view, mind or consciousness is the primary reality, and matter is an emergent property *created by mind* – the exact opposite of what our Cartesian-Newtonian 'common sense' leads us to believe!

More and more scientists are opening up to this possibility. Some are suggesting that consciousness might be the fundamental 'stuff' of physical reality, or that mind and matter are simply different manifestations of a higher-order reality. Some scientists are even considering the likelihood of a transcendent conscious being who might have created our universe (e.g. Sheldrake 1987). Perhaps, like Mahatma Gandhi, we have now crossed 'the Sahara of atheism', and are heading towards a spiritual renaissance?

As we approach this quantum leap in consciousness, I believe we are shifting from a physical to a *metaphysical* vision of reality – from matter to energy, from materialism to mentalism, from fragmentation to wholeness, from an inert universe to a conscious, evolving universe. We are moving beyond the limitations of the rational mind, beyond the five senses, beyond space and time, and beginning to explore the inner realms, to stretch the boundaries of our consciousness. We are reaching beyond our human potential towards our spiritual potential. (And to avoid becoming anachronistic and irrelevant, psychotherapy must rapidly follow suit.)

Of course, to those who are stuck in the Cartesian-Newtonian model, such speculations will seem nonsensical. After all, Thomas Kuhn's description of an individual who shifts to a new paradigm closely parallels one of religious conversion. Whereas nature once looked like a duck, it is now 'obvious' that she is a rabbit. The individual might have been aware of the shortcomings of the old paradigm for many years; but when the shift comes, it is often rapid and irreversible. (On a personal note, this was certainly true of my own experience. In an unforgettable and timeless moment, I suddenly 'knew', rather than merely believed in, a mystical world view. From that day, my life changed completely.)

Despite more and more people making this sudden shift, Kuhn observes that adherents of the old paradigm will continue to dismiss the revolutionary way-of-seeing as absurd and nonsensical:

'Of course the earth is flat!' 'Of course the sun revolves around the earth!' 'Of course the world is real and solid!' But as Alan Watts once remarked, 'If we are only open to those discoveries which will accord with what we already know, we might as well stay shut.'

(quoted in Klimo 1988: 13)

Psychology without a soul

After this brief excursion into the shifting metaphors of science, let us consider the possible implications for psychotherapy. Not surprisingly, as recent products of their culture, modern psychology and psychotherapy were built upon the shifting sands of Cartesian-Newtonian assumptions – with devastating consequences.

In an endeavour to gain status, psychology strived to emulate the materialist sciences, and lamentably rejected the more ephemeral, more subjective, more enthralling aspects of human experience in favour of the rational, tangible, measurable and quantifiable. It is easy to assess how long it takes rats to run through a maze, or whether someone's score on a depression inventory has increased or decreased. This might not reveal anything we did not know, much less anything very helpful or interesting, but it can be described in statistical terms and sound suitably 'scientific'.

The paradox is that while many physicists and biologists are now avidly discussing the nature of mind, the impact of consciousness upon physical reality, and even the possible nature of God, psychologists are still blindly pottering about in their offices and laboratories, measuring and quantifying anything that moves, in true Cartesian-Newtonian style, assuming there is an 'objective' reality which is gradually being discovered, and pooh-poohing parapsychology as irrational nonsense – as though nothing has changed.

Psychology should surely be the most fascinating topic on earth; instead it tends to be trivial, irrelevant, dehumanizing, limited and limiting. When I embarked upon an undergraduate course in psychology, eighteen years ago, my hopes and ideals centred upon exploring the nature and meaning of human existence, the complexity of personal relationships, the subtleties of our inner worlds. Little did I know! As Jacob Needleman (1988) puts it,

> modern psychology stands out among the sciences as a sort of strange disfigurement. The whole enterprise of modern, scientific psychology is rooted in an impossible contradiction: the attempt to subsume one level of reality under laws that govern a lower level.
>
> (Needleman 1988: 138)

Within a reductionist paradigm, we might fragment (break up, smash) the music of human behaviour into its component notes – but we can never hear the symphony. As a result, we have had to endure frankly embarrassing models of human psychology such as – borrowing an old phrase from Don Bannister – 'ping-pong balls with a memory'.

The mechanistic, reductionist, determinist assumptions of the Cartesian-

Newtonian world view are endemic in psychology and psychotherapy. The old paradigm gave birth to a positivist, materialist psychology which values objectivity, rationality and empiricism above caring, compassion and sheer humanity – which blindly assumes that we learn more from experimental data than from a novel or a poem.

In a recent letter to *The Psychologist* (March 1990: 124), a clinical psychologist claims to 'employ the scientific application of a problem-solving approach and functional analysis in conjunction with standardised assessments used within a developmental framework', and that her reports show a 'complete absence of "interpretation".' On reading this, with a heavy heart, I was reminded of Gooch's comment: 'I often feel like asking most psychologists if they have ever met a human being' (Gooch 1978: 79).

The aim of 'old paradigm' psychotherapy (along with organic psychiatry) is inherently conservative: to restore 'normal' functioning, to replace irrational thoughts and behaviour with rational, to encourage conformity, to plaster over the cracks so that the client can 'cope' again. It is a palliative-ameliorative approach. It assumes that 'normality' and 'coping' are synonymous with a desirable or optimal state. It searches for 'hard facts', failing to recognize the crucial importance of our fictions, of subjective perceptions, other than as a clue to what needs 'fixing', or as an aid to 'diagnosis'. It measures, categorizes and distances. It ignores our connectedness with others, our socio-political context (and thus labels depressed housewives as ill or inadequate). It assumes – however covertly – that the 'expert' is the therapist [see Chapter 6 by Mair], while the hapless client is the passive consumer of this invaluable expertise. And it claims, of course, to be value-free!

The old paradigm is also non-reflexive. Behaviourism, for example, which values 'objectivity' and detachment, does not require therapists to practise what they preach, nor to heal themselves as a prerequisite for healing others or be committed to their own personal growth. After all, it is scientific knowledge and technique which 'cures' people! Therapy is simply a professional job! As a result, how many of us know therapists whose personal lives are a mess – who are defensive, martyred, depressed, obsessional, lacking in self-esteem or devoid of *joie de vivre*? As Alan Watts (1975: 172) observes, 'The absence of spontaneity at almost any gathering of psychotherapists is one of the sorriest sights in the world.'

The psychoanalytic tradition of the aloof and detached 'observer', who dismisses any feelings the client has towards him or her as mere transference, and denies being involved in a two-person relationship, is another classic example of Cartesian-Newtonian thinking. The emphasis on rigid doctrine, jargon-ridden journals and prolonged training in psychoanalysis are reminiscent of initiation into a dogmatic religious sect. Professionalization of 'helping' – which goes hand-in-hand with scientific detachment – is an unfortunate legacy of the old world view, and inevitably empowers the professionals rather than their clients.

The early behaviourists adopted the old paradigm to the extent of dismissing consciousness altogether, defining psychology as the study of

behaviour – and attempting to understand human psychology via the study
of rats and pigeons. In 1914 John Watson suggested that 'Psychology . . . is
a purely objective, experimental branch of natural science which needs consciousness as little as do the sciences of chemistry and physics' (p. 27). Shortly
before physics began to expand to encompass psychology, psychology tried
to squeeze itself into the tiny glass slippers of Newtonian physics! As Capra
(1983: 177) notes, Watson would have been stunned to discover that, within
a couple of decades, physicists were saying that consciousness is intimately
bound up with the nature of physical reality.

> Sooner or later, nuclear physics and the psychology of the unconscious
> will draw together as both of them, independently of one another and
> from opposite directions, push forward into transcendental territory.
>
> (Jung 1951: ii)

Beyond dualism

The old paradigm is also dualistic. The very existence of psychology as a
discipline reveals our fragmented world view. In true Cartesian style – and
despite the growing impact of holistic medicine – we still tend to view mind
and body as separate. If people have thyroid problems, we refer them to a
medical doctor; if people have problems with stammering, or panic attacks
which rise into their throat, we are more likely to refer them to a psychotherapist. Yet a metaphysical viewpoint would suggest that all three problems
might have the same root cause: a blockage in communication or self-
expression, connected with the throat chakra (the chakras are energy centres
within the energy field, or etheric body, which surrounds and interpenetrates the human body), which might be expressed in different ways. Within
this paradigm, the body has its own wisdom and any 'symptom' – physical,
mental, emotional or spiritual – carries a metaphorical message which we
would do well to heed.

My experience is that clients often reveal long-standing physical problems
which perfectly mirror their difficulties – perhaps a 'weeping' skin problem
such as eczema in the case of unresolved grief, or cystitis in someone who
is 'pissed off' with their partner. At the same time, they tend to express
surprise that, as a clinical psychologist, I am interested in their *physical*
health. Equally, clients are often amazed when physical symptoms clear up
'spontaneously' as they deal with the underlying emotional issues. We have
been well indoctrinated with dualistic thinking.

If someone has a malignant tumour, the orthodox view – unquestioned by
many – is that the body-machine has acquired a random malfunction which
requires 'expert' intervention via chemicals, radiation and/or surgery. The
patient is a passive consumer of this 'treatment', and questions such as why
the tumour has formed, or what action the person might take to heal themselves, are unlikely to be asked. Machines do not have 'reasons', nor can
they fix themselves.

Yet at an intuitive level, I believe we are all aware of the metaphorical qualities of illness, and our potential for self-healing. Despite being taught to see illness as random and meaningless, we can readily see that our bodies mirror our inner selves. If people have cancer, might we not ask whether grief or resentment is 'eating away' at the person? Or whether they have resisted growth and change for so long that their body is expressing the 'need for growth' internally? Or whether this is their way of escaping an intolerable life situation, whether temporarily or permanently? Or whether these people have simply 'chosen' cancer as their means of dying? Such questions surely make sense to us, at an intuitive level. Yet how few cancer patients, even now, are routinely offered counselling or psychotherapy?

When I first saw someone with cancer – at her request – at a hospital renowned for its treatment of cancer, the consultant had patronizingly told her that he 'couldn't see it would do any harm', and apparently admitted that he had never heard of 'the cancer personality'. My client, who was much better informed than her consultant in this regard, 'knew' that suppressed anger and resentment, plus a recent bereavement, had played a major role in the aetiology of her disease.

Throughout the ages, physical illness has been treated with psychological approaches, yet, true to our reductionist world view, we now treat even *mental health* problems with physical methods: chemicals, electricity, surgery. If we continue to deny the meaning and significance of dis-ease in this way, to fragment therapy into countless specialisms, and to treat people as machines which can develop mechanical faults, we are reinforcing the destructive paradigm which is at the root of so much illness and distress, and assaulting our wholeness and humanity.

To borrow Lawrence LeShan's (1984) metaphor, we tend to behave like tinkering 'mechanics' where health is concerned, rather than like respectful 'gardeners' of the *whole* person: mind, body and spirit. (The question of whether psychotherapy, in its current form, should exist at all within the new holistic paradigm is certainly one to be seriously considered.)

With its concern with external appearance, observed behaviour and objectivity, the old paradigm has facilitated another form of dualism: the gulf between our public and private selves. (For an excellent analysis, see Smail 1984.) The widespread problems of child abuse and bulimia, for example, are two potent metaphors for the public 'mask' and private hell which so many people experience. Similarly, the Newtonian-based tendency to *weigh* an anorexic woman to assess whether she has 'recovered', rather than discuss her inner *experience*, would be laughable if it were not so damaging and destructive.

As a psychologist in the British National Health Service (NHS), I experienced this private–public split almost daily, and bit my tongue on countless occasions to avoid constantly challenging Cartesian–Newtonian assumptions – ranging from the medicalization of distress to sexism. (How rarely we speak from our heart and soul in these 'professional' settings.) When I eventually resigned from the NHS to become a metaphysical teacher and writer, it was partly because this gulf between my professional self and my personal, lived experience had become too great, too painful, too disempowering.

Steps to a new psychology

Of course, psychology has not adopted the Cartesian-Newtonian paradigm without having many dissenters – from William James to Gestalt psychology, from Carl Jung to Abraham Maslow. The 1960s saw the birth of humanistic and transpersonal psychology – representing many aspects of the new paradigm – with their focus on human potential rather than pathology, power rather than limitation, and growth through joy rather than suffering. The old paradigm had led to a focus on negativity, conflict and past trauma at the expense of delving into clients' strengths, talents and hidden potential. As Maslow (1962: 7) suggested, 'Freud supplied to us the sick half of psychology and we must now fill it out with the healthy half.'

The very concepts of 'treatment' or 'therapy', the still-used term 'patients', and 'clinical' psychology all reflect the assumption that unhappiness and distress are a sign that there is something wrong with the person – which needs to be fixed by a dispassionate 'expert'. A symptom-focused, old-paradigm therapist will often assume that the client's sole aim is to be free of 'symptoms'. A new-paradigm therapist is likely to help a client clarify her strengths, potential and hopes for the future, in the assumption that 'symptoms' indicate that the person is ready for growth and change, that her spirit is yearning to be fully embodied, that (at some level) she wishes to explore the deeper meaning and purpose of her life; thus, seeking personal growth or therapy is seen as a sign that there is something 'right' with the person.

Moreover, the new paradigm allows for transformation to occur through *dynamic interaction* of energy fields (or people), rather than via the mechanical *cause–effect* action of one particle (or person) on another. This provides a more holistic metaphor for the potential of therapist–client interactions, and emphasizes that – as most therapists would probably acknowledge – both therapist and client change when psychotherapy is 'effective'.

The old paradigm produced an essentially 'masculine' psychology: rational, analytic, linear, objectifying, fragmenting, distancing, controlling, disempowering and technique-based. In reflecting the patriarchal imbalance within society, psychology lost sight of its 'feminine' side. The new paradigm emphasizes the importance of maintaining a dynamic balance between the 'feminine' and 'masculine', between yin and yang. (Interestingly, Marilyn Ferguson (1982: 164) notes that those who have shifted to the new paradigm are typically involved in both science *and* the arts.)

While recognizing the value of rational thought and analysis, the new paradigm suggests that therapy *must* incorporate the feminine, that it should be a co-operative venture which values personal experience, which tolerates paradox and uncertainty, which sees context and wholes rather than isolated parts, which honours feelings and intuition, which recognizes that a therapist cannot be 'objective', and in which the client is encouraged to reclaim her inner wisdom and power.

Psychotherapy sprang from the ancient traditions of priests, shamans and healers. It was only in the late nineteenth century that its wellspring became science and clinical practice. Perhaps it is time to rediscover and reintegrate our roots, creating a novel synergy which will form the basis of twenty-first-century psychology. Nearly twenty years ago, Robert Ornstein (1972: 99) made a similar suggestion: 'For Western students of psychology and science, it is time to begin a new synthesis, to "translate" some of the concepts and ideas of traditional psychologies into modern psychological terms, to regain a balance lost.'

The new psychologies are certainly drawing more and more from philosophy, mysticism and spiritual traditions. Psychosynthesis, for example, draws upon Western and Eastern mysticism, classical Greek philosophy and neoplatonism, as well as twentieth-century psychotherapy (see Hardy 1987). In accord with mystical tradition, it has no rigid doctrine and encourages people to discover their own inner truth. (Neoplatonism and gnosticism likewise emphasize inner experience as the root of true knowledge, and see any doctrine as a mere approximation to the truth.)

What I gleaned from my own training in clinical psychology now seems trivial, inconsequential and even damaging in comparison with what I have learnt and experienced through metaphysics, Buddhism, Taoism, shamanism, mysticism and Western magical traditions, all of which embody intricate spiritually based psychologies which fully acknowledge human power and divinity, the impact of myth and storytelling, our interconnectedness, the wholeness of mind, body and spirit, and our potential ability to liberate ourselves from childhood and cultural conditioning.

Alan Watts (1975), in comparing the Eastern 'ways of liberation' with Western psychotherapy, suggests that they have two interests in common: the transformation of consciousness and the release of the individual from cultural conditioning. Perhaps he was being rather kind to Western psychotherapy here, since 'old paradigm' psychotherapy has no such aims!

So what are the essential characteristics of the 'new paradigm' psychology? First, the role of the therapist – as a fellow pilgrim in life's quest – is seen as supporting the individual in her journey towards wholeness, rather than as 'treating' or 'fixing' the client. The *client* is the expert, as she pursues exploration of her inner world, not the therapist. (The term 'therapist' should perhaps be abandoned in favour of 'guide', as in psychosynthesis and spiritual traditions, or perhaps the slightly more neutral term 'counsellor'.)

Second, the new psychology concerns itself with the *whole* person. This is not to say that it denies the role of allopathic medicine, but that it views physical symptoms and dis-ease as just as relevant in understanding a client's inner world as feeling depressed or anxious. The new psychology refuses to fragment people into mind and body, recognizing the inseparably interactive nature of the 'bodymind'.

It also makes the assumption – based upon intuitive knowledge rather than rational thought – that life is part of a spiritual journey, that each person's life is meaningful and purposeful, and that every challenge is a self-created opportunity to learn, grow and change, to move beyond the fears, doubts and limitations of the ego towards our higher self. (At this point, we lose many of the proponents of humanistic psychology.)

Instead of measuring and quantifying, reducing human beings to numbers and statistics, the new psychology's concern is with *quality*, with uniqueness and individual experience. It acknowledges the mystic within each of us which 'knows' that the personality, the ego, the 'I', is just a limited aspect of our unlimited Self. And it respects and values intuition, inner knowing, direct knowledge, which the old paradigm – '*cogito ergo sum*' – fails to recognize.

Rejecting the materialist goals and values of the old paradigm – such as competitiveness, domination, exploitation, sectarianism, fragmentation, blind rationality and detached objectivity – the new psychology encourages the development of *spiritual* values and qualities: love, trust, joy, creativity, co-operation, wisdom, compassion, intuition, humility, courage, vulnerability, caring, intimacy, clarity of purpose, responsibility, harmlessness, integrity, humour, authenticity and uniqueness. This is not, of course, to say that material goals and technological progress are inherently bad, but that they should be balanced with and directed by spiritual values such as love, wisdom and reverence. Within the new psychology, *love* is the primary healing power, the philosopher's stone – not theory or technique. (Therapists who see themselves as 'applied scientists' would, of course, cringe at this idea!)

> We see that when the activities of life are infused with reverence, they come alive with meaning and purpose. We see that when reverence is lacking from life's activities, the result is cruelty, violence and loneliness.
>
> (Zukav 1989: 22)

The new psychology is also present- and future-oriented – whereas old psychologies might focus on the traumas of the past, or aim to restore a *former* state of functioning. While recognizing the influence of childhood and cultural conditioning, the new psychology suggests that we get what we concentrate upon, and that we should therefore be *cautious* about re-energizing painful episodes from the past.

According to mysticism, time is an illusion that we create; the past is no more 'real', no more fixed and solid than the future. We constantly *recreate* our past in order to support or release our present beliefs, attitudes, thoughts, suppressed emotions and hidden agendas. The blockage is not caused by the past, but is created here-and-now. While we blame our childhood or other people for our difficulties, we are giving away our power. The present moment is our point of power.

Our memories of the past are therefore useful in reflecting the current state of our inner world, and what needs to be cleared out, depending upon which memories we choose to recall – but personal transformation comes from releasing the past, and reaching for the future. Unless we have personal and global visions for the future – desires, hopes, plans and dreams – we will simply recreate the past, or live out the life script set up in childhood.

According to the new paradigm, the inner realms – thoughts, beliefs, desires, imagination – are a powerful and creative force. ('Imagination' and 'magic' come from the same root.) Thus, many third-force and fourth-force psychologies make extensive use of creative visualization and guided imagery – first, as a way for clients to access their own inner wisdom, and second, as a way of actively 'creating' the future. Mystics and magicians have always known that the inner image carries extraordinary power, yet the old paradigm dismisses such activities as 'mere imagination', as witness the attitude of orthodox medicine towards visualization techniques in holistic approaches to cancer.

Within the old paradigm, change occurs slowly and often painfully. Sudden change is greeted with mistrust (as in the concept of 'flight into health'). The new psychology says that 'quantum leaps' in consciousness and health can and do occur, that rapid transformation *is* possible, if we allow it to be so.

More controversially, the cutting edge of the new world view suggests that our thoughts and beliefs *create* our experiences (see Edwards 1991). Each of us constructs our own personal world. This does not simply mean that we *distort* reality according to our beliefs and expectations, but that – since thoughts are energy, and similar energies resonate – we create and *attract* people, events and opportunities which reflect our inner world. As mystics say, the outer world mirrors our inner world. In this view, events are materialized experiences which have their origin in our thoughts, beliefs and attitudes. The world is not fixed and solid, but comprises dancing patterns of energy, which dance to the tune played by *consciousness*.

Such a view sounds quite crazy to our rational mind, since it turns our 'common sense' upside down. We generally assume that beliefs are based upon experience, rather than vice versa. We customarily see ourselves and others as victims of luck, fate and chance. A metaphysical world view suggests that *nothing* is random or meaningless; life is a lucid dream which *we* are creating, individually and collectively. It urges us to reclaim our power, to own our responsibility, through 'remembering' that we create our own reality. (This is not dogma to be swallowed, but a set of ideas to play with, to test out, to experience, to explore.)

If one starts from the assumption that we create our own reality – rather than from the traditional assumption that God, fate, luck or chance determines our lives – then *every* situation is seen as a self-created opportunity to learn and grow, to reclaim our power, our responsibility, our wholeness. When distorted and abused, this philosophy can become 'victim-blaming'

Table 8.1   Old paradigm and new paradigm psychology

Old paradigm psychology	New paradigm psychology
Cartesian-Newtonian.	Post-Einsteinian.
Materialist values/beliefs.	Spiritual values/beliefs.
Therapist as the expert.	Client as the expert.
Non-reflexive.	Reflexive.
Therapist as skilled technician, detached observer.	Therapist as participant in two-person relationship.
Therapist as expert.	Therapist as 'fellow pilgrim' (albeit with 'helping' role).
Therapy as one-way, cause-effect process.	Therapy as dynamic interaction, changing client *and* therapist.
Focus on measuring/quantifying and 'facts'.	Focus on quality and subjective experience.
Dualistic, reductionist.	Holistic, expansive.
Sees rationality and empiricism as only source of knowledge.	Accepts validity of intuitive knowledge and higher consciousness.
Tendency towards dogma and certainty.	Tolerates (or even welcomes) paradox and uncertainty.
Knowledge and technique seen as primary sources of change.	Love and wisdom seen as primary sources of change.
Focus on conflict, pathology and limitations.	Focus on strengths, potential and empowerment.
People seen as separate individuals.	People seen as part of a system.
Essentially 'masculine' approach.	Balances 'masculine' and 'feminine'.
Aim: restore 'normal' functioning, as defined by culture.	*Aim*: release client's future potential and wholeness.
Palliative-ameliorative approach.	Transformative approach.
Change seen as invariably slow and gradual.	Change can occur in 'quantum leaps'.
Focus on past creating the present.	Focus on future creating the present.
Symptoms seen as by-product of malfunction.	Symptoms seen as metaphorical message to self, when growth is blocked.
Life problems seen as negative stressors.	Life problems seen as self-created opportunities to grow.
Reality seen as fixed, solid and objective.	Reality seen as an 'illusion' that we create.
Life seen as mundane and essentially meaningless.	Life seen as part of our journey as conscious, evolving beings.

rather than 'victim-empowering', but every paradigm carries potential dangers. (The Cartesian-Newtonian paradigm, for example, has brought us to the brink of extinction ecologically – not to mention its brutal psychological impact.) When used lovingly and responsibly, this world view represents a quantum leap in consciousness – and might form the basis of the 'new psychology'.

Once you understand the symbolic nature of physical reality, then you
will no longer feel entrapped by it. You have formed the symbols, and
therefore you can change them.

(Roberts 1974: 436)

Beyond rationality

Might psychotherapy be seen as the process of helping people to shift to this
new paradigm – to restore meaning and significance to their lives, to recover
their sense of humanity, of connectedness, of authentic power, of wholeness,
of spirituality? As Proust said, 'The real voyage of discovery consists not in
seeking new lands but in seeing with new eyes'.

From its materialist perspective, the old psychology assumes that the goal
of life is, at best, happiness or pleasure – that life has no other meaning or
significance, no deeper purpose, no spiritual basis. Ever since the birth of
modern psychology, souls have been out of fashion. According to the old
world view, we cannot 'know' whether life is part of a spiritual journey,
since rationality and the five senses are our only source of 'knowledge', so
the question might as well be ignored.

Orthodox psychotherapy reinforces the 'meaninglessness' of life, and the
limited, rational self. ('Where id was, there shall ego be.') Mystical and
transpersonal approaches encourage us to expand beyond the ego, to realize
more and more of our potential, to open up to hidden dimensions of reality,
to 'remember' who we really are. The new psychology suggests that – once
our basic needs are met – our search for wholeness is our greatest single
drive, expressed in our *complementary* desires for individuality and for union
(or, if you prefer, in our search for the immanence and the transcendence of
God/dess).

In Maslow's terms, more and more people are now reaching beyond the
need for self-esteem and self-actualization, and becoming 'transcending self-
actualizers', in touch with superconscious material, aware of the 'God within'
or 'inner Light' along with an extraordinary sense of inner freedom and
power. (Maslow himself came to believe that humanistic psychology was
simply paving the way for transpersonal approaches.) Evelyn Underhill (1960)
notes that, for the limited self, 'sanity consists in sharing the hallucinations
of our neighbours'. To the mystic, everyday reality is but a pale shadow of
a far greater reality which can be experienced – an awareness which can
enhance every moment, and transform our everyday lives.

According to quantum physics, our reality *must* be a projection of higher
multidimensional realities (just as mystics have always claimed). Like prisoners in Plato's allegorical cave, we mistake our holographic illusions for
reality. If this is the case, it seems reasonable to suppose that, in certain
circumstances, we might perceive other dimensions of reality. A common
analogy is that our conscious mind is like a radio tuned into a certain
station. This station is so loud that we cannot hear other stations, and
might be unaware of their existence; but if we hush this noisy station – for

example, through meditation – we begin to 'hear' the subtle stations more clearly.

As William James (1977: 374) puts it, 'Our normal waking consciousness, rational consciousness as we call it, is but one special type of consciousness, while all about it, parted from it by the filmiest of screens, there lie potential forms of consciousness entirely different.'

Whereas Freud emphasized the neurotic side of human nature, and the dark side of the subconscious mind, and behaviourism focused upon the automatism of much learned behaviour, the new psychology throws light upon *higher* aspects of consciousness, showing how we can move beyond our conflicts or limitations by drawing upon inner resources of which our rational mind is unaware.

> This world is full of miracles. They stand in shining silence next to every dream of pain and suffering, of sin and guilt. They are the dream's alternative, the choice to be the dreamer, rather than deny the active role in making up the dream.
>
> *(A Course In Miracles*, 1985: vol. 1, p. 553)

Even when it has fully emerged from its chrysalis, the new psychology will not *supplant* cognitive-behavioural and psychodynamic approaches, nor the 'third force' psychologies which preceded it – any more than Einstein supplanted Newton, or Sheldrake supplants molecular biology. Instead, the new psychology *encompasses* the old within its greater vision, its broader perspective. (As a metaphysical counsellor, I still make use of psychodynamic, personal construct and Gestalt approaches, but always within a metaphysical vision – rather like using two-dimensional drawings in a three-dimensional world.)

Psychotherapy with a soul

Ken Wilber (1977) suggests there are four levels of consciousness, with corresponding forms of psychotherapy: the ego level (e.g. psychoanalysis, behaviourism), the biosocial level (e.g. family therapy, feminist therapy), the existential level (e.g. humanistic therapies) and the transpersonal level (which includes transpersonal therapies and spiritual paths). Each level of therapy will recognize and perhaps use methods from the levels 'beneath' it, but will tend to pathologize or invalidate the levels 'above' it; thus, in psychoanalytic tradition, mystical experiences are dismissed as signs of 'infantile regression' or 'narcissism'.

The new psychology is not synonymous with transpersonal psychology. Many transpersonal therapists use aspects of the old world view, while many behaviourists use aspects of the new paradigm. Very few of us embody a 'pure' form of either paradigm. As with any approach, it is essential to be sceptical, questioning and discerning – and not to assume that any one therapist speaks for others.

Some transpersonal therapists, for example, dogmatically insist that theirs is the one true path, or advocate suppressing rather than integrating emotions, or striving to be 'perfect', rather than to be 'perfectly oneself'. Some suggest that one should 'detach' from the world's problems rather than realize our connectedness and responsibility, or even that our main concern should be the after-life (in which case, one wonders why we're here at all!). Others hand over responsibility for their lives to God, or attempt to bypass the need to examine and transform one's inner world, in the hope that God or our higher self will do the work for us. Sadly, connecting with one's soul *can* be used as a way of avoiding personality issues and suppressed emotions which need to be dealt with *at a personality level*. 'Higher' is not necessarily 'better'. As I see it, spirituality needs to integrate psychology just as much as psychology needs to integrate spirituality.

The distinction between religion and spirituality is a crucial one here. The new paradigm is spiritual but non-religious. A religion is a dogmatic system of thought which urges us to seek truth *outside* ourselves – whether from priests, gurus, ancient texts, a transcendent (and non-immanent) God, or indeed from scientists or psychotherapists. Orthodox religions have been just as guilty of promoting the old world view as the current 'religion' of science. For example, both science and religion have portrayed humanity as the helpless pawns of forces beyond our control. While science sees our lives as determined by laws of nature or the whim of 'chance' or 'coincidence', religion has often pointed towards the dictates of God, fate or karma. Moreover, both world views have insisted that earth is mundane and physical: while science has merely pooh-poohed the non-rational and metaphysical, religion has often maintained a Cartesian dualism of matter and spirit, contrasting the mundaneness and suffering of life with the divinity and delight of the after-life ('Suffer, and get your reward in heaven!') – viewing earthly life as something to be endured until we ascend to the dubious pleasure of playing the harp for eternity, or vanish into the personal oblivion of nirvana.

The essence of a spiritual perspective is that we are conscious beings who happen to be embodied, rather than embodied beings who happen to be conscious – that is, that energy and consciousness rather than matter is the true 'stuff' of the universe. This is no less rational an assumption than materialism; indeed, it is more consistent with the emergent paradigm within natural science. If we accept these two assumptions – that time is an illusion, and that we are primarily conscious rather than material beings – then it makes little sense to suggest that we come into being at birth, or end at death. Life must be part of our journey as conscious beings. In the multi-dimensional reality which goes beyond spacetime, which transcends the limited personality self, we *must* be eternal.

> Our ordinary mind always tries to persuade us that we are nothing but acorns and that our greatest happiness will be to become bigger, fatter, shinier acorns; but that is of interest only to pigs. Our faith gives us knowledge of something much better: that we can become oak trees.
> (Schumacher 1978: 155)

One cannot reach a metaphysical world view purely through rational thought – at least while science is at its current stage in development. As in Dante's epic journey, we can be guided so far by Virgil (Reason), but in order to reach Paradise, we must be accompanied by Beatrice (Wisdom). We must go beyond rational thought, beyond the Cartesian-Newtonian paradigm, and trust our inner knowing and experience – and if *your* inner knowing contrasts with *mine*, that is perfectly fine. We are on different journeys, climbing the mountain from different sides. We need to relinquish the desire to be 'right', the outmoded belief that there is one objective reality, and trust that each individual is on their own path.

Our world view should always be provisional and vulnerable, open to revision, open to expansion, open to transformation, as we examine the inevitable puzzles and anomalies it raises. On the other hand, it seems crucial to make some *commitment* to a world view in order to explore its boundaries and limitations – just as Western culture has gradually exposed the strengths and weaknesses of the Cartesian-Newtonian paradigm. (For more than a decade, I *believed* in a metaphysical world view, but it had little impact upon my life and work until I began to *live* that world view, to explore its application and potential, tentatively slipping out of the materialist world view which I had been taught to believe in.)

The theory of dissipative structures – which has been applied to fields such as ecology, biology, economics and sociology – provides a useful metaphor here. Chemist Ilya Prigogine observed that any open system – for example, a world view, or a client–therapist relationship – is in a constantly fluctuating state. If these fluctuations become powerful enough, the system reaches a 'bifurcation point', a turning point, which leads either towards disintegration into chaos, or a sudden leap towards a higher and more stable level of organization. (The Chinese word for crisis – wei-chi – has two meanings: danger and opportunity.) When we are prepared to 'sit with' paradox and uncertainty for a while, to let go, to face the danger instead of retreating into the old and familiar, then space is created in which new patterns and possibilities can emerge at their own pace; in Prigogine's terms, a dissipative structure is formed (Prigogine and Stengers 1984).

Psychology and psychotherapy are perhaps heading towards such a bifurcation point, as the 'new science', Eastern philosophy, mysticism and transpersonal psychology begin to coalesce, challenging Cartesian-Newtonian approaches to psychology and pointing us towards a spiritually based psychology. The question is: will we descend into chaos, or make a quantum leap towards a higher level of understanding?

In Britain – where humanistic and transpersonal psychology have had little impact upon clinical psychology – many far-sighted individuals have been nudging psychology towards the new paradigm. Miller Mair, David Smail and Bob Hobson, for example, were all formative influences during my own clinical training and beyond (Hobson 1985; Smail 1987; Mair 1989). Each has, in his own unique way, challenged the Cartesian-Newtonian paradigm, and begun to construct a reflexive psychology which is personal, respectful, honest, loving and empowering, which recognizes context and connectedness, and which honours each client's inner wisdom and potential.

Part of the business of therapy is to help people to become explorers and makers of new maps. This is, of course, much more demanding than being simply a psychological tourist, simply following the map already prepared for you.

(Mair 1989: 37)

As one who deeply shares in this burning quest for 'personal knowledge', I long for psychology to be rescued from the blind alley of Cartesian-Newtonian science, and to witness its rebirth as an open inquiry into the meaning and nature of human existence, freed from dogma and certainty, and rooted in the inner qualities and metaphors of experience.

There is an old story of a university professor who visited a Zen master, Nan-In, to inquire about the philosophy of Zen. While Nan-In made tea for his visitor, the professor expounded on his own beliefs at great length. Eventually, Nan-In poured the tea into the professor's cup – and carried on pouring, even when the cup overflowed. 'Stop!' cried the professor. 'No more will go in!' 'Like this cup,' said Nan-In, 'you are already full of your own beliefs and speculations. How can I show you Zen unless you first empty your cup?'

Will psychology and psychotherapy cling to their faith in the Cartesian-Newtonian paradigm? Will we continue to pursue a soulless, fragmented psychology? Or will we find the courage and vision to 'empty our cup' – and listen to our hearts?

References

Bohm, D. (1980) *Wholeness and the Implicate Order*. London: Routledge & Kegan Paul.
Bohm, D. (1987) *Unfolding Meaning*. London: Routledge & Kegan Paul.
Capra, F. (1976) *The Tao of Physics*. London: Fontana.
Capra, F. (1983) *The Turning Point*. London: Flamingo.
A Course in Miracles (1985) London: Arkana.
Davies, P. (1982) *Other Worlds*. London: Sphere.
Davies, P. (1984) *God and the New Physics*. Harmondsworth: Penguin.
Edwards, G. (1991) *Living Magically: A New Vision of Reality*. London: Piatkus.
Ferguson, M. (1982) *The Aquarian Conspiracy*. London: Paladin.
Gauld, A. (1983) *Mediumship and Survival*. London: Paladin.
Gooch, S. (1978) *The Paranormal*. London: Fontana/Collins.
Gooch, S. (1980) *The Double Helix of the Mind*. London: Wildwood House.
Hardy, J. (1987) *A Psychology with a Soul*. London: Arkana.
Hobson, R. (1985) *Forms of Feeling: The Heart of Psychotherapy*. London: Tavistock.
James, W. (1977) *The Varieties of Religious Experience*. London: Fount/Collins. (First published 1902.)
Jung, C.G. (1951) *Aion, Collected Works*, vol. 9. London: Routledge & Kegan Paul.

Klimo, J. (1988) *Channelling*, Wellingborough, Northants: Aquarian.

LeShan, L. (1984) *Holistic Health*. Wellingborough, Northants: Turnstone. (Originally published as *The Mechanic and The Gardener*.)

Mair, M. (1989) *Between Psychology and Psychotherapy: A Poetics of Experience*. London: Routledge.

Maslow, A. (1962) *Towards a New Psychology of Being*. New York: Van Nostrand Reinhold.

Needleman, J. (1988) *A Sense of the Cosmos*. London and New York: Arkana. (First published 1975.)

Ornstein, R. (1972) *The Psychology of Consciousness*. San Francisco: Freeman.

Prigogine, I. and Stengers, I. (1984) *Order out of Chaos*. New York: Bantam.

Roberts, J. (1974) *Seth Speaks*. New York: Bantam.

Russell, P. (1988) *The Awakening Earth*. London: Arkana.

Schumacher, E.F. (1978) *Guide for the Perplexed*. London: Sphere.

Sheldrake, R. (1987) *A New Science of Life*. London: Paladin.

Smail, D. (1984) *Illusion and Reality*. London: Dent.

Smail, D. (1987) *Taking Care: An Alternative to Therapy*. London: Dent.

Talbot, M. (1981) *Mysticism and the New Physics*. New York: Bantam.

Talbot, M. (1988) *Beyond the Quantum*. New York: Bantam.

Targ, R. and Puthoff, H. (1978) *Mind-Reach*. London: Paladin.

Underhill, E. (1960) *Mysticism*. London: Methuen. (First published 1910.)

Walsh, R.N. and Vaughan, F. (1980) *Beyond Ego*, Los Angeles: Jeremy P. Tarcher.

Watson, J.B. (1914/1970) *Behaviourism*. New York: Norton.

Watts, A. (1975) *Psychotherapy East and West*. New York: Vintage.

Wilber, K. (1977) *The Spectrum of Consciousness*. Wheaton, Ill: Theosophical Publishing House.

Zukav, G. (1980) *The Dancing Wu-Li Masters*. London: Fontana.

Zukav, G. (1989) *The Seat of the Soul*. New York: Simon & Schuster.

RESPONSE – Albert Ellis

Gill Edwards has made an interesting and informative case for psychotherapists needing a 'soul' and for their adding a spiritual, mystical outlook and practice to empower and broaden their therapy. She makes a great number of points, many of which I agree with and many of which I, as a rational-emotive therapist, find exaggerated or misleading. Let me first point out my agreements, while noting that most practitioners of rational-emotive therapy (RET) and cognitive-behaviour therapy (CBT) would also tend to support these agreements today, although they may not have gone along with them, say, twenty years ago.

1 'Dogma lies firmly within the "old" psychology.' Yes, psychoanalysis, behaviourism and much of the 'old' positive thinking cognitive-therapy endorse the 'old' science of logical positivism and tend to be dogmatic. RET was somewhat on this false track in its beginnings (Ellis 1962) but is now in the constructivist, Popperian camp (Ellis 1989; 1990; 1991b).

2 Psychotherapy had better centre 'upon exploring the nature and meaning of human existence, the complexity of personal relationships, the subtleties of our inner worlds'. Yes! This is what RET and CBT today largely do (Beck 1976; Ellis 1988; 1990; 1991a; Ellis and Dryden 1987; 1990; 1991).

3 'Many of us know therapists whose lives are a mess.' Yes – including many transpersonal and mystical-minded therapists!

4 'The emphasis on rigid doctrine, jargon-ridden journals and prolonged training in psychoanalysis are reminiscent of initiation into a dogmatic religious sect.' Right on! I pointed this out in 1950 when I was still in the (liberal) psychoanalytic camp (Ellis 1950).

5 'Seeking personal growth or therapy is seen as a sign that there is something "right" with the person.' RET, along with Mahoney's (1991) brand of CBT, views therapy as helping people minimize their largely self-created symptoms *and* helping them to achieve more meaningful, and self-actualized lives (Ellis 1989; 1991b; Ellis and Dryden 1987; 1990; 1991).

6 'The new paradigm allows for transformation to occur through *dynamic interaction* of energy fields or people, rather than via the mechanical cause-effect action of one particle (or person) on another.' Many therapies stress interactionism today, especially RET and CBT (Ellis 1988; 1991b; Ellis *et al.* 1989; Huber and Baruth 1989; Mahoney 1991; Meichenbaum 1991).

7 Therapy 'should be a co-operative venture, which values personal experience, which tolerates paradox and uncertainty, which honours feelings and intuition, which recognizes that a therapist cannot be "objective", and in which the client is encouraged to reclaim her inner wisdom and power.' All of these goals are endorsed by modern RET and CBT.

8 'The new psychology . . . views physical symptoms and dis-ease as just as relevant in understanding a client's inner world as feeling depressed or anxious.' The 'science' that Edwards keeps taking pot shots at increasingly shows the important connections between disease and dis-ease; and therefore most clinicians, including RETers, today accept this 'new psychology'.

9 'We constantly *recreate* our past in order to support or release our present beliefs, attitudes, thoughts, suppressed emotions and hidden agendas.' The RET constructivist view agrees with this and even goes one step further: we partly accept *and* create our past 'experiences'; we also, as Edwards observes, *re*-create them today (Ellis 1990; 1991b; in press). So we are doubly constructive!

10 'According to the new paradigm, the inner realms – thoughts, beliefs, desires, imagination – are a powerful and creative force.' This has been one of the central theses – and practices – of RET for over thirty-five years (Ellis 1957; 1958; 1962).

11 If we start 'from the assumption that we create our own reality–rather than from the traditional assumption that God, fate, luck, or chance determines our lives – then *every* situation is seen as a self-created

opportunity to learn and grow, to reclaim our power, our responsibility, our wholeness'. Again, this has always been the approach of RET.

12 We had better be 'prepared to "sit with" paradox and uncertainty for a while, to let go, to face the danger instead of retreating into the old and familiar'. RET shows clients that certainty doesn't exist while paradox does; that they had better let go of dogmas, absolutes and musts; and that they preferably should often take risks, do what they are dysfunctionally afraid of doing, and look toward the present and future rather than the familiar past (Ellis 1962; 1988; Ellis and Dryden 1987; 1990; 1991).

My agreements with Gill Edwards, as can be seen from the above, are considerable; but so are my disagreements. I have already outlined several of them in my book, *Why Some Therapies Don't Work: The Dangers of Transpersonal Psychology* (Ellis and Yeager 1989), and shall probably devote another book to the mystical philosophy of many of the 'sages' that Edwards has followed, such as Ferguson (1982), Maslow (1973), Roberts (1974), Walsh and Vaughan (1980) and Wilber (1977). For lack of space, let me briefly – very briefly – specifically disagree with Edwards:

1 'A steady stream of books has suggested that physics is moving towards a world view which looks remarkably mystical.' No, a few physicists, like Bohm (1980) and Capra (1983), hold that science endorses mysticism. But the great majority of physicists deplore this view and hold that physics now emphasizes probability rather than certainty, and some amount of indeterminacy rather than overwhelming determinacy. 'Mysticism' is defined in *Webster's New World Dictionary* as:

> 1. The doctrine or beliefs of mystics; specifically the belief that it is possible to achieve communion with God through contemplation and love without the medium of human reason. 2. Any doctrine that asserts the possibility of attaining knowledge of spiritual truths through intuition acquired by fixed meditation. 3. Vague or obscure thinking or belief.

Actually, most mystics are certain that they can achieve communion with God and are positive that they can attain knowledge of spiritual truths through intuition. This is exactly what virtually no modern scientists, except a few like Capra, believe.

2 'Like ancient mysticism, the new physics suggests that the world of separate objects is just a superficial appearance, "maya", "illusion".' Yes, we don't see what separate objects, in themselves, are; but this hardly shows that they are nothing, have no existence, and are an illusion. Try kicking a stone and see!

3 'Quantum physics shows that consciousness not only has *impact* upon physical reality; it might even *create* physical reality!' It might, because almost anything is possible. But virtually all modern physicists believe that consciousness interprets – or 're-creates' – reality, not that it truly manufactures it.

4 'We are likely to be conscious *minds* which happen to be *embodied* at present. If so, perhaps the "software" of our minds can exist without the "hardware" of our brains.' Likely? Most improbably!

5 'We are reaching beyond our human potential towards our spiritual potential.' 'Spiritual' means, according to *Webster's New World Dictionary*:

> 1. Of the spirit or the soul, often in a religious or moral respect, as distinguished from the body. 2. Of, from, or concerned with the intellect, or what is thought of as the better or higher part of the mind. 3. Of or consisting of spirit; not corporeal. 4. Characterized by the ascendancy of the spirit; showing much refinement of thought and feeling. 5. Of religion or the church; sacred, devotional or ecclesiastical; not lay or temporal. 6. Spiritualistic or supernatural.

If therapists like Edwards would use the term in the second or fourth of the above definitions, they would get into little scientific trouble. For therapy, as in the case of RET, had better be intellectual, philosophic, and feeling oriented. But Edwards – following Alcoholics Anonymous and many other 'spiritual' therapies – wants to reach beyond our human potential: to communicate with, or actually to be, a supernatural Higher Power. This, I contend, is to denigrate our humanness, to increase our disturbed dependency, and to give up on our strictly human potential to help ourselves (Ellis 1983; 1985; Ellis and Schoenfeld 1990).

6 'In an unforgettable and timeless moment, I suddenly "knew", rather than believed in, a mystical world view.' By 'knew', Edwards obviously means she knew for certain instead of probabilistically believed. I wonder how any human can absolutely and certainly know that *any* world view is 'correct'. A world view is a belief; and beliefs or philosophies about the world are held probabilistically (by scientists) or with certainty (by devout non-scientific believers).

7 'The old paradigm gave birth to a positivist, materialist psychology which values objectivity, rationality and empiricism above caring, compassion and sheer humanity.' Virtually no modern form of psychological treatment – including, empirically, RET, CBT and behaviour therapy – is in the strawperson camp that Edwards describes. Therapies that do value objectivity, rationality and empiricism do so in the interest of caring, compassion and sheer humanity.

8 '"Old paradigm" psychotherapy is a palliative-ameliorative approach. It assumes that "normality" and "coping" are synonymous with a desirable or optimal state.' Another strawperson attack! RET, like many other 'rational' therapies, aims not only for symptom removal but also for helping people to make a profound philosophical change and to work for greater self-actualization (Ellis 1985; 1991a). Some New Age, faith healing therapies are palliative-ameliorative and only go for symptom removal, but most of the 'scientific' cognitive-behavioural therapies aim for genuine human growth and development.

9 'In true Cartesian style . . . we still tend to view mind and body as separate.' This is no longer true of even the majority of the educated public; and virtually no scientific psychologist still thinks this way.

10 'A metaphysical viewpoint would suggest that all three problems [thyroid trouble, stammering and panic attacks] might have the same root cause: a blockage in communication or self-expression, connected with the throat chakra'. Edwards defines the throat chakra as an energy centre 'within the energy field, or etheric body, which surrounds and interpenetrates the human body'. But if such an energy centre exists and blocks self-expression and causes diverse problems (like thyroid problems, stammering and panic attacks) it is obviously physical rather than metaphysical. Either it doesn't really exist, which is highly likely; or it exists but we cannot yet observe it, which is possible but unlikely; or it exists and for some reason can never be observed, which is most unlikely. Only if it exists and is not at all physical would it truly be metaphysical. But how can it then be called a field that has force? And how can Edwards seem so sure that it exists at all?

11 'A person with a malignant tumour is viewed by orthodox medicine as a machine, as a passive consumer of chemical, radiation, and surgery "treatment", and questions such as why the tumour has formed, or what action the person might take to heal themselves, are unlikely to be asked.' This is a travesty of modern medicine. Most 'spiritual' forms of healing, of cancerous tumours, moreover, do not ask (or answer) questions such as why the tumour has formed, and they require the afflicted persons to really heal themselves but also to rely on gurus, healers, religious figures, and assumed gods, and to use unproven and highly dubious medications (e.g. laetril).

12 'We now treat even *mental health* problems with physical methods: chemicals, electricity, surgery [thus] assaulting our wholeness and humanity.' But if, as Edwards keeps insisting, body-mind are one, disease clearly has mental *and* physical roots and it would be unethical and probably ineffective to *only* see mental disturbance as dis-ease and ignore its biological components. RET, although taking a highly phenomenological approach to many emotional problems, frequently combines chemical and psychological treatment for people with severe emotional problems (Ellis 1985; Ellis and Dryden 1987).

13 'Psychologists should be "gardeners" of the whole person: mind, body, and spirit. (The question of whether psychotherapy, in its current form, should exist at all within the new holistic paradigm is certainly one to be seriously considered.)' Suddenly, Edwards has brought body back into psychological treatment! But then she hints that all psychotherapy, presumably including spiritual therapy, is useless unless it is body-oriented, too, and is therefore 'holistic'. Maybe she means that it should only be spiritual. But then would it really be holistic?

14 'The Newtonian-based tendency to *weigh* an anorexic woman to assess whether she has "recovered", rather than discuss her inner *experience*,

would be laughable if it weren't so damaging and destructive.' Where does Edwards find these 'Newtonian-based' treaters of anorexia? In RET and practically all other scientific therapies, recovery from a woman's anorexia is assessed by her inner experience, her basic new philosophy of life, and several other important attitudes and behaviours, of which her increased weight is only one factor.

15 'Every concept of "treatment" or "therapy" . . . all reflect the assumption that unhappiness and distress are a sign that something is wrong with the person – which needs to be "fixed" by a dispassionate "expert".' Orthodox Freudian therapy somewhat went by this assumption, but virtually none of today's scientific therapies do. RET, for example, usually passionately and vigorously shows people how to question and challenge their own disturbance-creating assumptions, and how to do most of their self-help activities outside the therapy sessions.

16 'The "old paradigm" in psychology and medicine dismisses imagery and visualization as "mere imagination" as shown in their putting down visualization techniques to cure cancer.' Only partly true! Visualization is one of the most popular methods used by today's psychologist; and RET, for example, frequently employs positive imagery as well as its special brand of rational-emotive imagery. Medicine acknowledges that visualization may sometimes help cancer patients live longer and more happily, but is sceptical about its curing the disease itself.

17 In 'new paradigm' psychology, 'the client is the expert, as she pursues exploration of her inner world, not the therapist'. Yes, she is such an expert that she got herself into serious emotional problems and had to come for help! Besides, Edwards forgets the 'spiritual' psychology almost always teaches clients to follow – not lead! – a guru, a clergyperson, a mystical psychologist, a sacred scripture, a god, or some other kind of 'expert'.

18 The new psychology 'acknowledges the mystic within each of us which "knows" that the personality, the ego, the "I", is just a limited aspect of our unlimited self.' In RET we acknowledge that the ego, the 'I' is a limited aspect of our total self, but we are hardly contradictory (or grandiose) enough to claim that we have an *un*limited self. This sounds like mystical chutzpah!

19 'The new psychology encourages the development of *spiritual* values and qualities: love, trust, joy, creativity, co-operation, wisdom, compassion, intuition, humility, courage, vulnerability, caring, intimacy, clarity of purpose, responsibility, harmlessness, integrity, humour, authenticity, and uniqueness.' With the exception, perhaps, of vulnerability, these values and qualities are encouraged by virtually all scientific therapies, especially by RET. They are philosophic, meaningful values; but I fail to see how they have anything to do with spiritual or mystical values. Edwards previously said that a spiritual journey aims 'to move beyond the fears, doubts, and limitations of the ego toward our higher self' and 'at this point, we lose many of the proponents of humanistic psychology'.

But now she defines spiritual values and qualities only in humanistic terms!

20 'The new paradigm is spiritual but not religious.' I fail to see the difference. Spiritual, mystical and transpersonal psychologies all believe – and almost always *devoutly* believe – in higher powers; higher energies; higher consciousness; higher-order reality; a higher self; absolute truth; God-like intuition; creation of matter by mind; magical ways of communication, and survival after death; reaching beyond our human (to, presumably, superhuman) potential; *certain* knowledge of a true mystical world view; everyone's ability to completely cure himself or herself of physical and mental dis-ease; deification of 'inner experience'; full acknowledgement of human power and divinity; 'the unlimited self'; 'a metaphysical world view [in which] *nothing* is random or meaningless'; awareness of the 'God within' or 'inner light'; a 'world full of miracles'; the view that 'we *must* be eternal'; etc. If these aspects of spirituality and mysticism, all of which are endorsed by Edwards, are not the same thing as religiosity, I am not sure what is.

21 'If we accept these two assumptions – that time is an illusion, and that we are primarily conscious rather than material beings – then it makes little sense to suggest that we come into being at birth, or end at death. Life must be part of our journey as conscious beings. In the multidimensional reality which goes beyond spacetime, which transcends the limited personality self, we *must* be eternal.' What thinking! First, time is not an illusion that doesn't exist, but a phenomenon that has a relative, human-interpreted, but still 'real' existence. Second, we are conscious rather than just material beings. But we are most probably conscious and derived from material things. Third, conscious beings can easily come into being at birth and end at death; and it would look very much like they all do. Fourth, the 'multidimensional reality which goes beyond spacetime, which transcends the limited personality self' is an hypothesis, hardly a fact. Fifth, although she may vigorously deny it, this view of Edwards that our conscious self *must* be eternal is obviously a religious one.

22 In Edwards's Table 8.1, the items she places under 'New paradigm psychology' are subscribed to by virtually all modern scientific therapies, especially by RET and the cognitive-behaviour therapies, but a few items seem quite debatable: spiritual values/beliefs; client as the expert; accepts the validity of intuitive knowledge and higher consciousness; symptoms seen as metaphorical message to self, when growth is blocked.

These are merely *some* of the valuable and questionable points that I find in Edwards's chapter. I think that she has shown some of the limitations of the 'old psychology', but she has failed to note that its main aspects are no longer taken seriously by most modern non-mystical therapists. At the same time, she has clearly and accurately presented some of the main views of New Age, mystical, and spiritual psychotherapies and I hope that I have clearly and accurately shot them down.

References

Beck, A.T. (1976) *Cognitive Therapy and the Emotional Disorders.* New York: International Universities Press.

Bohm, D. (1980) *Wholeness and the Implicate Order.* London: Routledge & Kegan Paul.

Capra, F. (1983) *The Tao of Physics.* Boulder, Col: Shambhala.

Ellis, A. (1950) An introduction to the scientific principles of psychoanalysis. *Genetic Psychology Monographs* **41**: 147–212.

Ellis, A. (1957) *How to Live with a Neurotic.* New York: Crown. Revised edn 1975, Hollywood, Calif: Wilshire Books.

Ellis, A. (1958) Rational psychotherapy. *Journal of General Psychology* **59**: 35–49. Reprinted New York: Institute for Rational-Emotive Therapy.

Ellis, A. (1962) *Reason and Emotion in Psychotherapy.* Syracuse, NJ: Citadel.

Ellis, A. (1983) *The Case against Religiosity.* New York: Institute for Rational-Emotive Therapy.

Ellis, A. (1985) *Overcoming Resistance.* New York: Springer.

Ellis, A. (1988) *How to Stubbornly Refuse to Make Yourself Miserable about Anything – Yes, Anything!* Secaucus, NJ: Lyle Stuart.

Ellis, A. (1989) A rational-constructivist approach to couples and family therapy, in A. Ellis, J.L. Sichel, R.J. Yeager, D.J. DiMattia and R. DiGiuseppe, *Rational-Emotive Couples Therapy.* New York: Pergamon.

Ellis, A. (1990) Is rational-emotive therapy (RET) 'rationalist' or 'constructivist'?, in A. Ellis and W. Dryden (eds) *The Essential Albert Ellis.* New York: Springer.

Ellis, A. (1991a) Achieving self-actualization: the rational-emotive approach, in A. Jones and R. Crandall (eds) *Handbook of Self-Actualization.* Corte Madera, Calif: Select Press.

Ellis, A. (1991b) The revised ABCs of rational-emotive therapy, in J. Zeig (ed.) *Evolution of Psychotherapy, II.* New York: Brunner/Mazel.

Ellis, A. (in press) First- and second-order change in rational-emotive therapy: a reply to W.J. Lyddon. *Journal of Counseling and Development.*

Ellis, A. and Dryden, W. (1987) *The Practice of Rational-Emotive Therapy.* New York: Springer.

Ellis, A. and Dryden, W. (1990) *The Essential Albert Ellis.* New York: Springer.

Ellis, A. and Dryden, W. (1991) *A Dialogue with Albert Ellis.* Milton Keynes: Open University Press.

Ellis, A. and Schoenfeld, E. (1990) Divine intervention and the treatment of chemical dependency. *Journal of Substance Abuse* **2**: 459–68.

Ellis, A. and Yeager, R. (1989) *Why Some Therapies Don't Work: The Dangers of Transpersonal Psychology.* Buffalo, NY: Prometheus.

Ellis, A., Sichel, J., Yeager, R., DiMattia, D. and DiGiuseppe, R. (1989) *Rational-Emotive Couples Therapy.* New York: Pergamon.

Ferguson, M. (1982) *The Aquarian Conspiracy.* Los Angeles: Tarcher.

Huber, C.H. and Baruth, L.G. (1989) *Rational-Emotive and Systems Family Therapy.* New York: Springer.

Mahoney, M.J. (1991) *Human Change Processes.* New York: Basic Books.

Maslow, A.H. (1973) *The Farther Reaches of Human Nature.* Harmondsworth: Penguin.

Meichenbaum, D. (1991) Cognitive-behavior modification: an integrative approach in the field of psychotherapy, in J. Zeig (ed.) *Evolution of Psychotherapy: II.* New York: Brunner/Mazel.

Roberts, J. (1974) *Seth Speaks*. New York: Bantam.

Walsh, R.N. and Vaughan, F. (1980) *Beyond Ego*. Los Angeles: Tarcher.

Wilber, K. (1977) *The Spectrum of Consciousness*. Wheaton, Ill: Theosophical Publishing House.

REBUTTAL – Gill Edwards

Since I am familiar with Ellis's views on transpersonal psychology, there were few surprises in his response. Indeed, his comments often seem to refer to his own caricature of transpersonal psychology, rather than to what I actually said; but I'm sure that I have an equally prejudiced view of RET!

Since Ellis makes somewhat similar points several times, I shall reply under subheadings which cover his various comments.

Old vs new psychology

As I hope I made clear, I was not suggesting that humanistic psychology is 'old paradigm psychology', but rather – as Maslow suggested – that it is a staging post on the road towards a spiritually based psychology. (Ellis perhaps supports my case by emphasizing ways in which cognitive psychology has shifted over the years, although he would doubtless deny that RET shows any trace of mysticism!)

In order to clarify what I regard as 'old paradigm psychology', I agree with Ellis that I sometimes had to shoot at a strawperson; however, I still come across psychologists and others who are firmly stuck in the old paradigm. I wish I could agree with Ellis that all therapies are now based upon 'caring, compassion and sheer humanity' – but clearly he hasn't attended the kinds of case conferences which I have endured over the years! Likewise, I have seen remarkably little change in the hospital treatment of anorexia in Britain over the past fifteen years; the emphasis is still on weight and refeeding, with lip-service being paid to individual and family counselling (with a few rare and laudable exceptions).

The new science

I wholeheartedly agree with Ellis that the vast majority of scientists dispute the mystical views of Capra, Bohm, Davies, Sheldrake, Zohar and others. After all, such views challenge the status quo. (I personally know physicists who would not dare to mention Capra at work, but privately expound mystical views.) It is in the nature of a paradigm shift that a few courageous visionaries pave the way, while the bulk of the 'establishment' responds first by being smug and patronizing, then by attacking, and finally by being dragged reluctantly into a new vision of reality (often while claiming that they had known it all along). As John Kenneth Galbraith noted, 'Faced with having to change our beliefs or prove that there is no need to do so, most of us get busy on the proof.'

In my view, those scientists who are expounding mystical views are on the cutting edge of science, forming part of a global shift in consciousness which is moving beyond the Cartesian-Newtonian world view. As Bohm (1987: 7) says, 'I don't think the majority of physicists realizes how radical the implications of quantum mechanics are'.

Holistic health

First, my argument was against reductionism, not against a holistic view-point. I do have severe doubts about the wisdom of ever using drugs to suppress psychological distress, but I am in full agreement that making the body healthier (e.g. via diet and exercise) will have psychological impact. I am certainly not suggesting that psychotherapy is 'useless unless it is body-oriented' – healing can occur on many different levels – but that we perhaps need to move beyond the Cartesian model of having 'mind specialists' for 'mind problems' and 'body specialists' for 'body problems'.

Second, I totally agree with Ellis's criticism of some forms of 'faith healing', and have often made the point that too many alternative/complementary practitioners aim at symptom removal. However, modern medicine encourages people to treat *doctors* as 'faith healers' or 'gurus', in a way that is grossly disempowering and misleading. Holistic approaches to cancer, by contrast, invariably include counselling/psychotherapy and visualization techniques, and certainly require the person to understand why the cancer formed and to take responsibility for self-healing. I think Ellis overestimates the degree to which we have made the shift towards holistic thinking about health; as I see it, we have barely begun.

The chakras

I did not suggest that the throat chakra is metaphysical, merely that it is an energy centre unrecognized by orthodox science. I would refer Ellis to physicist Barbara Ann Brennan's excellent book *Hands of Light* (1988), in which she discusses the chakras from a research scientist's viewpoint.

Certainty and probability

Ellis makes an interesting point here. There is certainly a paradox in meta-physics over this issue (but one can enjoy wrestling with paradox!). The new metaphysics constantly refers to probable futures, probable selves and probable realities, and disputes old notions that our lives are predetermined by God, fate or karma. Similarly, it encourages us to rest easy in 'not knowing', suggesting that it is the limited, rational mind which constantly seeks 'certain, evident knowledge' of the kind that Descartes would recognize. As I stated, 'Our world view should always be provisional and vulnerable, open to revision, open to expansion, open to transformation'.

On the other hand, mystics have long distinguished between rational and intuitive knowledge – and this is where the apparent paradox arises. My own intuition makes me 'certain' of at least two things: first, that a creative Source exists (I resist the term 'God', with all its dogmatic, judgemental and patriarchal connotations); and second, that our separateness is an illusion. Once you ask what I *mean* by a Source, or what I *mean* by separateness or an illusion, I am thrown back upon my intellect, and therefore upon uncertainty. At this point, mysticism often seems woolly-minded or irrelevant. I doubt whether the human mind can even begin to grasp the true reality of 'God', yet I know that the existence of God is of profound significance to the way we understand our everyday lives.

Some years ago, I was deeply sceptical, even derisory, if anyone claimed to 'know' that God exists. How could they 'know', my rational mind would protest? Yet now, with some embarrassment – since I have long been anti-religious – I find myself in sympathy with those who say they have 'experienced' God. Carl Jung, when asked whether he believed in God (in a BBC interview with John Freeman), replied 'I do not have to believe. I know.' I now understand what Jung meant by this – 'knowing' in a non-rational way.

I disagree with Ellis's suggestion that this certainty is religious, since such knowledge is based upon *experience*, not upon received dogma. It is simply that the rational/'masculine' mind assures us that *rationality* is the only source of knowledge, and reinterprets intuitive/'feminine' experiences as superstition or mere 'belief'. The rational mind believes; the intuitive mind knows. As Plato suggested, true knowledge is remembering what the soul has always known. (I can only assume that Ellis has never had an experience of direct intuitive knowledge.)

Religion and spirituality

I do understand Ellis's confusion over the distinction between religion and spirituality, since mysticism – like any world view, including science – is, in a sense, a 'religion'. (Why do we accept that electron clouds exist? Because scientists tell us, and we trust and believe them; that is, we have 'faith' in their world view.)

For me, the crucial difference between religion and spirituality is that the latter rejects the view that there is any one 'true' religion, rejects dogma and external authority, respects inner experience and intuitive knowledge, and encourages us to seek our *own* ever-evolving and changing truth. It is the difference between accepting a statement because an 'expert' (whether scientist, priest or guru) tells you it is the case, and accepting it because you intuitively know it to be the case, because it 'feels right'. If one believes that knowledge has to be rational, then religion and spirituality might well seem indistinguishable.

Gurus and outside authorities

Ellis himself is attacking a strawperson here, since I made my position on this quite clear. It is time for us to stop 'worshipping' gurus, scientists, sacred texts, therapists or other so-called experts, and to find our inner guru. As Sheldon Kopp once put it, 'If you meet the Buddha on the road, kill him!' (1974). This isn't to say that we cannot learn from books, therapists and teachers – of course we can – but that the final arbiter on what we believe, or what we 'know', must be our own hearts. We should have no higher authority than ourselves. (And 'ourselves' includes our higher self – that wise, all-loving, far-sighted aspect of the self which the old psychology ignores.)

As for God, the new spirituality – from channelled metaphysics to liberation theology – is *panentheistic*, urging us to recognize the immanence (as well as transcendence) of God, and to forsake the childlike need for an 'authority figure in the sky'. It urges us to reclaim our power and responsibility, and recognize the God *within* us. Historically, the loss of the immanent God, with the rise of patriarchal religions, led us to view power and authority as external – and thus created an unholy mess. Part of the task of the new psychology is to help people to reclaim their own power, to learn to listen to their inner wisdom, to extend beyond their limited personality towards their true potential.

Human potential

When 'human potential' is defined by the Cartesian-Newtonian world view, then I would argue that it is limiting us to a small, dark cellar within the vast mansion of our selves. My guess is that most people are aware that we have scarcely begun to tap our potential, that we can reach *far* beyond what science and psychology currently tell us is possible. This is part of what I mean by our 'spiritual potential'; it is 'superhuman' only to the extent that one limits what it means to be human.

Creating our own reality

I'm quite sure Ellis *doesn't* believe that we create our own reality, despite his statement that 'this has always been the approach of RET' – unless he is a mystic in heavy disguise! My understanding is that he believes that we have *impact* upon physical reality, and *distort* it according to our inner world – the traditional psychological view. If someone's home is burgled (while the doors and windows were locked), would Ellis believe that the person created that event? If someone smashed into Ellis's parked car while he was in the supermarket, would he assume he had created that event? I doubt it. Yet a mystical view asserts that we create *every* event in our lives, and is thus a quantum leap beyond humanistic or psychoanalytic world views.

Having said this, there is a not-so-curious tendency for models which are becoming outmoded to begin sneakily to encompass the new, while denying that they are radically shifting their underlying assumptions! We saw this as behaviour therapy crept towards cognitive-behavioural approaches, and as the biomedical model began to acknowledge psychosocial factors in health. In view of this, I wouldn't be at all surprised if, in the twenty-first century, psychology claims to have been 'mystical' all along!

Eternal beings?

I am somewhat baffled as to why Ellis thinks it 'most improbable' that we can exist as conscious beings without bodies. It is only improbable to a materialist! There is plenty of 'scientific' evidence which supports this claim, and it is a view quite compatible with the new physics.

Ellis's objections simply arise from paradigm conflict. I would argue that Ellis is 'religiously' confining himself to orthodox science and rational materialism, while Ellis would counter that I am being 'irrational' and mystical. From the current orthodox viewpoint, I am the one who is crazy; but George Kelly spoke of the need to 'transcend the obvious' if we are to truly change. More and more people are now shaking up their core constructs, and coming to similar conclusions about the nature of reality.

By the end of the 1990s, I would predict that 'orthodoxy' and 'common sense' will have shifted quite considerably away from materialism, and towards a spiritual perspective on our everyday lives. If so, I hope that psychotherapy, with its history of 'transcending the obvious', will have little difficulty in following suit.

References

Bohm, D. (1987) *Unfolding Meaning*. London and New York: Routledge & Kegan Paul.

Brennan, B.A. (1988) *Hands of Light: A Guide to Healing through the Human Energy Field*. New York: Bantam.

Kopp, S. (1974) *If you meet the Buddha on the Road, Kill Him!* London: Sheldon Press.

Dryden. W. + (1992) Psychotherapy
Feltham . C. and its Discontents
Open University.

NINE

Psychotherapy and political evasions

DAVID PILGRIM

Introduction

This chapter will address the relationship between psychotherapy and politics
in two senses. First, I shall explore some of the occupational hazards surrounding the psychologizing of human distress. As all versions of psychotherapy are necessarily psychological in their reasoning, they are prone to
psychological reductionism. This tendency can be found in *all* branches of
counselling and psychotherapy (for my purposes these sets of occupational
practices will not be distinguished). I shall argue that this reductionism
takes different forms. In the case of the psychodynamic therapies the problem resides in the limitations of interpretative systems which focus narrowly
on intra-psychic events or group processes to the exclusion of their wider
social context. In the case of humanistic therapies the problem mainly
resides in overvaluing human agency and understating material constraints
on our ability to choose our destiny. Consequently, I shall argue that in
different ways, psychotherapy is condemned to psychological reductionism
and political ignorance.

My second exploration will be in the realm of professional power. This
issue will have been addressed in a particular way by Jeffrey Masson (see
chapter 2), which I consider to be important, but pre-emptively nihilistic.
My approach to this topic will be to argue that indeed professionalism in
the mental health industry is problematic but it is not inevitably tyrannical.
What is vital, in order to clarify *how much* it is problematic, is to refuse to
accept at face value what therapists say about themselves. Instead, it is

necessary to evaluate their claims using criteria set by others (particularly their clients). I hope to show that when this exercise is carried out, so much of what passes for either disinterested applied science (say in clinical psychology) or liberating art (say in the variants of human potential work) is a rhetorical gloss to the pursuit of self-interest.

I am holding these two critical exercises (about reductionism and professionalism) to be separate only as a paper exercise for clarity. In practice, I consider that they constantly reinforce one another and consequently mystify both their practitioners as well as the recipients of their services. For instance, when therapeutic experts articulate their preferred psychological understanding about nuclear weapons or infidelity in a woman's magazine or Sunday supplement, they are inducing a state of psychological mindedness in their audience and at the same time reinforcing their occupational authority and legitimacy. As a consequence, reductionism and professional rhetoric are often conflated. In order to begin a strategy of illumination about these conflated processes, we need to step back and try to unpack the sources of each.

Briefly, at the start, certain assumptions will be declared. First, I shall not aim to 'demonstrate' or 'prove' my case, although I shall stay with certain academic conventions associated with these processes. Instead, I want merely to *argue* a case, which I think is often not heard by a psychotherapeutic audience. Accordingly, and not in the academic tradition, I shall often use the first not third person. Second, and linked to this, it is important to declare that my own left-of-centre political values, held since early adulthood, have framed my way of understanding my experience of the mental health industry as a practitioner (between 1973 and 1986 in the British National Health Service) and thereafter, until 1990, as a trainer in higher education of counselling psychologists. During that time, I saw psychotherapy at first promising a role in personal and political liberation. At the time of writing (1991), in the wake of twelve years of New Right hegemony, I now view psychotherapists as holding a more dubious role in society. If they have not been personally captivated by aggressive individualism, they have become collectively preoccupied with professional survival and advancement. In the process, both intellectual integrity and social justice have been subverted, scorned or marginalized within their discourse. My attack on the two main issues in this chapter flows from, and has informed, this disillusionment with a culture to which I remain tentatively but ambivalently attached – a point I shall return to at the end.

In case it is misunderstood from a superficial reading, it is important to clarify what I do *not* want to claim. I do not claim that an exploration in personal terms in a safe relationship cannot often be of help in ameliorating mental distress. Also I do not want to claim that professionals are motivated *only* by self-interest and that their collective strategies are always reactionary in character. In other words, my concern in the rest of this chapter is to problematize professional therapy, not refute its legitimacy in total.

P attoologicium .

The problem of reductionism

To start with a recent example of this problem, I heard a psychotherapist contribute to a BBC Radio phone-in about the moral and political question about whether celibate women should be allowed to have artificial insemination from the health service (the so-called 'virgin mother' debate of March 1991). The therapist with total sincerity and occupational zeal explained to the listeners that from his experience of 'treating' female patients, applicants for such treatment were 'borderline personalities' or 'narcissists', who were psychologically incapable of the intimacy necessitated by a real heterosexual relationship. Moreover, he opined, if they were allowed to receive the help in conception they were demanding, the result would be children who themselves would become narcissistically disturbed, on account of their care at the hands of a damaged mother.

This stance about sexuality is not uncommon in therapists. Take another example from one of the doyens of British object-relations theory, Harry Guntrip. By all accounts Guntrip was a thoroughly decent and personable man. He eschewed the distant and deep interpretative framework of the Kleinians and considered that there was more to therapy than the transference interpretations, favoured by pure Freudians. However, this is his view of people who fail to conform to a settled heterosexual existence:

> Prostitution and homosexuality are clear cases of schizoid compromise in their evasion of the real relationship of marriage. That is one reason why they are so hard to cure.
>
> (Guntrip 1977: 303)

The problem with this type of statement (apart from the daft notion that he is trying to cure illnesses) is not that the claim might not be partially true, for some people some of the time. But it is unwise to take such a claim seriously for large groups of people. In any other context but that of psycho-therapeutic musings (say astrology), this type of claim would be laughed out of court as an example of an unsupportable stereotyping of complete strangers. So why should psychotherapists be immune from everyday expectations of truth-claims? Moreover, even when Guntrip's type of argumentation has some validity in a particular case, how does anyone (even a psychoanalyst) know that it is a <u>total explanation?</u> People are complicated. Their lives are constrained and shaped by many factors which psychologists of any school can only partly grasp (like the blind men and the elephant). As far as sexuality is concerned, all sorts of situational factors may determine its expression. Single-sex institutions encourage homosexuality for some temporarily and for others more permanently. As for prostitution, poverty is a pretty power-ful stimulus, as is the need to finance a drug habit. These external contex-tual factors are as relevant to consider in particular cases, as the antecedent biographical nuances which may have determined a person's proclivities.

Of course it could be argued that Guntrip was particularly prone to *reductio ad absurdum* arguments. However, I think the problem goes much deeper

228   *David Pilgrim*

than his particular intellectual foibles. It is probably traceable within psychoanalysis to Freudianism itself, which emerged as both a <u>hermeneutic</u> system *and* as a branch of <u>natural science.</u> As a medical procedure, which it still is in the main, psychoanalysis has built its knowledge upon the notion that scientific experts label the world in order to control it. (The world of psychoanalysis is the unconscious of its patients.) Whereas some psychoanalysts, since the Second World War, have been noteworthy for their critique of the objectification of patients by the biodeterminism of Kraepelinian psychiatry (the so-called 'medical model') (Laing 1964), they are exceptional. Most <u>psychoanalysts think 'diagnostically'</u>. The terminology of psychoanalysis is still that of medicine. Ever since Karl Abraham first systematized for the early Freudian circle a diagnostic typology (Abraham 1927) psychoanalysts have continued to play this scientific-medical game. Later on Fenichel (1945) and Winnicott (1958) both provided us with examples of this typing or, more accurately, stereotyping tendency within institutional psychoanalysis. Winnicott even argued on the basis of his three major diagnostic groups (neurotics, depressives and the narcissistically disturbed) that three therapeutic techniques naturally follow – respectively analysis, surviving and holding.

Thus both Guntrip and our phone-in psychotherapist (mentioned at the beginning of this section) are probably not eccentric. They personify a certain tradition within psychotherapeutic discourse, <u>which considers that generalizing about whole groups of people is a legitimate exercise</u>, which can even take place anonymously. At this stage I want to return then to the contradiction of psychoanalysis: its roots in both positivistic science and in hermeneutics. This contradiction entails a knowledge system which emphasizes on the one hand a particular form of biological determinism (Sulloway 1980) and on the other a notion of people as organisms who invest their lives with meanings. The latter can be decoded and renegotiated with their therapist. Thus the psychoanalytic expert has, from the beginning, had it both ways. He (or less often she) has been both a typologist and a hermeneut. This has left psychoanalysis as a body of knowledge tantalizingly ambiguous or 'ambivalent' (Ingleby 1984). It is almost like a Rorschach card which can induce innumerable responses from its acolytes, patients and commentators. These various reactions have been particularly evident in relation to political ideology.

Richards (1988) discussing this issue makes the following point:

What can be the political significance and value of a concept of 'the unconscious' if it can be inserted with equal conviction into both historical materialism . . . and classical liberalism? This is actually the wrong question although it is based on a fact which must be observed, namely that psychoanalysis does not bear with it a stable set of political values, which act as a constant factor in different combinations with other intellectual elements.

(Richards 1988: 6)

For Richards, the 'correct' question is whether the intellectual talent exists to generate credible connections between political theory (of any persuasion) and psychoanalysis. And of course this talent has been there. It has generated a number of hybrids between psychodynamic and political theory in the work, moving from left to right, of Reich, Althusser, Horkheimer, Habermas, Fromm, Eichenbaum and Orbach, Holbrook and Parsons. The political breadth of these thinkers demonstrates that psychoanalysis is open-textured and that it can be appropriated by many people from different political backgrounds. Accordingly, it is not possible to deduce, as many Leftist acolytes of psychoanalysis have, that Freud's work was inherently or unambiguously subversive (cf Turkle 1987). (If it was, Freud would not have been a conservative.) However, in line with the Nazis burning Freudian texts, I know of no attempt on the part of fascism to incorporate psycho-analysis, although this is not the case with Jungian psychology (Dalal 1988; Masson 1989). This may be explained specifically because psychoanalysis emerged from a predominantly Jewish intellectual culture. This ensured its vilification by an ideology which had anti-Semitism at its heart. Jung was a rare Gentile in Freud's early circle. With the rise of Nazism, this provided him with a privileged protection.

Why is psychoanalysis so open to incorporation by different political ideologies? The answer may reside in Freud's original generalization about psychopathology. This is so broad in its claim, that it potentially encourages wide sympathy. Essentially, in *Civilisation and its Discontents* (1930) he made it clear that civilization necessitates neurosis (which in turn necessitates psychotherapy). What he did not do was make a specific claim about any particular form of pathogenic society. There is a contradiction here when we consider the sympathies of many on the Left for psychoanalysis. Freud's grand meta-narrative about the human condition emphasized not class struggle but intrapersonal instinctual struggle. Here for instance:

> The meaning of the evolution of civilisation is no longer obscure to us. It must present the struggle between Eros and Death. This is what all life essentially consists of, and the evolution may therefore be simply described as the struggle for life of the human species.
>
> (Freud 1930: 122)

For psychoanalysis and its diluted therapeutic spin-offs, the consequences of frustration and repression imposed on all individuals in a civilized society are non-specific. They act like a blunderbuss, engendering some degree of psychopathology in all of us whatever our race, class or sex. This has led some sympathetic psychoanalytical commentators to commend Freud as a humanist who gave to us 'psychoanalytical compassion'. Turkle makes clear in this commendation that the boundaries of the family set the political limits on our shared predicament:

> we all suffer from the same processes, some of us merely suffer more than others. And . . . these processes are the fundamental tensions and

ambivalences that are set by our earliest lives as children growing up in a family . . . we have mothers and fathers, . . . we are in triangles and that's hard, we are ambivalent, we love, we hate and we are sexual, it's not clear we are in control all the time and we want to be.

(Turkle 1987: 80)

To quote an aphorism favoured by psychodynamic therapists, 'We are all ill'. We are all in the same boat, so we are all equally prone to the mental anguish generated by the quality of our family relationships in childhood. This type of 'totalizing' logic condemns its followers to reductionism. However, our race, class and sex are relevant because we live not only in civilization but also in a particular *society*, which is structured and politically divided along these three fracture lines (and others, such as disability and sexual orientation). What follows from this political fragmentation are empirically proven differences in mental health between rich and poor, men and women and white and black (Cochrane 1983; Busfield 1986). These findings suggest to me that something is going on outside of Turkle's family boundaries which contributes to mental pain. Moreover, I suspect that these events are also about current and real oppressions, not merely distant and fantastic inner conflicts. There is little wonder then that when a Leftist Freudian, Reich, insisted on a shotgun wedding between psychoanalysis and historical materialism (Reich 1933) he was vilified, isolated and probably eventually driven crazy by his efforts.

What are the conservative consequences of psychological reductionism by psychodynamic therapists? I shall mention three here, which I have personally experienced and encountered in accounts given by friends, students and clients. They are generalizations, so I shall simply say 'if the cap fits wear it'. I shall also cite other views, where relevant, to support my case.

First, clients are expected to suffer forbearance in the face of oppression. Action against oppression may be spotted as 'acting out' and so diagnosed as requiring further analysis. For instance, in a particularly mean-spirited attack on political action by representatives of Parisian psychoanalytical chic (Chasseguet-Smirgel and Gruneberger 1986), revolutionaries are deemed to be suffering from an omnipotent infantile fixation. If all societies are ubiquitously pathogenic, then personal education (analysis) and political passivity will be indicated or implicitly prescribed by therapists. These comfortable analysts issue the clear message that life is to be suffered in an oppressive society and that protest and the seeking of social justice are symptoms of individual pathology.

Second, notions of external reality are chronically questioned (as foci of the patient's projections) or ignored as being inconsequential. There is a constant therapeutic preoccupation not with externalities (and their lesser relevant 'signal anxiety') but with internal fictions. Their particular attendant neurotic anxieties, produced by the client's projections, repetition compulsions, repressions, fantasies, etc., then become the therapeutic foci. Faced with therapists who prioritize interpretative *élan* over practical problem-solving, clients unsurprisingly have a view of helpful events, which is often not shared with professionals (Llewelyn 1988).

Probably the most important and unresolved difficulty still facing psychodynamic therapists, in this regard, is the exposure of Freud's abandonment of the seduction theory (Masson 1985). This has led to two main responses. First, the bearer of the bad news has been metaphorically shot. Masson has been attacked in the *ad hominem* way typical of psychoanalytical reductionists. Alternatively, psychodynamic therapists have conceded that childhood sexual abuse is a reality and they entreat the public to approach them for help. Why anyone should trust these types of therapists given their past culpability, when they refused to accept the veracity of clients' accounts about abuse is, to say the least, curious.

The third general problem I touched on earlier, namely that of a continued underlying medical positivism which encourages diagnostic games. The retention of the medical discourse ('borderline personality', 'clinical depression', 'schizoid', 'paranoid', etc.) simply keeps lay (non-medical) therapists within the ambit of medical practice and it legitimizes the medical model. Psychotherapists, despite their inappropriate and anachronistic title, do not treat illness – they struggle with distress and meaning. This is also true of friends and lovers but without them picking up a salary or fee, and without them resorting to an alienating vocabulary. Diagnostic pigeon-holing does not enhance humanity – a truism for both biological and psychological therapists. When I have supervised trainee therapists and counsellors, I have been struck by the zeal with which some non-medical practitioners embrace the diagnostic discourse of medical psychotherapy. This may be seductive for this group because it enhances their sense of confidence, status or authority. Whatever the reason is, I have not heard any trainee following the trend, being able to defend their diagnostic pronouncements convincingly in terms of their client's interest. When I commit the same mistake (as I am a product of the same clinical socialization) I do so to encourage a sense of certainty in my own competence, but I recall no instance in which I have shared the 'diagnosis' with a client. This suggests that I have gained at their expense, as I do not have any confidence that their lives would be enriched by my labels.

Before leaving psychoanalysis, I want to mention another type of reductionism within its tradition. While Freud himself, and his followers, were blinkered by their preoccupation with individualism and an undiscriminating notion of 'civilization', social circumstances did not allow this occupational habit to persist indefinitely. For instance in Britain, as a result of the crisis created by battle fatigue during the Second World War, there were simply not enough individual therapists to go around. This supply and demand problem stimulated the emergence of group therapy. Thus the likes of Foulkes, Rickman, Bion and Main, all individual psychoanalysts, began to work, towards the end of the war, at Northfield Military Hospital. They creatively imported their professional ideas to group work. Whereas Bion returned to elitist individual private practice, others like Main, after the war, became highly influential in introducing psychoanalytical group work to the newly formed NHS, by heading up the Cassel Hospital. The Tavistock group, associated with Main and his colleagues, in 'Operation Phoenix', self-consciously viewed the circumscribed aim of the reform of the psychiatric hospital as a legitimate social experiment (Dicks 1970). This limited aim blinkered them from analysing the wider oppressive role of their profession; this task awaited the more anarchistic spirit of their younger colleague Ronald Laing.

The soldier-patient experiment in group work at Northfield was new terrain colonized by a tradition centred heavily upon the individual. At first it was a bit like a ship trying to move on land (witness Bion's struggles early on in his *Experiences in Groups*). Eventually an amphibian vehicle was constructed and psychoanalysis became adapted for group work. This shift of levels, from the individual to the group, was a potential growth point for psychoanalysis; it could have grown out of reductionism. It was not to be the case. What happened instead was that whereas previously the limits of attention of psychoanalysis were set by the skin-encapsulated individual, now they were set by the physical and psychological boundaries of the small or large group. The latter were thus separated from their wider societal context. This new form of reductionism not only came to characterize clinical innovations such as the therapeutic community movement (Manning 1989) but also the exploration of organizational problems and industrial relations. The latter, documented by Miller and Rose (1988), has been associated with the Institute of Human Relations, the organizational or non-clinical partner of the Tavistock Clinic. It has tended to remove organizational dynamics from their sustaining socio-political context: a form of reductionism which Silverman (1970) has correctly described as 'inadmissible'.

I have explored a concern about reductionism and its conservative consequences at the heart of European psychodynamic theory and practice. I now want to move to a different version of reductionism associated with American humanism. If the former has been hamstrung by the dead weight of medical-psychological positivism, then the latter has suffered from idealism in both senses of the word. It has been permeated by a whole set of utopian ideas about the growth or transcendence of the human spirit or mind unfettered by material reality. Certain key words display this character – 'growth', 'potential', 'choice', 'self', 'personal needs', 'responsibility', and so on. The soil in this horticultural model of psychological change is the dyadic or group relationship. The water and nutrients are the personal characteristics of the therapist. This is exemplified by the Rogerian central therapeutic triad of 'genuineness', 'non-possessive warmth' and 'accurate empathy'. It is a model of sharing and caring (like the American cartoon characters 'The Care Bears') which reduces problems of alienated life to problems of meeting and communicating. Pain and oppression can simply melt away given the correct relationship. As the guru of Gestalt therapy put it, 'You are you and I am I and if by chance we find each other, it's beautiful' (Perls 1972).

I would speculate that this personalistic US optimism has been bolstered and informed by three main cultural preconditions. The first of these is a political history of new beginnings (the USA as the great melting-pot for international immigration). In such a context, there is a high value placed upon an openness to new experiences and new faces. Friendliness and a generosity of spirit are engendered in US culture. The second is the narrow conflation of liberation with individual freedom (the resolution of the slave legacy and the consequent value placed upon civil rights in North American society). The third characteristic of modern US society is a refusal to respect boundaries. Examples of this expansionism were the violation of native territory, in the White man's genocide of the American Indians, and later the extensive military-imperialist adventures abroad in Indo-China, South and Central America and recently Arabia.

Together these historical features encourage certain personal character-istic values and attitudes in their populace which are then mirrored in a native therapeutic ideology. Specifically, these include optimism (anything is possible); voluntarism (anybody can do anything or be anything they want, provided that they try or fight hard enough); and opportunism (exploit the best choice available at the time). 'Go for it' is the slogan that says it all. Individualism and personal independence are not merely encouraged or expected (as in humanistic therapy) but dependants on the state are actively punished ('bums' and 'welfare scroungers'). Paying for one's personal liber-ation, by entering private psychotherapy, encapsulates and exemplifies the US way of life. The cash nexus highlights the notion that everything can be bought at a price in the market-place, including 'personal growth' or 'human potential'.

The standard of living of modern Americans may be predicated on a series of individual efforts but there is strong evidence that it may be based on the collective destruction of the rights and resources of other people (African slaves, native Indians, the Third World economy) by US imperialism. Moreover, nowhere is the gap between rich and poor more obvious than in US society. It is not surprising then that systematic studies of mental health services in the USA demonstrated that the personal liberties and sensitivities of the rich are highly valued (hence the prevalence of psychotherapy) while the 'dollar poor' get incarceration, chemicals and electro-shock (Hollingshead and Redlich 1958; Dohrenwend and Dohrenwend 1969). Personal growth is reserved for the rich, and social control is reserved for the poor, in the 'land of the free'. If you are wealthy enough to be able to afford regular psycho-therapy it is likely that your material resources are such that if you do not already have access to certain options to choose between, then they will soon be within your grasp. Making the best of what you already have ('positively connoting the experience') can be very helpful if you already have quite a lot. It can have a hollow ring if you are poor.

In this light it is not surprising that the fine grain of existence, explored by rich clients with their therapists consists of such foci as moral confron-tation and cognitive games. These have spawned respective aphorisms. The first of these is exemplified by Sheldon Kopp's dictum that 'You are free to

do whatever you like. You need only face the consequences' (Kopp 1974).
The second is exemplified by the dictum of George Kelly (1955) that 'Ulti-
mately a man sets the measure of his own freedom or his own bondage by
the level at which he chooses to establish his convictions'. (The reader of
Kelly can almost hear John Wayne in the wings prompting with the words
'A man's gotta do what a man's gotta do'.)

Indeed, returning to the wisdom of Kopp, he pronounces, 'The most important things each man must do for himself'. We also have other politically
loaded aphorisms from him, which imply that a shared underlying humanity
already makes us equal – 'No one is any stronger or any weaker than anyone
else'. And here echoing Freud: 'All of the significant battles are waged within
the self'. These moralisms give great comfort to conservative individualists.
The problem is that the messages simply do not stand up to scrutiny.
Sometimes our choices are irrelevant – and the poorer and more powerless
we are the more this claim becomes true. The notion that we are all of
equal strength must seem curious to the dispossessed throughout the world:
Black people in South Africa or the street children of Brazil. If your family
was burned to death by napalm, when the US Air Force was 'liberating'
Vietnamese villages by razing them to the ground, your view of which
battles were significant may not coincide with that held by Kopp.

As with my discussion of Guntrip earlier, I am not trying to argue that
moral responsibility and personal choice are not relevant considerations
when theorizing personal change. What I question though is whether these
are sufficiently central, or are of ubiquitous relevance, for a full understanding
about mental distress in all contexts. The emphasis on *individual* responsibility, strengths or cognitive ingenuity becomes more and more relevant
the richer and more powerful the client. The same is true in reverse: such
individualism simply degenerates into victim-blaming when people's lives
have been degraded by material poverty and racial, sexual or class oppression. As for the power of the individual in the face of an oppressive
state, try telling political prisoners in the gaols of tyrannies throughout the
world that they are ultimately responsible for their own bondage.

To show that I am not picking only on Americans in regard to the link
between opulence and psychological mindedness, I can cite a different example in one of their 'allies' in the recent Gulf War, reported just before
hostilities began, in *The Independent on Sunday*. Before Iraq vandalized
Kuwait's infrastructure, the oil riches of the Gulf had produced such material wealth for privileged Kuwaitis that their main difficulties were reported
to be 'existential'. Their lifestyle was so opulent that their problems in
living were being increasingly expressed in 'psychological' terms. By contrast,
the immigrant slave labour they employed (mainly from Palestine and the
Indian sub-continent) largely preoccupied itself with warding off poverty
and premature death, in a society awash with the fruits of oil profits. What
these exploited itinerants needed was not psychological care but social justice.
By contrast the rich Kuwaitis seemed to favour the opposite.

Returning to the main thrust of my argument about American humanism, there is an overlap with my previous focus: European psychoanalysis. While one reduces all of life to internal unconscious struggles and the other to the struggles of personal choice, the derivations of these personalistic reductions have much in common. Their discourses emerged in similar circumstances. Both came from male theorists and practitioners. Both came from privileged professional backgrounds. Both were White theories. Both emerged in countries with imperialistic histories. Their similarities should not be overdrawn though.

In particular, Freud's marginality as a Jew was compounded by his daring notions of sexuality. By contrast, Carl Rogers or George Kelly represent a mainstream WASP (White Anglo-Saxon Protestant) culture of liberalism and individualism in North America. Also, European imperialism was in decline, as American expansionism was springing to life. This may account for the different moral tone of the two broad therapeutic currents. The European one is more pessimistic. Indeed Freud's revised theory, which added Thanatos and was elaborated by Melanie Klein, is traceable to reflections on the carnage of the First World War. Likewise, while existential philosophy had resonances in both Europe and the USA, the latter took on a more optimistic form. Rollo May and Maslow came from a country of winners (on foreign soil), while Sartre's France was first host to a futile slaughter and then it was occupied and terrorized by Nazism. There is little wonder that Sartre was highly sensitive not only to the importance of human choice but also to 'the field of possibles', which constrain how those choices are made (Sartre 1963).

Having sketched my concerns about psychological reductionism and its conservative social consequences in both of the main currents of modern psychotherapy, I now want to turn to a second factor compounding these – professionalization.

Professional therapy and its vicissitudes

If the psychological basis of psychotherapeutic theory leads to the individualization of socially derived oppression, then this problem is aggravated by the politics of professionalization. To give Freud his due, he took on a cautious attitude towards the professional institutionalization of psychoanalysis. He tried to protect the rights of lay analysts opposed by his medical colleagues. Also, he feared that his legacy would end up as simply one among many treatments within psychiatry: the exact fate evident in terms of psychodynamic therapy becoming a 'sub-specialty' in the mental health professions. Freud was primarily interested in studying the unconscious, but he needed to make a living, so therapy became a necessary additional chore.

This ambivalence is still around. Psychoanalysts still issue both messages: their private practice hours have to be filled to pay for their consulting rooms, or to support their middle-class lifestyle, yet they can be found holding the notion of therapy in contempt. Hannah Segal (1987), a leading

Kleinian in Britain, in interview with Michael Ignatieff scolded him for
talking of 'therapies'. She insisted, 'Not therapies, psychoanalysis. I don't
like the word "therapy"'. Echoing the notion of the 'pure gold' of psychoanalysis she preferred a liquid metaphor. She accepted that 'not everyone
can have psychoanalysis' (this nearly constitutes a political insight!) and
commended the words of that arch-conservative Chesterton: 'I don't mind
where the water goes if it doesn't go into my wine'. The wine is psychoanalysis, which must be left undiluted. However, if it can be of help to that
lesser species (psychotherapy) Segal does not object to wine flowing into
water.

A few years ago a friend and colleague told me of being privately supervised by a Kleinian psychoanalyst. After a few sessions, she ventured to put
the point to her supervisor that her comments were insightful, but how
could she *help* the NHS clients she was seeing? 'Help?', the Kleinian mused,
'I'm a psychoanalyst. If you want to know how to help people you will have
to go and speak to those psychotherapists at the Tavistock Clinic'. This
story and the comments of Segal highlight a fundamental problem for
professionalized psychoanalysis. If it is not there to help people, why does
it offer itself as the response *par excellence* to modern neurosis? I wonder
how often professional analysts tell their 'patients' (yes, that is what they
call them) that actually they have a cultivated indifference to both pain and
personal change? Thus I am not convinced that clinical psychoanalysis should
be afforded the cultural status separate from therapy that people like Segal
demand. This elitist view that analysts merely continue to plough a lonely,
albeit well-paid, furrow in studying the unconscious, in one after another of
their patients, year after year, is more about image than reality. Unless
clients at some level were not seeking a helpful outcome (however vaguely
this might be defined) most of them would not be on the couch in the first
place.

There is another feature of clinical psychoanalysis, which necessarily puts
it in the therapeutic realm, rather than that of expertise about the unconscious: the claims made by therapists of all schools are little different to
those of psychoanalysts. That is, therapists tend to make claims about the
human condition in their own terms, as experienced during client contact.
Therapeutic knowledge (even that predicated speciously on experimental
evidence, such as behaviour therapy) is usually developed by a 'case law'
approach. When a theory is taken out to be aired by its advocates or a
practicum is exposed to the outside world, clinical experience with clients
underpins the therapist's legitimacy. The problem of course with this is that
the credibility or status of a preferred therapeutic approach is inextricably
bound up with an allegiance to a particular occupational group. In these
circumstances, therapists of any persuasion are not merely reporting an
example of their theory and practice, when they give the technical details
of a case study, they are also pinning their colours to the mast about their
professional club. They are saying effectively, 'this is not only about the
particular advantages of my approach for clients, but also it is a reason why

my occupational group (behavioural psychologists or medical psychotherapists, say) is particularly worthy of status and salaries'. In such circumstances,
it becomes problematic to distinguish knowledge claims about clients from
professional rhetoric. Accordingly it might be unwise to accept uncritically
what therapists say about their work.

For me, this interrelationship between knowledge and professional interests is not just about making a neat academic point. It has strong implications
for how 'the laity' might be able to evaluate the worthiness of therapists, as
secular priests in contemporary society. While those practitioners who have
a commitment to verbal psychotherapy were undoubtedly relieved to find
in the meta-analysis of Smith and Glass (1977) that all schools of therapy
could claim similar success levels, the finding also posed a new difficulty
for them. If 'all had won prizes', why should people (i.e. those party to
knowledge from psychotherapy research) now believe that a particular
approach is special?

As an indication of the power and inertia involved in professionals fighting
their corner or special pleading to the world, the old claims about being
unique persist, despite the research evidence. Eysenck and his followers
continue to dismiss verbal psychotherapy as pre-scientific nonsense,
commending 'evidence-based' technologies, while psychoanalysts still believe
in their wine or pure gold. In the Segal interview mentioned above she says
'I think that for most mental disorders the treatment of choice is actually
psychoanalytic'. Well, she would say that, wouldn't she? And whose choice
is involved in the notion of 'treatment of choice'? (An analogy from organic
psychiatry is that bio-determinists talk of major tranquillizers being the
'treatment of choice' for schizophrenia.) An even more extraordinary form
of special pleading about psychoanalysis is the reiteration of the dictum that
it is 'first and foremost about truth' (Menzies Lyth 1989). Given that truth
is perennially open to construction and reconstruction, why should psychoanalysis be trusted with being its guardian? Also, which psychoanalytical
brand of truth are ordinary mortals supposed to have faith in: Freudian
truth, Kleinian truth, the 'middle-group' truth?

Professional special pleading, and the mystification for outsiders (i.e. most
prospective clients) that it engenders, is the beginning not the end of the
problem. What we need to unpack further is what professionals are up to
when they deliver their rhetoric. As a case study of this, let me take my
own professional group (British clinical psychologists). Just as psychoanalysts
have expected the outside world to take on trust that they are in pursuit of
the truth, even though there has been vicious infighting between different
theoretical factions, so clinical psychologists have argued that their trade is
based on a stable and coherent set of scientific and therapeutic credentials.
This claim is made, even though they have lurched from one identity crisis
to another since the start of the profession in 1950.

At the outset, Eysenck (1950) argued that psychologists were scientific
psychometricians who could remain disinterested about their object of inquiry only if they eschewed therapy altogether. Later, he did a complete

about turn and was arguing that psychologists should take over jurisdiction for neurosis by treating it with behaviour therapy (Eysenck 1958). A precondition of this type of bid for legitimacy was the denigration of the established brand of medical psychology (psychoanalysis) (Eysenck 1952). Thus by the 1960s the profession's identity was increasingly associated with behaviour therapy and the aggressive displacement of 'pre-scientific' verbal psychotherapy. However, by the 1970s this position changed again when the profession began to incorporate a number of different approaches into an eclectic mish-mash (Richards 1983; Pilgrim and Treacher 1992). During this phase, clinical psychology brought psychotherapy back in from the cold. Also, following the dissolution of behaviourist hegemony in academic psychology and the rise of cognitivism, a new hybrid was born: cognitive-behaviour therapy. By 1980 clinical psychology had become 'homogenised and sterilised' (Smail 1982).

During the 1980s with clinical professions suffering a sustained attack from the 'new managerialism' of the protracted elected dictatorship of Margaret Thatcher, psychologists began to make shameless and grandiose claims about their therapeutic capability. They were worried that under conditions of an uncertain future, in a destabilized NHS, other occupational groups might encroach on their territory. Here is an example of a reaction to this threat. It comes from a group of clinical psychologists who expressed their concern that colleagues, such as psychiatric nurses, lacked appropriate training to be therapists:

> As trained clinical psychologists who have received intensive training, supervision and accreditation, we are skilled in all the various therapeutic methods such as anxiety management, psychodynamic psychotherapy, psychosexual and marital counselling, rational-emotive therapy, behaviour therapy, transactional analysis, guided grieving to name but a few.
>
> (Hallam *et al.* 1989)

I am not sure where these eclectic paragons of therapeutic virtue are supposed to exist in Britain. I have not encountered them. The Thatcher years encouraged this type of individual and collective self-aggrandizement. Humility became a rare virtue in the 1980s. The description in this quotation bears little relationship to the personal reality of the colleagues I trained with or trained during the 1970s and 1980s. Here is another example, this time from a new group of counselling psychologists who were making a bid to displace the therapeutic authority of clinical psychologists. It was in relation to sites of opportunistic employment, following a series of disasters (the Hillsborough football stadium deaths, the Zeebrugge sinking and the Lockerbie air explosion).

Clinical psychologists do excellent work in their own field, but it is only counselling psychologists, whose training in inter-personal and enabling skills specifically equips them to deal with the trauma of disasters.

(Noyes *et al.* 1989)

Having taught on the same course that two of these authors graduated from as trainees, I doubt whether such strong claims are sustainable. First of all, 'disaster counselling' did not appear on their syllabus (I am not sure that it appears on any course of this type at the moment). The vague allusion to 'skills' could be made equally plausibly by a whole range of helping professionals from social workers to health visitors or from nurses to occupational therapists. Also, how do they know that clinical psychologists do excellent work in their own field? Have they personally evaluated it as a profession or were these words just a softening up rhetorical device – a hook for their own overblown claims? I raise these questions simply to draw attention to the credibility problem that professional rhetoric poses. This is probably applicable to most forms of professionalism but it takes on a special irony when we consider that counsellors and therapists make a particular virtue of honesty or even 'truth' telling.

If it is so important for professional therapists to eschew self-criticism, in favour of positive or even exaggerated claims about their role and competence, why should they be trusted? In the case of clinical psychology for instance, in the past forty years a putative neutral onlooker has been asked to accept the following messages, sent apparently with equal conviction:

1 Science precludes psychologists from being therapists.
2 Science makes psychologists particularly good therapists.
3 Science rejects verbal psychotherapy.
4 Science enables psychologists to be good at all forms of therapy, including verbal psychotherapy.
5 Psychologists are trained to do things other mental health professionals cannot do.

Each of these five positions is problematic enough in itself. When they are put together in sequence to summarize the history of the profession, our honest onlooker probably is becoming confused or angry. It might seem that George Bernard Shaw's suspicion that professions are a conspiracy against the laity would be fair comment. If this conclusion were to be drawn, would that mark the end of my critique of the 'psy professions'? I think that there is a little more to be said, especially in relation to the aims of this chapter.

The first residual point is about democracy and accountability. The introverted preoccupation that now characterizes the psy professions necessarily makes them concerned to exclude not only competitors, but also critical scrutiny. The reliance on scientific research as a check against unfounded claims has failed. What psychoanalysis recognizes as research is simply more accumulated case law from within its own ranks. Its internal factionalism cannot even offer the public a coherent definition of what psychoanalysis is, let alone provide it with consistent specific claims about the human

Also: Rutter P (1991) Sex in the Forbidden Zone.
Mandale Press

240   *David Pilgrim*

condition. What behaviour therapy recognizes as research was either never carried out or used double standards. In the first case, behaviour therapy was not actually based upon experimental findings but upon case law (Portes 1971). In the second case, the standards of research evidence about behaviour therapy in its salad days were inferior to those being expected of the verbal psychotherapy it sought to discredit and supersede (Shapiro and Shapiro 1977). Also, the meta-analysis type of research has not stemmed the special pleading of particular factions of practitioners. Under these circumstances, the consumers of therapy cannot be confident that professionals have matched their rhetoric with even-handed self-evaluation. As in other quarters, allowing groups of people in authority to police themselves is tantamount to an invitation for them to please themselves.

There is a second additional point that is crucial. If it is conceded that psychotherapy is effective (Barkham 1990) then it also has to be conceded that it is of marginal utility. That is, while a gross claim of effectiveness may be tenable on empirical grounds, elaborated by psychotherapy researchers, buried in this claim is also evidence of negative effects. Some people deteriorate during therapy. Others are abused by their therapist, financially, sexually or emotionally. The sexual exploitation of clients by male therapists (Brown 1988) raises a question about the wisdom of training men at all. And if all practitioners were women they might be less prone to gratify their sexual desires, but the power asymmetry of the relationship would still invite other forms of abuse. This general point is both moral and political. If therapists are not going to repeat the paternalistic withholding of information about negative effects of therapy from clients (as in the case of drug treatment by organic psychiatrists) then they would have to come clean about the dangers involved in their work to all of their clients. The brief exploration of professional rhetoric, made above, showed that therapists are not keen on making public pronouncements which highlight their deficiencies – quite the reverse. This is hardly a propitious starting-point for democratic accountability.

Concluding comments

I have tried to examine some of the political evasions of psychotherapy in two senses. First, I argued that both psychoanalysis and humanistic psychology, the two broad currents underpinning verbal psychotherapy, are prone to particular forms of reductionism in their conception of the human condition. This leads to them being conservative-by-default in that they frame socially derived forms of oppression as individual problems.

Second, I went on to argue that this conservatism-by-default is compounded when self-interest is at work in professionalized therapy. Basically, where there is money, status, power or unemployment at stake, practitioners are likely to overstate their utility. This entails them putting their own interests before those of their clients – a strategy which is conservative and elitist.

Given that I have been so critical of therapy on these two general grounds, where does it leave me in relation to my own training and the practice of my friends and colleagues? (At the time of writing I have virtually given up being a therapist in favour of academic life.) I am reluctant prematurely to condemn therapy out of hand, although time may still take me to this position. In spite of everything I have said above, there are four grounds on which I might argue that therapy subsumes a progressive and desirable set of practices.

First, unlike Masson (1989), I take a different cue from disaffected users of psychiatric services. They have been pretty damning about physical treatments, such as ECT and tranquillizers. By contrast, their demands include the availability of free counselling from public mental health facilities (Survivors Speak Out 1987). They are suspicious of the 'power games' played by psychotherapists, but overall they still favour 'talking' to drugs and electricity (Rogers and Pilgrim 1991). Although Masson warns them that they are wrongheaded in this demand (Pilgrim 1989) (and time may still prove him to be correct) I believe that the request from users for alternatives to physical treatments deserves support.

A second grudging support I have for the continued availability of state-provided psychotherapy (I consider that fee-paying therapy is ultimately oppressive and elitist) is derived from the observation that while professional relationships risk the abuse of power, this can also take place in informal relationships, including self-help and friendships (Bell 1989). What is required though is an honest acceptance that therapists are potentially exploitative abusers. It behooves professional groups deploying versions of therapy to come clean about this problem and face it honestly. (At the moment, the signs are that generally professional groups deny the problem.)

My third faint-hearted support for therapy is that informal help or self-help is not always available to people in distress. In this light, it seems appropriate and desirable that the state should provide a facility in each locality, which offers a genuine and informed choice of approaches for clients to take up, if their social network is unsupportive or they have no opportunity or inclination to enter a self-help group.

Finally, a case can still be made for therapy forming part of a radical type of service delivery, which attempts self-consciously to use therapy as a stepping stone to empowerment and social change. Examples of this are given by Fulani (1988), Holland (1979) and Treacher (1989).

I hope that in rehearsing these four cautious arguments for supporting accessible and accountable therapeutic services I have avoided taking up a nihilistic or damning position, which may be evident elsewhere in this book. However, I hope that (as I promised at the outset), I have problematized therapy for the reader on reasonable and credible grounds. If the therapy trade is to continue, as is likely to be the case, I think that it is crucial that its associated rosy glow of humanism and moral rectitude (compared to the dehumanization of biological psychiatry) is dispersed. If the trade perseveres it should be treated with caution by its users. Of greatest importance is that

242   *David Pilgrim*

they evaluate it in their own terms and not necessarily those suggested by
therapists themselves.

References

Abraham, K. (1927) *Selected Papers*. London: Hogarth Press.
Barkham, M. (1990) Research in individual therapy, in W. Dryden (ed.) *Individual Therapy: A Handbook*. Milton Keynes: Open University Press.
Bell, L. (1989) Psychotherapy and user empowerment. *Clinical Psychology Forum* **23**: 12–14.
Brown, L.S. (1988) Harmful effects of post-termination sexual and romantic relationships between therapists and their former clients. *Psychotherapy* **25**(2): 249–55.
Busfield, J. (1986) *Managing Madness*. London: Hutchinson.
Chasseguet-Smirgel, J. and Gruneberger, B. (1986) *Freud or Reich? Psychoanalysis and Illusion*. London: Free Association Books.
Cochrane, R. (1983) *The Social Creation of Mental Illness*. London: Longman.
Dalal, F. (1988) The racism of Jung. *Race and Class* **29**(3): 1–22.
Dicks, H. (1970) *Fifty Years of the Tavistock*. London: Routledge & Kegan Paul.
Dohrenwend, B. and Dohrenwend, B.S. (1969) *Social Status and Psychological Disorder*. New York: Wiley.
Eysenck, H.J. (1950) Function and training of the clinical psychologist. *Journal of Mental Science* **96**: 710–25.
Eysenck, H.J. (1952) The effects of psychotherapy: an evaluation. *Journal of Consulting Psychology* **16**: 319–24.
Eysenck, H.J. (1958) (with Gwynne Jones) Paper on the psychological treatment of neurosis presented to the Royal Medico-Psychological Association, London.
Fenichel, O. (1945) *The Psychoanalytical Theory of Neurosis*. New York: Norton.
Freud, S. (1930) *Civilisation and its Discontents*. London: Hogarth Press.
Fulani, L. (1988) *The Psychopathology of Everyday Racism and Sexism*. New York: Harvester.
Guntrip, H. (1977) *Schizoid Phenomena, Object Relations and the Self*. London: Hogarth Press.
Hallam, R.S., Bender, M.P. and Wood, R. (1989) Use of psychological techniques. *The Psychologist* **2**(9): 375.
Holland, S. (1979) The development of an action and counselling service in a deprived urban area, in M. Meacher (ed.) *New Methods of Mental Health Care*. London: Pergamon.
Hollingshead, A. and Redlich, F. (1958) *Social Class and Mental Illness*. New York: Wiley.
Ingleby, D. (1984) The ambivalence of psychoanalysis. *Free Associations* Pilot Issue: 39–71.
Kelly, G.A. (1955) *A Theory of Personality*. New York: Norton.
Kopp, S. (1974) An eschatological laundry list, in *If You Meet the Buddha on the Road Kill Him!* London: Sheldon.
Laing, R.D. (1964) *The Divided Self*. London: Tavistock.
Llewelyn, S. (1988) Psychological therapy as viewed by clients and therapists. *British Journal of Clinical Psychology* **27**: 223–7.
Manning, N. (1989) *The Therapeutic Community: Charisma and Routinisation*. London: Routledge.

Masson, J.M. (1985) *The Assault on Truth: Freud's Suppression of the Seduction Theory.* Harmondsworth: Penguin.

Masson, J.M. (1989) *Against Therapy.* London: Collins.

Menzies Lyth, I. (1989) In *After Dark.* Channel Four, 22 September.

Miller, P. and Rose, N. (1988) The Tavistock Programme: the government of subjectivity and social life. *Sociology* 22(2): 171–92.

Noyes, L., Franklin, B. and Val Baker, J. (1989) Psychologists called in. *The Psychologist* 2(5): 214.

Perls, F. (1972) Gestalt Therapy Now. Harmondsworth: Penguin.

Pilgrim, D. (1989) Dangerous Liaisons: an interview with Jeffrey Masson. *Open Mind* December: 15–16.

Pilgrim, D. and Treacher, A. (1992) *Clinical Psychology Observed.* London: Routledge.

Portes, A. (1971) On the emergence of behaviour therapy in modern society. *Journal of Consulting and Clinical Psychology* 36: 303–13.

Reich, W. (1933) *Dialectical Materialism and Psychoanalysis.* Copenhagen: Sexual Political Press.

Richards, B. (1983) Clinical psychology, the individual and the state. Unpublished PhD thesis, North East London Polytechnic.

Richards, B. (1988) The Eupsychian Impulse: psychoanalysis and left politics since 1968. *Radical Philosophy* 48: 3–13.

Rogers, A. and Pilgrim, D. (1991) 'Pulling down churches': accounting for the British Mental Health Users' movement. *Sociology of Health and Illness* 13(2): 129–48.

Sartre, J.-P. (1963) *Search for a Method.* New York: Knopf.

Segal, H. (1987) Psychoanalysis after Freud, in B. Bourne, U. Eichler and D. Herman (eds) *Voices: Psychoanalysis.* London: Hobo Press.

Shapiro, D.A. and Shapiro, D. (1977) The 'double standard' in the evaluation of psychotherapies. *Bulletin of the British Psychological Society* 30: 209–10.

Silverman, D. (1970) *The Theory of Organisations.* London: Heinemann.

Smail, D. (1982) Clinical psychology: homogenised and sterilised. *Bulletin of the British Psychological Society* 35: 245–6.

Smith, M. and Glass, G. (1977) Meta-analysis of psychotherapy outcome studies. *American Psychologist* 32: 752–60.

Sulloway, F.J. (1980) *Freud: Biologist of the Mind.* London: Fontana.

Survivors Speak Out (1987) Charter. London: Survivors Speak Out.

Treacher, A. (1989) Technology and trickery. *Open Mind* August: 16–17.

Turkle, S. (1987) Psychoanalysis: nothing sacred? in B. Bourne, U. Eichler and D. Herman (eds) *Voices: Psychoanalysis.* London: Hobo Press.

Winnicott, D. (1958) Metapsychological and clinical aspects of regression in the psycho-analytical set up, in *Collected Works.* London: Hogarth Press.

RESPONSE – Ian Craib

Perhaps I should begin by declaring myself. I suspect I share at least some of David Pilgrim's political ideals; at any rate I regard myself as a left-of-centre socialist, but that phrase covers a multitude of views, most of which I have perhaps held at some stage in my life. In one professional guise, I am an academic sociologist; in another I work as a group therapist in the psychoanalytic tradition. My move from the former towards the latter was part of a process of disillusion that I thought might be reflected in Pilgrim's paper. At least we can stand as a warning to each other not to idealize our possible future professions.

Of course, no profession should be idealized, otherwise we might have to destroy it. It is tempting to respond to a polemic with a polemic, especially when it is as well written and enjoyable as Pilgrim's, and to find oneself giving flesh and blood to an animal that otherwise might not exist: in this case the reductionist, professionalized therapist. The tendencies that Pilgrim discusses are of course real, so perhaps I am simply fortunate in not knowing, among my friends and acquaintances in the therapeutic world, anyone I can recognize as a suitable target of his arguments. My response, if it can be summed up in a few words, is that psychotherapy, and the world in general, is more complicated than it is portrayed as being in his argument. While he makes some attempt to save the baby of psychotherapy from the bathwater of reductionism and professionalization, I would argue that they cannot be separated; if we decide we want the baby, we have to swim in the dirty bathwater. And even if we decide that we don't want this particular baby, I am not sure we can find any cleaner bathwater.

I shall respond as directly as possible to Pilgrim's points, limiting myself to the discussion of psychoanalytic therapy, which is the only form I feel I can discuss with any integrity, and I shall accept his division of the issues.

Reductionism

Pilgrim talks about two different forms of reductionism, which are worth distinguishing: a 'conceptual reductionism', to do with diagnostic categories, and an explanatory reductionism, to do with our understanding of the way the world is; he goes on to argue that this reductionism at least inhibits psychoanalysts' political understanding, or leads to a politics of which he disapproves.

I shall begin with 'diagnostic reductionism' which Pilgrim sees as reinforcing the medical model and juxtaposes to an idea of a properly human relationship, in which one partner is not seeking advantage over another, and the uniqueness and complexity of an individual is recognized.

Now a diagnostic category is a general category, covering a number of individual cases; we cannot actually think without such categories, nor can we have anything approaching working knowledge of any aspect of the world. In our process of understanding other people, such general categories act as signposts, a shorthand which can give us an idea of where we are. If I see a patient as 'clinically depressed' I immediately have a map which might or might not help me understand what is happening – that remains to be seen – but which enables me to *attempt* to understand what is happening. Without such categories, the person cannot be seen at all. We might prefer another set of categories to the ones that Pilgrim criticizes, but we cannot do without them. The work of Winnicott above all seems to me to show that we can think in diagnostic categories and leave plenty of space for individual complexity: it is not a matter of doing one or the other but of maintaining the tension between the two (see Winnicott 1987; Little 1985).

I am not sure that, by itself, the use of such categories reinforces the medical model, it is more a matter of *how* they are used. They are some-times rough and ready tools that can help or get in the way. Like Pilgrim, I find myself thinking in diagnostic categories but not necessarily sharing them with my patients; sometimes they help me to say something which is helpful; sometimes they help me to say things that are unhelpful; they help me stay with the patient, which I think is the minimum condition of any therapeutic work.

Of course, I also find myself using diagnostic categories to reinforce a sense of my own competence; I don't think it's the best way to hold on to my sense of competence, but sometimes it seems necessary. Sometimes I use them to give myself a sense of superiority and rightness, but this tends to be in relation to colleagues and friends. My point is not that Pilgrim is wrong; he is right but shows only half the picture. Diagnostic categories are good things and bad things at the same time; if we can hold on to the idea that 'we are all ill', then we acknowledge that diagnostic categories apply to the therapist as well, and we are less likely to use diagnoses in a damaging way. It is a pity that Pilgrim does not allow us this aphorism.

Moving on to explanatory reductionism, I agree that to see the world entirely in psychodynamic terms is misleading; in fact I think it is absurd, and when psychoanalysts step beyond their appropriate object, they some-times appear absurd. Psychoanalysis is concerned with the individual psyche and relationships between individuals. There are, quite clearly, other sources of misery in the world at the same time, but this does not mean that there are not psychological sources. Not every poor woman becomes a prostitute, not every member of a single-sex school becomes homosexual. We are dealing with different causal processes related in complex ways and psychoanalysis is concerned with only one process (see Craib 1989). In my experience, patients often have a rather better grasp of this complexity than Pilgrim. They can recognize that they are victims of social processes and situations, but they seek therapy because they are aware of something in themselves that contributes to, or prohibits them from dealing with, these problems. In these cases, the signs of therapeutic effectiveness are the op-posite of what I should, according to Pilgrim, expect. It is not forbearance in the face of oppression, but the growing ability to change a relationship, change a pattern of victimhood, deal creatively with employers, the ability to move, at last, from the parents' home, or to change tactics in seeking employment – these are the external signs of therapeutic change.

These are, of course, individual changes, with all the limitations of indi-vidual change. I also think social change is desirable, and within the limits of my personal energy, I would seek that as a socialist or trade unionist, not as a psychotherapist. Behind Pilgrim's argument is the assumption that psychotherapy and psychoanalysis *should* be politically radical, and should be radical in a particular way. The fact that various political positions can be associated with psychoanalysis seems to me the mark of an open system of thought. I think it *can* be radical, but in a way that I suspect would not be acceptable to Pilgrim. I find two aspects of psychoanalysis valuable in this respect. First, its emphasis on internal space and there being some degree of autonomy in interpersonal relationships; this counterbalances the impetus of *sociologically* reductionist explanations and the politics that stem from it. If we see everything as a result of social processes, then it seems to me we open the door to the sort of totalitarianism implicit in the slogan 'the personal is political' (Craib 1988). Our freedom, which is never absolute, lies not only in our ability to co-operate with other people in changing our world, but also in our ability to distance ourselves from others, make choices which separate ourselves from the collective, from the state: whether the state be capitalist, socialist, communist or whatever. In so far as psychoanalytic therapy achieves the aim of leaving ego where id has been, then it contributes to this freedom. The ego might go off and make political judgements of which I disapprove, but that is as it should be.

Second, I think it is right to say that psychoanalysis can add to the knowledge of other disciplines and sciences, but not replace it. My own view is that often this addition is not terribly significant. However, in relation to politics, it does, I believe, have something important to say about the motivation of some forms of political action. Politics is a dangerous game: it often, if not always, involves systematic dishonesty; often, but not always, corruption; sometimes it involves tyranny, murder and torture. It is important to recognize that however honourable a set of political ambitions, honour does not make us immune to any of these things. When Chasseguet-Smirgel and Gruneburger say that revolutionaries are suffering from an omnipotent infantile fixation, they are saying something about the dangers of some sorts of political motivation, and the blindness that it produces, something of which we ought to be aware, even, perhaps especially, if we are political revolutionaries. It can of course be read as a demand for political passivity if one chooses; it could be read, if one chooses, as a plea for self-understanding and a considered politics.

Professionalization

My response to Pilgrim's comments about professionalization are ambivalent in the extreme, but on the whole I am happy with my ambivalence and I shall begin by simply describing it.

I respond gratefully to Hannah Segal's desire to preserve the pure wine of psychoanalysis. I think the enterprise of knowing is an important and liberating enterprise, even if that knowledge is always provisional and incomplete, and even if it can be misused, and I think there is much to be said for the psychoanalytic method as a method of research, independently of its therapeutic value. However, I am happy to be called a psycho*therapist* and I think of my work as practical helping rather than research, although of course it is both at the same time. I have some specialist knowledge, that my patients do not (always) have; I do not consider this makes me better at life, although some people seem to think it should. Like the diagnostic categories, sometimes it is helpful to me and to my patients, sometimes it gets in my way, but not in my patients' way, sometimes vice versa. My work is aimed at enabling the patient to find a way of living free of me; I find that the early struggles in psychotherapy have more to do with the patient's attribution of power and knowledge to me rather than any power or knowledge I actually possess.

I am well aware of the rhetorical uses to which the term 'science' is put, that it can become a tool of self-seeking sectional interests, that the nature of a science is hotly disputed with a number of different positions each of which lays claim to some credibility. But it seems to me that we can argue about and establish epistemological criteria which can distinguish better from worse knowledge, and the fact that this is possible perhaps indicates that we should aim to tolerate differences rather than reject the enterprise altogether.

I wonder what Pilgrim's acquaintance meant by 'help'. Desiring to help a patient can get in the way of change (see esp. Milner 1969); or it can involve the projection of one's own damage into a patient, keeping it there – keeping the patient damaged, in order to avoid one's own pain; and of course, helping someone can make one feel good, without doing much for the person being helped (see Segal 1964). Helping can also be the best of activities; it can involve all the activities of holding, understanding and interpretation that can enable the patient to understand his or her-self. I don't understand how anyone remotely familiar with the Kleinian (or non-Kleinian) literature on counter-transference can argue that analysts have a 'cultivated indifference to both pain and personal change'; it is, of course, precisely through the experience of pain and many other things in the counter-transference, and the intelligent interpretation of that experience, that change can emerge. (The best account of this process I know of can be found in Casement 1985.)

I wonder what a patient is? I have used the word deliberately in my response. It seems to me that patienthood is a quality generally possessed in our society, perhaps in all societies; it is related to our dependence on others, to our original dependence, and perhaps to our intuition of future dependence. I do not want to hide this in the Newspeak that the use of 'client' can represent. Patients of course are also clients, just as clients are patients. Our problem is not so much that of avoiding our patienthood as of living with it in such a way that we do not, unless appropriate, become patients, dependent.

I wonder what success is, or what failure is, in therapeutic work? I feel constrained to tell my patients, when I first see them, that I cannot guarantee success. By some standards, my work always fails; by others I am

248   David Pilgrim

sometimes successful. I am happy, and sometimes depressed, to rely on the evaluation of the patients themselves. And, of course, that evaluation is likely to change over time.

I wonder what it means to pay for therapy? My experience as a patient and as a therapist is that sometimes it frees the patient from the need to be grateful, enabling criticism, anger, independence; sometimes it seems to be of comparatively little importance; sometimes, it seems to reinforce the patient's patienthood, the demand for inappropriate dependence.

I do make judgements about, for example, psychoanalysis being better than behavioural therapy, on all sorts of grounds; I like to earn a reasonable middle-class living, which I enjoy; I want to continue practising as a psychotherapist, and I want to feel that I am, most of the time, good-enough. I have some ambition. Sometimes any one of the desires and their associated fears can cloud my judgement, lead me to make exaggerated claims, unfair accusations, and whatever. I am sometimes very acutely aware of the possibilities of abuse, and it is simply not true that this receives no public discussion within the profession. In the weeks prior to reading Pilgrim's paper, I had read, without searching it out, a paper in the main British psychotherapy journal (Gerrard 1990), and received details of a conference on the issue (organized by the Institute of Group Analysis).

On the whole, I find my association with professional colleagues enables me to explore the ambiguity of all the things I have talked about in this section; we require standards of training and supervision and organizational forms that can enable all these issues to be discussed. I am also aware of all the dangers that Pilgrim attributes to professionalization, especially in the current political and economic climate. Yet the dangers and the benefits of belonging to a profession go together, and the paradox is that without the dangers, there can be no benefits. The problem is always to hold on to both sides at the same time. The baby of psychotherapy cannot be separated from its dirty bathwater; we have to remember that the baby is there and that the bathwater is dirty. It seems to me that this is a condition of any professional life.

References

Casement, P. (1985) On Learning from the Patient. London: Tavistock.
Craib, I. (1988) The personal and political. Radical Philosophy 48: 14–15.
Craib, I. (1989) Psychoanalysis and Social Theory: The Limits of Sociology. Hemel Hempstead: Harvester Wheatsheaf.
Gerrard, J. (1990) Use and abuse in psychotherapy. British Journal of Psychotherapy 7(2): 121–8.
Little, M.I. (1985) Winnicott working in areas where psychotic anxieties predominate: a personal record. Free Associations 3: 9–42.
Milner, M. (1969) The Hands of the Living God: An Account of a Psychoanalytic Treatment. London: Hogarth Press.
Segal, H. (1964) An Introduction to the Work of Melanie Klein. London: Heinemann.

Winnicott, D.W. (1987) *The Piggle: An Account of the Psychoanalytic Treatment of a Little Girl.* Harmondsworth: Penguin.

Acknowledgement

I would like to thank Fiona Grant and John Walshe for their comments on the first draft of this response.

REBUTTAL – David Pilgrim

I am grateful to Ian Craib for his comments on my chapter. Often my views are nearer to his than some of his strawmen might suggest. At other points in his argument he triggers strong reactions in me which actually drive me further away. Within the space available, I shall tackle the most salient of these.

The danger of idealization

Because Craib writes as an apologist for the therapy trade, rather than as the critical sociologist he is capable of being, he does no justice to the difference between the two professions that he and I straddle. It is much more difficult (though not impossible) to idealize sociology than it is psychotherapy. Indeed, during the training period of psychodynamic therapy, idolatory is not merely a hazard, it is an explicit expectation. Depending on the school, the works of Freud, Klein, Jung or Foulkes are the prescribed diet of trainees. (For instance, candidates in the British Institute of Psychoanalysis are obliged to purchase the complete hardback version of Freud's works, albeit at cut price, from the parent body.) This type of expectation during the socialization of analysts erodes their critical abilities.

Barbara Wooton (1959), in her classic critique of mental health practices, cites Edward Glover's confession that during their training period, analytical candidates have to abandon scepticism to mollify their training analysts. What chance intellectual rigour and honesty in such a quasi-religious atmosphere? By contrast, sociologists are hypercritical of one another, as well as those on the outside of their disciplinary boundaries. A minority of personal accounts of analytical training damn its bureaucratized, authoritarian and unaccountable character. Dissenting candidates are left dissatisfied and exasperated with the capacity of 'official' psychoanalysis to take external reality and legitimate political grievances seriously (Masson 1991; Modena 1986; Steltzer 1986). Steltzer's article centres on the tribulations of being asked to comply with and identify personally with a pre-existing body of knowledge. Masson's account bemoans the intellectual conformity required of trainees. It is true that there exists the 'Independent' group of analysts – the sort of freethinking Unitarians of the psychoanalytical culture (Rayner 1989). What this group demonstrate is the right to selectively mix and elaborate Freudianism and Kleinianism. This middle position still accepts a fundamental or broad allegiance to its sources. However, there are limits to how far an analyst can go before arriving beyond the pale. Some test this boundary to the limit (e.g. Peter Lomas). Others such as Jeffrey Masson and Ronald Laing had to leave the culture when their independent intellects asked one too many awkward questions.

The defence of diagnostic categories

Craib restates a truism, that we need cognitive categories in order to operate in the world. However, such a general proposition about the cognitive precondition for human functioning omits one vital point: categories are informed by value-laden information derived from their sustaining social context. While categories are required, *what type they are* can determine who gets the meat and who gets the gravy, who is honoured and who is disparaged, even who lives and who dies (remember 'racial hygiene'?). The positivistic categories of 'pathology' are traceable historically to the emergence of the clinical gaze of the physician, and the power differential this celebrates over patients. As C.S. Lewis (1943) noted, 'We reduce things to mere Nature in order that we may "conquer" them'. When the 'things' are people (or in the language of psychoanalysis 'objects') and their existential status is reduced to a 'natural' category of illness, the same logic of domination applies. Given this, there is little wonder that the odd honest psychoanalyst has struggled to rescue their trade from its own language traps. Szasz (1961; 1963) had to admit that people were not ill and that what was supposedly naturally in the patient's transference was actually a Freudian invention to protect the therapist from fear and desire. Laing (1967), a product of object-relations training, had to reject the language of objects. Schafer (1976) had to reject the objectifying notions of mental 'mechanisms' in favour of an action language to concede that human beings operated as agents in a moral order.

Nothing in what Craib argues dissuades me from the view that diagnostic notions are held back from patients for the very reason that they are pejorative, demeaning and stigmatizing. At the same time, the continued private use of such terms suggests that they bolster the power and confidence of therapists. Medical psychotherapists at least have the excuse of being a product of their own core socialization. Non-medical therapists (such as Craib and myself) have no such alibi. This leads to my next point.

The question of patienthood

Craib says 'I wonder what a patient is?' He notes that the social role of patient is ubiquitous and virtually inevitable. The language of inevitability usually points towards a conservative acceptance of the status quo. He wants to avoid dependency, and yet the word 'patient' implies such a fate – especially in protracted therapeutic relationships. When we shift from these theoretical speculations to what 'patients' actually say, then we find that the mental health users in Britain prefer 'survivor', 'recipient' or 'user' (Rogers and Pilgrim 1991). Moreover, surveys of their views of psychotherapy reveal that they want empathy and respect as ordinary human beings, not as 'patients', and they are distrustful of the 'power games' played by therapists (Rogers *et al.* 1992). The medical connotations of the word 'patient' must engender, and reveal, assumptions about asymmetry and power. To say that we are all patients does not dispose of these political issues.

The question of abuse

I am not satisfied that the discussion of abuse within the confines of a culture of therapists constitutes a genuine public airing. Equally, medical practitioners have researched and debated iatrogenic problems for decades but it has not stopped them plying their trade of prescribed dangerous drugs and surgical procedures. The lesson from this is that professionals, including psychotherapists, cannot be trusted to police themselves. As I mentioned in my chapter, the exposure of Freud's mistake on sexual abuse was simply incorporated by his descendants to their own advantage. Suddenly analytical therapists are entreating the public to believe that they are trustworthy experts on sexual abuse, when their tradition was the one which compounded the problem. Abuse itself just becomes another opportunity to create jobs and status for the boys (and girls). To take a related example, on BBC's *Newsnight* (27 May 1991) a child psychotherapist was interviewed about the 'pindown' scandal in the Staffordshire children's homes. She thought that the answer was to let her and her colleagues act as consultants to residential care staff. Well, she would say that, wouldn't she? Like the 'disaster' counsellors I mentioned previously, therapists show an unending ingenuity in preying on each new manifestation of human anguish.

The question of the dirty bathwater

Craib is fatalistically tolerant of his dirty bathwater. I am accused (in my omnipotent infantile way?) of throwing out the baby. The metaphor is a common rhetorical device to imply that an opponent in a debate lacks sensitivity or clarity in their arguments. Whether this is true or not can be judged by the reader. My suspicion is that Craib reaches for the metaphor because the difficult questions which I raise, about reductionism and professionalization, threaten his identity as a therapist. Let me make quite clear what I am not saying. I am not rejecting the depth psychology tradition out of hand. The variety of hermeneutic ventures it has spawned deserve to be considered carefully, on their merits, as having a potential role in explicating the personal dimension to social existence. I do not consider that they should be derided or dismissed in social science. However, this legitimate epistemological role, which could be disseminated for its consideration and potential utility to ordinary people, logically does not necessitate or endorse professionalized therapy.

My view is that the hermeneutic systems emanating from the Freudian legacy are often very useful in understanding personal relationships. My doubt is whether they inevitably convert to benign and user-friendly *professional* interventions for people in distress. Understanding and professionalized help cannot necessarily be conflated. As I argued in relation to the outcome debate (which Craib did not respond to) I suspect that dynamic psychotherapy is actually very effective in facilitating personal change – for better *and* for worse. It is the deterioration effects linked to sexual, emotional and financial abuse, at the hands of trained therapists, which are at the heart of my critique.

I am not crudely a social determinist about emotional distress. Psychological (and yes, even biological) factors may be relevant at times in this regard. However, to return to an example we dispute, if all poor people do not become prostitutes, it cannot be denied that poverty is the most important determinant of prostitution. Any attempt to privilege a psychological explanation over a social one is a victim-blaming insult and a comfort to reactionary elements who sustain poverty in their own interests. My criticism of therapists is that it is they who are one dimensional in their causal reasoning, by their tendency to see virtually everything in psychological terms.

Finally, Craib finds no difficulty in reconciling being a socialist, practising privately and promoting paying through the nose as a pathway to human freedom. Such ideological gymnastics are beyond my capability. To finish on the metaphor I have been lumbered with, I hope in writing my chapter that I have identified pollutants, not thrown out the baby. The question is: who will purify the water? My contribution is to help to identify the problem. Ultimately users of the therapy trade should determine its future. This is one of the key reasons why I hold back from dismissing therapy out of hand, for the time being. I am watching the users' space for the final judgement on the baby's fate.

References

Laing, R.D. (1967) *The Politics of Experience and the Bird of Paradise*. Harmondsworth: Penguin.
Lewis, C.S. (1943) *The Abolition of Man*. Oxford: Oxford University Press.
Masson, J. (1991) *The Final Analysis*. London: Harper Collins.
Modena, E. (1986) A chance for psychoanalysis to change. *Free Associations* 5: 7–22.
Rayner, E. (1989) *The Independent School of Psychoanalysis*. London: Tavistock.

Rogers, A. and Pilgrim, D. (1991) 'Pulling down churches': accounting for the British Mental Health Users' movement. *Sociology of Health and Illness* **13**(2): 129–48.
Rogers, A., Pilgrim, D. and Lacey, R. (1992) *Consenting Adults? Users' Views of Psychiatry.* London: Macmillan.
Schafer, R. (1976) *A New Language for Psychoanalysis.* New Haven, Conn: Yale University Press.
Steltzer, J. (1986) The formation and deformation of the identity during psychoanalytical training. *Free Associations* **7**: 38–58.
Szasz, T.S. (1961) *The Myth of Mental Illness.* New York: Hoeber-Harper.
Szasz, T.S. (1963) The concept of transference. *International Journal of Psychoanalysis* **44**: 432–43.
Wooton, B. (1959) *Social Science and Social Pathology.* London: Allen & Unwin.

TEN

Psychotherapy and its discontents: concluding comments

WINDY DRYDEN AND COLIN FELTHAM (1992)

Psychotherapy and Its Discontents
Open University –

It will be clear to readers that the critics presented here are a heterogeneous group, and the question therefore arises: what is the meaning of such diverse criticism, other than the trite conclusion that 'you can't please everyone'? We believe that the sum of the criticism represented here is significant in several ways, and we shall turn to these shortly.

Another matter of importance to us is a number of omitted or incomplete criticisms. We should like briefly to allude here to these in order to show the range of 'discontentment'. Our present critics between them have drawn attention to: the inadequacy of research validating the outcomes of psychotherapy (Kline); the possibility that therapy is no more effective than no treatment at all (Eysenck); the consumer's experience of therapy as harmful (Sutherland); the mystically self-protective nature of psychotherapy and its culture (Gellner); the pretentiousness of therapists' explanations (Mair); the widespread personal fallibility and exploitativeness of therapists (Masson); psychotherapy's anachronistic detachment from new-paradigm views (Edwards); and the psychological reductionism that weakens any political credibility that psychotherapy might have (Pilgrim). These are probably the major substantive criticisms. We now add other critiques, some of which have been elaborated before, and some not.

Schisms

First, it seems clear that there is something inherently schismatic in the field of psychotherapy which parallels the myriad splinter groups in the development of religions and political systems. ('Schismatic' here suggests that psychotherapy has never been and holds little prospect of becoming a unified field.) Although in its modern form psychotherapy is only a century old, subtle schisms and outright conflicts have plagued its development to the present day. While conflict in itself is not necessarily unhealthy, we believe the failure of proponents of psychotherapy even to approach agreement on vital issues of aetiology and remedy probably strains public credulity.

Trends

Stemming from this first point, one can see a number of apparently irreversible historical trends:

1 Schism versus schism within a tradition
2 Conservative versus innovative within and between schools
3 Pure versus eclectic
4 Long term versus brief
5 Psychotherapy versus counselling

These trends will now be discussed in turn.

Schism versus schism within a tradition

One can interpret Jung and Adler's moves away from Freud as either regrettable heresies or as healthy and enriching developments, but such splits and resulting therapeutic schools (and their attendant specialist languages) confuse rather than help the lay public. The situation is even more confusing when one looks at the divisions between one psychodynamic school and another, and further between the psychoanalytical, behavioural, humanistic and transpersonal schools, each with their own inner divisions. Again, this variety can be regarded as colourful pluralism, or as a kaleidoscope of unhelpfulness (or as anything in between). Horowitz (1989) recalls part of his journey through such schisms:

> I began a training analysis as part of my entry into the San Francisco Psychoanalytic Institute. My analyst, who saw my membership in Berne's didactic group therapy as a resistance to my psychoanalytic process with him, asked me to terminate it. When I discussed this request with Berne, who himself had trained in and dropped out of the same institute, he said that he saw my psychoanalytic treatment as a resistance to transactional analysis.
>
> (Horowitz 1989: 4)

Conservative versus innovative within and between schools

It is no secret that many humanistic and transpersonal therapists often view their behavioural and psychoanalytical colleagues as stiffly theory-bound;

conversely they are often regarded by analysts and behaviourists as undisciplined and wrongheaded. These positions are much more clearly stated in private conversations than in learned journals! But within schools too there are tensions between the classical dogma and new thinking.This raises the question as to whether psychotherapists are more or less dedicated to the pursuit of truth than anyone else. For a sceptical tour of the 'new psychotherapies' see Clare and Thompson (1981). For a rejection of the 'old psychologies' by the new, see Janov (1974: 206) or Mahrer (1989: 137).

Pure versus eclectic

Almost every school of psychotherapy but the frankly eclectic resists the notion that it is open to adaptation. This dynamic applies even to the most benign approaches like person-centred therapy (Mearns and Thorne 1988) which struggle to maintain the purity of their ideal as given by the founder. Interestingly, we now see an emerging trend towards 'integrative psychotherapy' which legitimizes eclecticism. (Is this a kind of pragmatic ecumenicism?)

Long term versus brief

Malan (1963) and others have drawn attention to the tendency of psychoanalytical therapies to become lengthy affairs. Malan has speculated that this may be due in part to the 'waning enthusiasm' of practitioners who, in their early practice, work energetically and empirically, only to tire, conform and protract treatment later. Shlien *et al.* (1962) among others have offered some evidence that brief psychotherapy is as effective as lengthy treatment. If this is actually the case, we are bound to ask why therapists go along with the lengthy and timeless models of therapy. (It could conceivably be because they require less enthusiasm or that they yield a higher rate of remuneration, and a more predictable one! An interesting theoretical inference here, then, might be the existence of an 'economic unconscious'.) Of course it is also arguable that many clients demonstrate a preference for long-term therapy. In response to this argument, one might ask whether they are truly getting long-term therapy, or long-term befriending, avoidance, or expensive companionship in a psychological hobby.

Psychotherapy versus counselling

Today there is possibly more confusion than ever in the public's mind about the difference between one brand of therapy and another, but also about the difference between psychotherapy and counselling. While many follow Patterson's (1973) view that there is no meaningful difference, others go to some lengths to suggest that psychotherapy is an altogether more serious, radical, personality-changing, time-consuming venture than counselling. Counselling ('Freud-and-water', as Gellner wittily calls it) is frequently caricatured as a rather superficial problem-solving exercise or as an inane process of head-nodding and repeating clients' words back to them. The experience and belief of the editors is that no meaningful distinction can be made, except by those likely to profit from such a distinction. We doubt that the general public are the intended beneficiaries.

In short, intra-professional disagreement commonly has more energy devoted to it than is expended on any objective pursuit of best methods for the alleviation or eradication of mental distress.

The myths of psychotherapy

Psychotherapists have apparently little enthusiasm for debate on central questions concerning the reality of mental illness and cure. It is a quite defensible proposition (see Wood 1983) that neurosis, for example, does not exist. Wood's argument is that the concept of mental illness has been extended to the point of absurdity; that much Freudian and neo-Freudian thinking has fostered an 'illness excuse'; that many of us hide from the realities of life and its demand for moral courage by appealing to the concept of neurosis. In this, Wood is echoing some of the same points raised by La Piere (1959). Wood commends a 'moral therapy' which is self-administered and places central importance on the need for courage, determination and responsibility. Most psychotherapists are anxious to undermine the idea that people can cure their own psychological ills by sheer effort, bibliotherapy or moral therapy. The interface between autotherapy and heterotherapy has received scant attention, yet how can we know just how resourceful people can be *without* therapy, when therapists by their very existence (as well as by their esoteric language) suggest that it is usually wiser to turn to professional others for help?

It is also a proposition to be taken seriously that psychotherapy (at least in all its established professional pretentiousness) offers only polished illusions (see Szasz 1988; Smail 1984; 1987). Szasz dwells on the misuse of the concept of illness for what are actually, he maintains, problems in living. He condemns the mis-use of power by the psychiatric establishment. He also adamantly refuses to accept the proliferation of aetiologies and remedies in the field of psychotherapy, finding it riddled with pretentiousness. Szasz's purpose is to show that what psychotherapy actually boils down to is 'healing words'. The empire of psychotherapy is, he argues, built on a misnomer and continues to exploit a medical metaphor. Smail's argument is in many ways similar to that of Szasz, but addresses more confrontatively the claims to success put forward by psychotherapists. The outcome of therapy is usually much more modest than is claimed by its proponents, says Smail, and the curative element of therapy probably has much more to do with the giving of comfort than with the many much-vaunted psychotechnologies (as Mair also argues).

Philosophical critiques of therapy are usually resisted or laughed out of court, yet we have much to learn from philosophical rigour. Perhaps it is significant that we live in an age that has little respect for the status of philosophy. It may also be significant that psychology and psychotherapy have roots in philosophy, but largely deny the usefulness of philosophy today. Humanistic psychologists in particular often dismiss anything that smacks of 'logical-positivism' as self-evidently anti-therapeutic; this, of course, leaves them free to pursue and promote any wild strain of 'therapeutic experience' unchecked by logic. The application of traditional philosophical analyses – in the fields of epistemology and semantics, for example – to the claims and language of psychotherapy, might at least rein in some of the wilder excesses of the profession. (For an example of one of the few such analyses, see Grunbaum 1984. While writers like Marcuse (1956) have brought philosophical analysis to bear on psychoanalysis, this has often been done in the broad brush strokes of social philosophy rather than with close attention to the clinical claims of psychotherapy.)

Much, if not most, psychotherapy seems to be conducted by enthusiasts with vested interests. What if Szasz were right, and therapy is no more than 'talking to people'? What if we stopped to consider Smail's contention that therapy offers no more (or less) than comfort (albeit in sophisticated guises)? Might not the tools of philosophical analysis help to answer such questions?

Psychotherapy and the medical model

The rejection by psychotherapists and counsellors of the 'medical model', with its reliance on power and labelling, may be coming full circle. On the one hand, the profession of psychotherapy is now anything but an accessible 'putting people first' enterprise. Yesterday's anti-psychiatrists are the people who, today, are strenuously trying to protect their profession from lay intruders. On the other hand, psychotherapy at present (at least in the UK) is a very demedicalized profession. An ironic consequence of this is the inadequacy of most assessment procedures (where there are any) and the tendency to psychologize problems willy-nilly. Sutherland (1976) has shown how woefully erroneous diagnoses can be. Striano (1988) cites several cases of misdiagnosis in her study of the damaging effects of psychotherapy. Many naive psychotherapists apparently cling to a belief that all personal problems (whether debt, migraine or cancer) are self-created and curable through psychotherapy.

Autonomy or dependency?

One of the great claims of psychotherapy is that it 'enables' its clients. By 'enabling', we imply we have at heart the restoration to clients of their own autonomy by means of specialized skills. Indeed, respect for the autonomy of clients is viewed by many (for example, Holmes and Lindley 1989) as the ethical centrepiece of psychotherapy. Arguably, therapists have a long way to go to give credibility to this claim. Psychotherapeutic theory grows more complicated by the day. Therapies claiming breakthroughs in treatment and simplification of technical language invariably become lengthy, jargon-ridden and equivocal in their results. Many clients find themselves hanging on to hope, attending their psychoanalysis or primal therapy year after year with little to show for it (Dinnage 1988; Striano 1988). One suspects that while many psychotherapists claim (and perhaps genuinely believe themselves) to be enablers, some covert process of vanity or ignorance prevents them from truly dedicating their efforts to liberating their clients. In his biography of Fritz Perls, for example, Shepard (1975: 170) speaks of Perls' 'conflict between his philosophy of encouraging others to be autonomous and then rewarding the sort of behaviour that he desired'.

Psychotherapy or a cult?

Growing out of the above point is the tendency of many clients, and psychotherapy trainees (and masters!) to congregate around institutes, workshops and charismatic leaders. For too many people therapy becomes an end in itself. There is a visible, palpable and incestuous sub-culture of psychotherapy, where you can witness people eating, sleeping and breathing therapy (dripping with therapy!); each day discovering yet another fascinating piece of pathology or ostensible micro-erosion of the hold of parental injunctions! While this may be viewed as a temporary stage of narcissism or of 'working-through' something, it can also be seen as demonstrating the likeness of therapy to (dependency-creating) religion, and a long way indeed from any goal of autonomy.

Psychotherapists – models of healthy parenthood?

Since a great deal of psychotherapeutic theory rests on observations of childhood and the damage done, one might expect a significant input from therapists into educative, preventive projects. Instead, therapists and their clients alike seem so eternally fascinated by pathology that there is no energy for preventing it. Masson has suggested (in Chapter 2) that therapists are frequently abusive to their clients. One must logically ask whether therapists are demonstrably better parents than their therapeutically un- treated peers, since if there is no sign that the children of therapists fare better (or in the poet Philip Larkin's words, are less 'fucked up') than others, then this is a significant research finding. While this is offered lightheartedly, the serious point is that after some decades of psychotherapy it is reasonable to expect to see some 'walking testimonies' to the power of therapy in the form of visibly mentally healthy therapists and their offspring. Referring again to Perls, Shepard (1975: 96) claims that he had 'a justly deserved reputation for being indifferent, at best, to children and was a failure as a father'.

Problems of class and feminism

Pilgrim has outlined the political failings of psychotherapy. Here we would make the observation that most therapy in practice is endemically middle-class and ethnocentric. It is only just beginning to react adequately to the realities of the socio-economic position of women and ethnic, and other, minorities. Therapists respond to urgent need and work at the level of clinical individualism, but perhaps this very work desensitizes them to the need for wider social changes. It must be questioned, too, whether psychotherapists are not by definition uninterested in or blind to social problems. In Britain, for example, the majority of counsellors are middle-class women, and much counselling (certainly counselling skills training) resembles, perhaps is often barely distinguishable from, the social skills and social graces of the middle classes. Albee (1990) makes the point that although the choice of psychotherapist as a career is as respectable as that of dentist or funeral director, in terms of making any real impact on 'the *incidence* of distress in the population', it is a futile endeavour. He therefore calls for greater resources for preventive projects (*not* for the training of more psychotherapists!). On the subject of vocational choice and concern for resources, Smail (1987: 86) talks of 'the worlds of difference between Mother Teresa of Calcutta and the average Hampstead psychoanalyst'.

In the preparation of this book we sought a contribution from a feminist perspective but were widely advised that while many women have objected to the grosser patriarchal assumptions of Freud, there is now a high degree of satisfaction with psychotherapy as an avenue for women to explore, express and alter some of the oppression they have lived with. This impression seems to agree with Masson's in Chapter 2. Chesler (1990: 317) confirms that 'despite my own early critique of institutional psychiatry and of private patriarchal therapy geared to high-income clients, I have come to believe that women can and do benefit from feminist therapy'. Perhaps where women have shown some implicit criticism of psychotherapy's structures is in the strength of the self-help and women's group movement.

Psychotherapy training and charisma

Turning to the problem of psychotherapy's power residing in professional individuals, we observe that all schools of therapy appear to have charismatic founders. Even within sober academic settings, courses in therapy and counselling tend to be dominated by the personalities of course leaders. The whole therapy world is shot through with personal influence, that is to say with leaders and with followers, yet this is rarely questioned. (Some people apparently refer to Carl Rogers, a champion of non-directiveness and enabling, as 'The Giant'!) This focus on founders and charismatic leaders aligns psychotherapy with religion (see e.g. Werkman 1986).

Psychotherapy – vehicle for radical change?

Finally, perhaps one of the saddest indictments of psychotherapy and its century of valiant efforts to plumb the depths of the human mind, is its moral triviality. Some of its best successes centre on clients becoming a little less depressed, able to leave the house, speak in front of a class, and so on. Many writers on psychotherapy take pains to demonstrate that while counselling may solve such problems, psychotherapy deals with fundamental personality change. How many ex-psychotherapy clients can be pointed to, however, as examples of people truly released from human suffering and folly? One of the distinctions of religions has been the promotion of a moral struggle to become a non-trivial, life-embracing person and citizen. How many psychotherapy clients have overcome vanity, lack of courage, self-deception, economic preoccupation and self-centredness? (And how many therapists?) Conversely, how many people who do embody admirable traits have got them through the medium of psychotherapy? It is, of course, one of the boasts of humanistic psychotherapy and the 'human potential movement' that just such gains *are* made through their methods. Yet it can seem sadly evident that the beards, hugs, vegetarian diets, espousing of radical causes and apparent spontaneity of people belonging to the subculture of the human potential movement, only thinly disguise the same suffering and folly that all flesh seems heir to.

This is not an exhaustive list of the shortcomings of psychotherapy but it is probably large enough. Certainly the advocates of psychotherapy can argue that therapy never set out to address non-clinical issues. They can also claim that there are examples within the world of psychotherapy of remarkable cures, remarkable people, and complete absences of the above-mentioned sins and foibles.

In order to pull together the criticisms of the eight chapter writers, as well as the points above, into something manageable and hopefully constructive, we suggest the following tripartite consideration of psychotherapy's problems:

Accountability

Whatever readers' judgements of Eysenck's or Kline's views, they do call for sharpened seriousness about research. Much psychotherapy is publicly funded and all of it is a publicly accountable activity. It deals with people's intimate concerns and most of them are vulnerable when seeking, and during, psychotherapy. It overlaps with the medical realm. It requires not only high levels of integrity from its practitioners, but also effectiveness. Therefore it must be shown both as a publicly available service and as a personal-professional skill to be based on fairly solid evidence. It is not enough to do piecemeal research and to convene profession-protecting committees.

It is remarkable to consider that psychotherapy, like aspects of the professions of law and medicine, is able to charge its customers for time spent with them with no guarantee of satisfaction. Dissatisfied consumers, other than those able to point to gross malpractice, seem to have little power to evoke an admission of accountability for 'failure to cure' or 'failure to make significant progress'. Psychotherapists often make contracts of sorts with their clients, but rarely, if ever, contracts committing themselves to particular results. This, of course, is understandable, given the complexity and frequent intractability of clients' personal problems. Psychotherapists are knowledgeable enough, therefore, not to commit themselves to promises they cannot be sure to keep – but are they honest enough to declare this uncertainty to their clients? Such honesty would preferably include ongoing soul-searching on the part of the therapist. Because therapists are in some sense both healers and salespeople (selling their service and promoting faith in their product to vulnerable people) they have to have enormous integrity. But even enormous integrity is not enough. The profession of psychotherapy must consider what it can and cannot deliver and represent this honestly to the public. There is plenty of therapeutic literature enticing people into therapy, but few consumer guides or safeguards. Perhaps Masson's call, seconded by Holmes, for an ombudsman (or ombudsperson) should be taken up urgently. Psychotherapists must learn to take seriously the views of consumers and critics.

Credibility

While many psychotherapists are excellent at writing both sensational and erudite books promising deliverance from painful symptoms, and also at establishing prestigious institutes filled with PhDs and brimming with mesmerizing technical language, as a whole the profession has failed to put across any credible, unified view of what it does. Indeed the schisms and warring schools that rather awkwardly constitute the profession of psychotherapy do very little to inspire confidence. It is our contention that psychotherapists need to 'leave' their institutes and reformulate their goals. When Guggenbühl-Craig (1971: 137) says that 'the psychotherapist needs erotic confrontation outside the analytical framework', he refers to the *eros* which is part of the drive towards truth, with truth being bigger than the institutes claiming to hold it. Is therapy a validly individualistic, clinical affair, or does it need to show its wider relevance?

Epistemology

Epistemology – 'the problem of knowledge' – is not a word often introduced into conversation about psychotherapy. Yet it must be apparent from the arguments of Gellner, Edwards, Masson and Mair, indeed of all our contributors, that psychotherapy is centrally concerned with questions of truth, judgement, decisions, common sense, learning, gullibility and deception. Psychotherapy, as Szasz (1988) says, is a matter of talking (even if the talking is accompanied by images, crying or 'bodywork') and of trying to reformulate 'problems in living'. One person consults another. One person in the role of 'relatively ignorant' consults another in the role of 'relatively knowledgeable'. In this interchange, psychotherapy is accepted as a body of knowledge. Yet we might say too that it is a provisional and pluralistic body of therapists' best guesses. Psychotherapists who adhere to a pure school of thought can and do regard their clients as fitting the theory. The job of a transactional analyst, for example, is to seize on the scripts, rackets and games of her client. It is not her job to look for other, uncharted phenomena. She tends, therefore, to see what she is looking for, and this is true for most (if not all) therapists.

The problem of knowledge in therapy is vast. How does the client know what is wrong with him, to whom to look for help, who to trust, who to remain with, how to evaluate success? (The short answer given by many therapists is that 'if it *feels* right for you, it probably *is* right'. A more mystical answer is along the lines of 'you and your therapist will find each other; these things have a way of happening at the appropriate time'. Are such answers sufficient and reliable?) And likewise, how does a trainee choose a training institute, know which model of therapy is most effective, know which intervention to use with each client at each moment, and so on? (Some schools of thought in psychotherapy, for example transactional analysis, have moved omnisciently towards answering this last question!)

Quite apart from the question of avoiding charlatans or power-seekers, clients have to contend with therapists who, in their fallible humanity, are as prone to error, vanity and plain ignorance, as themselves. The research of pseudo-patients cited by Sutherland clearly suggests a problem of knowledge in the area of diagnosis. Gergen (1990) draws attention to 'the language of mental deficit', pointing out that terms like 'stress', 'bulimia' and 'post traumatic stress disorder' tend to appear and achieve reification overnight. He argues that such language is of spurious value and likely to be 'enfeebling' for those for whom it is used (while comforting and profitable for those coining, owning and employing it). The numerous battles raging quietly within the world of psychotherapy are, in fact, a form of epistemological competition. Put crudely, can one perhaps detect, for example between the lines of debates between psychotherapists and their critics, a sense of 'I know better' and 'my knowledge-base is sounder than yours'? (And if this *is* the case, it suggests, perhaps, that both committed psychotherapists and critics may be prey to the *human* tendency to believe what one wishes to believe.) Is all this too gloomy an outlook? Perhaps the main reason we consult psychotherapists, as we consult priests, is that they appear to know the answers, even when they refuse to tell us – *especially* when (with many therapists being so opaque) they refuse to tell us!

Clients and therapists alike would do well to demand clearer explanations of what psychotherapy is. Consumers have a right to an ethical service (and ethics is a subject larger, as Rowe (1987) reminds us, than that which we spell out laboriously in our professional codes). Psychotherapists are obliged to promote better therapy. If Masson is right and psychotherapy had better be dismantled, there is no task but the dismantling. (Although in practice such a task would require, from those clinicians in agreement with Masson's radical disaffection, enormous personal sacrifice – and who is selfless enough to undergo such sacrifice?) However, while human suffering continues and we remain pragmatically involved in addressing it, we would do well to improve our training as therapists. Egan (1986: 6) urges that 'it would be unfair to tell those thinking of a career in the helping professions that all is well in Camelot. It is not. You are encouraged to acquaint yourself with the ongoing debate concerning the efficacy of helping'. Egan's way out of the discontentment is to call for better training focused on consistent helpfulness. We too share the call for better training, but it is hard to define better training (and continuing training) without noting that students and qualified practitioners will have to confront, not merely clinical issues, but the kinds of radical critiques put forward by the contributors to this book. Can psychotherapists not 'afford scepticism', as Mair suggests? On what grounds do we decide to entertain, dismiss or enter into dialogue with such critics?

References

Albee, G.W. (1990) The futility of psychotherapy, *Journal of Mind and Behaviour* **11** (3 and 4): 369–84.

Chesler, P. (1990) Twenty years since 'Women and Madness': towards a Feminist Institute of Mental Health and Healing. *Journal of Mind and Behaviour* **11** (3 and 4): 313–22.

Clare, A.W. and Thompson, S. (1981) *Let's Talk About Me*. London: British Broadcasting Corporation.

Dinnage, R. (1988) *One To One: Experiences Of Psychotherapy*. London: Viking.

Egan, G. (1986) *The Skilled Helper*. Pacific Grove, Calif: Brooks/Cole.

Gergen, K.J. (1990) Therapeutic professions and the diffusion of deficit. *Journal of Mind and Behaviour* **11** (3 and 4): 353–67.

Grunbaum, A. (1984) *The Foundations of Psychoanalysis*. Berkeley: University of California Press.

Guggenbühl-Craig, A. (1971) *Power in the Helping Professions*. Dallas, Tex: Spring.

Holmes, J. and Lindley, R. (1989) *The Values of Psychotherapy*. Oxford: Oxford University Press.

Horowitz, M.J. (1989) *Introduction to Psychodynamics: A New Synthesis*. London: Routledge.

Janov, A. (1974) *The Primal Scream*. London: Sphere.

La Piere, R. (1959) *The Freudian Ethic*. New York: Duell, Sloane & Pierce.

Mahrer, A.R. (1989) *Experiential Psychotherapy*. Ottawa: University of Ottawa Press.

Malan, D.H. (1963) *A Study of Brief Psychotherapy*. London: Plenum.
Marcuse, H. (1956) *Eros and Civilisation: A Philosophical Inquiry into Freud*. London: Routledge & Kegan Paul.
Mearns, D. and Thorne, B. (1989) *Person-Centred Counselling in Action*. London: Sage.
Patterson, C.H. (1973) *Theories of Counseling and Psychotherapy*. New York: Harper & Row.
Rowe, D. (1987) Avoiding the big issues and attending to the small, in S. Fairbairn and G. Fairbairn (eds) *Psychology, Ethics and Change*. London: Routledge & Kegan Paul.
Shepard, M. (1975) *Fritz*. Sagaponack, NY: Second Chance Press.
Shlien, J.M., Mosak, H.H. and Dreikurs, R. (1962) Effects of time limits: a comparison of two psychotherapies. *Journal of Counselling Psychology* 9: 31–4.
Smail, D. (1984) *Illusion and Reality*. London: Dent.
Smail, D. (1987) *Taking Care: An Alternative to Therapy*. London: Dent.
Striano, J. (1988) *Can Psychotherapists Hurt You?* Santa Barbara, Calif: Professional Press.
Sutherland, S. (1976) *Breakdown*. London: Weidenfeld & Nicolson.
Szasz, T. (1988) *The Myth of Psychotherapy*. New York: Syracuse University Press.
Werkman, S. (1986) Religious concepts in psychotherapies, in L.H. Robinson (ed.) *Psychiatry and Religion: Overlapping Concerns*. Washington, DC: American Psychiatric Press.
Wood, G. (1983) *The Myth of Neurosis*. London: Macmillan.

Index

McRae, R.B., 76
magic, psychotherapy and, 155–8, 205
see also mysticism
Mahrer, A.R., 151, 152, 153–4, 160, 256
Mair, Katherine, xvi, 161–6, 210–11, 254
Malan, D., 71–2, 105, 256
mania, 171
Marcuse, H., 54, 258
marital therapy, 175, 187, 189, 208
see also counselling
Martin, I., 114, 132
Marx, Karl: Marxism, 44, 47, 50
Maslow, A., 181, 202, 207
Masson, J.M., xv, 20, 229, 231, 249–50, 254, 259
Mearns, D., 166, 256
measurement/testing
methodology and, 67–8, 93
outcome studies and, 74–5, 192–3
and personality change, 75–80
psychoanalysis and, 55, 58
psychotherapy and, 49–50, 143–5
see also research
medication *see* drugs
Menaker, Esther, 14
Menninger Clinic project, 104, 105, 119, 129
mental hospitals
discharge from, 182–3
treatment at, 170, 172–85, 188, 191, 192
mentally ill, care and treatment
approaches to treatment, 169–70, 186–93, 201, 216
artificial nature of therapy, 174–6
attitudes of staff, 176–8, 180–1
boredom, 179–80 185
dependence, 173–4, 185, 258–9
information, lack of, 30–1, 178–9, 182–3, 185
powerlessness, 181–3
sensitivity, 171–3, 181, 185
stigma, 184
meta-analysis
evaluation of psychotherapy, 126, 128, 133, 192–3, 237
methodology and, 69
relevance of (in psychotherapy), 112–16
metaphysics
psychology and, 203, 208, 216
world view, 197, 205, 210, 218, 221–3
methodology in psychotherapy
experimental design, 80–1, 96–8
factor analysis design, 81–3, 93–4, 97
measurement of variables, 74–5
overview and conclusions, 83–4, 86–7, 94, 96–8
personality change, measurement of, 75–80
problems, 64–9
solutions, 69–74
validity threats, 87–92, 93
Miller, Alice, 16–17
Morris, L.A., 136, 145
mortality
belief in life after death, 197
bereavement and depression, 189
psychoanalysis and, 116–18
Mueller, B.S., 170, 172–3, 174, 177, 181–2
multiple personality disorder, 143, 164

mysticism
mind and consciousness, 197
new psychology, 203–5, 207, 210, 217–18, 222–4
and psychoanalysis, 41–4, 48, 51–3
science and, 214–15
myth: of psychotherapy, 147, 257–8

narcissistic disorders, 227, 228
National Health Service (British), 154, 201, 226, 231–2, 238
National Institute of Mental Health (USA), 87, 121, 127–8
Nazism
anti-semitism, 9–10, 12–13, 19, 24, 26–7, 229
atrocities, 25–6
and psychiatry, 19, 26–7, 34, 39
psychoanalysis and, 229
Needleman, J., 198
neoplatonism, 203
Neumann, K.F., 146
Neuro-Linguistic Programming (NLP), 10–11
neurosis
behaviour therapy, 65, 114, 116
Freud and, 49–50, 54, 139, 208
myth and, 257–8
psychoanalysis, 228
social origins, 229
treatment of, 100–12, 119–21, 125–9, 131, 139–40
'new' paradigm vs 'old' paradigm psychotherapy, 194, 198–224
Nicholi, A.M., 15
Northfield Military Hospital, 231–2
Noyes, L. *et al.*, 238–9
Nunnally, J.O., 78, 81

occupational therapy, 171, 180, 182
O'Connor, J. *et al.*, 110
'Oedipus Complex', 15, 20, 34
'old' paradigm vs 'new' paradigm psychotherapy, 194, 198–224
operations/'operationalization', 47–8, 49–50, 55–6, 57
Original Sin, doctrine of, 45–6
Orlinsky, D.E., 69, 143–4, 193
Ornstein, R., 203
outcome studies
measurement, 74–5
problems in psychotherapy, 100–33, 192–3
research, 69, 86, 143–5, 161–4
see also measurement/testing; research

paranoia, 179, 183
'paranormal', 155
'paraprofessionals', 150–1
parenthood: psychotherapists, 259–60
patients
dependency/autonomy, 173–4, 185, 258–9
effectiveness of treatment, 62, 87–92, 192–3, 240, 241, 247–8
impact of the new psychotherapy and, 202–3
information, lack of, 30–1, 178–9, 182–3, 185
interaction with therapists, 66, 81, 144, 148, 164, 187–8
personal experiences of, 170–84, 191–2

Psychodynamic theory(ies) and others create individualised pathologies from socially constructed (and derived) and politically maintained distress.

Therefore such theories are part of the controlling forces oppressing individuals under the guise of [individual] liberation.

Further, they are used to enhance prestige, [wealth] status, power [of practitioners] by pretension to diagnose these [individualised] pathologies often from within a pseudo medical [the status] setting.